D1563036

GEORGE HERBERT: THE CRITICAL HERITAGE

THE CRITICAL HERITAGE SERIES

GENERAL EDITOR: B. C. SOUTHAM, M.A., B.LITT. (OXON.)
Formerly Department of English, Westfield College,
University of London

For a list of books in the series see the back end paper

GEORGE HERBERT

THE CRITICAL HERITAGE

Edited by
C. A. PATRIDES

ROUTLEDGE & KEGAN PAUL
LONDON, BOSTON, MELBOURNE AND HENLEY

First published in 1983
by Routledge & Kegan Paul plc
39 Store Street, London WC1E 7DD,
9 Park Street, Boston, Mass. 02108, USA,
296 Beaconsfield Parade, Middle Park,
Melbourne, 3206, Australia, and
Broadway House, Newtown Road,
Henley-on-Thames, Oxon RG9 1EN
Printed in Great Britain by
Redwood Burn Ltd, Trowbridge, Wiltshire
Compilation, introduction, notes and index
Copyright © C. A. Patrides 1983

Library of Congress Cataloging in Publication Data

George Herbert, the critical heritage.

(The Critical heritage series)
Includes index.
1. Herbert, George, 1593–1633—Criticism and inter-
pretation—Addresses, essays, lectures.   I. Patrides,
C. A.   II. Series.
PR3508.G48 1983   821'.3   82–22959

ISBN 0–7100–9240–7

PR
3508
.G48
1983

General Editor's Preface

The reception given to a writer by his contemporaries and near-contemporaries is evidence of considerable value to the student of literature. On one side we learn a great deal about the state of criticism at large and in particular about the development of critical attitudes towards a single writer; at the same time, through private comments in letters, journals or marginalia, we gain an insight upon the tastes and literary thought of individual readers of the period. Evidence of this kind helps us to understand the writer's historical situation, the nature of his immediate reading-public, and his response to these pressures.

The separate volumes in the *Critical Heritage Series* present a record of this early criticism. Clearly, for many of the highly productive and lengthily reviewed nineteenth- and twentieth-century writers, there exists an enormous body of material; and in these cases the volume editors have made a selection of the most important views, significant for their intrinsic critical worth or for their representative quality—perhaps even registering incomprehension!

For earlier writers, notably pre–eighteenth century, the materials are much scarcer and the historical period has been extended, sometimes far beyond the writer's lifetime, in order to show the inception and growth of critical views which were initially slow to appear.

In each volume the documents are headed by an Introduction, discussing the material assembled and relating the early stages of the author's reception to what we have come to identify as the critical tradition. The volumes will make available much material which would otherwise be difficult of access and it is hoped that the modern reader will be thereby helped towards an informed understanding of the ways in which literature has been read and judged.

B.C.S.

for
Ted–Larry Pebworth and Claude J. Summers

ὸ μὲν κάλος ὄσσον ἴδην πέλεται κάλος
ὁ δὲ κἄγαθος αὔτικα κὔστερον ἔσσεται κὔστερον

Contents

Acknowledgments

My acknowledgments must necessarily begin with the expression of my gratitude to ten individuals in particular:
Mr C.B.L. Barr of the York Minster Library, who again placed
at my disposal his authoritative knowledge of Latin literature and scholarship; Professor Amy M. Charles of the University of North Carolina at Greensboro, the noted biographer of Herbert (1977) and editor of the Williams manuscript
of his poems (1977), who assisted me to an incalculable extent with Herbert's numerous seventeenth-century admirers;
Miss Margaret Crum of the Department of Western Manuscripts
at the Bodleian Library, who guided me with characteristic
alacrity through unpublished materials on Herbert; Dr Trevor
Joscelyne of the Polytechnic of North London, who wrote his
doctoral dissertation on Herbert at the University of York
under my supervision but now directed my own efforts,
especially in connection with Walton's reputation in the
nineteenth century; Dr Sebastian Köppl of the Bamberg
University Library, who called my attention to the crucial
passages in George Ryley's commentary on 'The Temple';
Professor David Novarr of Cornell University, the distinguished author of 'The Making of Walton's "Lives"' (1958),
who steered me with authority through the bibliographical
problems in Walton's life of Herbert here reprinted; Dr
Louise Schleiner, who generously imparted to me her impressive knowledge of the musical settings of Herbert's poems;
Professor Elaine Sisman of the University of Michigan at
Ann Arbor, who transcribed for the present volume John
Blow's setting of 'Ephes. 4.30' from Henry Playford's
'Harmonia sacra' (1688); Mrs Helen Wilcox of the University
of Liverpool, who advised me on several aspects of Herbert's
reputation in the seventeenth century and invited me to consider several writers (notably George Daniel, James Dunton,
and Oliver Heywood) I might have otherwise overlooked
(these writers were considered in her doctoral dissertation

on the subject); and my colleague Professor Ralph Williams,
who provided the essential translation of the poem by
James Duport (No. 27), moreover imitating the form of the
original Latin through alternating English iambic hexa-
meters and pentameters.

I am also grateful to Professor Thomas J. Collins of the University of Western Ontario for advice in connection with Browning; to Professor Alastair Fowler of the University of Edinburgh in connection with Saintsbury and Grierson; to Professor K.J. Höltgen of the University of Erlangen-Nuremberg in
connection with Ryley; to Professor Emeritus Walter E. Houghton of Wellesley College in connection with Clough; to Professor John Dixon Hunt of Bedford College, London, in connection with Ruskin; to Mr Gordon Phillips, Archivist of 'The
Times', for identifying the author of the anonymous essay (No.
73) as Basil de Selincourt; to Professor John R. Roberts of
the University of Missouri at Columbia in connection with Herbert's modern commentators; to Professor Charles Ryskamp,
Director of the Pierpont Morgan Library, in connection with
Cowper; to Professor Paul G. Stanwood of the University of
British Columbia in connection with Beaumont; to my colleague Professor R.H. Super in connection with Arnold; to
Professor Frank J. Warnke of the University of Georgia in
connection with Herbert's affinities with Continental
literature; and to Professor Emeritus Austin Warren of the
University of Michigan at Ann Arbor in connection with his
own essay (No. 74). I am equally grateful to still others
who provided me with materials I needed, most notably the
late Rosalie L. Colie and Professors Jared R. Curtis of
Simon Fraser University, Elsie Leach of San Jose State
College, Clayton D. Lein of Purdue University, Robert E.
Reiter of Boston College, Thomas S. Ryan of the University
of Texas at Arlington, Paul G. Stanwood (as above), William
E. Stephenson of East Carolina University, and R.A. Yoder
of Tufts University, as well as Mr M.A. Halls, Modern
Literary Archivist of King's College Library, Cambridge,
and Mr F. Thomas Noonan, Curator of Harvard's Houghton
Library Reading Room. Necessarily vital to my purposes
were the labours of my predecessors who did so much to
direct my attention to the major as well as to the obscure
exponents of Herbert since 1633. These predecessors include
in particular Joseph E. Duncan (1959), Saad El-Gabalawy
(1973), F.E. Hutchinson (1941), Trevor Joscelyne (1978),
Elsie Leach (1960), Arthur H. Nethercot (1924-5), Robert
H. Ray (1967), John R. Roberts (1978), Joseph H. Summers
(1954), and Karina Williamson (1962). The list of my obligations to individuals must conclude with an acknowledgment to the editorial staff at Routledge & Kegan Paul and
to the Series Editor, Mr Brian Southam.

Of libraries where my investigations were pursued, four
in particular should be named: the British Library, the
Bodleian Library, the University of Michigan Library at Ann
Arbor, and the New York Public Library. The manifold courtesies extended to me at all four are most gratefully
acknowledged.

Finally, acknowledgment is no less gratefully made to
the following publishers and individuals who allowed me access to the materials indicated: George Allen & Unwin Ltd for
permission to reprint an extract from 'The Works of John
Ruskin', ed. E.T. Cook and Alexander Wedderburn (1903 ff.)
(No. 44); the Keeper of Western Manuscripts in the Bodleian
Library for permission to print some verses by Polwhele
from MS Eng. poet. f. 16, fol. 11, and extracts from George
Ryley's commentary on 'The Temple' in MS Rawlinson D.199
(Nos 5 and 37, respectively); the Keeper of Manuscripts in
the British Library for permission to print some verses by
Ralph Knevet from Add. MS 27447 and an extract from
Coleridge's Notebook 26 in Add. MS 47524 (Nos 9 and 42,
respectively); Cambridge University Press for permission to
reprint an extract from 'The Ferrar Papers', ed. B. Blackstone (1938) (No. 3); Centaur Press Ltd and Southern Illinois University Press for permission to reprint the poem
on Herbert from 'Poems and Some Letters of James Thomson',
ed. Anne Ridler (1963) (No. 54); Éditions du Centre National
de la Recherche Scientifique for permission to reproduce
John Wilson's setting of Herbert's 'Content' from 'Poèmes
de Donne, Herbert et Crashaw', ed. André Souris (Paris,
1961) (App. I); the Governing Body of Christ Church, Oxford,
as well as The Odyssey Press (Bobbs-Merrill Company) and
Andrew J. Sabol, for permission to reproduce John Jenkins's
setting of Herbert's 'The Starre' as transcribed and edited
in 'Major Poets of the Earlier Seventeenth Century', ed.
Barbara K. Lewalski and Andrew J. Sabol (1973) (App. I);
Amy M. Charles and Ohio State University Press for permis-
sion to reprint extracts from her edition of 'The Shorter
Poems of Ralph Knevet' (1966) (No. 9); E.P. Dutton and Co.
Inc. for permission to reprint the essay on Herbert from
'Literary Criticisms by Francis Thompson', ed. Terence L.
Connolly (1948) (No. 68); Mrs Valerie Eliot and Faber & Faber
Ltd for permission to reprint T.S. Eliot's essay on Herbert,
first printed in the 'Spectator' for 12 March 1932 (Copy-
right T.S. Eliot 1932, © Valerie Eliot 1981) (No. 72);
Harvard University Press for permission to reprint extracts
from 'The Early Lectures of Ralph Waldo Emerson', Volume I,
1833-1836, ed. Stephen E. Whicher and Robert E. Spiller,
Cambridge, Mass.: The Belknap Press of Harvard University
Press (Copyright © 1959 by the President and Fellows of
Harvard College), and from 'The Journals and Miscellaneous

Notebooks of Ralph Waldo Emerson', ed. William H. Gilman
et al. (1960 ff.) (No. 43); the Librarian of the Houghton
Library at Harvard University, as well as Yale University
Press, for permission to print Clough's comments in MS bMS
Eng 1036 (8) as reproduced in Walter E. Houghton's 'The
Poetry of Clough' (1963) (No. 48); Trevor Joscelyne for
permission to draw on material in the introduction to his
'Architecture and Music in "The Temple"' (unpublished
D.Phil. dissertation, University of York, 1978); the
University Press of Kentucky for permission to reprint a
poem from Thomas B. Stroup's edition of 'The Selected
Poems of George Daniel of Beswick' (1959) (No. 14); Sebas-
tian Köppl for permission to reprint extracts from his
'Die Rezeption George Herberts im 17. und 18. Jahrhundert'
(1978) containing Ryley's commentary on 'The Temple' (No.
37); the Editors of 'Musical Quarterly', G. Schirmer Inc.,
and Louise Schleiner, for permission to reproduce John
Playford's setting of Herbert's 'The Altar' from her essay
in the journal mentioned (App. I); Novello and Co. Ltd for
permission to reproduce Purcell's setting of Herbert's
'Longing' from 'The Works of Henry Purcell', Vol. XXX,
'Sacred Music: Part VI', ed. Anthony Lewis and Nigel Fortune (1965) (App. I); Oxford University Press for permission to reprint extracts from 'The Poems English Latin and
Greek of Richard Crashaw', ed. L.C. Martin, 2nd edn (1957),
Davenant's 'Gondibert', ed. David F. Gladish (1971),
'Henry Vaughan: Poetry and Selected Prose', ed. L.C. Martin
(1963), 'The Letters and Prose Writings of William Cowper',
ed. James King and Charles Ryskamp (1979), 'Ruskin in
Italy: Letters to his Parents 1845', ed. Harold I. Shapiro
(1972) (©Oxford University Press 1972), 'The Correspondence of Gerard Manley Hopkins and Richard Watson Dixon',
ed. Claude C. Abbott (1955), and 'Metaphysical Lyrics and
Poems of the Seventeenth Century', ed. Herbert J.C.
Grierson (1921) (Nos 11-12, 15, 18, 40, 44, 58, and
71, respectively); G.P. Putnam's Sons for permission to
reprint Paul Elmer More's essay on Herbert from 'Shelburne
Essays', 4th series (1906) (No. 66); the University of
Reading's Department of Typography and Graphic Communica-
tion (Whiteknights Press) for permission to reprint an
extract from the preface to Cardell Goodman's 'Beawty in
Raggs', ed. R.J. Roberts (1958) (No. 6); the Editor of
'The Times Literary Supplement' for permission to reprint
Basil de Selincourt's essay on Herbert (1933) (No. 73);
Martin Secker & Warburg Ltd for permission to reprint the
comments on Herbert from 'Aubrey's Brief Lives', ed.
Oliver Lawson Dick (1950) (No. 23); Austin Warren and the
University of Michigan Press for permission to reprint an
abridged version of his essay on Herbert first printed in

the 'American Review' for 1936 and reprinted in his 'Rage
for Order' (1948; 1959) (Copyright © 1959 by The University
of Michigan Press) (No. 74); Helen Wilcox and the Editors
of 'Notes and Queries' for permission to reprint Polwhele's
verses from the 1979 volume (No. 5); the Librarian of Dr
Williams's Library, London, for permission to reprint the
preface to the anonymous 'Select Hymns' of 1697 (No. 34);
and the Librarian of Yale University Library, as well as
Yale University Press, for permission to print George
Eliot's letter in the Beinecke Rare Book and Manuscript
Library as reproduced in 'The George Eliot Letters', ed.
Gordon S. Haight (1954) (No. 45).

C.A.P.

Abbreviations

The place of publication is given only if it is other than London or New York.

Herbert's poetry is quoted from 'The English Poems of George Herbert', ed. C.A. Patrides (1974); and his prose, from Hutchinson's edition (see below).

The following abbreviations are used throughout:

Charles	Amy M. Charles (ed.), 'The Shorter Poems of Ralph Knevet' (Columbus, Ohio, 1966).
Duncan	Joseph E. Duncan, 'The Revival of Metaphysical Poetry: The History of a Style, 1800 to the Present' (Minneapolis, Minn., 1959).
Hutchinson	F.E. Hutchinson, [Herbert's] Contemporary and Later Reputation, in his edition of 'The Works of George Herbert' (Oxford, 1941), pp. xxxix-l.
Joscelyne	Trevor Joscelyne, George Herbert and the Walton Tradition, in 'Architecture and Music in "The Temple": The Aesthetic and Intellectual Context of George Herbert's Poetry', unpublished D.Phil. dissertation (University of York, 1978).
Köppl	Sebastian Köppl, 'Die Rezeption George Herberts im 17. und 18. Jahrhundert' (Heidelberg, 1978).
Leach	Elsie Leach, More Seventeenth-Century Admirers of Herbert, 'Notes and Queries', CCV (1960), 62-3.
Nethercot I	Arthur H. Nethercot, The Reputation of the 'Metaphysical Poets' during the Seventeenth Century, 'Journal of English and Germanic Philology', XXIII (1924), 173-98.
Nethercot II	Arthur H. Nethercot, The Reputation of the

	'Metaphysical Poets' during the Age of Pope, 'Philological Quarterly', IV (1925), 161–79.
Nethercot III	Arthur H. Nethercot, The Reputation of the 'Metaphysical Poets' during the Age of Johnson and the 'Romantic Revival', 'Studies in Philology', XXII (1925), 81–132.
Ray	Robert H. Ray, 'George Herbert in the Seventeenth Century: Allusions to him, Collected and Annotated', unpublished Ph.D. dissertation (University of Texas at Austin, 1967).
Roberts	John R. Roberts, 'George Herbert: An Annotated Bibliography of Modern Criticism 1905–1974' (Columbia, Mo., 1978).
Sloane	William Sloane, George Herbert's Reputation, 1650–1710: Good Reading for the Young, 'Notes and Queries', CCVII (1962), 213.
Summers	Joseph H. Summers, Time and 'The Temple', in his 'George Herbert: His Religion and Art' (Cambridge, Mass., 1954), Ch. I.
Walton, 'Lives'	Izaak Walton, 'The Lives of Dr. John Donne, Sir Henry Wotton, Mr. Richard Hooker, Mr. George Herbert', 4th rev. edn (1675). The second collected edition of the 'Lives'.
Williamson	Karina Williamson, Herbert's Reputation in the Eighteenth Century, 'Philological Quarterly', XLI (1962), 769–75.

Introduction

I HERBERT PAST AND PRESENT

'George Herbert is one of the best English lyric poets.'
The considered judgment of Joseph H. Summers at the very
beginning of his study of Herbert in 1954 (1) is by no
means representative of critical attitudes up to that time.
On the contrary, Herbert's reputation has fluctuated
greatly since his major work, 'The Temple', was first published soon after his death in 1633. Indeed, the eventual
'discovery' of Herbert - more properly, perhaps, his
're-discovery' - was not even the direct consequence of
the meteoric rise earlier in our century of the poet with
whom he has been most persistently associated, John Donne.
   The critical heritage of George Herbert was initially
determined by a gathering reputation centred largely on his
piety. As the publication of 'The Temple' in 1633 appeared
to confirm that piety, it should not surprise us that
scarcely any surviving opinion values its poetry as poetry.
So far, certainly, Walton's hagiography of Herbert - the
one literary masterpiece within the canon of Herbert's
critical fortunes - reflects perfectly the tendencies
shared by any number of seventeenth-century readers
whether Anglican or Puritan. At the same time, however,
the intrinsic merits of Herbert's poetic practice were
recognised by some of the numerous poets who strove to imitate him, especially where such imitators possessed the
talents of Henry Vaughan and, in New England, Edward
Taylor.
   Changes in critical taste during the eighteenth century
dictated a radical change in the attitude toward Herbert's
poetry ('gothic and uncouth'). But the ensuing century
reversed this judgment, especially once Coleridge in
England and Emerson in America expressed their enthusiastic
approval on a number of occasions. Yet opinions favourable

1

and adverse continued to coexist well into the twentieth century. In the event, Herbert was most decisively championed by a major fellow-poet, T.S. Eliot.

However extensive the influence of major figures is bound to be, Herbert's critical heritage is not comprised primarily of Vaughan and Walton in the seventeenth century, Coleridge and Emerson in the nineteenth, or Eliot in the twentieth. A host of lesser writers intervened to create, whether in their poetry or their prose, the texture of 'the moment' that conditioned the diverse responses to Herbert. The ensuing account necessarily takes into consideration the better part of such lesser writers, even though its starting point - and, eventually, its terminal point too - is a major poet.

II   HERBERT IN THE SEVENTEENTH CENTURY

Donne may be allowed the earliest noteworthy mention of Herbert (1615?): it is in the form of a laboured poem, to which Herbert responded with a poem no less laboured (No. 1). The attested kinship between the two poets deserves to be marked; for as a result of affinities that here as elsewhere are in fact only nominal, it was to be a very long time indeed before Herbert would finally be dissociated from Donne and the 'metaphysicals' to have his individual talents recognised. The confident generalisation ventured as recently as 1936 that Herbert is 'a metaphysical poet of the school of Donne with the same undivided consciousness of his tribe' (2) informs implicitly, and often quite explicitly, many of the judgments collected in the ensuing pages.

The second noteworthy mention of Herbert is by an even more illustrious figure, Sir Francis Bacon (No. 2). The connection between Bacon and Herbert should astonish but, astonishingly enough, does not. How was it that the father of modern scientific methodology - and if not its father, we have been told, certainly its godfather (3) - responded to the strictly devotional poet? One further oddity should also be noted, that Bacon had by 1625 actually seen evidence of Herbert's talents in religious poetry - a remarkable exception in itself, since we are fairly certain that the circulation of Herbert's poems in manuscript was as modest as that of Donne's was prodigal.

In advance of the publication of 'The Temple' in 1633, then, Herbert's reputation as a poet was confined to the very few. But his reputation as a pious man appears to have been extensively disseminated; and spreading rapidly from 1633 - a veritable annus mirabilis - it resulted in a

popularity no less immediate than it is impressive by any
standards. To the two editions of 'The Temple' that
appeared within 1633 were added nine others in 1634, 1635,
1638, 1641, 1656, 1660, 1667, 1674, and 1678, as well as a
pirated edition (c. 1647) and the reissue of the 1678 edition in 1695; while the handbook of 'holy Rules' for the
country parson, 'A Priest to the Temple', was published
thrice within the seventeenth century (1652, 1671, 1675).
(4) 'The Temple' is reported by Walton to have sold over
20,000 copies during the forty years to 1675, compared to
(say) the 3,000 copies that 'Paradise Lost' sold during the
first eleven years of its existence (below, pp. 127, 227).
Several individuals are, moreover, on record with statements attesting to the popularity of 'The Temple', or else
with demands for additional copies. Thus Nicholas
Ferrar's sister, Susanna Collett, reported in a letter to
her son in February 1634 that 'The Temple' is 'here (and
worthily) of great esteem', (5) while earlier still, in
October 1633, Joshua Mapletoft protested to Ferrar because
the printers to the University of Cambridge had underestimated the demand for the book:

> Touching Mr Herberts booke it hath ye most generall
> approbation y^t I haue knowne any as it well deserues I
> haue been importuned by diuerse friends for som of y^m
> London affords none & complaint att Cambridge y^t so few
> coppyes were printed. If you haue store I shalbe
> beholding for such a supply as you may afford. (6)

Even more arresting is the available evidence that a
number of aspiring poets, and at least one talented composer, began to study 'The Temple' practically from the
moment it was first published. The composer is John
Jenkins, by 1633 already mature as a musician, who
initiated a respectable tradition by providing six
settings - and necessarily as many interpretations - of
parts of four different lyrics by Herbert, one of which is
reproduced in Appendix I (pp. 357 ff.). (7) Of aspiring
poets, one was James Leeke, Fellow of Peterhouse, Cambridge, from 1630, who was sufficiently impressed by 'the
illustrious Herbertian Muse' to become Herbert's first
translator: at work within months of the appearance of
'The Temple', he rendered into Latin both 'Good Friday'
and - a heroic task indeed! - 'The Church Militant'. (8)
No less expeditious in his response to Herbert's poetry
was another minor versifier, John Polwhele, whose poetic
tribute to the 'Peircinge witt' of Herbert was probably
written before the end of 1633 (No. 5). Polwhele was
followed by one of the more appealing minor poets of the

period, Cardell Goodman, who demonstrated in his own poetry
the sense in which Herbert could be imitated as the 'best'
of models (No. 6). (9) The last poet within the decade of
the 1630s to remark favourably on Herbert was Robert
Codrington. His poetic tribute in 1638, surviving but in
a fragment, makes the vow already made by many others
about Herbert: 'Wee'le canonize him' (No. 7).

    And so they did. Walton's hagiography of Herbert was
still in the distant future, nearly four decades thence,
when the process of Herbert's canonisation began, partly
by reports of his 'most holy and exemplary' life, as his
brother, Lord Herbert of Chirbury, was to emphasise (No.
10), (10) partly by the concerted encomia of the poets
already enumerated, but especially by the biographical
portrait sketched by Nicholas Ferrar in the preface to
'The Temple' (No. 4). As Lord Herbert's emphatic statement was based on his familiarity with his brother's
character, so was Ferrar's elevation of the poet to the
status of 'a companion to the primitive Saints'. It would
after all be an understatement to assert that Herbert and
Ferrar were friends. According to Barnabas Oley, 'their
very souls cleaved together most intimately' (below,
p. 79); and according to Ferrar's brother John, 'it was
Said by them that knewe them booth there was one Soule in
twoe Bodys'. (11) In consequence, Herbert just before
his death entrusted the manuscript of 'The Temple' to
Ferrar (No. 3), and it may well be that the title of the
collection was in fact Ferrar's own, just as the title of
'A Priest to the Temple' was most likely Oley's. Herbert's
portrait in the preface to 'The Temple' was in any case
the result, his canonisation thereby advanced still further along the path leading to Walton.

    It was a path considerably smoothed by other factors
too. The encomiastic poets of the 1630s were succeeded
by equally encomiastic poets in the 1640s and 1650s, their
talents ranging from the utterly indifferent to the distinctly substantial. Pride of place among them must be
allotted to Christopher Harvey, not indeed because he was
possessed of any noteworthy abilities - he was, on the
contrary, consistently vapid - but solely because his
collection of poems, 'The Synagogue, or, The Shadow of
the Temple. Sacred Poems, and Private Ejaculations. In
imitation of Mr. George Herbert' (1640, revised in 1647
and 1657), proclaimed its loyalties so firmly that it commended itself to a public indiscriminately prepared to
tolerate any extension of the Herbertian canon. Harvey's
loyalties were clearly evident both in the poetic tribute
to Herbert made available here (No. 8) and in the numerous
other poems that alike testify to Herbert's inability to

fire Harvey's imagination. (12) Beginning with its second,
revised, edition of 1647, at any rate, 'The Synagogue' was
commonly bound with 'The Temple'. Thereafter Harvey's
poems were regarded as one with Herbert's, until they were
discerned in 1787 to be 'unworthy' of Herbert (No. 41) and
dismissed in 1862 as 'a poor imitation, almost a caricature, of "The Temple"' (below, p. 256). How far more
fortunate Sir Thomas Browne's 'Religio Medici' was to
prove! For it shed its own parasite, Sir Kenelm Digby's
pompous 'Observations upon Religio Medici', before the
seventeenth century even expired.
   Distinctly more talented than Harvey, Henry Colman ventured his 'Divine Meditations' in the same year that 'The
Synagogue' appeared (1640); but not being particularly
proficient in public relations, Colman displayed his
response to Herbert as 'a spiritual pattern and a literary
master' solely within his very capable poems. (13) A year
later, in 1641, Thomas Beedome echoed Herbert's mode of
articulation in three poems inclusive of the untitled one
beginning:

      When first of sinne I tooke survey,
         Sinne that first wrought poore mans decay,
      Mee thought the seeming pleasures that it wore
                     Betray'd a face
                     So full of grace
      That I desir'd it more and more.

The poem ends four stanzas later thus:

                     yet still I see
                  And heare the[e] say,
                  To thy poore clay,
      Is any thing too hard for me. (14)

In the meantime yet another poet, Ralph Knevet, was
beginning to discover his individual voice under Herbert's
guidance. Knevet's poetic labours encompassed an ambitious endeavour to complete 'The Faerie Queene'; but his
most important work was the cluster of eighty-two lyrics
constituting 'A Gallery to the Temple'. Meticulously
revised over three decades or so, the 'Gallery' suggests
the presence of Herbert 'more often as general guide than
as specific model'. (15) In line with Knevet's prefatory
celebration of Herbert as one 'who rightly knew to touch
Davids Harpe' (No. 9), his lyrics commonly respond as much
to Herbert's themes as to his verse forms and language:

Let mee not perish in the day
      Of thy displeasure:
But so prepare mee, that I may
      Become thy treasure:
Bruise mee not with an iron rodde,
      Oh breake mee not,
That am a despicable clod,
      An earthen pot. (16)

Knevet's sustained and constructive dialogue with Herbert
parallels the experience of only one other poet, Vaughan.
   'A Gallery to the Temple' asserts in its title a modest
link with 'The Temple' that is in fact quite substantial.
On the other hand, Crashaw's 'Steps to the Temple' (1646)
asserts in its title - if indeed the title is Crashaw's
own - a substantial link with 'The Temple' that is in fact
quite modest. True, Crashaw wrote an engaging poem centred
on Herbert (No. 11); equally true, he reminds one of Herbert in the occasional phrase and, most evidently, in the
tenor of his 'Charitas Nimia'. As the original poet that
he was, however, Crashaw developed along lines fundamen-
tally different from Herbert's, (17) given in particular
to a rousing lyricism dependent not on expostulation but
on meditation, nor on analysis but on celebration. The
anonymous preface to 'Steps to the Temple' does indeed hail
Crashaw as 'Herbert's second, but equall' (No. 12); the
claim, however, is a judgment appertaining rather to
Crashaw's own devotional commitments than to an admission
of his poetic affinities with Herbert. The author of that
preface, incidentally, may have been Joseph Beaumont,
whose own poem, the colossal 'Psyche', commends Herbert for
having cast 'Lyric's pure and precious Metal... / In holier
moulds' (No. 13). Yet Beaumont was in the final analysis
sympathetic not so much to Herbert as to Crashaw and to
lesser poets like Quarles. (18) The same may also be
asserted of another poet of the same period, Edward
Benlowes, whose equally colossal 'Theophila' (1652) confines the impact of Herbert to one or two allusions of
slight consequence. (19) One of these allusions, moreover, is to two lines at the outset of 'The Church-porch'
- 'A verse may finde him, who a sermon flies, / And turn
delight into a sacrifice' (11. 5-6) - which were so frequently quoted during the seventeenth century as to have
become a cliché.
   While Beaumont and Benlowes were only responding to
Herbert spasmodically, several minor poets were extending
the well-established tradition of celebrating Herbert even
when his actual influence was minimal. Foremost among them
was George Daniel, whose enthusiasm for Herbert in 1648 was

winsomely exorbitant even for an age much given to winsome
exorbitance. In an ode manifestly opposite to the Herbertian mode, Daniel agreeably if surprisingly described
Herbert as a 'Glorious Larke' and, more surprisingly still,
as 'Horace in voice; and Casimire in winge' (No. 14).
Confirming the aberrant configurations of the vision of
Herbert so evident by now, Mildmay Fane demonstrated in
the same year (1648) how a select few of Herbert's variable
verse forms could be adapted by a poet whose primary loyalty was to a very different talent, in this case Herrick.
(20) By the same token, Clement Barksdale in 1651
extolled the devotional poetry of Herbert and Crashaw but
was influenced by neither (No. 16); Henry Delaune, also in
1651, gestured toward 'Divine *Herbert*' by invoking the two
over-quoted lines from 'The Church-porch' ('A verse may
finde him', etc.), (21) but in the end proved far more
responsive to Jonson; Thomas Pestil in 1652 professed his
adherence less to the manner of the 'prince of poets,
illustrious *Dunne*' than to the 'inter-tissu'd *Wit* and *Holiness*' of Herbert and George Sandys (22) but said so in
language reminiscent not so much of his praised models as
of Benlowes; and Thomas Washbourne in 1654 quoted yet
again the statutory two lines from 'The Church-porch' on
his title-page but otherwise stood aloof from Herbert save
for one or two distant echoes of his actual phrasing. (23)
In 1657, moreover, Joshua Poole in the collection entitled
'The English Parnassus' provided materials for aspiring
poets in the form of quotations from the literature of the
English Renaissance; and though Herbert was at least
recognised as important enough to merit representation,
the extracts from his poetry were all too often accidentally mangled or, worse, intentionally 'improved' after the
fashion that was to become wellnigh standard during the
eighteenth century. (24) It is also indicative that the
commendation of Herbert in Poole's 'proeme' (No. 19) is
phrased in the increasingly more prevalent couplets.
  The changed outlook is clearly to be marked. The
earnestness behind the continuing encomia of Herbert
should not be doubted; but in practice, as we have
observed, the ongoing chorus of praise obscures the ever-
widening distance between the earlier proximity to Herbert's poetry and the evolving tendency to praise that
poetry at several removes. At the outset of the 1650s,
the prophetic soul of Hobbes perceived the new critical
attitudes clearly; and though he did not expressly mention
Herbert, his almost casual disapprobation of a very old
habit shared by Herbert (No. 15) is prologue to the omen
coming on. (25) For a considerable time yet to come,
however, the novel attitudes were resisted. The 1650s,

after all, witnessed three developments of cardical significance in Herbert's critical heritage: first, the signal
response to 'The Temple' on the part of Henry Vaughan;
secondly, the publication of the first substantial biography of Herbert, Oley's 'Prefatory View', as well as the
first public acknowledgments by Walton of the perspective
that was to inform the hagiography of 1670; and thirdly,
the startling adoption of Herbert by Puritans of the order
of Richard Baxter. (26)

'There is', we have been told of Vaughan's response to
Herbert, 'no example in English literature of one poet
adopting another poet's words so extensively.' (27)   From
Vaughan's first appearance as a poet in 'Silex Scintillans' (1650) to his last in 'Thalia Rediviva' (1678), Herbert's language as well as Herbert's verse forms remained
a constant presence.   Herbert in 'Obedience' (ll. 36-43)
had spoken of the deed whereby his heart was passed to God
and invited 'some kinde man' to 'set his hand / And heart
unto this deed' and 'thrust his heart / Into these lines'.
Responding, Vaughan in a poem first published in the first
edition of 'Silex Scintillans' wrote:

> Dear friend! whose holy, ever-living lines
>   Have done much good
>   To many, and have checkt my blood,
> My fierce, wild blood that still heaves, and inclines,
>   But is still tam'd
>   By those bright fires which thee inflam'd;
> Here I joyn hands, and thrust my stubborn heart
>   Into thy *Deed*,
>   There from no *Duties* to be freed,
> And if hereafter *youth*, or *folly* thwart
>   And claim their share,
>   Here I renounce the pois'nous ware.

Two years later, in 'The Mount of Olives' (1652) the 'holy'
lines of Herbert were said to reflect an equally holy life:

> We have had many blessed Patterns of a holy life in the
> *British Church*, though now trodden under foot, and
> branded with the title of *Antichristian*. I shall pro-
> pose but one to you, the most obedient *Son* that ever
> his *Mother* had, and yet a most glorious true *Saint* and
> a *Seer*. [Marginal reference to 'Mr. *George Herbert* of
> blessed memory; See his incomparable prophetick Poems,
> and particularly these, "Church-musick", "Church rents,
> and schisms", "The Church militant"'.] (28)

But the crucial year was 1655, for it was then that an

enlarged edition of 'Silex Scintillans' projected Vaughan's
adaptation of Herbert on an even larger canvas. Accompanied by an address that inter alia celebrates Herbert's
'holy *life* and *verse*' (No. 18), the more spacious tableau
illustrated far more conclusively than heretofore the verbal patterns and the diverse verse forms inspired by pre-
cedents in 'The Temple'. But the limits of Vaughan's
response to Herbert were now also evident, thematically in
his monochromatic emphasis on the light beyond the pheno-
menal world, and stylistically in the relaxed structure of
his designs. In themes as in style, nevertheless, it could
be more accurately said of Vaughan than of Traherne that
Herbert was the poet he 'most tried to emulate'. (29)

Barnabas Oley's vision of Herbert in 1652 (No. 17) was
the most generous confirmation yet of the reiterated emphasis on the poet's 'pious Life and Death', to quote a
pseudonymous writer of 1647. (30) A divine by calling and
a royalist by choice, Oley was tutor at Clare Hall, Cambridge, and over half a century a vicar in Huntingdonshire;
he was also Archdeacon of Ely and Prebendary of Worcester.
Personally acquainted with Herbert, he converted his subject generally into the pattern of 'holy life' and specifically into an exemplar of the ideal Anglican clergyman
worthy of imitation by a church 'now trodden under foot',
as we have observed Vaughan to remark in 'The Mount of
Olives'. Only too justly, indeed, Oley's labours were
later acknowledged by Walton as indispensable for 'some of
those Truths' he himself was to extend (below, p. 114).
Walton's own vision of Herbert evolved gradually. He first
referred to 'that holy Poet' on two different occasions
within 'The Compleat Angler' (1653): in Chapter I, where he
quoted three stanzas from 'Providence' (11. 17-20, 25-32),
and in Chapter V, where he quoted 'Vertue' in its entirety.
Before the end of the same decade, in 1658, he introduced
'that man of primitive piety' into his biography of Donne
(No. 20). In 1670, finally, he published 'The Life of
Mr. George Herbert' (No. 24), its nominal aims predicated
in a prefatory address:

> I profess it to be a *Free-will-offering*, and writ,
> chiefly to please my self; but not without some respect
> to posterity, for though he was not a man that the next
> age can forget, yet many of his particular acts and
> vertues might have been neglected, or lost, if I had not
> collected and presented them to the Imitation of those
> that shall succeed us. (31)

The nominal aims apart, Walton's ambition was to define the
office of the good parson by way of Herbert's holiness and

to commend that office as worthy by way of his background,
connections and talents. (32) The ambition may or may not
have obliged Walton to take liberties with some aspects of
Herbert's life; the artistic patterns he deployed, at any
rate, were of themselves adequate to shape the 'Life' into
an aesthetic entity (33) destined to become the foremost
single literary work in the entire range of Herbert's
critical heritage. So persuasive was Walton's performance, indeed, that his vision of Herbert has tended to
invite attention to itself at the expense of Herbert's
poetry. The critical fortunes of Herbert, in short,
parallel Marvell's, of whom it was once said - for very
different reasons, it is true - that 'his name has preserved his writings, rather than his writings his name'.
(34)

Walton affected Herbert's fortunes in yet another way,
quite indirectly, through the commendatory verses that
gathered about the 'Life'. Some of these verses are won-
drously torpid; but several are creditable as poetry and
noteworthy as interpretations of Herbert's life. In
advance of Walton, such verses had also been written to
honour the vapid poems of Christopher Harvey. The minor
poet John Legate - very minor, and hardly a poet - certainly knew what he liked, and whom:

> Herbert! whose every strain
> Twists holy Breast with happy Brain;
> So that who strives to be
> As elegant as he,
> Must climbe mount Calvary for Parnassus Hill.
> And in his Saviours sides baptize his Quill;
> A Jordan fit t' instill
> A Saint-like stile, back'd with an Angels skill. (35)

Of the poets who attended Walton, Samuel Woodford praised
Herbert's skill ('Herbert, who did its Chords distinctly
know, / More perfectly, than any Child of Verse below');
(36) Charles Cotton - a poet of considerable merit eventually praised by Coleridge in 'Biographia Literaria' -
claimed exorbitantly that Herbert was 'deeply tainted
with Ambition' (No. 25); while James Duport honoured
Herbert with two poems written in Latin: one by way of a
tribute to Walton, first published in the fourth edition
of the 'Lives' (1675), and another in his own 'Musae
subsecivae' (1676), translated for the present volume by
Ralph Williams (No. 27).

Herbert was throughout the period to the 1650s regarded
by Anglicans as an Anglican poet who wrote primarily if not
exclusively for Anglicans. Entirely in keeping with such

possessiveness, Archbishop Robert Leighton of Glasgow
quoted from 'The Temple' frequently; and it is also
reported by Anthony à Wood that among the few works that
Charles I 'delighted to read' was Herbert's poetry - a
report much qualified by Sir Thomas Herbert, whose list of
the books 'read often' by His Majesty ranges from 'The
Temple' and the sermons of Lancelot Andrewes to 'The
Faerie Queene', Fairfax's version of 'La Gerusalemme
liberata', 'and the like'. (37) By and large, of course,
the Anglican proprietorial claims on Herbert were most
effectively upheld by Vaughan and Oley, and eventually by
Walton. In the 1650s, however, Herbert the Anglican began
also to appear in the guise of Herbert the Puritan. The
unexpected development was in the first instance the
achievement of Richard Baxter, who appropriated Herbert in
his widely read masterpiece, 'The Saints Everlasting Rest'
(1650), by quoting several lines from 'The Temple' but
especially 'Dotage' and 'Home' in their entirety and the
last stanza of 'The Glance'. (38) Thirty-one years later,
in the preface to his 'Poetical Fragments' (1681), Baxter
attributed the Puritans' enthusiastic regard for 'the
Divine poet' Herbert strictly to the nature of his religious commitment. Herbert's poetry was, as poetry, dismissed as of no consequence: the fashionable poet Abraham
Cowley - 'and others' - were expressly said 'far [to]
excel *Herbert* in Wit and accurate composure' (No. 29).
Characteristically, Baxter's own poems, inclusive of
'Divine Love's Rest (written on *Herbert*'s Poems)', echo
'The Temple' neither in their outer form nor in their
inner structure and language. In parallel fashion, it
should be noted, Puritans in colonial America welcomed
Herbert because he appeared to share their own emphasis on
'the direct relation of the individual to God'; (39) yet
they, too, remained aloof from his poetry as poetry, witness the debatable impact of Herbert on Philip Pain (40)
or the solitary allusion to 'The Temple' in the verses of
John Danforth. (41) The distinguished exception is
Edward Taylor, whose estimable poetry attests 'a mind
saturated with Herbert's poetry'. (42)
     The thirty-one years from Baxter's 'The Saints
Everlasting Rest' in 1650 to his 'Poetical Fragments' in
1681 witnessed no other major developments in the attitudes toward Herbert. The proprietorial claims of Anglicans were extended variously, as by the generalised influence of Herbert on John Norris, rector of Bemerton for
nearly twenty years from 1692, and - much more dubiously -
by the plagiarism of a large portion of 'Providence' in
J.H.'s 'Miscellanea' (1669) and of three lines from 'Vertue' in John Hall's 'Jacobs Ladder' (1676). (43) The newly

aroused commitment to Herbert on the part of nonconformists
also continued apace, perhaps through the commendation of
'The Temple' by Peter Sterry and Philip Henry, or through
the extensive quotations from Herbert - 'that incomparable
sweet Singer of our *Israel*' - in John Bryan's 'Dwelling
with God' (1670) and Oliver Heywood's 'The Sure Mercies of
David' (1672). (44)   Concurrently, five well-established
traditions were prolonged still further: the composition of
poetic tributes to Herbert, as in Thomas Forde's verses of
1660 (No. 21); the invocation yet again of the two oft-
quoted lines from 'The Church-porch' ('A verse may finde
him', etc.), as on the title-page of Samuel Crossman's
'The Young Mans Meditation, or some few Sacred Poems'
(1664); the fabrication of commendatory verses, as in the
poems prefixed to the tenth edition of 'The Temple' in
1674; (45) the provision of a preface attacking 'the
looseness of this Age' joined to a celebration of Herbert,
as in Samuel Speed's 'Prison-Pietie' of 1677 (No. 28); and
the translation into Latin of poems from 'The Temple', as
in William Dillingham's versions of 'The Sacrifice',
'Charms and Knots', 'Providence', 'Mans Medley', and -
another heroic task indeed! - 'The Church-porch'. (46)
Securing a place in the emerging encyclopedic compilations,
moreover, Herbert appeared first in Thomas Fuller's 'The
History of the Worthies of England' (No. 22) and next in
Edward Phillips's 'Theatrum Poetarum' (No. 26), the account
in the latter destined to reappear twelve years later in
William Winstanley's strictly derivative 'Lives of the
most Famous English Poets' (No. 31).   By now canonised not
only as 'a most glorious true *Saint*' but as a classic too,
Herbert was absorbed into the educational curriculum
through his enrolment by Charles Hoole among 'Authours
useful for the fourth Form'; (47) while Thomas White, in a
perfectly ghastly poem most likely written in the 1670s but
extant only in a version published in 1702, maintained the
value of Herbert in moral education, especially that of
'little children' (No. 35).   As a further contribution to
this ambitious programme, 'The Temple' was equipped with
an index detailing Herbert's beasts ('Sheep', 'Horse',
etc.) but also a diversity of moral dicta ('Mirth becometh
not a Sinner') and political axioms ('Antichrist's various
policies ... *see* Rome') not even remotely sanctioned by
Herbert. (48)   David Lloyd's report in 1668 that 'all' are
'ravished' with 'The Temple' (49) may or may not be an
exaggeration; but the forms that the ravishment assumed
are clearly surprising.
      A year after the endorsement of 'the Divine poet' in
Baxter's 'Poetical Fragments', the advent of the novel
outlook prophesied long since by Hobbes (No. 15) was

confirmed by Dryden in an explicitly pejorative allusion
to Herbert's mode of articulation (No. 30). (50) But Dryden's failure to respond to Herbert, it should be empha-
sised, was increasingly shared even by Herbert's most
devoted admirers. The ongoing praise of 'The Temple' notwithstanding, one can scarcely avoid the gathering impression that Herbert was lauded rather by force of habit than
by virtue of conviction. One clear indication of this
development is the lengthy tribute by Daniel Baker (No.
33); another, the mechanical quotation of those abused two
lines from 'The Church-porch' within contexts dramatically
different from Herbert's interests; (51) and a third, the
commendation of 'The Temple' by versifiers who deplored
the secularisation of poetry even as they themselves
advanced it materially. In 1686, for example, Thomas Flatman expressed his boundless enthusiasm for two predecessors in particular:

> While Reverend *Donn*'s, and noble *Herbert*'s Flame
> A glorious immortality shall claim,
> In the most durable Records of Fame,
>
> Our modish Rhimes, like Culinary Fire,
> Unctuous and Earthy, shall in smoak expire.... (52)

But Flatman himself continued cheerfully along pastoral-
comical-tragical lines. One of his poems, all too characteristic, is addressed to cats ('Ye Cats that at midnight
spit love at each other, / Who best feel the pangs of a
passionate Lover, / I appeal to your scratches...').
    Yet Herbert endured; but he endured near the end of the
seventeenth century by appearing in still another guise,
that of the author of hymns intended sometimes for congregational use but habitually for private devotions too.
One expects that Herbert would have been delighted by this
development, for he was much in love with music and it
would seem that he shaped several of his stanzas with
various contemporary tunes in mind, both sacred and secular. (53) As if in response to Herbert's partiality to
music, John Jenkins, as we noted (p. 3), began the
honourable tradition of providing settings for Herbert's
lyrics that was to encompass by the middle and later
seventeenth century four other composers: John Wilson,
John Playford, John Blow, and Henry Purcell (see Appendix
I, Seventeenth-Century Musical Settings of Lyrics by
Herbert, pp. 357 ff.). The collections in which these
settings were first published are primarily two, John Playford's 'Psalms & Hymns in Solemn Musick' (1671) and Henry
Playford's 'Harmonia sacra' (1688). Still other

collections gave only Herbert's texts - in all cases with
many amendments - for example, Joseph Boyse's book of
hymns for the use of Presbyterians, which includes Herbert's adaptation of Psalm 23, (54) but especially the
collection of 'Select Hymns, Taken out of Mr. Herbert's
Temple' which, replete with a preface in praise of 'Our
Divine Poet' (No. 34), was first published in 1697 for the
use of Dissenters. Far from expiring at the end of the
seventeenth century, the tradition was extended thereafter
not only by John Wesley, as we are to observe later, but
by a number of composers to our own time. The poems most
often transmuted into hymns have been 'Antiphon' (I),
'Vertue', and 'The Elixer', followed in terms of their
popularity by 'The 23rd Psalme', 'Praise' (II), and
'L'Envoy'. (55)

Herbert was in the last decade of the seventeenth century adopted by a journal, the 'Athenian Mercury'. Beginning in 1692, a series of favourable judgments - nearly
all, perhaps, by the journal's editor, John Dunton - range
from a commendation of 'The Temple' to a 'Poetical Lady'
('one that's Young, and extremely delights in poetry') to
a celebration of Herbert in verse ('Sweet *Herbert*! who
can ever *weary* be, / That *writes* or *reads*, or *thinks* of
thee?'). (56) One sustained judgment, ventured in 1694,
surprises by its endorsement of 'most' of Herbert's poetry
as 'fine' (No. 32). It was to prove the last statement
of its kind for well over a century; for Herbert's poetry
was about to ebb noticeably, not that it ceased to be read
but that it was read primarily in 'improved' versions.

III HERBERT IN THE EIGHTEENTH CENTURY

'The Temple' had during the first six decades since its
publication (1633-95) appeared in eleven editions and one
reissue. Enjoying a like prominence at the outset of the
eighteenth century, it reappeared in 1703 and 1709 but
then faded for nine decades to 1799. The absence of any
edition during this long span of time need not have been
significant in itself had it not been joined to a concerted disapprobation of Herbert on the part of the
period's major literary figures. The first expressly to
condemn Herbert was Addison, whose adverse remarks in 1711
stand in the line of descent from Hobbes and especially
Dryden (No. 36; cf. Nos 15 and 30). Even worse, however,
was the stony silence of both Pope and Johnson. The views
of Pope are known to us only distantly, through the
reports by Joseph Warton and Joseph Spence. Warton
informs us that Pope had actually read Thomas Flatman -

the same who sang of 'Cats that at midnight spit love at
each other' - and adds, coarsely, that from such a 'dung-
hill, as well as from the dregs of Crashaw, of Carew, of
Herbert, and others (for it is well known he was a great
reader of all those poets) POPE has very judiciously
collected gold'. (57) For his part, Spence assures us that
Pope was of the opinion that 'Herbert is lower than Crashaw, Sir John Beaumont higher, and Donne, a good deal
so'. (58) How fortunate for Johnson that no second-hand
reports of *his* views exist! Like Pope, Johnson was
evidently familiar with Herbert's poetry but preferred
Crashaw's; and if statistics are of any relevance, his
Dictionary cites Herbert 78 times but Crashaw 103 and
Cowley 290. (59) The low fortunes of Herbert the poet
among the creators of literature in the eighteenth century
were not even redeemed by a sustained enthusiasm for the
'Divine Herbert' (as Gray once called him in passing). (60)
True, Cowper was on one occasion attracted by Herbert's
'strain of piety'; but it was a short-lived experience,
hardly fortified by a respect for what Cowper dismissed as
Herbert's 'gothic and uncouth' poetry (No. 40). During the
entire eighteenth century, indeed, 'The Temple' appears to
have elicited the response not of any poet but of a
novelist. In Book V of 'Tristram Shandy', first published
in 1762, Sterne's hero reports, 'Everything in this world,
said my father, is big with jest, - and has wit in it, and
instruction too, - if we can but find it out'. It is the
clearest allusion to 'The Temple' in eighteenth-century
literature, in this case to one of the more luminous passages in 'The Church-porch':

> All things are bigge with jest: nothing that's plain,
> But may be wittie, if thou hast the vein. (61)

Yet a number of other claims advanced during this
period would seem considerably to qualify the sombre sketch
just provided. Giles Jacob in 1720, for example, reported
that Herbert's poems are 'very much admired' (No. 38); and
John Wheeldon in 1768, introducing the 'select pieces' he
edited from Herbert's poetry and Jeremy Taylor's prose,
affirmed:

> Would it not be wasteful and ridiculous Excess to write
> a Panegyric on the divine Herbert? It would be gilding
> refined Gold, and throwing a Perfume on the Violet. His
> Memory like the Phoenix survives his Ashes, immortal as
> his Poems.... (62)

But Jacob's sense of discrimination can scarcely be trusted

since he thought that Harvey's 'The Synagogue' constituted
Part II of 'The Temple'; nor can Wheeldon's enthusiasm be
regarded as absolute since he thought it advisable to reprint only three poems from 'The Temple' - 'The Church-
porch' and, far less predictably, 'Dotage' and 'The Sacrifice' - in deference to the general distaste for Herbert's
'gothic and uncouth' poetry. At the same time it would be
unfair to Wheeldon to detract from his achievement, for in
refusing 'to alter or retouch one original Feature' of
Herbert's poems he displayed a boldness truly remarkable
for his time. By 1768, after all, Herbert's poems were
already being amended habitually, and often beyond recognition.

Herbert's poems had been amended during their translation into hymns, initially in the collections already noted
of John and Henry Playford as well as in the anonymous
'Select Hymns, Taken out of Mr. Herbert's Temple' (1697),
and thereafter in such volumes as Samuel Bury's 'A Collection of Psalms, Hymns, and Spiritual Songs' (1707), Henry
Playford's 'The Divine Companion' (3rd edn, 1709), John
Hill's 'A New Book of Psalmody' (1730?), John Gambold's
'Collection of Hymns of the Children of God in All Ages'
(1754), and others. (63) As was to be expected, many of
the amendments were dictated by the demands of the common
metre, even though in one exceptional instance, the anonymous 'Select Hymns' of 1697, a valiant effort was made to
remain 'painstakingly faithful' to Herbert's diction and
imagery. (64) If Wesley was not concerned to be similarly
faithful, it is because he never tried. He loved Herbert
so profoundly, so totally, that it was later said - by
William Jerdan, in 1853 - that

> Had there not been a Herbert, it is probable there might
> never have been a Wesley; for in the founder of the
> Methodists, it is impossible not to recognise almost
> every impulse and emotion he expressed, every doctrine
> he preached, and every duty he practised. (Below,
> p. 199)

The judgment is extreme and invites scepticism. As symbolic testimony, however, it accounts for Wesley's procla-
mation that Herbert's poems are 'scarce inferior either in
sense or language to most compositions of the present age';
it justifies, too, the inordinate time he spent transcrib-
ing, amending, and invariably 'singing George Herbert'; and
it annotates the numerous references to Herbert throughout
his correspondence. (65) His remarkable collection of
'Hymns and Sacred Poems' (1739) - the foremost among the
several collections that include adaptations of Herbert's

poems – may to a novice appear merely risible because
Wesley's version of 'The Collar' begins:

> No more, I cry'd, shall Grief be mine,
>   I will throw off the Load;
> No longer weep, and sigh, and pine
>   To find an Absent GOD.

So, too, with the transmutation of Herbert's cry of wonder

> Who would have thought my shrivel'd heart
> Could have recover'd greennesse?
>
> ('The Flower', 11. 8-9)

into the emasculated composure of

> Who would have thought my wither'd Heart
> Again should feel thy sov'reign Art,
>   A kindly Warmth again should know?

Line for line and phrase for phrase, Wesley will ever be
found wanting. But to regard his total performance is to
become aware that a poem by Herbert such as 'The Elixer'
has not simply been pruned – 'ruthlessly pruned' (66) –
but has ceased to be Herbert's:

> Teach me, my God and King,
>   In All things Thee to see;
> And what I do in any Thing,
>   To do it as for Thee!
>
> To scorn the Senses' Sway,
>   While still to Thee I tend:
> In all I do, be Thou the Way,
>   In all be Thou the End.
>
> A Man that looks on Glass,
>   On That may fix his Eye;
> Or unoppos'd may thro' it pass,
>   And Heav'n behind descry.
>
> All may of Thee partake:
>   Nothing so small can be,
> But draws, when acted for thy Sake,
>   Greatness and Worth from Thee.
>
> If done t' obey thy Laws,
>   Ev'n Servile Labours shine;
> Hallow'd is Toil, if this the Cause,
>   The meanest Work Divine.

> Th' Elixir this, the Stone
> That All converts to Gold:
> For that which GOD for His doth own,
> Cannot for less be told. (67)

Wesley's adaptation of Herbert's poems to his own purposes
can also be appreciated if his version of one poem in particular, 'Vertue', is compared with the drastic revisions
ventured first in 'Universal Harmony' (1745) and, four
decades later, in 'Universal Magazine' (1788). Deemed to
be 'perhaps the most astonishing revisions of a pre-
Restoration poem', (68) the earlier of these endeavours
transformed 'Vertue' into a celebration of wedded love, and
the latter into an extension of the *carpe diem* tradition!
(See Appendix II, Eighteenth-Century Versions of Herbert's
'Vertue', pp. 374 ff.) Simon Patrick's version of 'The
'Banquet' in 1719, it may also be recorded, was not nearly
as brutally secularised, yet its connection with Herbert's
poem was no less remote. Suffice it to quote but its opening lines:

> O Welcome, sweet, and sacred Cheer,
> The Banquet of my Saviour dear!
> O! with me, in me, ever dwell!
> Thy Charms pass Tongue to taste or tell!
> Thy Neatness entertains my Sight
> With Admiration and Delight!
> Thy Spry Flavour of the Bowl,
> Enflames, transports, fills all my Soul.... (69)

Distinctly more remote from Herbert was an anonymous effort
of much later vintage (1789) that reduced 'Affliction' (I)
to a mere jingle. It begins:

> When first the Lord my heart engag'd,
>   I thought his service brave;
> For I rejoic'd I ransom'd was
>   From being Satan's slave.... (70)

The amendments of Herbert's poetry during the eighteenth
century are one testimony to the change in critical taste.
Another is the compilation of a massive commentary on
'The Temple' by George Ryley in 1714/15 and the composition
of the longest ever poetic tribute by John Reynolds in
1725. Ryley's commentary, still unpublished, aspired to
'explain and improve' 'The Temple':

> The Whole Design of this Undertaking being to Gratifie
> 2 or 3 of my friends who Desired a better acquaintance

with the Divine Poet I Look't upon my Self as happily
freed from studying to be Elaborate & Chose to write
only what occur'd to my first Tho'ts under Each Poem To
which if I add my frequent Avocations I promise myself
I shall need no further Excuse for the Errata Both of
Judgement & Pen Should I enumerate these which mySelf
am Conscious of It would take up as many more Sheets as
I have allready Blotted.

'The uttermost I please myself with', Ryley added, 'is that
a Tollerable Sence is put upon Every poem & there are not
many that have Escaped a Genuine Denundation.' (71)   In
short, as the extracts made available here demonstrate
(No. 37), 'The Temple' was judged sufficiently removed
from the comprehension of the eighteenth-century reader to
require explication in depth. The alternative was so to
interpret Herbert's poetry as to align it with the period's
rampant optimism, witness the engaging labours of John
Reynolds (No. 39). The presuppositions once established,
and the amendments to his poetry effected, Herbert could
be esteemed one of the most unimpeachable teachers of
'*Moral* and *Divine* Subjects'. As Moses Browne declared of
such teachers in 1739, 'We have yet (be it own'd to our
Praise) a SPENCER, and HERBERT, a MILTON, and WALLER; and
those present living Ornaments, our POPE, our YOUNG, and
WATTS to boast.' (72)
       Spasmodic though the endorsements of 'The Temple' during
the eighteenth century were, and still fewer the commenda-
tions of 'A Priest to the Temple', the common denominator
even of eulogistic utterances is clearly to be marked: the
poetry of Herbert had, qua poetry, declined precipitously.
The creators of literature, we should again remind ourselves, pointedly failed so much as to mention Herbert; and
so, by and large, did critics like John Oldmixon in 1728 and
the formidable editors of the 1780s and the 1790s - John
Nichols, Henry Headley, George Ellis, Robert Anderson, and
John Ritson - of whom Headley and Ellis provided space for
only a single poem by Herbert ('Church monuments' in one
case, 'Life' in the other), as against six poems by William
Cartright, eight by Wither, and ten by Carew. (73) Equally
indicative of the prevailing critical temper are the biographical entries on Herbert in the period's encyclopedias.
Thus the adjusted English version of Pierre Bayle's
'General Dictionary' was content to describe Herbert as
'an eminent English Poet and Divine'; Erasmus Middleton in
1784 devoted twenty-two pages to Herbert as 'a pattern of
grace to posterity' but not a single phrase to his poetry;
while the third edition of the 'Encyclopaedia Britannica'
in 1797 laconically termed Herbert a 'pious divine' - and

the seventh edition of 1842 bypassed him altogether. (74)
The handful of biographical accounts that did mention Herbert's poetry were patronising at best and contemptuous at
worst. James Granger in 1769, for example, declared that
'such was [Herbert's] character that we cannot but revere
so great and good a man, as little as we esteem his
poetry.' (75) 'Little' is an understatement; for as
Headley asserted in 1787, Herbert is 'infinitely inferior
to both Quarles and Crashaw' (No. 41).

IV   HERBERT IN THE NINETEENTH CENTURY

In 1800, Dawson Warren observed in an unpublished sketch of
Herbert that there is 'no reason to doubt that he excelled
most of his contemporaries, though to the refined ear of a
modern his verses seem unmusical'. (76) Herbert's sudden
elevation to a rank inaccessible at least since the 1680s,
and the distinctly cautious tone that his verses only
'seem' unmusical, appear to herald a gradual change in
critical attitudes. In fact, however, the burden of convention lay most heavily on that considerable production
of the nineteenth century's first decade, Robert Southey's
continuation of the Ellis collection in 1807, which dismisses 'metaphysical poetry' as a manifestation of a taste
'rather retrograde than progressive' and mentions Donne and
Cowley but sidesteps Herbert in silence. (77) The most
accurate report of the consensus of opinion then current
is most likely the statement in 'The General Biographical
Dictionary' of 1814: 'As a poet Mr. Herbert ranks with
Donne, Quarles, and Crashaw; but, as some critics have
asserted, is inferior to these'. (78)
     Coleridge disagreed; and in disagreeing on expressly
literary grounds, he redirected critical opinion in Herbert's favour and paved the way for his eventual recognition as 'one of the best English lyric poets'. As the
extracts reprinted here testify (No. 42), (79) Coleridge's
initial response to Herbert was conventional enough ('I
used to read [him] to amuse myself with his quaintness, in
short, only to laugh at'). Upon consideration, however,
he determined that 'the quaintness of some of his thoughts
(not of his diction, than which nothing can be more pure,
manly, and unaffected,) has blinded modern readers to the
great general merit of his Poems, which are for the most
part exquisite in their kind'. The consequence was in the
first instance the influential remarks on Herbert in 'Biographia Literaria', and in the last the frequently
reprinted notes on 'The Temple' that invited a total
involvement with Herbert as 'a true poet, but a poet *sui*

generis'. Coleridge's enthusiasm was not transmitted
immediately either to Wordsworth or to Lamb. (80)
Mediately, however, it affected a host of lesser critics
and stimulated the response of at least one major figure,
Emerson.

Emerson's earliest substantive comment on Herbert, in a
letter of 1829, is eloquently simple: 'I dearly love Geo.
Herbert's Poems'. (81) Throughout his long career, he
placed Herbert first among the exemplars of 'etherial
poesy' ('Herbert, Shakespeare, Marvell, Herrick, Milton
Ben Jonson'), enrolled him among the foremost representatives of the English genius ('Shakespeare, Chaucer, Spenser, Herbert'), or numbered him among the select few who
articulated thoughts or feelings in an unforgettably
'virile manner' ('Luther, Montaigne, Pascal, Herbert').
(82) His enthusiasm was hospitable enough to admit even
Herbert's much maligned pattern poems ('What eggs,
ellipses, acrostics, forward, backward and across, could
not his liquid genius run into, and be genius still and
angelic love?'). (83) It was a lasting enthusiasm, too, for
the extracts reprinted here (No. 43) extend all the way to
1874, when Emerson's anthology 'Parnassus' praised Herbert
unreservedly even as its preface maintained, with characteristic extravagance, that 'So much piety was never
married to so much wit'. One consequence was that Emerson's own poetry was influenced by 'The Temple' to such an
extent that William Henry Channing once mistook Emerson's
'Grace' (1830?) for a poem by Herbert; and a second was
that Emerson by quoting from Herbert's 'Man' in the final
chapter of 'Nature' (1834) transformed him into a primitive
transcendentalist. (84) The advantage in either case was,
clearly, Herbert's.

Still another major figure of the nineteenth century who
entertained a lifelong enthusiasm for Herbert was Ruskin.
But where Coleridge and Emerson responded as much to Herbert's thought as to its articulation – his 'most correct
and natural language' according to Coleridge, 'the inimitable felicity of his diction' according to Emerson – Ruskin
was capitally concerned with Herbert's embodiment of Protestantism 'in a perfectly central and deeply spiritual
manner'. It is within such a framework that Ruskin's numerous judgments on Herbert are to be understood (No. 44).
True, he was to confess in 'Praeterita' (1885-9) the 'most
innocent' of his juvenile affections, 'the affection of
trying to write like Hooker and George Herbert'. (85) But
the confession appertains rather to modes of thought than
to style and more specifically to language. A declaration
as early as 1840 of his enthusiasm for Herbert ('I admire
George Herbert above everything') was joined to a revealing

qualification ('and shall learn "The Church-porch" by heart
as soon as I have time'). (86)   In 1845, addressing his
parents from Italy, a casual reference that he 'had been
reading George Herbert all the morning' was subsequently
annotated thus:

> I really *am* getting more pious than I was, owing pri-
> marily to George Herbert, who is the only religious per-
> son I ever could understand or agree with, and second-
> arily to Fra Angelico & Benozzo Gozzoli, who made me
> believe everything they paint, be it ever so out of the
> way. (87)

Ruskin invoked Herbert on any number of occasions, and in
an appendix to 'Modern Painters' named him among such
cardinal guides as 'Wordsworth, Carlyle, and Helps; to
whom (with Dante and George Herbert, in olden time) I owe
more than to any other writers; - most of all, perhaps, to
Carlyle'.   As always, however, Herbert was made to serve a
particular purpose, in the case of Ruskin best disclosed in
one of his lectures at Oxford in 1874: 'Perfect Christianity is the Christianity of Sir Philip Sidney and George
Herbert, not of John Knox or Calvin'. (88)   In short, two
centuries after 'pious' Herbert was hailed as 'a most
glorious true *Saint*', his piety was transformed into an
aesthetic principle and his saintliness into a symbolic
experience fraught with cultural implications.
   The favourable attitude of Coleridge and Ruskin in
England, and of Emerson in America, did not reduce everyone
else to silence.   Dissenting views, however decreasing
their force, continued to be expressed.   In 1821, for
instance, an anonymous essayist in the 'Retrospective
Review' was persuaded that 'The Temple' is 'such a mass of
uninviting and even repulsive matter' that a few poems
should be singled out for praise; yet not himself convinced
by the examples chosen - 'The Church-porch' is 'for the
most part written in an uncouth and ungraceful style',
'Jordan' (I) begins 'with a very fantastical stanza',
'Vertue' is 'defaced by a vulgar expression or two', and
so on - concluded that 'no reader of taste, and rational
views of religion, but must lament and wonder at the
strange and almost incomprehensible turn of some of the
poems'. (89)   Only slightly more charitable, James Montgomery remarked in 1827 that Herbert's poems,

> amidst innumerable conceits and quaintnesses, have a
> sufficient proportion of natural and beautiful thoughts,
> simply or elegantly expressed to redeem them from
> oblivion.   His piety is unquestionable, but his taste

so perverted, that devotion itself is turned into
masquerade throughout his writings. (90)

The biographical entries in the period's encyclopedic
compilations, all equally influenced by Walton, were at
the same time moving in a variety of directions. Thus the
entry in 'The Penny Encyclopaedia' (1838) codified the
increasing sense of the similarities between 'The Temple'
and John Keble's 'The Christian Year' (1827): 'there is the
same zeal and energy in pastoral duties, the same love of
paradox in language, the same reverence for antiquity and
for the ceremonies of the church'. (91) The entry in
Robert Chambers's survey of English literature (1844)
reiterated the common disapprobation of Herbert's 'ridiculous conceits or coarse unpleasant similes' and the
equally common regret that his taste should have been so
'very inferior' to his genius (No. 46). The entry in
'Lives of the Illustrious' (1855) outdid even Walton by
picturing Herbert as a student at Cambridge awaiting the
descent of the Holy Spirit ('In the silent watches of the
night, whilst all his fellow-students were asleep, he sat
alone waiting for this holy coming; the sad stars looking
sorrowfully at him through the window-panes...'). The
poetry as poetry was mentioned only coincidentally. 'The
thought', we are told, 'is always quaint and original, and
so is the dressing of it; but, in an artistic sense, the
verse is not always perfect or musical.' Of the poems
specifically commended, the 'most perfect' are said to be
'Sunday', 'Mortification', and 'The Flower'; and the 'most
beautiful', 'Vertue'. But the final judgment is the familiar one that Herbert's fame 'does not rest so much upon
his talents as a writer, as upon his character as a man'.
(92) In a like frame of mind, the entry in 'Chambers's
Encyclopaedia' - written as late as 1863 - generously maintained that 'The Temple', 'although disfigured by fantastic
conceits, contains several passages of the purest pious
verse which the language possesses'; yet added the generally accepted premise that Herbert owes his immortality
rather to Walton's 'quaint and loving pen' than to his own
poems. (93)
     Notwithstanding the most adverse of opinions, however,
the nineteenth century regained what the eighteenth had so
completely lost, the actual text of the entire 'Temple'.
After nine decades of hybernation, Herbert's poems began to
appear from 1799 with a frequency reminiscent of the height
of their popularity from 1633 to the late 1690s. The proliferating editions were often extravagantly handsome in
demeanour (94) and, even more often, encompassed Herbert's
complete works as Pickering in his pioneering issue of

'The Remains of that Sweet Singer of The Temple' in 1836
quite proudly announced ('the only edition in which all his
works are to be found'). One's expectation that an ulter-
ior motive informed these enterprises is confirmed by the
concurrent appearance of 'A Priest to the Temple' not only
as an appendix to 'The Temple' but in its own right - for
example, in 1832 - as well as within collections like
'The Clergyman's Instructor' (1807) and the American
effort entitled 'The Preacher and Pastor' (1845). (95)
Even more eloquent is the constant presence of Walton in
the biographical entries already cited and in the several
editions that reprinted his hagiography in full or in
abridged form, (96) also in the more formal biographical
portraits written by William Hazlitt the Younger in England and George L. Duyckinck in America, (97) and especially in the three major editions of the 1850s by William
Jerdan, George Gilfillan, and Robert Aris Willmott.
Habitually florid in their articulation and often crude in
their reduction of Walton's subtle insights, the introductions to the three editions (Nos 49-51) were alike conditioned by the presupposition ringingly stated at the very
outset of Jerdan's account: 'The Mission of Poetry is
refining, pure and holy'. 'The Temple' thus converted into
a collection of poems replete with edifying matter, Herbert
emerged as a proper Victorian, 'one of the most thoroughly
Christian gentlemen that ever breathed'. (98) Not surprisingly, Herbert was thereafter included in the standard
Victorian collections of poetry. The process began, hesi-
tantly, first with Francis Palgrave's enormously popular
'Golden Treasury' (1861), which included only 'The Pulley'
- retitled for the sake of clarity 'The Gifts of God'! -
and next with Archbishop Richard Trench's equally popular
'Household Book of English Poetry' (1868), which included
'The Flower' and 'Mortification'. (99) The ultimate
endorsement of Herbert occurred in 1889, when thirty-three
of his poems were included by Palgrave in 'The Treasury
of Sacred Song'.
    The editions of Jerdan, Gilfillan, and Willmott have
their limitations; but their virtues should be marked too.
For one, they made Herbert's poetry familiar to a wider
public; and for another, they contributed substantially to
an increasing appreciation of his strictly literary
achievement. With various degrees of emphasis, all three
introductions - but especially Gilfillan's - upheld the
'very rare, lofty, and original order' of 'The Temple'.
Perhaps it could not have been otherwise, certainly because Coleridge's decisive endorsement of Herbert could
hardly have been disregarded, but also because De Quincey's
enthusiastic approval of Donne in 1838 ('he combined what

no other man has ever done - the last sublimation of dia-
lectical subtlety and address with the most impassioned
majesty') (100) was forcing readers to reconsider the
accumulated critical prejudices against the 'metaphysicals'. The most unexpected reader of Herbert in the early
1840s was George Eliot; and though her response was
entirely personal (No. 45), it suggests that 'The Temple'
was being read outside the prevailing critical climate.
Equally original was George L. Craik, whose influential
'Sketches of the History of Literature in England' (1845)
adventurously observed that Herbert's poetry

> has been to a great extent preserved from the imitation
> of Donne's peculiar style, into which it might in other
> circumstances have fallen, in all probability by its
> having been composed with little effort or elaboration,
> and chiefly to relieve and amuse his own mind by the
> melodious expression of his favourite fancies and con-
> templations. His quaintness lies in his thoughts
> rather than in their expression, which is in general
> sufficiently simple and luminous. (101)

Herbert's reception in America was even more cordial.
Reservations about 'The Temple' were indeed expressed, but
the final decision tended to incline in the direction
indicated by Whittier in 1847:

> We have been delighted with 'Holy George Herbert'.
> Some of his conceits are not agreeable to our taste,
> and we cannot always sympathise with his Church eulo-
> gies. But there is enough beside to make us love him.
> (102)

Instrumental in the creation of a favourable attitude in
America was, of course, Emerson. He appears to have conditioned the response of Thoreau, some of whose poems
display an 'obvious' debt to 'The Temple'; and he may have
occasioned, too, the 'distinct relationship' claimed to
have existed between Herbert and Emily Dickinson. (103)
When all is said, however, Emerson's most substantial convert to Herbert was Margaret Fuller, who in 1846 ventured
'perhaps her most completely successful attempt at creative criticism' (104) within the most unique format in
Herbert's critical heritage: an imaginary conversation between him and his elder brother, Lord Herbert of Chirbury
(No. 47).
   Arthur Hugh Clough in the 1850s decided to reproach
Herbert (No. 48) even though his own improbably-named poem
'Epi-Strauss-Ion' appears to have been influenced by his

predecessor's 'The Windows'. (105)   Another minor poet,
John Keble, behaved no less oddly, for his oblique statement about Herbert (No. 52) stands in diametric opposition
to the period's frequent juxtaposition of 'The Temple'
and 'The Christian Year'.   Eventually, at any rate, Keble
would recede into obscurity as ever more readers began to
discern Herbert's superiority in 'terseness and vigour'
(below, p. 253).   The decisive judgment against Keble was
voiced in 1896, by A.C. Benson (No. 59), who leads to the
persuasion in our time that while Herbert is possessed of
'excessive refinement of feeling', Keble displays but
'dimness and blandness'. (106)

The 1850s also witnessed the last substantial effort to
speak adversely of Herbert.   It appeared anonymously in
the 'British Quarterly Review' for 1854 (No. 53); and
though hostile comments would persist for several decades
yet to come, none would match the ambition so evidently
impressed upon it.   Within four years, however, the pendu-
lum swung to the other extreme with the most hysterical
praise of Herbert ever, in an essay by Samuel Brown. (107)
Such is Brown's baroque exuberance over Herbert's 'fervid
and beautiful productions' that no purpose would be served
by reproducing his paean at length.   It should nevertheless be recorded that Brown boldly proclaimed that
Herbert's poetry is 'resonant with genuine music, to the
sense as well as to the soul', that 'in true poetic genius'
it surpasses 'immeasurably' much of religious poetry, and
that in it 'the most uncompanioned poetic taste is sure to
find far more delight than weariness and offence'.
Commenting on a number of individual poems, Brown spoke
shrewdly of the anagram on the Virgin Mary as a 'sublime
prank'; but he also said of 'The Church-porch', blissfully
unaware of any irony, that it is like 'old Polonius
bestowing wise and elegant advices on his son'.

The ensuing decade, the 1860s, was to prove one of the
most crucial in Herbert's critical fortunes.   The curious
verses of James Thomson apart (No. 54), the decade is distinguished in the first instance by a major apologia for
Herbert's poetry that appeared anonymously in the 'Christian Remembrancer' for 1862 (No. 55).   A stunning performance by any account, it belongs to its time to the extent
that it was written 'now that so many of the clergy strive
to raise themselves to Herbert's high standard'.   Swiftly
transcending such limitations, however, it crosses swords
with every adversely inclined critic of Herbert, disputes
the traditional extension of the Waltonesque portrait of
Herbert by asserting that the poet was not a recluse but
'emphatically a man of social sympathies', and urges 'all
true lovers of poetry' to seek Herbert's treasure 'below

the surface'. A year later, in 1863, Herbert's poetry was
edited anew by Charles Cowden Clark with an introduction by
John Nichol, who as Professor of English literature at the
University of Glasgow became Herbert's first academic
critic (No. 56). Nichol's introduction is a disappointment so far as it reiterates the usual complaints about
Herbert's 'want of condensation', his lack of musicality,
and the like; but it is also refreshing in its distant
awareness of the 'unity of thought and purpose' that pervades 'The Temple' and in its firm declaration that some
of his poems seem 'inspired by a deeper flow of imagination than the rest, and will bear comparison with the best
of all but our greatest poets'. As Herbert's 'defects'
were being reconsidered one by one, the charge that he is
wanting in musicality was itself inverted in 1868, by the
poet and novelist George Macdonald, who averred that Herbert 'excels' in nothing so much as in the sound of his
verses. One of the most considerable essays in the history of Herbert criticism, Macdonald's evaluation of 'The
Temple' (No. 57) maintained also that Herbert is 'seldom
other than graceful' and that his 'exquisite art' is marred
only by its association with the poetry of the other members of 'Dr. Donne's school' – to use the phrase that was
thereafter to be heard repeatedly. Even so, however, the
contributions of the remarkable 1860s were not yet exhaus-
ted, for in 1867 a far greater literary figure, Arnold,
included Herbert in a list of poets he was to read. The
task must have been accomplished expeditiously, for soon
Arnold's notebooks began to cite Herbert, while in 1868,
responding to Lord Coleridge's view of Herbert, Vaughan,
and Cowley as 'mannerists and affected', he wrote:

I should be inclined to put George Herbert – perhaps
because I have read him within this last year – in
another category from Vaughan and Cowley, to use many
qualifications in calling him 'a mannerist and affected', and to attribute to him more hold on men and more
prospect of keeping it than you do. (108)

Herbert exerted no influence on Arnold's poetry, and
even less on Tennyson's. But he did affect two other
later nineteenth-century poets, Christina Rossetti and
Gerard Manley Hopkins. Rossetti's familiarity with 'The
Temple' was evidently an early experience that extended to
her later poems, most notably 'Up-Hill'; but, as T.S. Eliot
warned, the apparent resemblance in the temperament of the
two poets is much qualified by their 'profound differences' (No. 72). (109) Hopkins, on the other hand,
absorbed Herbert's example much more constructively within

his own powerful poetry. Whether or not Hopkin's 'strongest tie to the English Church' was Herbert, (110) it is
significant that he mentioned neither his fellow-Catholic
Crashaw nor the Anglican Donne but remarked favourably on
the 'rich and nervous' Marvell and certainly on Herbert
(No. 58). Given such discriminating concern with poetry as
poetry, we are not surprised to discover, as has been said,
that 'Herbert's frank avowal of Christ; his passionate yet
restrained colloquies with God; his vigorous and subtle
expression of doctrine; his significant quaintness and
happy conceits, - all these elements are found, in duly
modified form, in the later Hopkins'. (111) Herbert's partiality for orthodox paradoxes - and incidentally to compound epithets like 'Christ-side-piercing spear' ('Prayer'
(I), l. 6) - could hardly fail to attract Hopkins.

Yet by the end of the nineteenth century it was not Herbert but Donne who was increasingly praised by critics of
the order of Arthur Symons ('Donne's quality of passion is
unique in English poetry. It is a rapture in which the
mind is supreme, a reasonable rapture, and yet carried to a
pitch of actual violence'). (112) It is nevertheless
worthy of consideration that while the resuscitation of
Donne was a phenomenon confined to the very end of the
nineteenth century and the outset of the twentieth, the
reputation of Herbert remained steadily high ever since the
early 1800s. Throughout the century, moreover, Herbert
enjoyed a popularity not even remotely matched by Donne or
Crashaw or Vaughan or Cowley. As editions, reissues, and
anthologies of his poetry multiplied, the anonymous editor
of his 'Works' for The Lansdowne Poets (1878) grouped
Donne, Herbert, and Cowley only in order to separate them
without hesitation: 'Herbert is the best of the three', he
declared, 'and remains the only one of them popularly read
in the present day.' (113) Oddly enough, only the indus-
trious Alexander B. Grosart, in editing the period's
greatest scholarly text of Herbert's complete works (1874),
refused explicitly to commit himself one way or the other.
Brilliant though Grosart was as a scholar - he discovered
the Williams manuscript of Herbert's poems and contributed
many biographical details of fundamental importance - he
was restricted by his subjective approach to Herbert and
by his retreat into Walton's hagiography as contemplated
through the spectacles of Victorian sentimental piety.(114)
His extremely lengthy 'critical examination' of Herbert is
but extremely lengthy; and where he ventured judgments,
they were either derivative as in the endorsement of George
Macdonald's praise of Herbert's 'exquisite art in combination with quaintness', or else shrouded in Victorian pom-
posity ('HERBERT was autochthonal after a remarkable type,

alike in his thinking and imaginativeness, and wording and art'). (115)

Anglicans were in the meantime extending their claim on Herbert through a number of strategies. Apart from the provision of still further editions like that of Ernest Rhys for The Canterbury Poets (1885), J. Henry Shorthouse wrote for his novel 'John Inglesant' (1881) an evocative account of Nicholas Ferrar's community at Little Gidding - but an account, alas, blatantly plagiarised. (116) Far more creditable was Bishop John Jeremiah Daniell's 'Life of George Herbert of Bemerton', published in 1893 by the Society for Promoting Christian Knowledge. Based on documentary evidence accumulated after laborious research, it is an indispensable biography to students of Herbert's life. But it is also a biography that zealously eschews the poetry, while its orotund style and unwarranted fancifulness converge to picture Herbert's last days, for example, thus:

> towards the middle of January 1632-3, his strength decayed rapidly. He took his last walk into the garden; stood for the last time on the bank of the river; looked for the last time on its crystal waters; lifted his eyes for the last time to the cathedral; and then returned to his home, never to leave it again. (117)

Across the Atlantic, too, the pious could be exalted by the 'Beauties of the Rev. George Herbert', edited with piquant irresponsibility by Bostwick Hawley, D.D. (1877). Like Warton's Pope, however, Hawley managed to collect gold from dregs:

> Mr. Herbert was a quaint thinker and strong writer. Sympathetic, vigorous, and deeply religious, he wrote for the people. Strongly characterized for common sense, his fancy was fruitful, his language pure and racy, and his style true to nature. (118)

Herbert's American admirers were so far from being circumscribed within any ecclesiastical orbit that they included James Russell Lowell and Oliver Wendell Holmes. (119) But his admirers in Britain were equally diverse, numbering as they did the vivacious Alice Meynell, who borrowed his own words to describe his poetry as 'perfectly a box where thoughts "compacted lie"'. (120) On the other hand, Herbert failed to secure the support of the period's foremost academic authority, George Saintsbury, who pronounced in 1898 that Herbert was equal only to Keble, less than equal to Crashaw or Vaughan, and decidedly inferior to Christina

Rossetti (No. 60). Whatever the accuracy of a later
description of Saintsbury as 'indefatigable and omniscient
but sometimes blundering and tasteless', (121) his adverse
view of Herbert was by no means a deviation from the attitudes current at the turn of the century. In spite of
Francis Thompson's optimism in 1903 ('The seventeenth century poets are coming to their own'), (122) the immediate
future belonged not to Herbert but - *pace* Arthur Symons and
others - to Donne. For some three more decades, Herbert
continued to elicit divided responses.

V HERBERT IN THE TWENTIETH CENTURY

The divided responses to Herbert at the outset of the
twentieth century appear at first glance less than divided
since Frances Duncan dismissed him as a 'comparatively un-
important poet' and Saintsbury continued to credit that he
is devoid of the 'rarest touch' of Crashaw or Vaughan.
(123) But the sequence of extracts made available here
suggests the varieties of experience that in fact obtained.
Edward Dowden in 1900 endeavoured to transcend Victorian
premises with an earnest consideration of Herbert's poetic
range (No. 61), while three readers in 1903 sounded all but
one of the remaining possible notes: Archbishop William
Alexander of Armagh, who confessed to his occasional anger
with Herbert, and certainly to his contempt (No. 62);
Canon H.C. Beeching, who hovered between the traditional
disparagement of Herbert's conceits and the increasing
respect for his 'exquisite' style (No. 63); and W.J. Courthope, Professor of Poetry at Oxford, who did not allow his
preference for Crashaw and Vaughan to interfere with his
sympathetic and refreshingly literary appreciation of 'The
Temple' (No. 64). The ultimate sound was generated by the
formidable edition of Herbert in 1905, the work of an
American scholar, George Herbert Palmer ('bearing Herbert's
name, I have had him as a companion throughout my life and
have studied him elaborately').
    'I am attempting', Palmer declared, 'a kind of critical
dictionary of Herbert, in which his meaning may be system-
atically fixed with reference to the text itself, to the
facts of the author's life, and to the literary conditions
under which his poetry arose.' (124) The crucial factor
was 'the facts of the author's life', so interpreted as to
yield four periods - Education, Hesitation, Crisis, Consecration - within which the various poems were located in
an audacious rearrangement of their given order. Accurately described as 'the apotheosis of the psychological
approach', (125) Palmer's method is in fact an extension of

Walton's strategy, however unaffected it is by Walton's
emphases and however much Palmer protested that 'Walton's
fascinating portraiture has taken so firm a hold on the
popular imagination that it may truly be said to constitute
at present the most serious obstacle to a cool assessment
of Herbert'. (126) The unwarranted rearrangement of the
poems apart, however, Palmer's edition is a major achievement because of his infectious enthusiasm for the poetry,
his manifest conviction that Herbert is a conscious artist,
and his expansive commentary on the general as on the particular. His sophistication is apparent especially in his
reiterated affirmation of Herbert's 'ever-present use of
art', *id est*, 'a solidity of structure hitherto unknown'
conflated with a 'compact abundance of thought'. Felicities abound, as when Palmer maintains that Herbert's use of
an unrhymed line as a refrain creates an effect of 'a dis-
jointed cry', or when he defines conceits as so many cases
of 'condensed imagination'. (127) Most perceptive on Herbert's 'unique' metres, variable stanzas, and form, Palmer
repeatedly pleaded for a recognition of his favourite
poet's depth - for example:

> What can have made a writer whose diction is on the
> whole sound, and who is ever alert, artistic, and highly
> rational, so difficult to read? For difficult he is.
> No other English poet, not even Donne or Browning,
> gives his reader such frequent pause. Nearness of
> acquaintance does not remove the intricacy. It is per-
> petual. Or if at times poems like 'The Elixer',
> 'Gratefulnesse', 'The Method', 'Submission', the second
> 'Temper', 'Unkindnesse', show that he might have been
> as simple in verse as he regularly is in prose, the
> moment's lucidity merely makes the prevailing darkness
> deeper. A trait of style so marked in a man of unmis-
> takable power is apt to be connected with his genius.
> What at first appears a surface blemish, - and a strange
> one, - traced intimately, runs down to the sources of
> his strength. (128)

As Palmer's edition cannot adequately be represented
through a single extract, its essential arguments are
sketched here through his own efforts at a summary statement, ventured thirteen years later in 'Formative Types in
English Poetry' (No. 65).
   Distressed by the implications of Palmer's edition,
Paul Elmer More attempted in an impressionistic essay
(1906) to defend the threatened traditional view of Herbert
(No. 66). But others learned to react differently, appre-
ciating that Palmer's edition made it possible to claim -

as A. Clutton-Brock claimed later, in 1921 - that it was
no longer conceivable to describe as merely 'quaint' a
poet who is 'so continually interesting' (No. 70). Pre-
eminently pious accounts of Herbert as 'tender, humble,
devoted' did not cease automatically, of course, witness
Arthur Waugh's vacuous introduction to The World's
Classics edition of Herbert (1907), in time the object of
T.S. Eliot's scorn (No. 72). It is nevertheless significant that while A.G. Hyde's biography of Herbert - the
first in the twentieth century (1906) - regarded its subject as primarily 'the Poet of the Church' and thought his
tactics 'often repellent' as traditionally charged, it
demonstrated in the end that 'The Temple' is 'full of
music' and bears 'all the marks of the great style' (No.
67). In parallel fashion, Edward Bliss Reed in 1912 reconsidered some of Herbert's decried aspects and discovered them to be 'not a mere ornament' but intrinsic to
the aims of 'The Temple' (No. 69).

    Herbert's emergence ever since the late seventeenth
century as the author of hymns was earlier said to have
been extended into the twentieth (above, p. 14). A
related development in 1911 centred on the provision by
Vaughan Williams of musical settings for five of Herbert's
poems, while later 'The Temple' would even be transmuted
into an oratorio. (129) But the twentieth century also
witnessed the extension of yet another tradition, Herbert's
continuing though distinctly humble influence on some of
his fellow-poets. Early in the century this influence was
distantly exerted on Francis Thompson, whose enthusiasm
for Herbert is well-attested (No. 68). (130) Yeats also
responded, absorbing Herbert's lines in 'Vertue' -

    Onely a sweet and vertuous soul,
    Like season'd timber, never gives;
    But though the whole world turn to coal,
              Then chiefly lives.

- into his own in 'A Friend's Illness':

    Why should I be dismayed
    Though flame had burned the whole
    World, as it were a coal,
    Now I have seen it weighed
    Against a soul?

Herbert also appears to have affected both Dylan Thomas and
Louis MacNeice. (131) If his influence on the early T.S.
Eliot was minimal, (132) one factor must have been Eliot's
'discovery' of Herbert sometime after the appearance of all

the poems up to and including 'The Waste Land' (1922).   In
the event, Eliot became the most decisive champion of Herbert in the twentieth century.

Eliot's initial response to Herbert was conditioned by
H.J.C. Grierson's editions first of Donne (1912) and then
of 'Metaphysical Lyrics and Poems of the Seventeenth
Century' (1921).   Grierson's own attitude toward Herbert
appears to have deteriorated from 1906, when he could at
least aver that 'Herbert's quaint figures are managed with
great rhetorical effectiveness', (133) to 1921, when he
thought that Herbert's mind was indeed acute but 'not profound', nor his poetry 'greatly imaginative' (No. 71).
Grierson's approbation in the first instance of Donne, and
in the second of Marvell, was adapted in the review of his
labours by Eliot in the enormously influential essay The
Metaphysical Poets (1921).   But Eliot's developing interests as a poet dictated in time a decreasing enthusiasm for
Donne and Marvell, and a correspondingly increasing enthusiasm
for Herbert. (134)   Marvell was the first adversely to be
affected (1923), his erstwhile stature reduced to a level
below that of the distinctly minor poet Henry King.   Donne
was reproached next (1931), chided for his 'manifest fis-
sure between thought and sensibility'.   'His learning',
added Eliot, 'is just information suffused with emotion,
or combined with emotion not essentially relevant to it.'
(135)   On the other hand, elevating Herbert in 1932, Eliot
praised his 'spiritual stamina' and remarked apropos anthologies inclusive of Grierson's that as throughout 'The
Temple' 'there is brain work, and a very high level of intensity', Herbert's poetry should be considered 'definitely an *oeuvre*, to be studied entire' (No. 72).   Confirming this attitude thirty years later in 'George Herbert', the longest essay he wrote on any of the 'metaphysicals', Eliot argued that 'we must study "The Temple"
as a whole' because Herbert is 'a major poet'. (136)

The decade of the 1930s is the most crucial in Herbert's
critical heritage, the turning point in his recognition as
a poet.   Eliot's contribution, spacious as it was in its
generosity, remains of cardinal importance both in itself
and in its influence.   But one would wish to note that it
coincided with a number of other developments in other
quarters and under other assumptions: the increased regard
for Coleridge's critical perception in general and his
judgment on Herbert in particular; the cumulative impact
of Herbert's partisans in America beginning with Emerson;
the creation of a climate favourable to Herbert even if
some of the preceding century's more impressive essays,
notably the one in the 'Christian Remembrancer' (No. 55),
were not actually read widely; the great number of
ecclesiastically sanctioned editions of 'The Temple' and

indeed of Herbert's complete works, which kept his popularity at uncommonly high levels; the 'discovery' of Donne,
which may at the outset have affected Herbert adversely
but in the end obliged a reassessment of his achievement
too; the publication of reputably literary essays in
advance of Eliot's, for example, Dowden's and especially
Courthope's and Clutton-Brock's (Nos 61, 64, 70); and, of
course, the ambitious edition by Palmer. In 1933, moreover, the novelist Aldous Huxley responded to Herbert much
as another novelist, Sterne, had responded in the far more
hostile context of the eighteenth century (above, p. 15).
Huxley in 'Texts and Pretexts' quoted from several of Herbert's poems, endorsed in particular 'The Collar' ('one of
the finest he ever wrote and among the most moving, to my
mind, in all our literature'), and remarked after citing a
number of verses from 'The Flower' (11. 8-21 and 36-42)
that

> The climate of the mind is positively English in its
> variableness and instability. Frost, sunshine, hope-
> less drought and refreshing rains succeed one another
> with bewildering rapidity. Herbert is the poet of this
> inner weather. Accurately, in a score of lyrics un-
> excelled for flawless purity of diction and apposite-
> ness of imagery, he has described its changes and inter-
> preted, in terms of a mystical philosophy, their signi-
> ficance. Within his limits he achieves a real perfec-
> tion. (137)

A year after Eliot's contribution, in 1933, several
essays on Herbert appeared apropos the tercentenary of his
death and the first publication of 'The Temple'. Except
for Basil de Selincourt's essay in 'The Times Literary
Supplement' (No. 73), none of them merits one's attention
now save as an indication that the emergence of Herbert as
'a major poet' had not yet been disseminated widely. One
reader, indeed, generously inclined to the view that Herbert 'by no means deserves a polite obscurity', while
another went so far as to dismiss him as 'a signpost to be
recorded rather than a writer to be read'. (138) Within
three years, however, attitudes had changed perceptibly.
Of three major reconsiderations of Herbert published in
America in 1936, one (by George M. Harper) was concerned
with 'the excellence of Herbert's poetry', (139) while
another (by Helen C. White) voiced the persuasion that
'Herbert is no naïve and innocent dévot singing with un-
premeditated spontaneity, but a highly conscious and
deliberate artist, as is coming to be more and more appreciated among Herbert scholars'. (140) The third and best

of these studies, by Austin Warren, is made available here
(No. 74).

Before the remarkable 1930s expired, Herbert also
appeared on the Continent for the first significant time
since the publication of 'The Temple'. A humble appearance, it involved his influence on Simone Weil - 'une
influence décisive', as a scholar assures us - that included the commendation of the third of his poems entitled
'Love' as 'le plus beau poème du monde'. (141)   In 1938,
moreover, Louis Untermeyer gave attention to Herbert's
'combination of solemnity and virtuosity', arguing in
particular that his pattern poems do not constitute
'irresponsible playfulness, but a mixture of play and
passion which allows Herbert to embody his most profound
thoughts in anagrams and acrostics, shaped whimsies and
puns'. (142)

Herbert's progress thereafter was irreversible.
Scholarship provided the necessary implements: first,
F.E. Hutchinson's text of 'The Works of George Herbert'
(Oxford, 1941), the most responsible edition up to its
time; and by the 1970s, an edition of the English poems
based on the collation of the available sources (143) as
well as Amy M. Charles's facsimile of the Williams manuscript and her thoroughly researched 'Life of George
Herbert' (both in 1977), Mario A. DiCesare and Rigo
Magnami's 'Concordance' (also 1977), John R. Roberts's
annotated bibliography and collection of 'essential
articles' (1978-9) (144) - and now, of course, the present
volume of Herbert's critical heritage. New material has
also come to light: two poems in Latin, their existence
unknown prior to 1962; and two poems in English, their
existence known but their authoritative texts not available
before 1979. (145)   The major scholarly studies commenced
with Rosemond Tuve's 'reading' in the background to Herbert's thought (1952); and the major critical reassess-
ments, with Joseph H. Summers's seminal evaluation of the
poetry (1954).   Summers's study, whose opening statement
initiates the present volume too - 'George Herbert is one
of the best English lyric poets' - has been followed by a
number of other sustained discourses, particularly those
by Mary Ellen Rickey, Arnold Stein, Helen Vendler, and
Stanley Fish. (146)   'Today', it was said in 1954, 'Herbert's reputation is higher than it has been since the
end of the seventeenth century'.   At present, certainly,
Herbert is commonly seen as 'one of the strongest poetic
personalities in English' or even as 'one of the best
English poets in most things, and the best of all in some
things'. (147)   Consenting, a fellow-poet, W.H. Auden,
maintained in 1973 that 'Of all the so-called

"metaphysical" poets, he has the subtlest ear'. Auden invoked Coleridge in support: 'Herbert is a true poet, but a poet *sui generis*, the merits of whose poems will never be felt without a sympathy with the mind and character of the man' (No. 42). 'My own sympathy', Auden wrote, 'is unbounded'. (148)

NOTES

1   Summers, p. 11. The abbreviations in use throughout are listed above, p. xvi.
2   Helen C. White, 'The Metaphysical Poets' (1936, repr. 1962), p. 185. Interestingly, Herbert did not once borrow directly from Donne; but Donne did borrow a line from Herbert's 'The Church-porch' (1. 80) for his own poem 'To Mr Tilman after he had taken orders' (1. 30).
3   Douglas Bush, 'English Literature in the Earlier Seventeenth Century', 2nd rev. edn (Oxford, 1962), p. 275.
4   According to the inventory by A.F. Allison, 'Four Metaphysical Poets ... A Bibliographical Catalogue of the Early Editions of their Poetry and Prose' (Folkestone and London, 1973), pp. 13-23.
5   'Nicholas Ferrar: Two Lives', ed. J.E.B. Mayor, being Part I of 'Cambridge in the 17th Century' (Cambridge, 1855), p. 313.
6   Ferrar Papers (No. 796), Magdalene College, Cambridge; quoted by Amy M. Charles, 'A Life of George Herbert' (Ithaca, NY, 1977), p. 125.
7   Jenkins's settings survive in a set of partbooks in a manuscript now in the Library of Christ Church, Oxford (MSS 736-8); they are of 'Christmas' (11. 15 ff.), 'The Dawning', 'Ephes. 4.30: Grieve not the Holy Spirit' (11. 1-18 and 19-36), and 'The Starre' (11. 1-16 and 17-32). They are discussed in detail by Duckles (as below, p. 357). Another composer of the same period, Henry Lawes, provided a setting of Herbert's version of Psalm 23 (in the British Library's Add. MS 53723).
8   In a manuscript in the Durham Cathedral Library (MS Hunter 27, Part 8), described by Paul G. Stanwood, Poetry Manuscripts of the Seventeenth Century in the Durham Cathedral Library, 'Durham University Journal', n.s., XXXI (1970), especially pp. 88-90. Of Leeke's translation of 'The Church Militant', 11. 1-48 are in Stanwood; 11. 235-52 in Grosart (as below, note 115: II, xxii-xxv); and the entire poem in Köppl, Ch. II.

9   Goodman has been noted by Saad El-Gabalawy, Two
    Obscure Disciples of George Herbert, 'Notes and
    Queries', CCXXII (1977), 541-2.
10 On the relationship between the two brothers, consult
    Mario M. Rossi, 'La vita, le opere, i tempi di Edoardo
    Herbert di Chirbury' (Florence, 1947), 3 vols, passim;
    and on their poetry: Mary E. Rickey, Rhymecraft in
    Edward and George Herbert, 'Journal of English and
    Germanic Philology', LVII (1958), 502-11.
11 'The Ferrar Papers', ed. B. Blackstone (Cambridge,
    1938), p. 303. Blackstone's edition, together with
    Mayor's (above, note 5), are indispensable sources on
    the Ferrar circle; but see also 'The Story Books of
    Little Gidding', ed. E. Cruwys Sharland (1899), and
    'Conversations at Little Gidding ... Dialogues by
    Members of the Ferrar Family', ed. A.M. Williams (Cam-
    bridge, 1970). Other accounts include T.O. Beachcroft,
    Nicholas Ferrar and George Herbert, 'Criterion', XII
    (1932), 24-42; R. Balfour Daniels, George Herbert's
    Literary Executor, in his 'Some 17th Century Worthies'
    (Chapel Hill, NC, 1940), pp. 80-90; Margaret Cropper,
    'Flame Touches Flame' (1949), pp. 29-72; C. Leslie
    Craig, 'Nicholas Ferrar Junior' (1950); and especially
    Alan L. Maycock, 'Nicholas Ferrar of Little Gidding'
    (1938), with its continuation in 'Chronicles of Little
    Gidding' (1954).
12 See A.C. Howell, Christopher Harvey's 'The Synagogue'
    (1640), 'Studies in Philology', XLIX (1952), 229-47.
    Howell is far too kindly disposed toward his insipid
    subject.
13 Henry Colman, 'Divine Meditations', ed. Karen E.
    Steanson (New Haven, Conn., 1979), pp. 20-5.
14 Thomas Beedome, 'Poems, Divine and Humane' (1641),
    sig. H2. The other two poems mentioned occur on sigs
    H1v and H6-H7.
15 Charles, pp. 63-72; consult also her substantial study,
    Touching David's Harp: George Herbert and Ralph Knevet,
    'George Herbert Journal', II (1978), 54-69. On
    Knevet's labours over Spenser, see C. Bowie Millican,
    Ralph Knevett, Author of the 'Supplement' to Spenser's
    'Faerie Queene', 'Review of English Studies', XIV
    (1938), 44-52, and Charles, pp. 53-62. Karl Höltgen
    in Ralph Knevet under the Commonwealth, 'Notes and
    Queries', CCXV (1970), 407-8, marks some aspects of
    Knevet's spiritual development.
16 Ralph Knevet, 'The Sute', 11. 5-12; in Charles, p. 310.
17 See Hamish Swanston, The Second 'Temple', 'Durham
    University Journal', n.s., XXV (1963), 14-22.
18 Notwithstanding Beaumont's allusions to and

reminiscences of Herbert, as well as the twenty-one
titles they share (listed in 'The Minor Poems of Joseph
Beaumont', ed. Eloise Robinson (Boston, Mass., 1914),
pp. xxxi and xxxvi-xxxvii).

19 See Elsie Duncan-Jones, Benlowes's Borrowings from
George Herbert, 'Review of English Studies', n.s., VI
(1955), 179-80.

20 Mildmay Fane, 2nd Earl of Northumberland, 'Otia Sacra'
(1648). Originally published anonymously, the volume
was later edited by the indefatigable Alexander B.
Grosart (1879).

21 Henry Delaune, 'Πατρικὸν Δῶρον. Or, a Legacy to his
Sons, being a Miscellany of Precepts; Theological,
Moral, Political, Oeconomical' (1651), sig. A3v.

22 Thomas Pestil, in the commendatory poem prefixed to
Benlowes's 'Theophila' (1652).

23 Of prayer, for example, he says that it 'can tower /
As high as heaven, and tie the hands / Of God himself
in bands' (Thomas Washbourne, 'Divine Poems' (1654),
pp. 3-4). The use of the two lines from 'The Church-
porch' by Washbourne, Delaune, et al., is cited by
Saad El-Gabalawy, George Herbert: The Preacher Poet
'Notes and Queries', CCXXVIII (1973), 165.

24 Most of Poole's extracts from 'The Temple' are listed
by Ray, pp. 136-42. On 'The English Parnassus'
see further Robert H. Ray, Two Seventeenth-Century
Adapters of George Herbert, 'Notes and Queries',
CCXV (1980), 331-2. A slightly earlier work,
the anonymous 'The Mirrour of Complements',
reprinted in its fourth edition (1650) seven
poems by Herbert in full and one poem in part.

25 On Hobbes's critical theory, see George Watson,
Hobbes and the Metaphysical Conceit, 'Journal of the
History of Ideas', XVI (1955), 556-62, and the reply
by T.M. Gang, ibid., XVII (1956), 418-21.

26 Where one might have expected yet another development
- Herbert's impact on Continental poetry - there was
none. Huygens possessed a copy of 'The Temple', and
there are some intriguing parallels between his poems
and Herbert's (see Rosalie L. Colie, Constantijn
Huygens and the Metaphysical Mode, 'Germanic Review',
XXXIV (1959), 59-73). But I am assured by Professor
Frank J. Warnke that Herbert's influence is no less
inconclusive on Huygens than it is absent from Revius.

27 Hutchinson, p. xliii: the statement might have been
revised in the light of Knevet's practice (above,
pp. 5-6) had Knevet been a more substantial poet than
he is. On Vaughan's response, consult E.C. Pettet,
'Of Paradise and Light: A Study of Vaughan's "Silex
Scintillans"' (Cambridge, 1960), Ch. III, and Mary
E. Rickey, Vaughan, 'The Temple', and Poetic Form,

'Studies in Philology', LIX (1962), 162-70. Many of
the echoes of Herbert's poetry are tabulated - largely
from L.C. Martin's edition of 'The Works of Henry
Vaughan', 2nd edn (Oxford, 1957) - by Ray, pp. 76-89,
90-1, 95-9, 114-16, 125-31, and 215-16. The title of
Vaughan's major collection of poems may also have been
suggested by Herbert: see Philip Dust, Sources for the
Title of Vaughan's 'Silex Scintillans' in Herbert's
Neo-Latin Poetry, 'Studies in English and American
Literature', I (1978), 110-12. Vaughan's brother
Thomas, it should also be noted, was no less familiar
with Herbert; but he adapted him to his own distinctly
esoteric purposes (see Elizabeth Holmes, 'Henry Vaughan
and the Hermetic Philosophy' (1932), p. 15).

28   In Martin's edition (previous note), p. 186.
29   The claim about Traherne, so far unsubstantiated in
terms of his actual practice, is advanced by Stanley
Stewart, 'The Expanded Voice: The Art of Thomas
Traherne' (San Marino, Calif., 1970), p. 80.
30   'Philo-Dicaeus', 'The Standard of Equality' (1647),
Epistle Dedicatory to Sir John Danvers.
31   From the first collected edition of the 'Lives' (1670),
sig. A6. On Walton's achievement, consult Donald A.
Stauffer, 'English Biography before 1700' (Cambridge,
Mass., 1930), Ch. IV; John Butt, Izaac Walton's Method
in Biography, 'Essays and Studies by Members of the
English Association', XIX (1933), 67-84; Marchette
Chute, Walton's Biography of Herbert, in her 'Two
Gentle Men' (1959), pp. 277-82; Robert E. Reiter,
George Herbert and his Biographers, 'Cithara', IX
(1970), ii. 18-31 (also on Oley and several biographers of the nineteenth and early twentieth centuries); but especially David Novarr, 'The Making of
Walton's "Lives"' (Ithaca, NY, 1958), Ch. X, and
Clayton D. Lein, Art and Structure in Walton's 'Life
of Mr. George Herbert', 'University of Toronto Quarterly', XLVI (1976-7), 162-76.
32   Thus Novarr (previous note), p. 315.
33   See particularly Lein (as above, note 31).
34   'Andrew Marvell: The Critical Heritage', ed. Elizabeth
S. Donno (1978), p. 153. The remark belongs to an
anonymous reviewer in 1832.
35   Postfixed to 'The Synagogue', 2nd rev. edn (1647), sigs
C8-C8v.
36   Prefixed to the first edition of Walton's 'Life of
Mr. George Herbert' (1670), p. 8.
37   Anthony à Wood, 'Athenae Oxonienses', ed. Philip Bliss
(1813), III, 99, and Sir Thomas Herbert, 'Memoirs of
the Two Last Years of ... King Charles I' (1702), p. 43.

38   Richard Baxter, 'The Saints Everlasting Rest' (1650),
      pp. 814, 818, and 853-6. Baxter's references to and
      statements about Herbert are collected by Köppl,
      pp. 61-72, and Ray, pp. 71-6, 233-5.
39   Kenneth B. Murdoch, 'Literature and Theology in Colo-
      nial New England' (Cambridge, Mass., 1949), p. 149;
      see also p. 153-4. 'The Temple' evidently crossed the
      Atlantic soon after its publication. By 1650, in
      Virginia, Edward Johnson was so grateful to receive a
      copy that he fell on his knees and prayed (Maycock,
      'Chronicles' (as above, note 11), p. 75).
40   Philip Pain, 'Daily Meditations: or, Quotidian Pre-
      parations for, and Conversations of Death and Eternity'
      (Cambridge, Mass., 1668); reproduced in facsimile, with
      an introduction by Leon Howard (San Marino, Calif.,
      1936). Howard's claim that Herbert exerted a 'direct
      and persuasive influence' on Pain is shared by Theo-
      dore Grieder, Philip Pain's 'Daily Meditations' and
      the Poetry of George Herbert, 'Notes and Queries',
      CCVII (1962), 213-15; but Norman Farmer in The Literary
      Borrowings of Philip Pain, ibid., CCIX (1964), 465-7,
      detects the influence rather of Quarles than of Her-
      bert.
41   Occurring in the opening lines of Danforth's elegy on
      Mrs Mary Gerrish, the allusion is to Herbert's ana-
      gram on the Virgin Mary (noticed by Thomas A. Ryan,
      The Poetry of John Danforth, 'Proceedings of the
      American Antiquarian Society', LXXVIII (1968), 133 and
      156).
42   Louis L. Martz, in his extended foreword to 'The Poems
      of Edward Taylor', ed. Donald E. Stanford (New Haven,
      Conn., 1960), p. xiv. Herbert's influence on Taylor
      is mapped, and the differences in their creative ex-
      pressions are delineated, in Martz's foreword, pp.
      xiii-xviii (reprinted in 'The Poem of the Mind' (1960),
      Ch. IV), and in Stanford's notes, passim; but see also
      William J. Scheik, Typology and Allegory: A Comparative
      Study of George Herbert and Edward Taylor, 'Essays in
      Literature' (Western Illinois University), II (1975),
      76-86, as well as the more general study by Thomas H.
      Johnson, Edward Taylor: A Puritan 'Sacred Poet', 'New
      England Quarterly', X (1937), 290-322.
43   On Herbert and Norris, see John Hoyles, 'The Waning of
      the Renaissance 1640-1740' (The Hague, 1971), pp.
      128-9; on the 'Miscellanea' of J.H. (Joseph Henshaw?):
      Harold Reese, A Borrower from Quarles and Herbert,
      'Modern Language Review', LV (1940), 50-2; and on John
      Hall: Leach, p. 63. William Croune also adapted a part
      of 'Love' (I) for a poem of his own in 1679 (see

Robert H. Ray, in the 'Notes and Queries' article
mentioned in note 24).

44 Sterry and Henry are cited by Hutchinson, p. xliv.
Bryan quotes three poems of the 'Divine *Herbert*' in
full - 'The H. Communion', 'The Banquet', 'Church-
musick' - and parts of several others ('Dwelling with
God', especially pp. 32-3, 34-5, and 54-5). Heywood
also quotes three poems in full - 'Clasping of hands',
'Death', 'The Church-floore' - usually at the climactic
points of his argument ('The Sure Mercies of David',
pp. 119-20, 237-8, and 252-3).

45 Quoted in full by Ray, pp. 190-7.

46 William Dillingham, 'Poemata varii argumenti' (1678),
pp. 1-44. It should be noted that Herbert is given
pride of place in a collection that includes figures of
the order of Erasmus, Sir Thomas More, Théodore de
Bèze, and Hugo Grotius.

47 Charles Hoole, 'A New Discovery of the old Art of
Teaching Schoole' (1660), sig. A10v.

48 I consulted the 33-page index appended to the 11th
edition of 'The Temple' in 1678. See also Saad El-
Gabalawy, A Seventeenth-Century Reading of George
Herbert, 'Papers on Language and Literature', VII
(1971), 159-67.

49 David Lloyd, 'Memoires of the Lives, Actions, Sufferings & Deaths of those ... that suffered ... for the
Protestant Religion' (1668), p. 619 (marginal nota-
tion).

50 Dryden's remarks on the 'metaphysical' Donne do not
encompass Herbert (see Arthur H. Nethercot, The Term
'Metaphysical Poets' before Johnson, 'Modern Language
Notes', XXXVII (1922), 11-17). But the connection
between Donne and Herbert was to be made soon enough.

51 The two lines are quoted on the title-page of John
Rawlet's 'Poetick Miscellanies' (1687) as well as by
Edmund Spoure in 'A Booke of Poems, on Severall sub-
jects, Persons, and occasions, now transcrib'd, Anno
Domini 1695', fol. 44v (Bodleian MS Eng. poet. c. 52).
Nahum Tate also quotes the lines in 'Miscellanea
Sacra: or, Poems on Divine and Moral Subjects' (1696),
sig. A7v; but, as his title suggests, the coincidence
with Herbert's interests is not casual.

52 On Dr. Woodford's Paraphrase on the Canticles, in
Thomas Flatman's 'Poems and Songs', 4th rev. edn
(1686), p. 178; not in the first edition of 1674.

53 See Louise Schleiner, Jacobean Song and Herbert's Metrics, 'Studies in English Literature', XIX (1979),
109-26.

54 Joseph Boyse, 'Sacramental Hymns' (Dublin, 1693),
pp. 52-3.

55   See John Julian (ed.), 'A Dictionary of Hymnology',
     2nd rev. edn (1907, repr. 1957), I, 511-12; Louis F.
     Benson, 'The English Hymn' (1915, repr. Richmond, Va.,
     1962), pp. 87-8; Frederick J. Gillman, 'The Evolution
     of the English Hymn' (1927), p. 167; C.S. Phillips,
     'Hymnody Past and Present' (1937), p. 156; H.A.L.
     Jefferson, 'Hymns in Christian Worship' (1950), pp.
     213-14; et al. Fifty-three arrangements of 24 poems
     by Herbert are listed by Samuel A. and Dorothy R.
     Tannenbaum, 'George Herbert: A Concise Bibliography'
     (1946), pp. 18-21; but I was unfortunately unable to
     locate Edna D. Parks's 'Early English Hymns: An Index'
     (Metuchen, NJ, 1972), which lists nearly 70 relevant
     items. In our time, adaptations of Herbert poems sung
     as hymns include, among Lutherans, 'Antiphon' (I) and
     a much altered version of 'The Elixer' ('Service Book
     and Hymnal, authorized by the Lutheran Churches'
     (Philadelphia, Pa, 1967), nos 418 and 451); among
     Canadian Presbyterians, 'Discipline', 11. 1-4 (Harvey
     B. Marks, 'The Rise and Growth of English Hymnody'
     (1937), p. 88); and among Anglicans and Episcopalians,
     'Antiphon' (I), 'Praise' (II), and 'The Elixer' (Amy
     M. Charles, George Herbert: Priest, Poet, Musician,
     in Roberts's 'Essential Articles' (as below, note 144),
     pp. 254-5).
56   'Athenian Mercury', in the issues of 24 October 1963
     (vol. 12, no. 1) and 17 September 1692 (vol. 8, no. 6),
     respectively. The former of these comments has been
     ascribed to Samuel Wesley, the father of John Wesley
     (Gilbert D. McEwen, 'The Oracle of the Coffee House:
     John Dunton's "Athenian Murcury"' (San Marino, Calif.,
     1972), p. 100). For remarks by Dunton which certainly
     can be ascribed to his pen, consult Nethercot I, p. 186,
     and II, pp. 163-4.
57   Joseph Warton, 'An Essay on the Writings and Genius of
     Pope' (1756), pp. 87-8.
58   Joseph Spence, 'Anecdotes, Observations, and Charac-
     ters, of Books and Men, collected from the Conversation
     of Mr. Pope, and other eminent persons of his time'
     (1820), p. 22.
59   Thus W.B.C. Watkins, 'Johnson and English Poetry before
     1660' (Princeton, NJ, 1936), p. 83, and - on the sta-
     tistics given - David Perkins, Johnson on Wit and
     Metaphysical Poetry, 'Journal of English Literary His-
     tory', XX (1953), 210. Johnson's only comment on Her-
     bert is ventured in passing, on his letters (in the
     'Life of Pope', in 'Lives', Everyman edn (1925, repr.
     1968), II, 183).
60   Letter to Horace Walpole, 19 September 1763; in

'Correspondence of Thomas Gray', ed. Paget Toynbee and Leonard Whibley (Oxford, 1935), II, 816. Gray did not ever again mention Herbert.

61   Laurence Sterne, 'Tristram Shandy', Bk V, Ch. 32; and 'The Church porch', 11. 239-40. The allusion was first noted by Herbert Rauter, Eine Anleihe Sternes bei George Herbert, 'Anglia', LXXX (1962), 290-4.

62   'Sacred Prolusions: or, Select Pieces from Bishop Taylor and Mr. Herbert', ed. John Wheeldon (1768), p. vii.

63   Bury includes Herbert's 'Home', 'Gratefulnesse', 'Antiphon' (I), 'The 23rd Psalme', etc., while John Playford and Hill include settings of 'The Altar' (see below, pp. 366 ff.). On Gambold's collection, see John Sparrow, George Herbert and John Donne among the Moravians, in 'Hymns Unbidden', by Martha W. England and John Sparrow (1966), pp. 1-29.

64   Williamson, pp. 774-5. Thus also Stephenson (see head-note to No. 34).

65   Seriatim: T.B. Shepherd, 'Methodism and the Literature of the Eighteenth Century' (1940), p. 100; 'The Journal of the Rev. John Wesley', ed. Nehemiah Curnock, 'standard edition' (1909-16), I, 242; and 'The Letters of the Rev. John Wesley', ed. John Telford, 'standard edition' (1931), I, 66 and 169, II, 205, III, 45, VII, 163 and 170, etc. On Herbert's impact on Wesley, see F.E. Hutchinson, John Wesley and George Herbert, 'London Quarterly and Holborn Review', CLXI (1936), 439-55; Thomas W. Herbert, 'John Wesley as Editor and Author' (Princeton, NJ, 1940), pp. 54-8, 82-4; Martha W. England, The First Wesley Hymn Book, in 'Hymns Unbidden' (as above, note 63), pp. 31-42; and Elsie A. Leach, John Wesley's Use of George Herbert, 'Huntington Library Quarterly', XVI (1952-3), 183-202.

66   Hutchinson, p. xlvii.

67   John and Charles Wesley, 'Hymns and Sacred Poems' (1739), pp. 33-4; the quotations from 'The Collar' and 'The Flower' are on pp. 42 and 49, respectively.

68   Earl R. Wasserman, 'Elizabethan Poetry in the Eighteenth Century', Illinois Studies in Language and Literature, XXXII (Urbana, Ill., 1947), ii-iii, pp. 179-80.

69   Simon Patrick, 'Poems upon Divine and Moral Subjects' (1719), pp. 124-5.

70   'A Collection of Poems on Spiritual Subjects ... By a Citizen of Glasgow, a lover of Truth' (Glasgow, 1789), pp. 62-4. Mercifully, Herbert's name is not mentioned anywhere in this collection.

71   Bodleian MS Rawlinson D. 199, fol. 1; in Küppl, p. 92.

The commentary has been inadequately edited by John M.
Heissler (unpublished Ph.D. dissertation, University
of Illinois at Urbana, 1960). On Ryley's labours
consult especially Summers, Appendix A.

72 Moses Browne, 'Poems on Various Subjects' (1739), sig.
A2v.

73 John Oldmixon, 'The Arts of Logick and Rhetoric'
(1728: a free adaptation of Dominique Bouhours, 'La
manière de bien penser dans les ouvrages d'esprit',
1687); John Nichols (ed.), 'Select Collection of
Poems' (1780-2); Henry Headley (see No. 41); George
Ellis (ed.), 'Specimens of the Early English Poets'
(1790), p. 312; Robert Anderson (ed.), 'A Complete
Edition of the Poets of Great Britain' (1792-1807),
13 vols; and Joseph Ritson (ed.), 'The English Anthology' (1793-4), 3 vols. But Herbert did appear -
strictly edited as always - in Thomas Hayward's edition
of 'The British Muse, or, A Collection of Thoughts
Moral, Natural, and Sublime, of our English Poets; who
flourished in the Sixteenth and Seventeenth Centuries'
(1738), 3 vols, passim.

74 Pierre Bayle, 'A General Dictionary, Historical and
Critical', augmented by J.P. Bernard, Thomas Birch,
et al. (1738), VI, 124; Erasmus Middleton, George
Herbert, in 'Biographia Evangelica: or, an Historical
Account of the Lives and Deaths of the most eminent and
evangelical authors or preachers, both British and
Foreign, in the several denominations of Protestants'
(1784), III, 48-70; and 'Encyclopaedia Britannica', 3rd
edn (Edinburgh, 1797), VIII, 469.

75 James Granger, 'A Biographical History of England'
(1769), I (ii), 394. Granger's critical acumen led
him also to claim that 'The anonymous poems subjoined
to Herbert's [i.e. Harvey's 'The Synagogue'] were
written by Crashaw'.

76 Dawson Warren, The Life of George Herbert, in Bodleian
MS Eng. hist. e. 318, fol. 37. Dawson's sketch was
first noted by Amy M. Charles (as above, note 6),
p. 203.

77 Robert Southey, 'Specimens of the Later English Poets'
(1807), I, xxiv. On the Ellis collection see above,
note 73.

78 Herbert (George), in 'The General Biographical Dictionary: containing an historical and critical account of
the lives and writings of the most eminent persons in
every nation', revised by Alexander Chalmers (1814),
XVII, 380. The entry inter alia corrects Granger for
having 'very improperly' attributed Harvey's poems to
Crashaw (above, note 75).

79   Also available in Roberta F. Brinkley (ed.), 'Coleridge
     on the Seventeenth Century' (Durham, N.C., 1955),
     pp. 533-40, where they are marred by a number of
     inaccuracies, two of them serious.
80   On Lamb, see below, p. 168. Wordsworth in 1800-2 read
     widely in Anderson's collection (as above, note 73)
     which bypasses Herbert completely; later, in a letter
     to Anderson on 17 September 1814, he advised him - as
     urged by 'several of my Friends Messieurs Coleridge and
     Southey in particular' - to enlarge his collection by
     adding several poets inclusive of Herbert ('The Letters
     of William and Dorothy Wordsworth', ed. Ernest de
     Selincourt, 2nd edn (Oxford, 1970), III, ii, 153).
     But in spite of Wordsworth's tribute to 'the heaven-
     taught skill of Herbert' ('The River Duddon', Sonnet
     XVIII, 11. 12-13), it is debatable whether he was inti-
     mately acquainted with 'The Temple' (consult Jared R.
     Curtis, William Wordsworth and English Poetry of the
     Sixteenth and Seventeenth Centuries, 'Cornell Library
     Journal', I (1966), 28-39). The similarities between
     Herbert's 'Constancie' and Wordsworth's 'Character of
     Happy Warrior' - first noted by Emerson (as below,
     note 82: VII, 45) - have been asserted with various
     degrees of conviction by G.C. Moore Smith and S. But-
     terworth in 'Notes and Queries', 12th series, XII
     (1923), 30 and 113; Theodore T. Sternberg in 'Modern
     Language Notes', XL (1926), 252-3; Elbert N.S. Thompson
     in 'Publications of the Modern Language Association',
     LIV (1939), 1023; et al.
81   Letter to William Emerson, 20 February 1829; in 'The
     Letters of Ralph Waldo Emerson', ed. Ralph L. Rusk
     (1939), I, 264. On Emerson's Herbert, consult Norman
     A. Brittin, Emerson and the Metaphysical Poets,
     'American Literature', VIII (1936), 1-21, and R.A.
     Yoder, 'Emerson and the Orphic Poet in America'
     (Berkeley, Calif., 1978), especially pp. 80-2; see
     further F.O. Matthiessen, 'American Renaissance'
     (1941), pp. 100 ff., and J. Russell Roberts, Emerson's
     Debt to the Seventeenth Century, 'American Literature'.
     XXI (1949), 298-310.
82   'The Journals and Miscellaneous Notebooks of Ralph
     Waldo Emerson', ed. William H. Gilman et al. (Cam-
     bridge, Mass., 1960 ff.), III, 148; XIII, 132; and
     XIV, 277. Chronologically, the three remarks range
     from 1828 to 1859. See also the frequent quotations
     from 'The Temple' in III, 255, 321; IV, 255; V, 199;
     VI, 103, 230; VII, 59; VIII, 249; IX, 94; XII, 422;
     etc.
83   'Journals of Ralph Waldo Emerson', ed. Edward W.

Emerson and Waldo E. Forbes (Boston, Mass., 1911),
V, 5.

84 See Brittin (as above, Note 81); John C. Broderick.
The Date and Source of Emerson's 'Grace', 'Modern
Language Notes', LXXIII (1958), 91-5; and Duncan,
pp. 74-5, as well as Summers, pp. 22-3.

85 John Ruskin, 'Praeterita' (1899), I, 3 (section 2).
For a detailed study of Ruskin's lifelong admiration of
Herbert as 'an ally for prophetic teachings and an
artist to be ranked with some of the world's best',
see John L. Idol, Jr, George Herbert and John Ruskin,
'George Herbert Journal', IV (1980), i, 11-28.

86 'The Works of John Ruskin', ed. E.T. Cook and
Alexander Wedderburn, Library Edition (1903 ff.), I,
409.

87 Letters of 6 April and 9 June 1845; in 'Ruskin in
Italy: Letters to his Parents 1845', ed. Harold I.
Shapiro (Oxford, 1972), pp. 8 and 108.

88 John Ruskin, 'Works' (as above, note 86), V, 427, and
XXIII, 252, respectively. Sir Arthur Helps (1813-75)
was a popular English essayist and historian.

89 'Retrospective Review', III (1821), 215-22.

90 James Montgomery, 'The Christian Poet; or, Selections
in Verse, on Sacred Subjects' (Glasgow, 1827), p. 237.
The anthology reprints eight of Herbert's poems and
two extracts from 'The Church-porch'.

91 'The Penny Encyclopaedia of the Society for the Diffusion of Useful Knowledge' (1838), XII, 147. The same
entry figures in 'The English Encyclopaedia', 'con-
ducted by' Charles Knight: 'Biography', III (1856),
391.

92 George Herbert, in 'Lives of the Illustrious (The Biographical Magazine)' (1855), VI, 58-69.

93 'Chambers's Encyclopaedia' (1863), V, 329. The
remark is hardly unique: Thomas Campbell, whose extensive collection of 'Specimens of the British Poets'
allotted space only to a single poem by Herbert,
'Vertue' ((1819), III, 81-2), was of the opinion that
Herbert's 'memory is chiefly indebted to the affectionate mention of old Isaac Walton'.

94 Perhaps the most handsome edition ever is 'The Works of
George Herbert', published by Bell and Daldy in 1859
(2 vols).

95 Seriatim: 'A Priest to the Temple' (1832), to which are
appended 'The Church-porch', 'The Priesthood', 'The
Church-floore', and 'Gratefulnesses'; 'The Clergyman's
Instructor, or a Collection of Tracts on the Minister-
ial Duties' (Oxford, 1807), pp. 1-93; and 'The
Preacher and Pastor', ed. Edwards A. Park (Andover,

Mass., and New York, 1845), pp. 163-222. The first
scholarly edition was provided half a century later:
'Herbert's Country Parson', ed. H.C. Beeching (Oxford,
1898).

96 Thus Walton's 'Life' was prefixed to 'Herbert's Poems:
with his Country Parson. A new edition' (1809) and
appeared in abridged form in 'Herbert's Poems: and
Country Parson. A New Edition' (1824).

97 Aspiring to repair Dr Johnson's omission, Hazlitt's
Waltonesque George Herbert, in 'Johnson's Lives of the
British Poets Completed' (1854), I, 286-8, touched on
the poems only 'incidentally', commending them solely
for their 'most earnest piety'. Duyckinck's full-
length 'Life of George Herbert' (1858), written with
the blessings of the General Protestant Episcopal Sunday School Union, and Church Book Society, aimed to
make Herbert suitable for Sunday School reading.
According to its preface, 'Walton has furnished our
chief authority'.

98 George Gilfillan, On the Life and Poetical Works of
George Herbert, in 'The Poetical Works of George Herbert' (Edinburgh, 1853), p. xvii. The Waltonesque
burden of the mid-century accounts of Herbert is best
delineated by Joscelyne, pp. 15 ff. A visual interpretation of the gentlemanly Herbert was also attempted
by William Dyce in 'George Herbert at Bemerton' (oil on
canvas), first exhibited at the Royal Academy in 1861
and now at the Guildhall Art Gallery, City of London;
it is reproduced and discussed by Marcia Pointon,
'William Dyce 1806-1864: A Critical Biography'
(Oxford, 1979), pp. 175-6 and Plate 112.

99 In the fifth edition of 1889, Trench added still
another poem, 'Sinne' (I).

100 Rhetoric (1828), in 'De Quincey's Literary Criticism',
ed. H. Darbishire (1909), p. 50.

101 George L. Craik, 'Sketches of the History of Literature in England', 2nd series (1845), IV, 17.

102 Letter of 6 May 1847; in 'The Letters of John Green-
leaf Whittier', ed. John B. Pickard (Cambridge, Mass.,
1975), II, 89.

103 Summers, p. 22, calls attention to two poems of
Thoreau in particular, 'I am a parcel of vain striv-
ings tied' and 'Friendship' ('Collected Poems of Henry
Thoreau', ed. Carl Bode, rev. edn (Baltimore, 1964),
pp. 81-2 and 89-91). On Herbert and Dickinson, consult
especially Judith Banzer, 'Compound Manner': Emily
Dickinson and the Metaphysical Poets, 'American Literature', XXXII (1961), 421 ff. Summers points out that
eight lines from Herbert's 'Mattens' were ascribed in

1945 to Dickinson (in her 'Bolts of Melody', ed. Mabel
L. Todd and Millicent T. Bingham (1945), p. 125
(no. 232)).

104   Helen N. McMaster, Margaret Fuller as a Literary
Critic, 'University of Buffalo Studies', VII (1928),
iii, 79. Harry R. Warfel in Margaret Fuller and
Ralph Waldo Emerson, 'Publications of the Modern Language Association', L (1935), 576-94, provides the
best account of their close friendship.

105   R.A. Forsyth, Herbert, Clough, and their Church-
Windows, 'Victorian Poetry', VII (1969), 17-30.

106   Jean Wilkinson, Three Sets of Religious Poets,
'Huntington Library Quarterly', XXXVI (1973), 224-5.
For a more sustained comparison of Herbert and Keble,
see Elbert N.S. Thompson, 'The Temple' and 'The
Christian Year', 'Publications of the Modern Language
Association', LIV (1939), 1018-25.

107   Samuel Brown, 'Lectures on the Atomic Theory and
Essays Scientific and Literary' (Edinburgh, 1858),
II, 103-30.

108   For the reading list citing Herbert, see 'The Notebooks of Matthew Arnold', ed. Howard F. Lowry, Karl
Young, and Waldo H. Dunn (1952), p. 581; and for the
other references to Herbert: pp. 68, 77, 97, 102,
etc. Lord Coleridge's remark occurs in The President's Address, 'Report and Transactions of the
Devonshire Association for the Advancement of Science,
Literature, and Art', II (1867), 293; and Arnold's
reply, dated 25 September 1868, in 'Life and Correspondence of John Duke Lord Coleridge Lord Chief Justice of England', ed. Ernest Hartley Coleridge (1904),
II, 160. Among a number of Arnold's subsequent
references to Herbert, one in 'St Paul and Protestantism' cites him as an example of 'the more eminently
and exactly Christian type of righteousness' ('The
Complete Prose Works of Matthew Arnold', ed. R.H.
Super (Ann Arbor, Mich., 1968), VI, 104).

109   On the two poets' superficial and fundamental differences, see especially M.M. Mahood, Two Anglican
Poets, in her 'Poetry and Humanism' (1950), Ch. II.

110   As Hopkins's intimate friend William Aldis said
(quoted by Eleanor Ruggles, 'Gerard Manley Hopkins'
(1944), p. 73; apud Duncan, p. 91).

111   W.H. Gardner, 'Gerard Manley Hopkins: A Study of
Poetic Idiosyncrasy in Relation to Poetic Tradition'
(1944-9), II, 73-4; see also I, 170-2, and II, 84 and
196, as well as Duncan, pp. 95-6, 98, 100, and
Summers, p. 22. Still another considerable literary
figure who read Herbert in the 1860s was Robert Louis

Stevenson. As he reported to his mother on 5 September 1868, 'I have been reading a good deal of Herbert. He's a clever and devout cove; but in places awfully twaddley (if I may use the word)...' ('Letters', ed. Sidney Colvin, new edn (1911), I, 19). Stevenson was at the time just short of his eighteenth birthday. He did not mention Herbert ever again. It may be added that Browning's references to Herbert are also minimal - all the more surprising since his interest in Donne was substantial.

112 Arthur Symons, John Donne, 'Fortnightly Review', LXVI (1899), 740-1. See also the parallel statements by Swinburne et al. in 'John Donne: The Critical Heritage', ed. A.J. Smith (1975), pp. 482 ff.

113 'The Works of George Herbert', 'Edited from the latest editions' (1878), p. v.

114 Joscelyne, pp. 22-5.

115 Alexander B. Grosart (ed.), 'The Complete Works in Verse and Prose of George Herbert' (1874), II, lxxi and xcic-c; the 'critical examination' extends to about 130 130 pages (II, ix ff.). Later, Grosart served scholarship still further by editing an 'absolute facsimile in every way' of 'The Temple' (1876).

116 See W.K. Fleming, Some Truths about 'John Inglesant', 'Quarterly Review', CCXLV (1925), 130-48; and Maycock, 'Ferrar' (as above, note 11), App. I. Shorthouse also edited a facsimile of 'The Temple' (1882), the florid introduction to which claims, inter alia, that Keble's poetry is 'finer' than Herbert's (p. xxiv).

117 John Jeremiah Daniell, 'The Life of George Herbert of Bemerton' (1893), p. 229.

118 Bostwick Hawley (ed.), 'Beauties of the Rev. George Herbert' (1877), p. 28. It may be worth recording that another American anthology, at once more catholic and secular, included seven of Herbert's poems: it was edited by William Cullen Bryant as 'A Library of Poetry and Song, being Choice Selections from the Best Poets' (1871).

119 Holmes spoke of 'the purity of holy George Herbert'; and Lowell, of 'that fine old poet Herbert' (Duncan pp. 69 and 70).

120 Alice Meynell (ed.), 'The Flower of the Mind: A Choice among the Best Poems' (1897), p. 335. The anthology reprints eight of Herbert's poems, which Meynell was occasionally 'greatly tempted' to amend - as she did, displacing 'rest' (in 'The Pulley', 1. 10) by 'peace'. In a later collection, 'The School of Poetry: An Anthology chosen for Young Readers' (1923), she reprinted five of Herbert's poems, remarking that

he is 'a poet of great gravity, who yet lets his
fancy play with his religious dutifulness' (p. 36).

121   George M. Harper, 'Appreciations' (as below, note
139), p. 20.

122   In the review cited below (note 130).

123   Duncan, in the 'Critic', XLIX (1906), 83, and
Saintsbury in 'A History of English Prosody' (1908),
II, 332 (both in Roberts, pp. 3 and 5).

124   George Herbert Palmer (ed.), 'The English Works of
George Herbert' (Boston, Mass., 1905), 1, xiv-xv. Of the
edition's three volumes, the first includes a sustained commentary and reprints Herbert's prose,
while the other two provide the controversial
rearrangement of the poems.

125   Joscelyne, p. 29. For evaluations of Palmer's edition, see Joscelyne, pp. 28-32, and Reiter (as
above, note 31), pp. 25-8.

126   'Works' (as in note 124), I, 46.

127   Ibid., I, 116, 141, 157, 132, 163.

128   Ibid., I, 151.

129   Vaughan Williams's settings in 'Five Mystical Songs'
(1911) are of 'Antiphon' (I), 'The Call', 'Easter'
(ll. 1 ff. and 19 ff.), and 'Love' (III). The oratorio is by Joseph W. Clokey, 'The Temple' (1944).
For a lengthy list of modern cantata and anthem
settings of Herbert poems, see Louise Schleiner,
'Herbert's "Divine and Moral Songs"', unpublished
Ph.D. dissertation (Brown University, 1973),
Appendix B.

130   Duncan argues that Thompson's 'Any Saint' suggests
Herbert's 'Man' and 'Mans medley'; but he also con-
trasts the former poet's 'precipitate prodigality'
to the latter's 'controlled, contained calm'
(pp. 104, 105-6, 108). In addition to the review
reprinted here, Thompson wrote a briefer one for
the 'Academy and Literature', LXIV (28 February
1903), 198-9. He was aware of Hopkins's favourable
attitude toward Herbert: it may not be an accident
that Hopkins spoke of Herbert's 'fragrant sweetness'
(No. 58), and Thompson of 'the fragrant common-sense
of Herbert' ('Literary Criticisms', ed. Terence L.
Connolly (1948), p. 66).

131   On Herbert and Yeats, see Duncan, pp. 132, 133-6,
140, and Elsie Leach, Yeats's 'A Friend's Illness'
and Herbert's 'Vertue', 'Notes and Queries', CCVII
(1962), 214. On Herbert and Thomas, see Bill Read,
'The Days of Dylan Thomas' (1964), p. 59, reporting
that Herbert was Thomas's 'old favorite', and Aneirin
T. Davies, 'Dylan: Druid of the Broken Body' (1964),

pp. 40-1, as well as Vincent B. Leitch, Herbert's
Influence in Dylan Thomas's 'I See the Boys of
Summer', 'Notes and Queries', CCVII (1972), 341. On
Herbert and MacNeice, see Babette Deutsch, 'Poetry in
our Time' (1952), 364-6, as well as MacNeice's own
'Varieties of Parable' (Cambridge, 1965), p. 45, where
he observes that Herbert anticipated Bunyan 'not only
in his household and everyday images but also in the
plainness of his diction'. Herbert's influence on
modern poets demands a sustained discussion, not the
occasional references we obtain in studies like Henry
W. Wells, 'New Poets from Old' (1940), or Sonya
Raiziss, 'The Metaphysical Passion' (Philadelphia,
1952).

132   But not entirely so, according to Robert D. Thornton
in Polyphiloprogenitive: The Sapient Stulers, 'Anglican Theological Review', XXXV (1953), 28-36. On the
other hand, David Ward in 'T.S. Eliot between two
Worlds' (1973), pp. 283-5, marks the differences in
the outlook of the two poets.

133   H.J.C. Grierson, 'The First Half of the Seventeenth
Century', being vol. VII of 'Periods of European
Literature', ed. George Saintsbury (Edinburgh, 1906),
p. 166. Another academic critic, Émile Legouis, much
more militantly observed that Herbert's poetry 'constantly offends taste, but often gives the impression
of a sort of sublimity' ('A History of English Literature', trans. Helen D. Irvine (1926), I, 352). The
word 'constantly' was later displaced by 'frequently'
(ibid., rev. edn (1960)).

134   The contours of Eliot's changing attitudes are skil-
fully mapped by Elsie Leach, T.S. Eliot and the
School of Donne, 'Costerus: Essays in English and
American Language and Literature', III (1972), 163-80.

135   The remark on Marvell occurs in a review in 'Nation
and Athenaeum' (29 September 1923), repr. in 'Marvell',
ed. Michael Wilding (1969), p. 58; and the one on
Donne, in Donne in our Time, in 'A Garland for John
Donne', ed. Theodore Spencer (Cambridge, Mass., 1931),
p. 8. Eliot first signalled his altered view of
Donne in the unpublished Clark Lectures of 1926 (the
original typescript is in King's College Library,
Cambridge, and a carbon copy is in Harvard's Houghton
Library).

136   T.S. Eliot, 'George Herbert' (Writers and their Work,
1962) p. 17. Igor Stravinsky also reported that
Eliot told him, 'Herbert is a great poet ... and one
of a very few I can read again and again' (Memories of
T.S. Eliot, 'Esquire', August 1965, p. 92; in Roberts,
p. 174).

137   Aldous Huxley, 'Texts and Pretexts' (1933), pp. 12-13.
      The remark on 'The Collar' is on p. 90.

138   U.M.D. Orange, The Poetry of George Herbert, 'Poetry
      Review', XXIV (1933), 118-27, and Gilbert Thomas,
      George Herbert, 'Contemporary Review', CXLII (1933),
      706-13, respectively. In 1933 not even F.E. Hutchin-
      son - Herbert's great editor less than a decade later
      - could manage anything but a merely appreciative
      survey (George Herbert: A Tercentenary, 'Nineteenth
      Century', CXIII (1933), 358-68).

139   George M. Harper, George Herbert's Poems, 'Quarterly
      Review', CCLXVII (1936), 58-73; reprinted in his
      'Literary Appreciations' (Indianapolis, Ind., 1937),
      pp. 19-45. Harper's study is marred only by his
      elevation of Herbert at the expense of Donne.

140   Helen C. White, 'The Metaphysical Poets' (1936, repr.
      1962), p. 157; the reassessment of Herbert is in Chs
      VI-VII. White's study partakes of the general ten-
      dency to regard Herbert as a member of 'the school of
      Donne' (see above, p. 2).

141   Jean Mambrino, Simone Weil et George Herbert,
      'Études', CCCXL (1974), 247-56.

142   Louis Untermeyer, The Religious Conceit: Play for
      God's Sake, in his 'Play in Poetry' (1938), Ch. II.

143   The edition is the one I provided for Everyman's
      University Library: 'The English Poems of George Her-
      bert' (1974).

144   Amy M. Charles, 'The Williams Manuscript of George
      Herbert's Poems: A Facsimile Reproduction' (Delmar,
      NY, 1977) and 'A Life of George Herbert' (Ithaca,
      NY, 1977); Mario A. DiCesare and Rigo Magnami, 'A
      Concordance to the Complete Writings of George
      Herbert' (Ithaca, NY, 1977); John R. Roberts,
      'George Herbert: An Annotated Bibliography of Modern
      Criticism 1905-1974' (Columbia, Mo., 1978), and
      'Essential Articles for the Study of George Herbert's
      Poetry' (Hamden, Conn., 1979).

145   Leicester Bradner, New Poems by George Herbert: The
      Cambridge Latin Gratulatory Anthology of 1613,
      'Renaissance News', XV (1962), 208-11; Kenneth A.
      Hovey, George Herbert's Authorship of 'To the Queene
      of Bohemia', 'Renaissance Quarterly', XXX (1977),
      45-50; and Ted-Larry Pebworth, George Herbert's Poems
      to the Queen of Bohemia: A Rediscovered Text and a
      New Edition, 'English Literary Renaissance', IX
      (1979), 108-20.

146   Seriatim: Rosemond Tuve, 'A Reading of George Herbert'
      (Chicago, 1952); Joseph H. Summers, 'George Herbert:
      His Religion and Art' (Cambridge, Mass., 1954);

Mary Ellen Rickey, 'Utmost Art: Complexity in the
Verse of George Herbert' (Lexington, Ky, 1966);
Arnold Stein, 'George Herbert's Lyrics' (Baltimore,
Md, 1968); Helen Vendler, 'The Poetry of George
Herbert' (Cambridge, Mass., 1975); and Stanley Fish,
'The Living Temple: George Herbert and Catechizing'
(Berkeley, Calif., 1978). More recently still, Claude
J. Summers and Ted-Larry Pebworth have edited '"Too
Rich to Clothe the Sunne": Essays on George Herbert'
(Pittsburgh, Pa, 1980).

147   Seriatim: Margaret Bottrall, 'George Herbert' (1954),
p. 146; D.J. Enright, George Herbert and the Devotional Poets, in 'From Donne to Marvell', ed. Boris
Ford (1956), p. 142; and Jim Hunter, 'The Metaphysical Poets' (1965), p. 122. All three statements are
also in Roberts, pp. 106, 116, and 171.

148   W.H. Auden, from the introduction to his selections
from 'The Temple', in 'George Herbert' (1973).

Herbert in the Seventeenth Century

1. JOHN DONNE, 'TO MR GEORGE HERBERT'

1615?

First published in the posthumous edition of Donne's 'Poems'
in 1650, the address 'To Mr *George Herbert*' appeared also
in the subsequent editions of 1654 and 1659, in Herbert's
'Remains' (1652), and in Walton's 'Life of Dr. John Donne'
(see No. 20); it is sensitively discussed by David Novarr,
'The Disinterred Muse: Donne's Texts and Contexts' (Ithaca,
NY, 1980), pp. 103-7. The poem is said by I.A. Shapiro and
Helen Gardner - in each case for different reasons - to
have been written in 1615 ('Notes and Queries', CXCIV
(1949), 473-4, and Gardner's edition of Donne, 'The Divine
Poems', 2nd edn (Oxford, 1978), App. G). Herbert, at any
rate, responded as shown below. The two poems were preceded by Latin versions, available in 'The Poems of John
Donne', ed. Herbert J.C. Grierson (Oxford, 1912), I, 398-9,
and in Hutchinson, pp. 438-9, respectively. See further
above, p. 2.
     Source: Donne, 'Poems' (1650), pp. 377 and 379.

             To Mr *George Herbert*, with one of my
             Seal[s], of the Anchor and Christ.

     A Sheafe of Snakes used heretofore to be
     My Seal, the Crest of our poore Family. (1)
     Adopted in Gods Family, and so
     Our old Coat lost, unto new armes I go.
     The Crosse (my seal at Baptism) spred below,

Does, by that form, into an Anchor grow.
Crosses grow Anchors; Bear, as thou shouldst do
Thy Crosse, and that Crosse grows an Anchor too.
But he that makes our Crosses Anchors thus,
Is Christ, who there is crucifi'd for us.
Yet may I, with this, my first Serpents hold,
God gives new blessings, and yet leaves the old;
The Serpent, may, as wise, my pattern be;
My poison, as he feeds on dust, that's me.

To Doctor *Donne* upon one of his Seales:
The *Anchor*, and *Christ*. *In Sacram
Anchoram Piscatoris*.

Although the Crosse could not Christ here detain,
Though nail'd unto't, but he ascends again,
Nor yet thy eloquence here keep him still,
But onely while thou speak'st; This Anchor will.
Nor canst thou be content, unlesse thou to
This certain Anchor adde a Seal, and so
The Water, and the Earth both unto thee
Doe owe the symbole of their certainty.
Let the world reel, we and all ours stand sure,
This holy Cable's of all storms secure.

When Love being weary made an end
Of kinde Expressions to his friend,
He writ; when's hand could write no more,
He gave the Seale, and so left o're.

How sweet a friend was he, who being griev'd
His letters were broke rudely up, believ'd
'Twas more secure in great Loves Common-weal
(Where nothing should be broke) to adde a Seal.

Note

1   The first two lines are evidently the title - in
Walton's case, a descriptive one (below, p. 87).

2. SIR FRANCIS BACON, DEDICATION OF HIS 'TRANSLATION OF CERTAINE PSALMES INTO ENGLISH'

1625

Bacon's dedication of his 'Translation of Certaine Psalmes into English' to his 'very good friend' Herbert is the first public acknowledgment of the emerging poet's talents. Herbert returned the compliment in two Latin poems, the short 'Ad Autorem Instaurationis Magnae' and the lengthier and more effusive 'In Honorem Illustr. D.D. Verulamij' (translated by Mark McCloskey and Paul R. Murphy in 'The Latin Poetry of George Herbert' (Athens, Ohio, 1965), pp. 167, 169-71; discussed by Summers, App. B). See also above, p. 2.

Source: Bacon, 'Translation of Certaine Psalmes into English' (1625), sigs A3-A3v.

To his very good friend, Mr. George Herbert

The paines, that it pleased you to take, about some of my Writings, (1) I cannot forget: which did put mee in minde, to dedicate to you, this poore Exercise of my sicknesse, Besides, it being my manner for Dedication, to choose those that I hold most fit for the Argument, I thought, that in respect of Diuinitie, and Poesie, met (whereof the one is the Matter, the other the Stile of this little Writing) I could not make better choice. So, with signification of my loue and Acknowledgment, I euer rest

Your affection Frend,
FR: St. ALBAN.

Note

1   Herbert had assisted in rendering 'The Advancement of Learning' into Latin. According to Thomas Tenison's introduction to 'Baconiana' (1679), Bacon caused what he had written in English 'to be translated into the *Latine* Tongue by Mr. *Herbert*, and some others, who were esteemed Masters in the *Roman* Eloquence' (apud Hutchinson, p. xi).

3.   JOHN FERRAR, FROM 'A LIFE OF NICHOLAS FERRAR'

post 1633

Nicholas Ferrar, the leader of the community at Little
Gidding, was Herbert's devoted friend (see above, p. 4).
Herbert just before his death asked Arthur Woodnoth to
deliver the manuscript of 'The Temple' to Ferrar. The
episode, related by Walton who also provides a portrait of
Ferrar (below, pp. 123 ff. and 127 ff.), was first mentioned in the 'Life' of Ferrar by his brother John - here
reprinted from a composite of manuscripts ultimately
deriving from the original 'Life'.
     Source: 'The Ferrar Papers', ed. B. Blackstone (Cam-
bridge, 1938), p. 59.

...when Mr Herbert dy'd, he recommended only of all his
Papers, that of his Divine Poems, & willed it to be
delivered into the hands of his Brother N.F. appointing
him to be the Midwife, to bring that piece into the World,
If he so thought good of it, else to [burn it.] The w^{ch}
when N.F. had many & many a time read over, & embraced &
kissed again & again, he sayd, he could not sufficiently
admire it, as a rich Jewell, & most worthy to be in y^e
hands & hearts of all true Christians, that feared God, &
loved the Church of England. It was licensed at Cambridge
(with some kind of Scruple by some, if I was not mis-
informed) only for those his Verses upon America &c: (1)
But it did pass, with the epistle that N.F. made to it....

Note

1   In licensing 'The Temple' for publication, the Vice-
    Chancellor at Cambridge objected to two lines in 'The
    Church Militant': 'Religion stands on tip-toe in our
    land, / Readie to passe to the *American* strand'
    (ll. 235-6). But Nicholas Ferrar 'would by no means
    allow the Book to be printed, and want them' (Walton,
    below, p. 128).

4. NICHOLAS FERRAR, PREFACE TO 'THE TEMPLE'

1633

The anonymous preface to the first edition of 'The Temple'
in 1633 was written by Nicholas Ferrar, as is attested
both by John Ferrar (No. 3) and by Walton (below, p. 123).
    Source: 'The Temple' (Cambridge, 1633); reproduced from
'The English Poems of George Herbert', ed. C.A. Patrides
(1974), pp. 30-1.

The Printers to the Reader

The dedication of this work having been made by the Authour
to the *Divine Majestie* onely, how should we now presume to
interest any mortall man in the patronage of it? Much
lesse think we it meet to seek the recommendation of the
Muses, for that which himself was confident to have been
inspired by a diviner breath then flows from *Helicon*. The
world therefore shall receive it in that naked simplicitie,
with which he left it, without any addition either of support or ornament, more than is included in it self. We
leave it free and unforestalled to every mans judgement,
and to the benefit that he shall finde by perusall. Onely
for the clearing of some passages, we have thought it not
unfit to make the common Reader privie to some few par-
ticularities of the condition and disposition of the
Person;
    Being nobly born, and as eminently endued with gifts of
the minde, and having by industrie and happy education
perfected them to that great height of excellencie, whereof
his fellowship of Trinitie Colledge in Cambridge, and his
Orator-ship in the Universitie, together with that knowledge which the Kings Court had taken of him, could make
relation farre above ordinarie. Quitting both his deserts
and all the opportunities that he had for wordly prefer-
men, he betook himself to the Sanctuarie and Temple of God,
choosing rather to serve at Gods Altar, then to seek the
honour of State-employments. As for those inward enforce-
ments to this course (for outward there was none) which
many of these ensuing verses bear witnesse of, they
detract not from the freedome, but adde to the honour of
this resolution in him. As God had enabled him, so he
accounted him meet not onely to be called, but to be com-
pelled to this service: Wherein his faithfull discharge was
such, as may make him justly a companion to the primitive
Saints, and a pattern or more for the age he lived in.

To testifie his independencie upon all others, and to
quicken his diligence in this kinde, he used in his
ordinarie speech, when he made mention of the blessed name
of our Lord and Saviour Jesus Christ, to adde, *My Master.*

Next God, he loved that which God himself hath magnified above all things, that is, his Word: so as he hath
been heard to make solemne protestation, that he would not
part with one leaf thereof for the whole world, if it were
offered him in exchange.

His obedience and conformitie to the Church and the
discipline thereof was singularly remarkable. Though he
abounded in private devotions, yet went he every morning
and evening with his familie to the Church; and by his
example, exhortations, and encouragements drew the greater
part of his parishioners to accompanie him dayly in the
publick celebration of Divine Service.

As for worldly matters, his love and esteem to them was
so little, as no man can more ambitiously seek, then he
did earnestly endeavour the resignation of an Ecclesiasticall dignitie, which he was possessour of. (1) But God
permitted not the accomplishment of this desire, having
ordained him his instrument for reedifying of the Church
belonging thereunto, that had layen ruinated almost
twenty yeares. The reparation whereof, having been
uneffectually attempted by publick collections, was in the
end by his own and some few others private free-will-
offerings successfully effected. With the remembrance
whereof, as of an especiall good work, when a friend (2)
went about to comfort him on his death-bed, he made
answer, *It is a good work, if it be sprinkled with the
bloud of Christ:* otherwise then in this respect he could
finde nothing to glorie or comfort himself with, neither
in this, nor in any other thing.

And these are but a few of many that might be said,
which we have chosen to premise as a glance to some parts
of the ensuing book, and for an example to the Reader. We
conclude all with his own Motto, with which he used to
conclude all things that might seem to tend any way to his
own honour;

Lesse then the least of Gods mercies.(3)

Notes

1   Herbert had wanted to transfer his benefice at Leighton
    Bromswold in Huntingdonshire to Ferrar.
2   Arthur Woodnoth (see below, p. 129).
3   The phrase - the refrain of Herbert's 'The Posie' -
    derives from the words of Jacob after he had wrestled

with God and had been renamed Israel: 'I am not worthy
of the least of all the mercies ... which thou has
shewed unto thy servant; for with my staff I passed
over this Jordan' (Genesis 32.10). The motto was also
adopted at Little Gidding ('The Ferrar Papers',
ed. B. Blackstone (Cambridge, 1938), p. 178).

5. JOHN POLWHELE, 'ON MR. HERBERTS DEVINE POEME THE
CHURCH'

1633?

Typical of the numerous poetic tributes to Herbert during
the seventeenth century, the ensuing one by the Reverend
John Polwhele of Tremorgan was presumably written not long
after the poet's death in 1633. First published in 1972
and again in 1979, the poem is headed 'Post mortem author
mestris posuit' ('After the death [of Herbert] the sad
author sets down [the following poem]'). See also above,
p. 3.
     Source: Bodleian MS Eng. poet. f. 16, fol. 11. First
published by Amy M. Charles in 'Renaissance Papers 1971'
(Durham, NC, 1972), p. 73, and reprinted in 'Essential
Articles for the Study of George Herbert's Poetry', ed.
John R. Roberts (Hamden, Conn., 1979), pp. 428-9; here
reproduced from the version transcribed by Helen Wilcox
in 'Notes and Queries', CCXXIV (1979), 153.

On Mr. Herberts Devine poeme the church.

     Haile Sacred Architect
   Thou doest a glorious Temple raise
      stil ecchoinge his praise.
who taught thy genius thus to florish it
with curious gravings of a Peircinge witt.

     Statelye thy Pillers bee,
   Westwards the Crosse, the Quier, and
      thine Alter Eastward stande,
where Is most Catholique Conformitie
with out a nose-twange (1) spoylinge harmonie.

     Resolve to Sinne noe more,
   from hence a penitent sigh, and groane

cann flintye heartes unstone;
and blowe them to their happye porte heaven's doore,
where Herberts Angell's flowen awaye before.

Note

1 An allusion to a peculiarity of Puritan speech and
   therefore symbolic of the threat to the 'harmonie'
   celebrated by Herbert (according to Wilcox; see head-
   note).

6. CARDELL GOODMAN, FROM THE PREFACE TO HIS 'BEAWTY IN
RAGGS'

1633 ff.

A tribute to Herbert of a different order was paid by
Cardell Goodman, Fellow of St John's College, Cambridge.
In a very appealing cluster of poems he wrote periodically
from 1633 through the late 1640s and the early 1650s - but
first published in 1958 - Goodman not only displayed the
influence of Herbert throughout but proclaimed that influence explicitly in the prefatory epistle given below. See
also above, p. 4.
    Source: Goodman, 'Beawty in Raggs or Divine Phansies
putt into Broken Verse', ed. R.J. Roberts (Reading, 1958),
p. xiv.

I need not tell you whence I took my pattern, for these
Meditations; the Author is so well knowne to you, that you
will soone discover the mark I aime ~tt, though every
shaft I deliver fall many bowes short of it.
    The Example indeed is farr above my imitation, and I
know my weakness will appeare so much the more, because I
scribble under so faire a Coppy: butt my ambition (I confess) was allwayes to look upon the best Patternes, though
with weak and tender eyes; and heerin my aime is, not to
bee a fellow, butt a follower, att distance, of my Leader:
It shall bee honour enough for mee, to bee accompted His
Eccho, endeavouring to say somthing after him, though I
reach no farther, than the repetition of half words and
sentences.

7.   ROBERT CODRINGTON, 'ON HERBERTS POEMS'

1638

Another poetic tribute to Herbert occurs in a manuscript of
poems by Robert Codrington of Corpus Christi College, Cambridge. Dated 30 May 1638, the poem breaks off at a point
where several pages in the manuscript are unfortunately
missing. The surviving fragment is printed here for the
first time.
   Source: Bodleian MS Eng. poet. f. 27, p. 296.

On Herberts poem

Veiw a true Poet, whose bare lines
Include more goodnesse then some shrines.
Wee'le canonize him, and what er
Befalls, style him heauens Chorister.
No Muse inspird his quill, the three
Graces, ffaith, Hope, and Charitie
Inflamd that breast, whose heat farre higher....

8.   CHRISTOPHER HARVEY, FROM 'THE SYNAGOGUE'

1640

Seven years after the publication of 'The Temple', the
devotional poet Christopher Harvey proclaimed his debt to
Herbert on the title-page of his distinctly uncertain performance, 'The Synagogue' ('In imitation of Mr. George
Herbert'). The collection of twenty-four poems begins,
after 'The Dedication', with a sustained tribute to Herbert, first in Latin, and next in English as given below.
   Source: Harvey, 'The Synagogue, or, The Shadow of the
Temple. Sacred Poems, and Private Ejacvlations. In imitation of Mr. George Herbert' (1640), pp. 1-2. Initially
published anonymously.

A stepping-stone to the threshold of Mr.
Herberts Church-porch.

What Church is this? Christs Church. Who builds it?
Mr. *George Herbert*. Who assisted it?

Many assisted: who, I may not say,
So much contention might arise that way.
If I say Grace gave all, Wit straight doth thwart,
And sayes all that is there is mine: but Art
Denies and sayes ther's nothing there but's mine:
Nor can I easily the right define.
Divide: say, Grace the matter gave, and Wit
Did polish it, Art measured and made fit
Each severall piece, and fram'd it all together.
No, by no means: this may not please them neither.
None's well contented with a part alone,
When each doth challenge all to be his owne:
The matter, the expressions, and the measures,
Are eqyally Arts, Wits, and Graces treasures.
Then he that would impartially discusse
This doubtfull question, must answer thus:
In building of this temple Mr. *Herbert*
Is equally all Grace, all Wit, all Art.
    Roman and *Grecian* Muses all give way:
    One *English* Poem darkens all your day.

9. RALPH KNEVET, FROM 'A GALLERY TO THE TEMPLE'

1640s ff.

A learned and spasmodically talented poet, Ralph Knevet
has been deemed 'the most interesting of Herbert's
avowed disciples after Vaughan' (Summers, p. 200). Of
several collections of poems he composed, 'A Gallery to
the Temple' is doubtless his best - and, as its title
suggests, was heavily influenced by Herbert. Most
likely written in the 1640s though amended over the next
two decades, the 'Gallery' remained in manuscript until
its publication in 1966. The ensuing extract is from
the prefatory address To the Reader. See further
above, pp. 5-6.
    Source: Knevet, 'A Gallery to the Temple. Lyricall
Poems vpon Sacred Occasions', in British Library Add.
MS 27447; reproduced from Charles, pp. 280-1.

I wonder ... at the inadvertencye of our moderne wittes,
who in this maturity of sciences, have appeared so barren
concerning the production, of this most divine sorte of
Poesye, that the species thereof might have bene number'd
among lost Antiquities if our Pious Herbert (a name which

I dare confidently affirme most aptly aggrees with the
past and present condition of the person whom it denoted)
had not by a religious cultivation, added new life to the
wither'd branches, of this celestiall Balme Tree. - whereby Hee hath not onely surpassed those of his owne Nation,
but even the haughty Italians, who chalenge a priority in
art, as well as devotions. It is true, that their glorious Temples abounde with musicke, both vocall, and instru-
mentall, But all their Academicall Societyes of wittes (1)
cannot showe a Paralell to Herberts Temple. Their Inflam-
mati of Padua, their Elevati of Ferrara, their Affidati of
Pavia, their Intronati of Sienna &c: were so taken up with
court-Corinna's, or countrey Laura's, that they quite for-
gott those lawes of duety, and gratitude, wherein they
stood obliged to Heaven, for their endowments. Dante
affordes us better matter then words: Petrarch better
words then matter: Ariosto, and Marino have done well in
heroicke Moralls, but Tasso best of all. Yet concerning
that divine Poesye, which immediately aymes at the glory
of the Almighty (which at first was, and ever ought to bee
the principall end of Poesye) They are all as mute as
Seriphian Frogs: (2) And in their bookes they render more
expressions that tend to the flatterye of Man, then to the
praises of the liveing God: And though they pretend to
deliver incentives to vertue, yet they intend nothing more,
then the interest of their owne vaineglory. Onely that
incomparable Dame Vittoria Colonna, Lady Dowager to the
heroicke Ferdinando D'avalos Marques of Pescara may seeme
to have rescued the honour of the Italian Academyes,
(which were lyable to censure, for their deficiencye in
this kind of divine lyricke Poemes) by those excellent
Canzonetts, which shee composed upon th'occasion of the
death of her beloved Consort. But it hath bene the
ordinary taske of the moderne, and sublimated wittes of
our Nation, to idolize some silly scornfull woman into a
fooles Paradise of self admiration, and with store of such
stuffe our late Rapsodyes abound; but in respect of these
ingenious Brutes, I may say of Herbert: Sanctius his animal, mentisq capacius altae Deerat adhuc (3) - For it was
Hee who rightly knew to touch Davids Harpe: and though
Heaven affordes me not so much favour that I may come
neare him in the excellencye of his high Enthusiasmes,
yet I am comforted in that I am permitted to follow Him in
his Devotions.

Notes

1 Knevet speaks from experience, the result of his visit

to Italy in 1638-9. The response to these societies by
Milton, also a visitor to Italy at the time, was distinctly more favourable.
2 '...the frogs on the island of Seriphus were said never
to croak as long as they remained on the island'
(Charles, p. 398).
3 'A being more holy than these, a more capable mind was
lacking until now' (Ovid, 'Metamorphoses', I, 76-7).

10. EDWARD LORD HERBERT OF CHIRBURY, FROM HIS 'AUTOBIOGRAPHY'

1643?

Lord Herbert, the poet's eldest brother, was by far the
most celebrated member of his family, both as a statesman
and as a philosopher (see the portrait by Walton, below,
p. 92). His autobiography, probably written in 1643 but
left incomplete on his death in 1648, contains but the
following solitary reference to the poet.
   Source: 'The Autobiography of Edward, Lord Herbert of
Cherbury', ed. Sidney Lee, 2nd rev. edn (1906), pp. 11-12,
where the text is that of the first printed edition from
Horace Walpole's private press (1764).

My brother George was so excellent a scholar, that he was
made the public orator of the University in Cambridge;
some of whose English works are extant; which, though they
be rare in their kind, yet are far short of expressing
those perfections he had in the Greek and Latin tongue,
and all divine and human literature; his life was most
holy and exemplary; insomuch, that about Salisbury,
where he lived, beneficed for many years, he was little
less than sainted. He was not exempt from passion and
choler, being infirmities to which all our race is subject,
but that excepted, without reproach in his action.

11.   RICHARD CRASHAW, 'ON MR. G. HERBERTS BOOKE INTITULED
THE TEMPLE'

ante 1646

The title of Crashaw's 'Steps to the Temple' may or may not
have been his own.   But he did include within its pages a
substantial tribute to Herbert, the ensuing poem, first
published in 1646 but presumably written before he departed
for Italy, where he died three years later (1649).   See
also above, p. 6.
   Source: Crashaw, 'Steps to the Temple. Sacred Poems,
with other Delights of the Muses' (1646); reproduced from
'The Poems ... of Richard Crashaw', ed. L.C. Martin, 2nd
edn (Oxford, 1957), pp. 130-1.

> *On Mr.* G. Herberts *booke intituled the Temple*
> *of Sacred Poems, sent to a Gentlewoman.*

Know you faire, on what you looke;
Divinest love lyes in this booke:
Expecting fire from your eyes,
To kindle this his sacrifice.
When your hands unty these strings, (1)
Thinke you have an Angell by th' wings.
One that gladly will bee nigh,
To wait upon each morning sigh.
To flutter in the balmy aire,
Of your well perfumed prayer.
These white plumes of his heele lend you,
Which every day to heaven will send you:
To take acquaintance of the spheare,
And all the smooth faced kindred there.
And though *Herberts* name doe owe
These devotions, fairest; know
That while I lay them on the shrine
Of your white hand, they are mine.

Note

1   I.e. used to tie the book.

12.   JOSEPH BEAUMONT (?), FROM THE PREFACE TO CRASHAW'S
'STEPS TO THE TEMPLE'

1646

The anonymous preface to Crashaw's 'Steps to the Temple'
has been supposed to be the work of Joseph Beaumont, a
close friend of the poet's and given much to the florid
style characteristic of the following lines (see Austin
Warren, 'Richard Crashaw' (Ann Arbor, Mich., 1939),
p. 220). Beaumont was Fellow of Peterhouse, Cambridge,
and, after the Restoration, the College's Master; his well-
attested tribute to Herbert is given in No. 13.
     Source: from The Preface to the Reader, in 'Steps to the
Temple' (as in No. 11); reproduced from Martin's edition,
p. 75.

Learned Reader,

The Authors friend, (1) will not usurpe much upon thy eye:
This is onely for those, whom the name of our Divine Poet
hath not yet seized into admiration, I dare undertake, that
what *Jamblicus (in vita Pythagorae)* (2) affirmeth of his
Master, at his Contemplations, these Poems can, *viz.* They
shal lift thee Reader, some yards above the ground: and, as
in *Pythagoras* Schoole, every temper was first tuned into a
height by severall proportions of Musick; and spiritual-
iz'd for one of his weighty Lectures; So maist thou take a
Poem hence, and tune thy soule by it, into a heavenly
pitch; and thus refined and borne up upon the wings of
meditation, in these Poems thou maist talke freely of God,
and of that other state.
     Here's *Herbert's* second, but equall, who hath retriv'd
Poetry of late, and return'd it up to its Primitive use;
Let it bound back to heaven gates, whence it came.
Thinke yee, St. *Augustine* would have steyned his graver
Learning with a booke of Poetry, had he fancied their
dearest end to be the vanity of Love-Sonnets, and Epitha-
lamiums? No, no, he thought with this, our Poet, that
every foot in a high-borne verse, might helpe to measure
the soule into that better world: *Divine Poetry*; I dare
hold it, in position against *Suarez* on the subject, (3)
to be the Language of the Angels; it is the Quintessence
of Phantasie and discourse center'd in Heaven; 'tis the
very Outgoings of the soule; 'tis what alone our Author is
able to tell you, and that in his owne verse....

[The comments immediately ensuing are an attack – only
slightly less virulent than Vaughan's (below, p. 84) – on
secular poetry.]

Notes

1 I.e. the author of the preface on hand.
2 Actually, Eunapius's life of Iamblichus, not Iamblichus's life of Pythagoras.
3 The Spanish theologian Francisco Suárez (d.c. 1615) had
   denied that angels use the language of men.

13. JOSEPH BEAUMONT, FROM 'PSYCHE'

post 1648 / mid-1650s

Beaumont's meandering, ambitiously 'cosmic' poem 'Psyche'
– nearly three times the length of 'Paradise Lost' – contained no reference to Herbert in its first edition (1648).
But the posthumously published second edition (1702) included the ensuing stanza, its precise date of composition unknown but most likely penned – as I am informed by Paul G.
Stanwood – sometime between 1648, when Beaumont began to
revise the poem's first edition, and the mid-1650s, when
Beaumont was still interested in Herbert as a poet. See
also above, p. 6.
   Source: Beaumont, 'Psyche, or Love's Mystery', 2nd rev.
edn (Cambridge, 1702), p. 46 (Canto IV, stanza 102).

[Apropos the roll-call of poets inclusive of Pindar and
the Roman poet Flaccus (first century AD), Beaumont adds:]

   (Yet neither of their Empires was so vast
   But they left *Herbert* too full room to reign,
   Who Lyric's pure and precious Metal cast
   In holier moulds, and nobly durst maintain
       Devotion in Verse, whilst but the spheres
       He tunes his Lute, and plays to heav'nly ears.)

14.   GEORGE DANIEL, 'AN ODE UPON ... "THE TEMPLE"'

1648

Poetic tributes to Herbert had become a well-established
tradition by the time the spasmodically capable poet Daniel
wrote his in 1648 (first published in 1959). The characteristic of this poem is, clearly, its galloping enthusiasm. See also above, pp. 6-7.
  Source: British Library Add. MS 192555; reproduced from
'The Selected Poems of George Daniel of Beswick 1616-1657',
ed. Thomas B. Stroup (Lexington, Ky, 1959), pp. 66-7.

An Ode upon the Incomparable Liricke Poesie written
     by Mr George Herbert; entituled: *The Temple*

          LORD! yet how dull am I?
              When I would flye!
     Up to the Region, of thy Glories where
              Onlie true formes appeare;
     My long brail'd (1) Pineons, (clumsye, and unapt)
                 I cannot Spread;
          I am all dullnes; I was Shap't
     Only to flutter, in the lower Shrubbs
          Of Earth-borne-follies. Out alas!
              When I would treade
     A higher Step, ten thousand, thousand Rubbs
              Prevent my Pace.

     This Glorious (2) Larke; with humble Honour, I
              Admire and praise;
              But when I raise
     My Selfe, I fall asham'd, to see him flye:
     The Royall Prophet, (3) in his Extasie,
              First trod this path;
     Hee followes neare; (I will not Say, how nigh)
          In flight, as well as faith.
     Let me asham'd creepe backe into my Shell;
          And humbly Listen to his Layes:
     Tis prejudice, what I intended Praise;
     As where they fall soe Lowe, all Words are Still.
          Our Untun'd Liricks, onlie fitt
              To Sing, our Selfe-borne-Cares,
          Dare not, of Him. Or had wee Witt,
              Where might wee find out Ears
     Worthy his Character? if wee may bring
              Our Accent to his Name?

This Stand, of Lirick's, Hee the utmost Fame
Has gain'd; and now they vaile, (4) to heare Him Sing
Horace in voice; and Casimire (5) in winge.

Notes

1 Fastened by thongs.
2 'happie', according to another (earlier?) version of
   the poem.
3 I.e. Donne.
4 Stoop before.
5 The Polish epigrammatist and lyric poet Maciej Kazi-
   mierz Sarbiewski (1595-1640).

15. THOMAS HOBBES, FROM THE ANSWER TO DAVENANT

1650

Heralding the advent of novel attitudes, the 'answer' that
the formidable philosopher Hobbes provided to - and first
published with - Sir William Davenant's 'Discourse upon
Gondibert' (Paris, 1650) did not specifically mention Herbert. Yet his one generalised comment about a habit
shared by Herbert is symptomatic of the outlook that was
adversely to affect the poet's fortunes in the century
following. See further above, p. 7.
    Source: The Answer of Mr. Hobbes to Sir Will. D'Aven-
ant's Preface before Gondibert; reproduced from 'Gondibert', ed. David F. Gladish (Oxford, 1971), p. 47.

In an Epigramme or a sonnet, a man may vary his measures,
and seeke glory from a needlesse difficulty, as he that
contrived verses into the formes of an Organ, a Hatchet,
an Egge, an Altar, and a payre of Winges; but in so great
and noble a worke as is an Epique Poeme, for a man to
obstruct his owne way with unprofitable difficulties, is
great imprudence.

16.   CLEMENT BARKSDALE, FROM 'NYMPHA LIBETHRIS'

1651

Barksdale was a versifier possessed of a minimal talent.
The following poetic tribute juxtaposes 'The Temple' and
Crashaw's 'Steps to the Temple', even though Barksdale was
stylistically influenced by neither. See also above,
p. 7.
    Source: Barksdale, 'Nympha Libethris or the Cotswold
Muse' (1651), pp. 93-4.

Herbert and Crashaw.

When into *Herbert's Temple* I ascend
By *Crashaws Steps*, I do resolve to mend
My lighter Verse, and by low notes to raise,
And in high Accent sing my *Makers* praise.
Mean while these *sacred Poems* in my Sight
I place, and *read*, that I may learn to *write*.

17.   BARNABAS OLEY, 'A PREFATORY VIEW OF THE LIFE OF
MR GEO. HERBERT'

1652

The first substantial biography of Herbert, Oley's 'A
Prefatory View of the Life of Mr Geo. Herbert', was
prefixed to Herbert's 'Remains' (1652). Anonymous on
its first appearance, the biography was claimed later
by Oley as his own work. On Oley himself, and on the
impact of his account on subsequent biographers inclusive of Walton, see above, pp. 9 f.
    Source: 'Herbert's Remains. Or, Sundry Pieces of
that sweet Singer of the Temple, Mr George Herbert'
(1652), sigs a1-c6v. The volume includes 'A Priest to
the Temple', which Oley in the following pages refers to
as 'this Book'.

To the *Christian*, more designedly, to the *Clergy*-Reader
of the same Time, and Rank, and Mind, and in like Condition with the Epistler. Grace *&c*. and Recovery, and Profit
by the ensuing Tract.

My poor and deer Brother,
    Do not expect (I humbly beseech thee) the High and
Glorious Titles of *Companion in tribulation, and in the
patience of JESUS*, &c.   I could most willingly (if I
thought that I could truely) give thee them; knowing, that
what lustre I cast upon thee, would by rebound lite upon
my self.   But my mouth is stopped: Let God be true, and
the Justice of God be Justified.
    1. The reading of those piercing Scriptures *I Sam. 2.
& 3.* chap. *Jer. 23. Exek. 3 & 33. Hos. 4. Mal. 2.*   2. The
view of this ensuing Tract; which (mee thinks) is not a
Book of 37 Chapters, but *a Bill of seven times 37 Indict-
ments* against thee and me: a strange *Speculum Sacerdotale*;
(1) in its discovery (me thinks) something resembling the
secret of the *holy Urim*: As if this good *Bezaleel* (2) had
invented a living, pure looking-Glasse, in most exact proportions of Beauty, that should both present it self as a
Body of unblemished perfections, and shew all the beholders deformities at once: that should shew thee both *Aaron
in the Holy of Holyes*, before the Mercy-Seat, in all his
pure Ornaments: and *Hophni* or *Phineas*, ravening for their
Fees of Flesh, and wallowing in their lust at the door of
the Tabernacle.   3. The reflecting on common Conversation
in the day of our prosperity, and the paralelling the Book
of mine own Conscience with the Authors Book (in both
which I finde my self (not to say Thee) written highly
defective in every duty the good man commends, and not a
little peccant in every particular taxed by him.)   These
three have convinced, and even inforced me to confesse,
that I am sure mine (and I fear, thy) sifferings are not
the meer sufferings of *pure and perfect Martyrs,* but of
Grievous Transgressors.   Not only under the rods of Gods
just judgment, but the scorpions of his heavy displeasure,
fierce wrath, and sore Indignation.   Not only from the
smoaking of Gods jealousie, or the sparks of his Anger,
but the flames of his furnace, (heat seven times more then
ever,) yea, even from the Furiousnesse of the wrath of
God. *Psal. 78. 50.*
    Gods sinking the Gates, his destroying the wals, his
slighting the strong holds of Zion; his polluting the
Kingdom, his swallowing the Palaces, his cutting off the
Horn of Israel: Gods hating our Feasts, his abominating our
Sabboths, his loathing our solemnities, *Esa. I.* (3) Gods
forgetting his Footstool, his abhorring his Sanctuary, his
casting off his Altar, are (to me) signes that the glory of
God is departed to the Mountain, *Ezek. II. 23.*   That God
hath in the indignation of his anger despised the *King and
the Priest, Lam. 2.* [6].   It must be acknowledged sure! that
the hand of God hath gone out against us, more then against

others of our Rank at other times; at least, that God hath
not restrained violence against us, so as he did that
against those of our Profession in the dayes of old: *The
portion of the Egyptian Priests (that served the Oxe, the
Ape, and the Onion), escaped sale in time of the Famine.*
Learned *Junius* (in his Academia, Chap. 4.) (4) sayes, that
the *Philistines spared the Schooles of the Prophets in
their Warrs with Israel*: and that the *Phoenicians, Cald-
eans, and Indians were tender over such places*: Thus then
did God restraine the spirits of Princes: yet that God
(who in his own Law, *Lev. 25. 32. gave the Levits a special priviledg of redeeming Lands* (sold by themselves) *at
any time*, when other Tribes were limited to a set Time)
hath not stayed the madnesse of the people against us, but
that our portions are sold unto others *without Redemption*.

We must acknowledg, that Gods word hath taken hold of
us, *Zec. 1. 5.* That the Lord hath devised a device against
us, hath watched upon the evil, and brought it upon us;
For, under the whole heaven hath not been done, as hath
been done upon Jerusalem, *Dan. 9. 14.*

Let us not flatter our selves presumptuously! The
punishment answers the sin, as the wax the seal, and as
the Mould owns the Figure: And let us own both. It is very
dangerous to blesse our selves too boldly; God has cursed
our Blessings, *Mal. 2. 2.* And that he may blesse to us our
very Curses; Let us take with us words and say, To the
Lord our God belong mercies and forgivenesses, and multi-
plyed pardons, to us shame and confusion, as at this day.
The most compendious way to get what belongs to God, is,
to take to our selves what belongs to us. If we would
Judge your selves, and every man, knowing the plague of
his own heart, lay Gods Dealing to heart; and accepting of
our punishment, give glory to God, and humble our selves
under his mighty hand; then shall God exalt us, and accept
us and take away our Reproach.

If we shall confesse our sins, that like *Simeon* and
Levi, we have been Brethren in evil, have broken the
Covenant of *Levi*, have done violence to, and been partial
in the law, have made our selves vile, and therefore are
justly, by God, made contemptible and base before the
people, *Mal. 2. [9].* If wee shall confesse, that wee
neither understood nor valued our High and Holy Calling as
Christians, much lesse as Ministers of Christ; That we
did not thrive kindly, when Providence had planted and
watered us in *those Horns of Oyl, the two Universities*; or
removed us into *Countrey Cures*, we did not fructifie (as
this Book will shew) in any proportion to his encouragements, & therfore are justly cashiered out of his service,
and stript of his Rewards: God is faithfull and just to

forgive us: For, *Job. 33. 27.* He looks upon men; if any
say, I have sinned, I have perverted that which was right,
and it profited me not; he will deliver his soul from the
pit, his life shall see the light.

And now, let none think, that this Confession will give
advantage to the Adversary; They may take, where none is
given: They may say, *Let the Lord be glorified:* By their
own confession, *we offend not, though we devour them,
because they have sinned against the Lord, the habitation
of Justice,* Jer. 50. 7. But they will finde at last,
That to forsake the Levite is a sin; That it is a bitter
thing to *Help forward affliction,* when *God is but a little
displeased:* That Jerusalem will be a cup of trembling, and
a burdensome stone to every one that cryes but *Downe with
it.* Woe to thee, O Assur, the Rod of Gods anger; the
staffe in thine hand is Gods Indignation. Thou, Lord,
hast ordained him for judgment, and established him for
correction; Even for Our correction, to purifie Us sons
of *Levi* from our drosse; (Howbeit, hee meaneth not so) and
by his hand, who punisheth us not onely for that which is
sin, to put on us Martyrs Robes; by that contrivance both
Chastning and Covering our sins; As the *Persians* use
their Nobles, beating their Clothes, and saving their
Persons.

There can be no credit lost by giving glory to God: Did
Achan lose any thing by confessing that God had found him
out, and his Garment, and his Wedg? Hath not *Adonibezek
got a Fame of Ingenuity, for acknowledging Gods Art of
Justicing, in that most exact way of Counter passion or
Retaliation?* which is so frequent in these times, though
it is not considerd.... (5)

I hope no man will think, though I speak thus, that I
give him leave to *construe my words Mathematically,* as if
there was not an atome, or hair of a good man, or man of
God in our Church. There were divers *primitive* (and are
at this day, Blessed be God, The Lord make them 1000 times
more then they are,) *holy* and *heavenly souls,* vessels
chosen and fitted for the service of the Sanctuary. I
shall be bold to *instance* in *Three,* who died in peace; few
considering (some did) that they were taken away from the
evil to come, lest their eys should see (what their spirits
foresaw) what is come on us, on whom the days, not of visi-
tation only, but of vengeance, even the ends of the world
are come.

The first of these was *Thomas Jackson* D.D. late President of Corpus Christi College in *Oxford,* and sometimes
Vicar of St. *Nicholas* Church in *Newcastle* upon *Tyne;* two
places that must give account to God for the good they had,
or might have had by that Man; as all Scholers must for

his neglected Works.

The second was Mr. *Nicholas Ferrer* (6) of little *Gidding* in Huntington Shire, sometimes fellow-Commoner and Fellow of Clare-hall in Cambridge.

The third was the Author of this book, *Master GEORGE HERBERT*, Fellow of Trinity Colledge, Orator of the University of Cambridge, and Rector of Bemmorton in Wiltshire. All three Holy in their lives, eminent in their gifts, signall Protestants for their Religion, painfull in their several stations, pretious in their deaths, and sweet in their memories.

First, I will give thee a briefe of some confrontments common to them all, and then some of their, at least this Authors proper excellencies apart.

1. They all had that inseparable Lot and signe of Christ and Christians, *Isa. 8. 18. Heb. 2. 13. Luke 2. 34.* To be signes of Contradiction (or spoken Against) men wondred at, and rated at by the world.... (7) [F]or our Authour (*The sweet singer of the Temple*) though he was one of the most prudent and accomplish'd men of his time, I have heard sober men censure him as a man that did not manage his brave parts to his best advantage and preferment, but lost himself *in an humble way;* That was the phrase, I well remember it.

The second thing wherein all Three agreed, was a singular sincerity in Imbracing, and transcendent Dexterity in Defending the Protestant Religion established in the Church of *England....* (8) [H]e that reads Mr *HERBERT's* Poems attendingly, shall finde not onely the excellencies of Scripture Divinitie, and choice passages of the Fathers bound up in Meetre; but the Doctrine of *Rome* also finely and strongly confuted; as in the Poems, *To Saints and Angels, The British Church, Church Militant,*&c.

Thus stood they in aspect to Rome and her children on the left hand. As for our Brethren that erred on the right hand, (*Doctor Jackson* speaks for himself) and *Mr. F.* though he ever honoured their persons (that were pious and learned) and alwayes spoke of them with much Christian respect, yet would hee bewaile their mistakes, which (like mists) led them in some points back again to those errors of Rome which they had forsaken.... [T]he chiefe aime of Master *F.* and this Authour, (9) was to win those that disliked our Liturgy, Catechisme, &c: by the constant, reverent, and holy use of them: Which, surely had we all imitated, having first imprinted the virtue of these prayers in our own hearts, and then studied with passionate and affectionate celebration, (for voyce, gesture, &c:) as in God's presence to imprint them in the mindes of the people, (as this Book teaches,) our prayers had been

generally as well beloved as they were scorned. And for
my part, I am apt to think, That our prayers stood so long,
was a favour by God granted us at the prayers of these men,
(*who prayed* for *these prayers as well as* in *them:*) and that
they fell so soon, was a punishment of our negligence, (and
other sins) who had not taught even those that liked them
well, to use then aright; but that the good old woman
would absolve, though not so loud, yet as confidently as
the Minister himselfe.

Lastly, *The blessed Three in One* did make these three
men agree in one point more. That one spirit, which divides to every man gifts as he pleases, seems to me to have
dropt upon these three Elect vessels all of them some unction or tincture of the Spirit of prophesie. Shal I say,
I hope, or Fear Mr. *Herbert's lines* should be verified?

[Quotes 'The Church Militant', 11. 235-58.]

I pray God he may prove a true prophet for *poor America*,
not against *poor England*. Ride on *Most Mighty Jesu*, because of the word of truth. Thy Gospel is a light big
enough for them and us: But leave us not. The people of
thine holinesse have possessed it but a little while,
Isaiah. 63. 15. &c.... (10)

This Authour, *MR. G. HERBERT*, was extracted out of a
Generous, Noble, and Ancient Family: His Father was *RICH-
ARD HERBERT* of *Blachehall,* in *Mountgomery*, Esq; descended
from the *Great Sir RICHARD HERBERT* in *Edward* the Fourth's
time; and so his Relation to the Noble Family of that Name,
well known. His Mother was Daughter of Sir *Richard Newport*
of *Arcoll,* who doubtlesse was a pious daughter, she was so
good and godly a mother; She had ten children, *Job*'s number, and *Job*'s distinction, seven sons; for whose education she went and dwelt in the University, to recompence
the losse of their Father, in giving them two Mothers.
And this great care of hers, this good son of hers studied
to improve and requite, as is seen in those many Latin and
Greek Verses, the Obsequious *Parentalia,* he made and printed in her memory: which though they be good, very good,
yet (to speak freely even of this man I so much honour)
they be dull or dead in comparison of his *Temple Poems.*
And no marvel; To write those, he made his ink with water
of *Helicon*, but these Inspirations propheticall were dis-
tilled from above: In those are weake motions of Nature,
in these Raptures of Grace. In those he writ Flesh and
Blood: A fraile earthly Woman, though a MOTHER, but in
these he praysed his Heavenly FATHER, the God of Men and
Angels, and the Lord Jesus Christ *His Master;* For so (to
quicken himself in Duties, and to cut off all depending on

man, whose breath is in his nosthrils) hee used ordinarily
to call our *Saviour*.

I forget not where I left him: He did thrive so well
there, that he was first chosen fellow of the Colledge,
and afterward Oratour of the Universitie. The Memorials
of him left in the Orators Book, shew how he discharged
the Place: and himself intimates, *Church*. That whereas his
Birth and Spirit prompted him to Martiall Atchievements,
The way that takes the Town; and not to sit simpering
over a Book; *God did often melt his spirit,* and entice him
with Academick Honor, to be content to wear, and *wrap up
himselfe in a gown,* so long, till he durst not put it off,
nor retire to any other calling. However, propably he
might, I have heard (as other Orators) have had a Secretary of States place.

But the good man like a genuine son of *Levi* (I had like
to have said *Melchisedeck*) balked all secular wayes, saw
neither father, nor mother, childe nor Brother, birth nor
friends (save in Christ Jesus) chose the Lord for his portion, and his service for employment. And he knew full
well what he did when he received Holy orders, as appears
by every page in this Book, and by the Poems call'd
Priesthood, and *Aaron*: And by this unparalell'd *vigilancy*
which he used over his Parish, which made him (sayes that
modest Authour of the *Epistle* before his Poems, *N.F.* who
knew him well) *A Peer to the primitive Saints, and more
then a pattern to his own age.* (11)

Besides his Parsonage, he had also a Prebend in the
Church of *Lincoln*; which I think (because he lived far
from, and so could not attend the duty of that place,) he
would faine have resigned to Master *Ferrer*, and often
earnestly sued to him to discharge him of it; but Master *F.*
wholly refused, and diverted or directed his charity (as I
take it) to the re-edifying of the ruined Church of *Leighton*, where the corps of the Prebend lay. So that the
Church of *England* owes to him (besides what good may come
by this Book, towards the repair of us Church-men in point
of morals,) the reparation of a *Church-materiall*, and
erection of that costly piece (of Mosaick or Solomonich
work,) *the Temple*; which flourishes and stands inviolate,
when our other Magnificences are desolate, and despised.

These things I have said are high; but yet there is
one thing which I admire above all the rest: The right
managing of the *Fraternall duty of reproof* is (me thinks)
one of the most difficult offices of Christian Prudence.
O Lord! what is then *the Ministeriall*? To do it as wee
should, is likely to anger a whole world of waspes, to set
fire on the earth. This, I have conjectured, was that
which made many holy men leave the world, and live in

wildernesses; which, by the way, was not counted by
Ancients, an act of Perfection, but of Cowardise and poor
spiritednesse: of Flight to shade and shelter, not of
Fight in dust and blood, and heat of the day. This
Authour had not only got the courage to do this, but the
Art of doing this aright.

There was not a man in his way (be he of what Ranke hee
would) *that spoke awry* (in order to God) *but he wip'd his
mouth with a modest, grave and Christian reproof:* This was
Heroicall; Adequate to that Royall Law, Thou shalt in any
case reprove thy Brother, and not suffer sin upon him.
And that he did this, I have heard from true Reporters,
and thou mayst see he had learned it himselfe, else he
never had taught it us, as hee does in divers passages of
this Book.

His singular Dexterity in sweetning this Art, thou mayst
see in the Garb and phrase of his writing. Like a wise
Master-builder, he has set about a forme of Speech, transferred it in a Figure, as if he was all the while learning
from another man's mouth or pen, and not teaching any.
And whereas we all of us deserved the sharpnesse of
Reproofe, ἔλεγχε ἀποτόμως, (12) He saith, *He does this,
and he does that*; whereas, poor men, we did no such thing.
This dart of his, thus dipped, pierces the soul.

There is another thing (some will call it a Paradox)
which I learned from Him (and *Mr. Ferrer*) in the *Managery*
of their most cordiall and *Christian Friendship*. That
this may be maintained in vigour and height without the
Ceremonies of Visits and Complements; yea, without any
Trade of secular courtesies, meerly in order to spirituall
Edification of one another in love. I know they loved each
other most entirely, and their very souls cleaved together
most intimately, and drove a large stock of Christian
Intelligence together long before their deaths: yet saw
they not each other in many years, I think, scarce ever,
but as Members of one Universitie, in their whole lives.

There is one thing more may be learn'd from these Two
(I may say, these Three) (13) also: Namely, That *Christian
Charity* will keep Unity of souls, amidst great differences
of Gifts and Opinions. There was variation considerable
in their Indowments: *Doctor Jackson* had in his youth (as
if he then had understood Gods calling) laid his grounds
carefully in Arithmetick, Grammer, Philology, Geometry,
Rhetorick, Logick, Philosophy, Orientall Languages, His-
tories, *&c.* (yea, he had Insight in Heraldry and Hieroglyphicks,) hee made all these serve either as Rubbish
under the Foundation, or as drudges and day labourers to
Theology. He was copious and definitive in Controversies
of all sorts. *Master Ferrar* was Master of the Westerne

Tongues; yet cared not for Criticismes and curiosities.
He was also very modest in points of controversie, and
would scarce venture to *Opine*, even in the points wherein
the world censured him possessed. Our Authour was of a
midle Temper betwixt, or a Compound of both these; yet
having rather more of *Master Ferrer* in him: And to what he
had of him, he added the Art of Divine Poesie, and other
polite learning, which so commended him to persons most
Eminent in their time, that *Doctor Donne* inscribed to him
a paper of Latine verses in print; and the *Lord Bacon*
having translated some Psalmes into English meetre, sent
them with a Dedication prefixed, To his very Good friend,
Master GEORGE HERBERT, thinking that he had kept a true
decorum in chusing one so fit for the Argument, in respect
of Divinity and Pöesy (the one as the Matter, the other as
the Stile) that a better choice he could not make. (14)

In summ, To distinguish them by better Resemblances out
of the Old and New Testament, and antiquity: Me thinks,
Doctor *J.* has somewhat like the spirit of *Jeremy*, Saint
James, and *Salvian*. Master *Herbert*, like *David*, and other
Psalm-men, Saint *John*, and *Prudentius*. Master *F.* like
Esay, Saint *Luke*, and Saint *Chrysostome*; yet in this diver-
sity, had they such an Harmony of souls as was admirable.
For instance, In one who differ'd in some points from them
all, yet in him they so agreed all, as that Master *F.* out
of a great liking of the Man, translated him into *English*,
Master *Herbert* commented on him, and commended him to use;
And Doctor *J.* allowed him for the Presse, It was *Valdesso's*
110 Considerations.

It would swell this Preface too much to set down the
severall excellencies of our Authour: His *consciencious*
expence of Time, which he even measured by the *pulse*, that
native watch God has set in every of us. His eminent
Temperance, and *Frugality*, (the two best Purveyors for his
Liberality and Beneficence,) his private *Fastings*, his
mortification of the body, his extemporary exercises
thereof, at the sight or visit of a *Charnell House*, where
every Bone, before the day, rises up in judgement against
fleshly lust and pride: at the *stroke of a passing bell*,
when ancient charity used (said he) to run to Church, and
assist the dying Christian with prayers and tears (for
sure that was the ground of that custome;) and at all
occasions he could lay hold of possibly, which he sought
with the diligence that others shun and shift them.
Besides his carefull, (not scrupulous) observation of
appointed Fasts, Lents, and *Embers*: The neglect and defect
of this last, he said, had such influx on the children
which the Fathers of the Church did beget at such times,
as malignant Stars are said to have over naturall

Productions; Children of such Parents, as be Fasting and
Prayers, being like *Isaak*, and *Jacob*, and *Samuel*; most
likely to become Children of the Promise, Wrastlers with
God, and fittest to wear a linnen *Ephod*. (15)   And with
this *Fasting* he imp'd his prayers both private and publick: His private must be left to God, who saw them in
secret; his publick were the *Morning and Evening Sacrifice*
of the *Church Liturgie*, which he used with consciencious
devotion, not of Custome, but serious Judgement; Knowing,
1. That the Sophism used to make people hate them, was a
solid reason to make men of understanding love them;
Namely, because taken out of the Masse Book: Taken out,
but as gold from drosse, the precious from the vile.   The
wise Reformers knew *Rome* would cry *Shism, schism*, and
therefore they kept all they could lawfully keep, being
loth to give offence; as our blessed Saviour, being loth
to offend the *Jews* at the great Reformation, kept divers
old Elements, and made them new Sacraments and Services,
as their frequent Washings he turned into one Baptisme;
some service of the Passeover into the Lord's Supper.
2. That *the homelinesse and coursenesse*, which also was
objected, was a great commendation.   The Lambes poor of
the Flock are forty, for one grounded Christian: propor-
tionable must be the care of the Church to provide milk;
that is, plain and easie nourishment for them: and so had
our Church done, hoping that stronger Christians, as they
abounded in Gifts, so they had such a store of the Grace of
of Charity, as for their weak Brethren's sakes to be content therewith.
     He thought also that a set Liturgy was of great use in
respect of those without, whether erring Christians, or
unbelieving men.   That when we had used our best arguments
against their errours or unbeliefe, we might shew them a
Form wherein we did, and desired they would serve Almighty
God with us: That we might be able to say, *This is our
Church, Here would we land you*.   Thus we believe, *see the
Creed*.   *Thus we pray, baptize, catechise, celebrate the
Eucharist, Marry, Bury,* Intreat the sick, *&c.*
     These, besides Unity, and other accessary benefits, he
thought grounds sufficient to bear him out in this prac-
tise: wherein he ended his life, calling for the Church
Prayers a while before his death, saying, *None to them,
none to them* at once both commending them, and his soul to
God in them, immediately before his dissolution, as some
Martyrs did, *Mr. Hullier* by name, Vicar of *Babram*, burnt
to death in *Cambridge*; who having the *Common-Prayer Book*
in his hand, in stead of a Censor, and using the prayers as
incense, offered up himselfe as a whole Burnt Sacrifice to
God; with whom the very Book it selfe suffered Martyrdome,

when fallen out of his consumed hands, it was by the
Executioners thrown into the fire and burnt as an Hereti-
call Book.

He was moreover so great a Lover of *Church-Musick*, That
he usually called it *Heaven upon earth*, and attended it a
few days before his death. But above all, his chief
delight was in the *Holy Scripture*, One leafe whereof he
professed he would not part with, though he might
have the whole world in Exchange.   That was *his
wisdome, his comfort, his joy*, out of that he took
his Motto; *LESSE THEN THE LEAST OF ALL GOD'S MERCIES.*
(16) In that he found the substance, Christ, and in Christ
Remission of sins, yea, in his blood he placed the goodnesse of his good works.   *It is a good Work*, (said he of
Building a Church,) *if it be sprinkled with the Blood of
Christ*.

This high esteem of the *Word of life*, as it wrought in
himselfe a wondrous expression of high Reverence, when ever
he either read it himselfe, or heard others read it, so it
made him *equally wonder, that those which pretended such
extraordinary love to Christ Jesus, as many did*, could
possibly give such leave and liberty to themselves as to
hear that word that shall judge us at the last day, *without any the least expression* of that *holy feare* and *trembling* which they ought to charge upon their souls in private, and in publick, to imprint upon others.

Thus have I with my foul hands soiled this (and the
other) fair piece, and worn out thy patience: yet have I
not so much as with one dash of a pensill, offered to
describe that person of his, which afforded so unusuall a
Contesseration (17) of Elegancies, and set of Rarities to
the Beholder; nor said I any thing of his Personall Relation, as an *Husband*, to a *loving* and *vertuous Lady*; as a
Kinsman, Master, &c. yet will I not silence his spirituall
love and care of Servants: Teaching Masters this duty, To
allow their Servants daily time, wherein to pray privately,
and to enjoyne them to do it: holding this for true
generally, *That publick prayer alone to such persons, is
no prayer at all*.

I have given thee onely these lineaments of his mind,
and thou mayest fully serve thy selfe of this Book, in
what vertue of his thy soul longeth after. *His* practice it
was, and *His Character* it is, *His* as *Authour*, and *His* as
Object: yet, Lo, the humility of this gracious man! He
had small esteem of this Book, and but very little of his
Poems.   Though God had magnified him with extraordinary
Gifts, yet said he, *God has broken into my Study, and
taken off my Chariot wheels, I have nothing worthy of God*.
And even this lowlinesse in his own eyes, doth more

advance their worth, and his vertues.

I have done, when I have besought the R[everend] Fathers, some Cathedrall, Ecclesiasticall, and Academicall men, (which Ranks the modest Authour meddles not with,) to draw *Idaea's* for their severall Orders respectively.... If it do no other good, yet will it help on in the way of *Repentance*, by discovery of former mistakes or neglects; which is the greatest, if not the onely Good that can probably be hoped for, out of this Tract: which being writ nigh *twenty years since,* will be lesse subject to misconstruction. The Good Lord prosper it according to the pious intent of the Authour, and hearty wishes of the Prefacer; who confesses himselfe unworthy *to carry out the Dung of Gods Sacrifices.*

Notes

1   'Mirror for priests'.
2   Who constructed the tabernacle (Exodus 31.2 ff., 35.30 ff., 36.1 ff.)
3   I.e. Isaiah 1.
4   Franciscus Junius (François Du Jon) the Elder, 'Academia' (1587).
5   Some other examples parallel to the cases of Achan (Joshua 7.1 ff.) and Adonibezek (Judges 1.5-7) are here omitted.
6   See above, p. 4.
7   The cases of Jackson and Ferrar, detailed at this point, are here omitted.
8   Ditto.
9   I.e. Herbert.
10 Some remarks on Ferrar and Jackson at this point are here omitted.
11 Above, No. 4.
12 'He confutes sharply'.
13 The third is Jackson (above, p. 75).
14 On Donne and Bacon, see above, pp. 55-7.
15 Jewish priestly vestment.
16 See above, No. 4 (note 3).
17 Combination.

18.   HENRY VAUGHAN, FROM HIS PREFACE TO 'SILEX SCINTILLANS'

1655

The second edition of Vaughan's 'Silex Scintillans' opens
with a violent denunciation of secular poetry and terminates with a paean to Herbert.   Both in this collection and
elsewhere, Herbert's impact on Vaughan is demonstrable if
not without its limits (see further above, pp. 8 f.).
Source: from The Authors Preface to the following
Hymns, in 'Silex Scintillans: Sacred Poems and Private
Ejaculations', 2nd edn (1655); reproduced from his 'Poetry
and Selected Prose', ed. L.C. Martin (1963), pp. 217 and
220-1.

That this Kingdom hath abounded with those ingenious persons, which in the late notion are termed *Wits*, is too
well known.   Many of them having cast away all their fair
portion of time, in no better imployments, then a deliberate search, or excogitation of *idle words*, and a most
vain, insatiable desire to be reputed *Poets*; leaving
behind them no other Monuments of those excellent abilities conferred upon them, but such as they may (with a
Predecessor of theirs) term *Parricides*, and a soul-killing
Issue; for that is the Βραβεῖον, (1) and Laureate *Crown*,
which idle *Poems* will certainly bring to their unrelenting
Authors.
    And well it were for them, if those willingly-studied
and wilfully-published vanities could defile no *spirits*,
but their own; but the *case* is far worse.   These *Vipers*
survive their *Parents*, and for many ages after (like
Epidemic diseases) infect whole Generations, corrupting
always and unhallowing the best-gifted *Souls*, and the most
capable *Vessels*....

[Four equally virulent pages later, Vaughan considers the
exceptions:]

    The first, that with any effectual success attempted a
diversion of this foul and overflowing *stream*, was the
blessed man, Mr. *George Herbert*, whose holy *life* and *verse*
gained many pious *Converts*, (of whom I am the least) and
gave the first check to a most flourishing and admired *wit*
of his time. (2)   After him followed diverse, - *Sed non
passibus aequis*; (3) they had more of *fashion*, then *force*:
And the *reason* of their so vast *distance* from him, besides
differing *spirits* and *qualifications* (for his *measure* was

eminent) I suspect to be, because they aimed more at
verse, then *perfection*; as may be easily gathered by their
frequent *impressions*, and numerous *pages*: Hence sprang
those wide, those weak, and lean *conceptions*, which in the
most inclinable *Reader* will scarce give any nourishment or
help to *devotion*; for not flowing from a true, practick
piety, it was impossible they should effect those things
abroad, which they never had acquaintance with at home;
being onely the productions of a common spirit, and the
obvious ebullitions of that light humor, which takes the
pen in hand, out of no other consideration, then to be seen
in print. It is true indeed, that to give up our thoughts
to pious *Themes* and *Contemplations* (if it be done for
pieties sake) is a great *step* towards *perfection*; because
it will *refine*, and *dispose* to devotion and sanctity. And
further, it will *procure* for us (so easily communicable is
that *loving spirit*) some small *prelibation* of those heavenly *refreshments*, which descend but seldom, and then very
sparingly, upon *men* of an ordinary or indifferent *holyness*;
but he that desires to excel in this kinde of *Hagiography*,
or holy writing, must strive (by all means) for *perfection*
and true *holyness*, that a *door may be opened to him in
heaven*, Rev, 4.1. and then he will be able to write (with
Hierotheus (4) and holy *Herbert*) A *true Hymn*. (5)
    To effect this in some measure, I have begged leave to
communicate this my poor *Talent* to the *Church*, under the
protection and *conduct* of her *glorious Head*....

Notes

1 Award, prize.
2 Donne? Or possibly Herrick?
3 'But with steps that match not his' (Virgil, 'Aeneid',
   II, 724).
4 Mythical first-century bishop of Athens, the teacher of
   pseudo-Dionysius the Areopagite.
5 The title of a poem by Herbert.

19.   JOSHUA POOLE, FROM 'THE ENGLISH PARNASSUS'

1657

Poole's handbook for aspiring poets, 'The English Parnassus', is a collection of extracts from the poetry and prose
of the late sixteenth and early seventeenth centuries.

Herbert, represented by a number of rather mangled phrases and lines, is also mentioned in the following counsel to poets in the book's Proeme. See also above, p. 7.

    Source: Poole, 'The English Parnassus: or, A Helpe to English Poesie' (1657), sigs A7v–A8.

   Many have been, which Pulpits did eschew,
   Converted from the Poets reading pew,
   And those that seldome do salute the porch
   Of Solomon, will come to Herberts Church;
   For as that English Lyrick sweetly sings,
   Whilst angels danc'd upon his trembling strings,
   A verse may find him who a Sermon flies,
   And turn delight into a sacrifice. (1)
   Then let the Poet use his lawfull bait,
   To make men swallow what they else would hate,
   Like wise Physicians that their pills infold
   In sugar, paper, or the leaves of gold,
   And by a vertuous fraud and honest stealth,
   Cozen unwilling Patients into health.

Note

1   The oft-quoted couplet is borrowed from 'The Church-porch', 11. 5–6.

20.   IZAAK WALTON, FROM 'THE LIFE OF DR. JOHN DONNE'

1658

First published in 1658, Walton's life of Donne includes these remarks on Herbert, clearly anticipatory of the later, more sustained performance centred on Herbert (No. 24). The episode here recounted is reiterated in the life of Herbert (below, p. 101).

    Source: 'The Life of Dr. John Donne', in 'Lives', pp. 55–8.

...in this enumeration of [Donne's] friends, though many must be omitted, yet that man of primitive piety, Mr. *George Herbert* may not; I mean that *George Herbert*, who was the Author of the *Temple*, or *Sacred Poems and*

Ejaculations.   A Book, in which by declaring his own
spiritual Conflicts, he hath Comforted and raised many a
dejected and discomposed Soul, and charmed them into sweet
and quiet thoughts: A Book, by the frequent reading whereof, and the assistance of that Spirit that seemed to inspire the Author, the Reader may attain habits of *Peace*
and *Piety*, and all the gifts of the *Holy Ghost* and *Heaven*:
and may by still reading, still keep those sacred fires
burning upon the Altar of so pure a heart, as shall free
it from the anxieties of this world, and keep it fixt upon
things that are above;) betwixt this *George Herbert* and
Dr. *Donne* there was a long and dear friendship, made up by
such a Sympathy of inclinations, that they coveted and
joyed to be in each others Company; and this happy friendship, was still maintained by many sacred indearments; of
which, that which followeth may be some Testimony.

   To Mr. *George Herbert*; sent him with one of my Seals of
the *Anchor* and *Christ*. (A sheaf of Snakes used heretofore
to be my Seal, which is the Crest of our poor Family.)

[Quotes Donne's poem and Herbert's reply (as above,
No. 1).]

21.   THOMAS FORDE, '[LINES] WITH HERBERTS POEME'

1660

As the poetic tributes to Herbert continued apace, the
distinctly minor versifier Thomas Forde attempted yet
another one in 1660.   In this case, as in others like
Daniel's (No. 14), the enthusiasm for Herbert is palpably
evident.   See also above, p. 12.
   Source: Forde, 'Fragmenta Poetica: or, Poetical Diver-
sions' (1660), pp. 17-18.

[Lines] *With* Herberts *Poeme*.

The *Poet*'s now become a *Priest*, and layes
His Poem at your feet, expects no *Bayes*,
But your *acceptance*; *kind'le* it with your eyes,
And make this *Offering* prove a *Sacrifice*.
The Vestal fire that's in your breast, will burn
Up all his drosse, and make it *Incense* turne;

And then your smile a second life will give,
Hee'l fear no death, if you but bid him live.
Pardon this bold ambition, tis his drift,
To make the *Altar* sanctifie the *Gift*.
Visit this *Temple*, at your vacant houres,
Twas *Herberts* Poem once, but now tis *Yours*.

22. THOMAS FULLER, FROM 'THE HISTORY OF THE WORTHIES OF
ENGLAND'

1662

Eight years before the publication of Walton's hagiography
of Herbert (No. 24), the poet's sanctification was
advanced a step further by the celebrated antiquary
Thomas Fuller - 'the least prejudiced great man in an age
that boasted a galaxy of great men', said Coleridge.
Walton, it is clear, was not an exception to the evolving
attitudes. See also above, p. 12.
   Source: Fuller, 'The History of the Worthies of England'
(1662), Montgomery-shire, p. 46.

GEORGE HERBERT was born at *Montgomery-Castle*, younger
Brother to *Edward* Lord *Herbert* ... bred Fellow of *Trinity
Colledge* in *Cambridge*, and Orator of the *University*, where
he made a speech no less learned than the occasion was
welcome, of the return of Prince *Charles* out of *Spain*.
   He was none of the Nobles of *Tekoa*, who at the building
of *Jerusalem put not their necks to the work of the Lord;*
(1) but waving preferment, chose serving at Gods Altar
before State-employment. So pious his life, that as he
was a copy of primitive, he might be a pattern of Sanctity
to posteritie, to testifie his independency on all others,
he never mentioned the name of *Jesus Christ*, but with this
addition, *My Master*. Next God the Word, he loved the Word
of God, being heard often to protest, That he *would not
part with one leaf thereof for the whole world*.
   Remarkable his conformity to Church-Discipline, whereby
he drew the greater part of his Parishioners to accompany
him daily in the publick celebration of Divine Service.
Yet had he (because not desiring) no higher preferment
than the Benefice of *Bemmerton* nigh *Salisbury* (where he
built a fair house for his Successor) and the Prebend of
Leighton (founded in the Cathedral of *Lincoln*) where he

built a fair Church, with the assistance of some few
Friends free Offerings. When a Friend on his death bed
went about to comfort him with the remembrance thereof, as
an especial good work, he returned, *It is a good work if
sprinkled with the Blood of Christ*. But his Church (that
inimitable piece of Poetry) may out-last this in structure.
His death hapned *Anno Dom*. 163—. (2)

Notes

1   Nehemiah 3.5 (author's marginal note).
2   I.e. 1633.

23.   JOHN AUBREY, FROM 'BRIEF LIVES'

post 1667

The gossipy antiquary Aubrey began to compile his 'Brief
Lives' from 1667 although the first edition was not to
appear until 1897. His entry on Herbert, even if known to
writers in the intervening two centuries, would not have
amended their view of the poet in any substantive way. The
entry begins with some antiquarian details concerning the
Herbert family and continues as shown below.
    Source: from George Herbert, in 'Aubrey's Brief Lives',
ed. Oliver Lawson Dick (1950), p. 137.

Mr. George Herbert was kinsman (remote) and Chapelaine to
Philip, Earl of Pembroke and Montgomery, and Lord Chamber-
layn. His Lordship gave him a Benefice at Bemmarton (between Wilton and Salisbury) a pittifull little chappell of
Ease to Foughelston. The old house was very ruinous. Here
he built a very handsome howse for the Minister, of Brick,
and made a good garden and walkes. He lyes in the Chan-
cell, under no large, nor yet very good, marble grave-
stone, without any Inscription.
    In the Chancell are many apt sentences of the Scripture.
At his Wive's Seate, *My life is hid with Christ in God* (he
hath verses on this Text in his Poëms). Above, in a
little windowe - blinded, with a Veile (ill painted) *Thou
art my hideing place*.
    He maried Jane, the third daughter of Charles Danvers,
of Bayntun, in com. Wilts. Esq. but had no issue by her.

He was a very fine complexion and consumptive. His mari-
age, I suppose, hastened his death. My kinswoman was a
handsome *bona roba* and ingeniose.

When he was first maried he lived a yeare or better at
Dantesey house. H. Allen, of Dantesey, was well acquainted with him, who has told me that he had a very good hand
on the Lute, and that he sett his own Lyricks or sacred
poems.

Scripsit: - Sacred Poems, called 'The Church', printed,
Cambridge, 1633; a Booke entituled 'The Country Parson',
not printed till about 1650, 8vo. He also writt a folio
in Latin, which because the parson of Hineham could not
read, his widowe (then wife to Sir Robert Cooke) condemned
to the uses of good houswifry. (This account I had from
Mr. Arnold Cooke, one of Sir Robert Cooke's sonnes, whom I
desired to aske his mother-in-lawe for Mr. G. Herbert's
MSS.)

He was buryed (according to his owne desire) with the
singing service for the buriall of dead, by the singing
men of Sarum. Francis Sambroke (attorney) then assisted
as a Chorister boy; my uncle, Thomas Danvers, was at the
Funerall.

'Tis an honour to the place, to have had the heavenly
and ingeniose contemplation of this good man, who was
pious even to prophesie; e.g.

> Religion now on tip-toe stands,
> Ready to goe to the American strands.
> ['The Church Militant', ll. 235-6]

24.   IZAAK WALTON, 'THE LIFE OF MR. GEORGE HERBERT'

1670; 1675

First published in 1670, Walton's life of Herbert was to
prove of incalculable importance in the formation of all
subsequent attitudes to Herbert until our own time (see
further above, pp. 9 ff.). It is reprinted here from
the carefully reconsidered edition of 1675.
    Source: Walton, 'Lives', pp. 260-328.

The Introduction.

In a late retreat from the business of this World, and

those many little cares with which I have too often cumbred my self, I fell into a Contemplation of some of those
Historical passages that are recorded in *Sacred Story*; and,
more particularly, of what had past betwixt our *Blessed
Saviour*, and that wonder of Women, and Sinners, and Mourners, *Saint Mary Magdalen*. I call her *Saint*, because I did
not then, nor do now consider her, as when she was possest with seven Devils; not as when her wanton Eyes, and
dissheveld Hair, were designed and manag'd, to charm and
insnare amorous Beholders: But I did then, and do now consider her, as after she had exprest a visible and sacred
sorrow for her sensualities; as after those Eyes had wept
such a flood of penitential tears as did wash, and that
hair had wip't, and she most passionately kist the feet of
hers, and our blessed *Jesus*. And I do now consider, that
because she lov'd much, not only much was forgiven her:
but that, beside that blessed blessing of having her sins
pardoned, and the joy of knowing her happy Condition, she
also had from him a testimony, that her *Alabaster box* of
precious oyntment poured on his head and feet, and *that
Spikenard*, and those Spices that were by her dedicated to
embalm and preserve his sacred body from putrefaction,
should so far preserve her own memory, that these demonstrations of her sanctified love, and of her officious, and
generous gratitude, should be recorded and mentioned wheresoever his Gospel should be read: intending thereby, that
as his, so her name should also live to succeeding generations, even till time it self shall be no more.
    Upon occasion of which fair example, I did lately look
back, and not without some content (*at least to my self*)
that I have endeavour'd to deserve the love, and preserve
the memory of my two deceased friends, Dr. *Donne*, and Sir
Henry Wotton, by declaring the several employments and
various accidents of their Lives: And though Mr. *George
Herbert (whose Life I now intend to write)* were to me a
stranger as to his person, for I have only seen him: yet
since he was, and was worthy to be their friend, and very
many of his have been mine; I judge it may not be unaccept-
able to those that knew any of them in their lives, or do
now know them by mine, or their own Writings, to see this
Conjunction of them after their deaths; without which, many
things that concern'd them, and some things that concern'd
the Age in which they liv'd, would be less perfect, and
lost to posterity.
    *For these Reasons I have undertaken it, and if I have
prevented any abler person, I beg pardon of him, and my
Reader.*

The *LIFE*

George Herbert was born the third day of *April*, in the
Year of our Redemption 1593. The place of his Birth was
near to the Town of *Montgomery*, and in that *Castle* that
did then bear the name of that Town and County; that
Castle was then a place of state and strength, and had
been successively happy in the Family of the *Herberts*, who
had long possest it: and, with it, a plentiful Estate, and
hearts as liberal to their poor Neighbours. A Family,
that hath been blest with men of remarkably wisdom, and a
willingness to serve their Country, and indeed, to do good
to all Mankind; for which they are eminent: But alas! this
Family did in the late Rebellion suffer extreamly in their
Estates; and the Heirs of that *Castle* saw it laid level
with that earth that was too good to bury those Wretches
that were the cause of it.

The Father of our *George*, was *Richard Herbert* the Son
of *Edward Herbert* Knight, the Son of *Richard Herbert*
Knight, the Son of the famous Sir *Richard Herbert* of *Cole-
brook* in the County of *Monmouth* Banneret, who was the
youngest Brother of that memorable *William Herbert* Earl of
Pembroke, that liv'd in the Reign of our King *Edward* the
fourth.

His Mother was *Magdalen Newport*, the youngest Daughter
of Sir *Richard*, and Sister to Sir *Francis Newport* of *High
Arkall* in the County of *Salop* Kt. and Grand-father of
Francis Lord *Newport*, now Comptroller of His Majesties
Houshold. A Family, that for their Loyalty, have suffered
much in their Estates, and seen the ruine of that excellent Structure, where their Ancestors have long liv'd, and
been memorable for their Hospitality.

This Mother of *George Herbert* (of whose person and wisdom, and vertue, I intend to give a true account in a
seasonable place) (1) was the happy Mother of seven Sons,
and three Daughters, which she would often say, was *Job's
number*, and *Job's distribution*; and as often bless God,
that they were neither defective in their shapes, or in
their reason; and very often reprove them that did not
praise God for so great a blessing. I shall give the
Reader a short accompt of their names, and not say much of
their Fortunes.

Edward the eldest was first made Kt. of the *Bath*, at
that glorious time of our late Prince *Henries* being
install'd Knight of the Garter; and after many years useful travel, and the attainment of many Languages, he was
by King *James* sent Ambassador Resident to the then *French*
King, *Lewis* the Thirteenth. There he continued about two
Years; but he could not subject himself to a compliance

with the humors of the Duke *de Luines*, who was then the
great and powerful Favourite at Court: so that upon a com-
plaint to our King, he was call'd back into *England* in
some displeasure; but at his return he gave such an honourable account of his employment, and so justified his Com-
portment to the Duke, and all the Court, that he was suddenly sent back upon the same Embassie, from which he
return'd in the beginning of the Reign of our good King
Charles the first, who made him first Baron of *Castle-
Island*; and not long after of *Cherbery* in the County of
*Salop: He was a man of great learning and reason, as
appears by his printed Book* de veritate; *and by his
History of the Reign of K.* Hen. *the Eight, & by several
other Tracts.* (2)

The second and third Brothers were *Richard* and *William*,
who ventur'd their lives to purchase Honour in the Wars of
the *Low Countries*, and died Officers in that employment.
Charles was the fourth, and died Fellow of *New-College* in
Oxford. *Henry* was the sixth, who became a menial servant
to the Crown in the daies of King *James*, and hath continued to be so for fifty years: during all which time he
heath been Master of the Revels; a place that requires a
diligent wisdom, with which God hath blest him. The seventh Son was *Thomas*, who being made Captain of a Ship in
that Fleet with which Sir *Robert Mansel* was sent against
Algiers, did there shew a fortunate and true English valor.
Of the three Sisters, I need not say more, then that they
were all married to persons of worth, and plentiful fortunes; and liv'd to be examples of *vertue*, and to do good
in their generations.

I now come to give my intended account of *George,* who
was the fifth of those seven Brothers.

George Herbert spent much of his Childhood in a sweet
content under the eye and care of his prudent mother, and
the tuition of a Chaplain or Tutor to him, and two of his
Brothers, in her own Family (for she was then a Widow)
where he continued, till about the age of twelve years;
and being at that time well instructed in the Rules of
Grammar, he was not long after commended to the care of
Dr. *Neale*, who was then Dean of *Westminster*; and by him to
the care of Mr. *Ireland*, who was then chief Master of that
School; where the beauties of his pretty behaviour and wit,
shin'd and became so eminent and lovely in this his innocent age, that he seem'd to be marked out for piety, and
to become the care of Heaven, and of a particular good
Angel to guard and guide him. And thus, he continued in
that School, till he came to be perfect in the learned
Languages, and especially in the Greek Tongue, in which he
after prov'd an excellent Critick.

About the age of Fifteen, he, being then a Kings Scholar, was elected out of that School for *Trinity Colledge* in *Cambridge*, to which place he was transplanted about the year 1608, and his prudent mother well knowing, that he might easily lose, or lessen that virtue and innocence which her advice and example had planted in his mind; did therefore procure the generous and liberal Dr. *Nevil*, who was then Dean of *Canterbury*, and Master of that Colledge, to take him into his particular care, and provide him a Tutor; which he did most gladly undertake, for he knew the excellencies of his Mother, and how to value such a friendship.

I have told her birth, her Marriage, and the Number of her Children, and have given some short account of them: I shall next tell the Reader, that her husband dyed when our *George* was about the Age of four years: I am next to tell that she continued twelve years a Widow: that she then married happily to a Noble Gentleman, the Brother and Heir of the Lord *Danvers* Earl of *Danby*, who did highly value both her person and the most excellent endowments of her mind.

In this time of her Widowhood, she being desirous to give *Edward* her eldest son, such advantages of Learning, and other education as might suit his birth and fortune: and thereby make him the more fit for the service of his Country: did at his being of a fit age, remove from *Montgomery Castle* with him, and some of her younger sons to *Oxford*; and having entred *Edward* into *Queens Colledge*, and provided him a fit *Tutor*, she commended him to his Care; yet she continued there with him, and still kept him in a moderate awe of her self: and so much under her own eye, as to see and converse with him daily; but she managed this power over him without any such rigid sourness, as might make her company a torment to her Child; but with such a sweetness and complyance with the recreations and pleasures of youth, as did incline him willingly to spend much of his time in the company of his dear and careful Mother: which was to her great content: for, she would often say, 'That as our bodies take a nourishment sutable to the meat on which we feed: so, our souls do as insensibly take in vice by the example or Conversation with wicked Company:' and would therefore as often say, 'That ignorance of Vice was the best preservation of Vertue: and, that the very knowledge of wickedness was as tinder to inflame and kindle sin, and to keep it burning.' For these reasons she indeared him to her own Company: and continued with him in *Oxford* four years: in which time, her *great* and *harmless wit*, her *chearful gravity*, and her *obliging behaviour*, gain'd her an acquaintance and friendship with

most of any eminent worth or learning, that were at that
time in or near that University; and particularly, with
Mr. *John Donne*, who then came accidentally to that place,
in this time of her being there: it was that *John Donne*
who was after *Doctor Donne*, and Dean of *Saint Pauls
London*: and he at his leaving *Oxford*, writ and left there
in verse a Character of the Beauties of her body, and
mind; of the first, he saies,

>   No *Spring nor Summer-Beauty*, has such grace
>   As I have seen in an *Autumnal* face.

Of the latter he sayes,

>   In all her words to every hearer fit
>   You may at *Revels*, or at *Council sit*.

The rest of her Character may be read in his printed
Poems, in that Elegy which bears the name of the *Autumnal
Beauty*. (3) For both he and she were then past the meri-
dian of mans life.
    This Amity, begun at this time, and place, was not an
Amity that polluted their Souls; but an *Amity* made up of a
chain of sutable inclinations and vertues; an *Amity*, like
that of St. *Chrysostoms* to his dear and vertuous *Olimpias*;
whom, in his Letters, he calls his *Saint*: Or, an *Amity*
indeed more like that of St. *Hierom* to his *Paula*; whose
affection to her was such, that he turn'd Poet in his old
Age, and then made her *Epitaph; wishing all his Body were
turn'd into Tongues, that he might declare her just
praises to posterity*. And this *Amity* betwixt her and Mr.
Donne, was begun in a happy time for him, he being then
near to the Fortieth year of his Age (which was some years
before he entred into Sacred Orders:) A time, when his
necessities needed a daily supply for the support of his
Wife, seven Children, and a Family: And in this time she
prov'd one of his most bountiful Benefactors; and he, as
grateful an acknowledger of it. You may take one testimony for what I have said of these two worthy persons,
from this following *Letter*, and *Sonnet*.

MADAM,
Your Favours to me are every where; I use them, and have
them. I enjoy them at *London*, and leave them there; and
yet find them at *Micham*: such Riddles as these become
things unexpressible; and such is your goodness. I was
almost sorry to find your Servant here this day, because
I was loth to have any witness of my not coming home last
Night, and indeed of my coming this Morning: But my not

coming was excusable, because earnest business detein'd
me; and my coming this day, is by the example of your St.
Mary Magdalen, who rose early upon *Sunday*, to seek that
which she lov'd most; and so did I. And from her and my
self, I return such thanks as are due to one to whom we
owe all the good opinion, that they whom we need most,
have of us - by this Messenger, and on this good day, I
commit the inclosed *Holy Hymns* and *Sonnets* (which for the
matter, not the workmanship, have yet escap'd the fire) to
your judgment, and to your protection too, if you think
them worthy of it; and I have appointed this inclosed *Sonnet* to usher them to your happy hand.

Your unworthiest Servant,
unless your accepting him to be so,
have mended him.

Micham,
  July 11.
   1607.   JO. DONNE.

To the Lady *Magdalen Herbert*; of St. *Mary
Magdalen.*

[Quotes the dedicatory poem prefixed to 'La Corona'.]

These *Hymns* are now lost to us; (4) but doubtless they were
such, as they two now sing in *Heaven.*
  There might be more demonstrations of the Friendship,
and the many sacred Indearments betwixt these two excellent
persons (for I have many of their Letters in my hand) and
much more might be said of her great prudence and piety:
but my design was not to write hers, but the Life of her
Son; and therefore I shall only tell my Reader, that about
that very day twenty years that this Letter was dated,
and sent her, I saw and heard this Mr. *John Donne* (who was
then Dean of *St. Pauls*) weep, and preach her Funeral Sermon, in the Parish-Church of *Chelsey* near *London*, where
she now rests in her quiet Grave: and where we must now
leave her, and return to her Son *George*, whom we left in
his Study in *Cambridge.*
  And in *Cambridge* we may find our *George Herberts* behaviour to be such, that we may conclude, he consecrated the
first-fruits of his early age to vertue, and a serious
study of learning. And that he did so, this following
Letter and Sonnet which were in the first year of his
going to *Cambridge* sent his dear Mother for a New-years
gift, may appear to be some testimony.

  'But I fear the heat of my late *Ague* hath dried up
those springs, by which Scholars say, the Muses use to
take up their habitations. However, I need not their

help, to reprove the vanity of those many Love-poems, that
are daily writ and consecrated to *Venus*; nor to bewail
that so few are writ, that look towards *God* and *Heaven*.
For my own part, my meaning (*dear Mother*) is in these
Sonnets, to declare my resolution to be, that my poor
Abilities in *Poetry* shall be all, and ever consecrated to
Gods glory; and beg you to receive this as one testimony.

My God, where is that ancient heat towards thee,
    Wherewith whole showls of *Martyrs* once did burn,
    Besides their other flames? Doth Poetry
Wear *Venus* Livery? only serve her turn?
Why are not *Sonnets* made of thee? and layes
    Vpon thine Altar burnt? Cannot thy love
    Heighten a spirit to sound out thy praise
As well as any she? Cannot thy *Dove*
Out-strip their *Cupid* easily in flight?
    Or, since thy ways are deep, and still the same,
    Will not a verse run smooth that bears thy name!
Why doth that fire, which by thy power and might
    Each breast does feel, no braver fuel choose
    Than that, which one day, *Worms* may chance refuse.

Sure Lord, there is enough in thee to dry
    Oceans of *Ink*; for, as the Deluge did
    Cover the Earth, so doth thy Majesty:
Each cloud distils thy praise, and doth forbid
Poets to turn it to another use.
    Roses and *Lillies* speak thee; and to make
    A pair of Cheeks of them, is thy abuse.
Why should I *Womens eyes* for Chrystal take?
Such poor invention burns in their low mind
    Whose fire is wild, and doth not upward go
    To praise, and, on thee Lord, some *Ink* bestow.
Open the bones, and you shall nothing find
    In the best *face* but *filth*; when Lord, in thee
    The *beauty* lies, in the *discovery*.

                                                    G.H.

This was his resolution at the sending this Letter to
his dear Mother; about which time, he was in the Seventeenth year of his Age; and, as he grew older, so he grew
in learning, and more and more in favour both with God and
man: insomuch, that in this morning of that short day of
his life, he seem'd to be mark'd out for vertue, and to
become the care of Heaven; for God still kept his soul in
so holy a frame, that he may, and ought to be a pattern of
vertue to all posterity; and especially, to his Brethren

of the Clergy, of which the Reader may expect a more exact
account in what will follow.

I need not declare that he was a strict Student,
because, that he was so, there will be many testimonies in
the future part of his life. I shall therefore only tell,
that he was made *Batchelor of Art* in the year 1611. *Major
Fellow* of the *Colledge, March* 15. 1615. And that in that
year, he was also made *Master of Arts*, he being then in
the 22*d* year of his Age; during all which time, all, or
the greatest diversion from his Study, was the practice of
Musick, in which he became a great Master; and of which,
he would say, 'That it did relieve his drooping spirits,
compose his distracted thoughts, and raised his weary soul
so far above Earth, that it gave him an earnest of the
joys of Heaven, before he possest them.' And it may be
noted, that from his first entrance into the Colledge, the
generous Dr. *Nevil* was a cherisher of his Studies, and
such a lover of his person, his behaviour, and the excellent endowments of his mind, that he took him often into
his own company; by which he confirm'd his native gentile-
ness; and, if during this time he exprest any Error, it
was, that he kept himself too much retir'd, and at too
great a distance with all his inferiours: and his cloaths
seem'd to prove, that he put too great a value on his
parts and Parentage.

This may be some account of his disposition, and of the
employment of his time, till he was Master of Arts, which
was *Anno* 1615. and in the year 1619. he was chosen Orator
for the University. His two precedent Orators, were Sir
Robert Nanton, and Sir *Francis Nethersoll*: The first was
not long after made Secretary of State; and Sir *Francis*,
not very long after his being Orator, was made Secretary
to the Lady *Elizabeth* Queen of *Bohemia*. In this place of
Orator, our *George Herbert* continued eight years; and
manag'd it with as becoming, and grave a gaiety, as any
had ever before, or since his time. For *He had acquir'd
great Learning, and was blest with a high fancy, a civil
and sharp wit, and with a natural elegance, both in his
behaviour, his tongue, and his pen*. Of all which, there
might be very many particular evidences, but I will limit
my self to the mention of but three.

And the first notable occasion of shewing his fitness
for this employment of *Orator*, was manifested in a Letter
to King *James*, upon the occasion of his sending that University his Book, called *Basilicon Doron*; and their Orator
was to acknowledge this great honour, and return their
gratitude to His Majesty for such a condescension; at the
close of which Letter, he writ,

    Quid Vaticanam Bodleianamque objicis hospes!
       Vnicus est nobis Bibliotheca Liber. (5)

    This Letter was writ in such excellent Latin, was so
full of Conceits, and all the expressions so suted to the
genius of the King, that he inquired the Orators name,
and then ask'd *William* Earl of *Pembroke*, if he knew him?
whose answer was, 'That he knew him very well; and that he
was his Kinsman, but he lov'd him more for his learning and
vertue, than for that he was of his name and family.'   At
which answer, the King smil'd, and asked the Earl leave,
'that he might love him too; for he took him to be the
Jewel of that University.'
    The next occasion he had and took to shew his great
Abilities, was, with them, to shew also his great affection to that Church in which he received his *Baptism*, and
of which he profest himself a member; and the occasion was
this: There was one *Andrew Melvin*, (6) a Minister of the
Scotch Church, and Rector of St. *Andrews*; who, by a long
and constant Converse, with a discontented part of that
Clergy which oppos'd Episcopacy, became at last to be a
chief leader of that Faction: and, had proudly appear'd
to be so, to King *James*, when he was but King of that
Nation, who the second year after his Coronation in *England*, conven'd a part of the *Bishops* and other Learned
Divines of his Church, to attend him at *Hampton-Court*, in
order to a friendly Conference with some Dissenting Brethren, both of this, and the Church of *Scotland:* of which
Scotch party, *Andrew Melvin* was one; and, he being a man
of learning, and inclin'd to *Satyrical Poetry*, had scatter'd many malicious bitter Verses against our *Liturgy*,
our *Ceremonies*, and our *Church-governments:* which were by
some of that party, so magnified for the wit, that they
were therefore brought into *Westminster-School*, where Mr.
George Herbert then, and often after, made such answers to
them, and such reflexion on him and his *Kirk*, as might un-
beguile any man that was not too deeply pre-ingaged in
such a quarrel. - But to return to Mr. *Melvin* at *Hampton-
Court Conference*, he there appear'd to be a man of an
unruly wit, of a strange confidence, of so furious a Zeal,
and of so ungovern'd passions, that his insolence to the
King, and others at this conference, lost him both his
Rectorship of St. *Andrews*, and his liberty too: for, his
former Verses, and his present reproaches there used
against the Church and State, caus'd him to be committed
prisoner to the Tower of *London*: where he remained very
angry for three years.   At which time of his commitment,
he found the Lady *Arabella* an innocent prisoner there; and
he pleas'd himself much in sending the next day after his

Commitment, these two Verses to the good Lady, which I
will under-write, because they may give the Reader a taste
of his others, which were like these.

    Causa tibi mecum est communis, Carceris, Ara-
        Bella; tibi causa est, Araque sacra mihi. (7)

I shall not trouble my Reader with an account of his
enlargement from that Prison, or his Death; but tell him,
Mr. *Herberts* Verses were thought so worthy to be preserv'd,
that Dr. *Duport* the learned Dean of *Peterborough*, hath
lately collected, and caus'd many of them to be printed,
as an honourable memorial of his friend Mr. *George Herbert*,
and the Cause he undertook. (8)
    And, in order to my third and last observation of his
great Abilities, it will be needful to declare, that about
this time King *James* came very often to hunt at *New-Market*
and *Royston*; and was almost as often invited to *Cambridge*,
where his entertainment was Comedies suted to his pleasant
humor; and where Mr. *George Herbert* was to welcome him
with *Gratulations*, and the *Applauses* of an *Orator*; which
he alwaies perform'd so well, that he still grew more into
the Kings favour, insomuch, that he had a particular
appointment to attend His Majesty at *Royston*, where after
a Discourse with him, His Majesty declar'd to his Kinsman,
the Earl of *Pembroke*, 'That he found the Orators learning
and wisdom, much above his age or wit.' The year following, the King appointed to end His progress at *Cambridge*,
and to stay there certain days; at which time, he was
attended by the great Secretary of Nature, and all Learning, Sir *Francis Bacon* (Lord *Verulam*) and by the ever
memorable and learned Dr. *Andrews* Bishop of *Winchester*,
both which did at that time begin a desir'd friendship
with our *Orator*. Upon whom, the first put such a value on
his judgment, that he usually desir'd his approbation,
before he would expose any of his Books to be printed, and
thought him so worthy of his friendship, that having trans-
translated many of the Prophet *Davids* Psalms into English
Verse, he made *George Herbert* his Patron, by a publick
dedication of them to him, as the best Judge of *Divine
Poetry*. (9) And for the learned Bishop, it is observable,
that at that time, there fell to be a modest debate betwixt them two about *Predestination*, and *Sanctity of life*;
of both which, the *Orator* did not long after send the
Bishop some safe and useful *Aphorisms*, in a long Letter
written in Greek; (10) which Letter was so remarkable for
the language, and reason of it, that after the reading it,
the Bishop put it into his bosom, and did often shew it to
many Scholars, both of this, and forreign Nations; but did

alwaies return it back to the place where he first lodg'd
it, and continu'd it so near his heart, till the last day
of his life.

To these, I might add the long and intire friendship
betwixt him and Sir *Henry Wotton*, and Doctor *Donne*, but I
have promis'd to contract my self, and shall therefore
only add one testimony to what is also mentioned in the
Life of Doctor *Donne*; namely, that a little before his
death, he caused many Seals to be made, and in them to be
ingraven the figure of *Christ crucified* on an *Anchor* (the
emblem of hope) and of which Doctor *Donne* would often say,
Crux mihi Anchora. (11) - These Seals, he gave or sent to
most of those friends on which he put a value; and, at Mr.
Herberts death, these Verses were found wrapt up with that
Seal which was by the Doctor given to him.

When my dear Friend could write no more,
He this *Seal*, and so gave ore.

When winds and waves rise highest, I am sure,
This *Anchor* keeps my *faith*, that me secure.

At this time of being *Orator*, he had learnt to understand the *Italian, Spanish*, and *French* Tongues very perfectly; hoping, that as his Predecessors, so he might in
time attain the place of a *Secretary of State*, he being
at that time very high in the Kings favour; and not meanly
valued and lov'd by the most eminent and most powerful
of the Court-Nobility: This, and the love of a Court-
conversation mixt with a laudible ambition to be something
more than he then was, drew him often from *Cambridge* to
attend the *King* wheresoever the Court was, who then gave
him a *Sine Cure*, which fell into his Majesties disposal, I
think, by the death of the Bishop of St. *Asaph*. It was
the same, that Queen *Elizabeth* had formerly given to her
Favourite Sir *Philip Sidney*; and valued to be worth an
hundred and twenty pounds *per Annum*. With this, and his
Annuity, and the advantage of his Colledge, and of his
Oratorship, he enjoued his gentile humor for cloaths, and
Court-like company, and seldom look'd towards *Cambridge*,
unless the King were there, but then he never fail'd; and,
at other times, left the manage of his Orators place, to
his learned friend Mr. *Herbert Thorndike*, who is now Prebend of *Westminster*.

I may not omit to tell, that he had often design'd to
leave the University, and decline all Study, which he
thought did impair his health; for he had a body apt to a
Consumption, and to *Fevers*, and other infirmities which he
judg'd were increas'd by his Studies; for he would often

say, 'He had too thoughtful a Wit: a Wit, like a Pen-knife
in too narrow a sheath, too sharp for his Body:' But his
Mother would by no means allow him to leave the University, or to travel; and, though he inclin'd very much to
both, yet he would by no means satisfie his own desires at
so dear a rate, as to prove an undutiful Son to so affectionate a Mother; but did always submit to her wisdom. And
what I have now said, may partly appear in a Copy of
Verses in his printed Poems; 'Tis one of those that bears
the title of 'Affliction': And it appears to be a pious
reflection on Gods providence, and some passages of his
life, in which he saies,

[Quotes 'Affliction' (I), ll. 37-66.]

   In this time of Mr. *Herberts* attendance and expectation
of some good occasion to remove from *Cambridge*, to Court;
God, in whom there is an unseen Chain of Causes, did in a
short time put an end to the lives of two of his most
obliging and most powerful friends, *Lodowick* Duke of *Rich-
mond*, and *James* Marquess of *Hamilton*; and not long after
him, King *James* died also, and with them, all Mr. *Herbert's* Court-hopes: So that he presently betook himself to
a Retreat from *London*, to a Friend in *Kent*, where he liv'd
very privately, and was such a lover of solitariness, as
was judg'd to impair his health, more then his Study had
done. In this time of Retirement, he had many Conflicts
with himself, Whether he should return to the painted
pleasures of a Court-life, or betake himself to a study of
Divinity, and enter into Sacred Orders? (to which his dear
Mother had often persuaded him.) These were such Con--
flicts, as they only can know, that have endur'd them; for
ambitious Desires, and the outward Glory of this World,
are not easily laid aside; but, at last, God inclin'd him
to put on a resolution to serve at his Altar.
   He did at his return to *London*, acquaint a Court-friend
with his resolution to enter into *Sacred Orders*, who persuaded him to alter it, as too mean an employment, and too
much below his birth, and the excellent abilities and endowments of his mind. To whom he replied, 'It hath been
formerly judged that the Domestick Servants of the King of
Heaven, should be of the noblest Families on Earth: and,
though the Iniquity of the late Times have made Clergy-men
meanly valued, and the sacred name of *Priest* contemptible;
yet I will labour to make it honourable, by consecrating
all my learning, and all my poor abilities, to advance the
glory of that God that gave them; knowing, that I can
never do too much for him, that hath done so much for me,
as to make me a Christian. And I will labour to be like

my Saviour, by making Humility lovely in the eyes of all
men, and by following the merciful and meek example of my
dear Jesus.'

This was then his resolution, and the God of Constancy,
who intended him for a great example of vertue, continued
him in it; for within that year he was made Deacon, but
the day when, or by whom, I cannot learn; but that he was
about that time made Deacon, is most certain; for I find
by the Records of *Lincoln*, that he was made Predend of
Layton Ecclesia, in the Diocess of *Lincoln, July* 15. 1626.
and that this Prebend was given him, by *John*, then *Lord
Bishop of that See*. And now, he had a fit occasion to
shew that Piety and Bounty that was deriv'd from his
generous Mother, and his other memorable Ancestors, and
the occasion was this.

This *Layton Ecclesia*, is a Village near to *Spalden* in
the County of *Huntington*, and the greatest part of the
Parish Church was fallen down, and that of it which stood,
was so decayed, so little, and so useless, that the Parish-
Parishioners could not meet to perform their Duty to God
in publick prayer and praises; and thus it had been for
almost 20 years, in which time there had been some faint
endeavours for a publick Collection, to enable the
Parishioners to rebuild it, but with no success, till Mr.
Herbert undertook it; and he, by his own, and the contribution of many of his Kindred, and other noble Friends,
undertook the Re-edification of it; and made it so much
his whole business, that he became restless, till he saw
it finish as it now stands; being, for the workmanship, a
costly *Mosaick:* for the form, an *exact Cross*; and for the
decency and beauty, I am assur'd it is the most remarkable
Parish-Church, that this Nation affords. He lived to see
it so wainscoated, as to be exceeded by none; and, by his
order, the Reading Pew, and Pulpit, were a little distant
from each other, and both of an equal height; for he
would often say, 'They should neither have a precedency or
priority of the other: but that *Prayer* and *Preaching* being
equally useful, might agree like Brethren, and have an
equal honour and estimation.'

Before I proceed farther, I must look back to the time
of Mr. *Herberts* being made Prebend, and tell the Reader,
that not long after, his Mother being inform'd of his
intentions to Re-build that Church: and apprehending the
great trouble and charge that he was like to draw upon
himself, his Relations, and Friends, before it could be
finisht; sent for him from *London* to *Chelsey* (where she
then dwelt) and at his coming, said – '*George*, I sent for
you, to perswade you to commit Simony, by giving your
Patron as good a gift as he has given to you; namely, that

you give him back his Prebend; for, *George*, it is not for
your weak body, and empty purse, to undertake to build
Churches.' Of which, he desir'd he might have a Days time
to consider, and then make her an Answer: And at his
return to her the next Day, when he had first desired her
blessing, and she given it him, his next request was,
'That she would at the Age of Thirty three Years, allow
him to become an *undutiful Son*; for he had made a Vow to
God, that if he were able, he would Re-build that Church':
And then, shew'd her such reasons for his resolution, that
she presently subscribed to be one of his Benefactors: and
undertook to sollicit *William* Earl of *Pembroke* to become
another, who subscribed for fifty pounds; and not long
after, by a witty, and persuasive Letter from Mr. *Herbert*,
made it fifty pounds more. And in this nomination of some
of his Benefactors, *James* Duke of *Lenox*, and his brother
Sir *Henry Herbert*, ought to be remembred; as also, the
bounty of Mr. *Nicholas Farrer*, and Mr. *Arthur Woodnot*; the
one, a Gentleman in the Neighbourhood of *Layton*, and the
other, a Goldsmith in *Foster-lane, London*, ought not to be
forgotten: for the memory of such men ought to out-live
their lives. Of Master *Farrer*, I shall hereafter give an
account in a more seasonable place; (12) but before I proceed farther, I will give this short account of Master
Arthur Woodnot.

He was a man, that had consider'd, overgrown Estates do
often require more care and watchfulness to preserve, than
get them, and consider'd that there be many Discontents,
that Riches cure not; and did therefore set limits to himself as to desire of wealth: And having attain'd so much
as to be able to shew some mercy to the Poor, and preserve
a competence for himself, he dedicated the remaining part
of his life to the service of God; and to be useful for
his Friends: and he prov'd to be so to Mr. *Herbert*; for,
beside his own bounty, he collected and return'd most of
the money that was paid for the Re-building of that Church;
he kept all the account of the charges, and would often go
down to state them, and see all the Workmen paid. When I
have said, that this good man was a useful Friend to Mr.
Herberts Father, and to his Mother, and continued to be so
to him, till he clos'd his eyes on his Death-bed; I will
forbear to say more, till I have the next fair occasion to
mention the holy friendship that was betwixt him and Mr.
Herbert. - From whom Mr. *Woodnot* carryed to his Mother
this following Letter, and delivered it to her in a sickness which was not long before that which prov'd to be her
last.

A Letter of Mr. *George Herbert* to his
Mother, in her Sickness.

MADAM,
At my last parting from you, I was the better content because I was in hope I should my self carry all sickness
out of your family: but, since I know I did not, and that
your share continues, or rather increaseth, I wish earnestly that I were again with you: and would quickly make
good my wish, but that my employment does fix me here, it
being now but a month to our *Commencement*: wherein, my
absence by how much it naturally augmenteth suspicion, by
so much shall it make my prayers the more constant and the
more earnest for you to the God of all Consolation. - In
the mean time, I beseech you to be chearful, and comfort
your self in the God of all Comfort, who is not willing to
behold any sorrow but for sin. - What hath Affliction
grievous in it more then for a moment? or why should our
afflictions here, have so much power or boldness as to
oppose the hope of our Joys hereafter? - Madam! As the
Earth is but a point in respect of the heavens, so are
earthly Troubles compar'd to heavenly Joys; therefore, if
either Age or Sickness lead you to those Joys, consider
what advantage you have over *Youth* and *Health*, who are now
so near those true Comforts. - Your last Letter gave me
Earthly preferment, and I hope kept Heavenly for your
self: but, wou'd you divide and choose too? our Colledge
Customs allow not that, and I shou'd account my self most
happy if I might change with you; for, I have always
observ'd the thred of Life to be like other shreds or
skenes of silk, full of snarles and incumbrances: Happy is
he, whose bottom is wound up and laid ready for work in
the New *Jerusalem*. - For my self, *dear Mother*, I alwaies
fear'd sickness more then death, because sickness hath
made me unable to perform those Offices for which I came
into the world, and must yet be kept in it; but you are
freed from that fear, who have already abundantly dis-
charg'd that part, having both ordered your Family, and so
brought up your Children that they have attain'd to the
years of Discretion, and competent Maintenance. - So that
now if they do not well the fault cannot be charg'd on
you, whose Example and Care of them, will justifie you
both to the world and your own Conscience: insomuch, that
whether you turn your thoughts on the life past, or on the
Joys that are to come, you have strong preservatives
against all disquiet. - And for temporal Afflictions: I
beseech you consider all that can happen to you, are
either afflictions of *Estate*, or *Body*, or *Mind*. - For
those of Estate, of what poor regard ought they to be,

since if we had Riches we are commanded to give them away:
so that the best use of them is, having, not to have them.
- But perhaps being above the Common people, our Credit
and estimation calls on us to live in a more splendid
fashion? - but, O God! how easily is that answered, when
we consider that the Blessings in the holy Scripture, are
never given to the rich, but to the poor. I never find
Blessed be the Rich; or, Blessed be the Noble; but,
Blessed be the Meek, and, *Blessed be the poor*, and,
Blessed be the Mourners, for they shall be comforted -
And yet, Oh God! most carry themselves so, as if they not
only not desir'd, but even fear'd to be blessed. - And for
Afflictions of the Body, *dear Madam*, remember the holy
Martyrs of God, how they have been burnt by thousands,
and have endur'd such other Tortures, as the very mention
of them might beget amazements; but their Fiery-trials
have had an end: and yours (which praised be God are less)
are not like to continue long. - I beseech you let such
thoughts as these, moderate your present fear and sorrow;
and know, that if any of yours shou'd prove a *Goliah*-like
trouble, yet you may say with *David*, - *That God who hath
delivered me out of the paws of the Lion and Bear, will
also deliver me out of the hands of this uncircumcised*
Philistin. - Lastly, for those Afflictions of the Soul:
consider, that God intends that to be as a *sacred Temple*
for himself to dwell in, and will not allow any room
there for such an in-mate as Grief; or allow that any sad-
ness shall be his Competitor. - And above all, If any care
of future things molest you, remember those admirable
words of the Psalmist: *Cast thy Care on the Lord and he
shall nourish thee.* To which join that of *St.* Peter,
Casting all your Care on the Lord, for he careth for you.
(13) - What an admirable thing is this, that God puts his
shoulder to our burthen! and, entertains our Care for us
that we may the more quietly intend his service. - To
Conclude, Let me commend only one place more to you
(Philip. 4.4.) St. *Paul* saith there: *Rejoice in the Lord
alwaies, and again I say rejoice.* He doubles it to take
away the scruple of those that might say, What shall we
rejoice in afflictions? yes, I say again rejoice; so that
it is not left to us to rejoice or not rejoice: but whatsoever befalls us we must always, at all times rejoice in
the Lord, who taketh care for us: and it follows in the
next verse: *Let your moderation appear to all men, the
Lord is at hand: be careful for nothing.* What can be said
more comfortably? trouble not your selves, God is at hand
to deliver us from all, or in all. - Dear Madam, pardon my
boldness, and accept the good meaning of,

Trin. Col.   *Your most obedient Son,*
May 29.   George Herbert.
  16 22.

/

About the year 1626. and the 34*th* of his Age, Mr. *Herbert* was seiz'd with a sharp *Quotidian Ague*, and thought to remove it by the change of Air; to which end, he went to *Woodford* in Essex, but thither more chiefly, to enjoy the company of his beloved Brother Sir *Henry Herbert*, and other Friends then of that Family. In his House he remain'd about Twelve Months, and there became his own Physitian, and cur'd himself of his Ague, by forbearing Drink, and not eating any Meat, no not Mutton, nor a Hen, or Pidgeon, unless they were salted; and by such a constant Dyet, he remov'd his Ague, but with inconveniencies that were worse; for he brought upon himself a disposition to Rheums, and other weaknesses, and a supposed Consumtion. And it is to be Noted, that in the sharpest of his extream Fits, he would often say, *Lord abate my great affliction, or increase my patience; but, Lord, I repine not, I am dumb, Lord, before thee, because thou doest it.* By which, and a sanctified submission to the Will of God, he shewed he was inclinable to bear the sweet yoke of *Christian Discipline*, both then, and in the latter part of his life, of which there will be many true Testimonies.

And now his care was to recover from his Consumption by a change, from *Woodford* into such an air as was most proper to that end. And his remove was to *Dantsey* in *Wiltshire*, a noble House which stands in a choice Air; the owner of it then was the Lord *Danvers* Earl of *Danby*, who lov'd Mr. *Herbert* so very much, that he allow'd him such an apartment in it, as might best sute with his accommodation and liking. And, in this place, by a *spare Dyet*, declining all *perplexing Studies, moderate exercise*, and a *cheerful conversation*, his health was apparently improv'd to a good degree of strength and chearfulness: And then, he declar'd his resolution both to marry, and to enter into the Sacred Orders of Priesthood. These had long been the desires of his Mother, and his other Relations; but she liv'd not to see either, for she died in the year 1627. And, though he was disobedient to her about *Layton* Church, yet, in conformity to her will, he kept his Orators place, till after her death; and then presently declin'd it: And, the more willingly, that he might be succeeded by his friend *Robert Creighton*, who is now Dr. *Creighton*, and the worthy Bishop of *Wells.*

I shall now proceed to his Marriage; in order to which, it will be convenient, that I first give the Reader a short view of his person, and then an account of his Wife, and of some circumstances concerning both. - *He was for his person of a stature inclining towards Tallness; his Body was very strait, and so far from being cumbred with too much flesh, that he was lean to an extremity. His*

aspect was chearful, and his speech and motion did both
declare him a Gentleman; for they were all so meek and
obliging, that they purchased love and respect from all
that knew him.

These, and his other visible vertues, begot him much
love from a Gentleman, of a Noble fortune, and a near
kinsman to his friend the Earl of *Danby*; namely, from Mr.
Charles Danvers of *Bainton*, in the County of *Wilts* Esq;
this Mr. *Danvers* having known him long, and familiarly,
did so much affect him, that he often and publickly
declar'd a desire that Mr. *Herbert* would marry any of his
Nine Daughters (for he had so many) but rather his
Daughter *Jane*, than any other, because *Jane was his*
beloved Daughter: And he had often said the same to Mr.
Herbert himself; and that if he could like her for a Wife,
and she him for a Husband, *Jane* should have a *double*
blessing: and Mr. *Danvers* had so often said the like to
Jane, and so much commended Mr. *Herbert* to her, that *Jane*
became so much a Platonick, as to fall in love with Mr.
Herbert unseen.

This was a fair preparation for a Marriage; but alas,
her father died before Mr. *Herberts* retirement to *Dantsey*;
yet some friends to both parties, procur'd their meeting;
at which time a mutual affection entred into both their
hearts, as a Conqueror enters into a surprized City, and
Love having got such possession govern'd, and made there
such Laws and Resolutions, as neither party was able to
resist; insomuch, that she chang'd her name into *Herbert*,
the third day after this first interview.

This haste might in others be thought a *Love-phrensie*,
or worse: but it was not; for they had wooed so like
Princes, as to have select Proxies: such, as were true
friends to both parties; such as well understood Mr.
Herberts, and her temper of mind; and also their Estates
so well, before this Interview, that, the suddenness was
justifiable, by the strictest Rules of prudence: And the
more, because it prov'd so happy to both parties; for the
eternal lover of Mankind, made them happy in each others
mutual and equal affections, and compliance; indeed, so
happy, that there never was any opposition betwixt them,
unless it were a Contest which should most incline to a
compliance with the others desires. And though this begot,
and continued in them, such a mutual *love* and *joy*, and
content, as was no way defective: yet this mutual *content*
and *love* and *joy*, did receive a daily augmentation, by
such daily obligingness to each other, as still added such
new affluences to the former fullness of these divine
Souls, as was only improvable in Heaven, where they now
enjoy it.

About three months after his Marriage, Dr. *Curle*, who
was then Rector of *Bemerton* in *Wiltshire*, was made Bishop
of *Bath* and *Wells* and not long after translated to *Winchester*, and by that means the presentation of a Clerk to
Bemerton, did not fall to the Earl of *Pembroke* (who was
the undoubted Patron of it) but to the King, by reason of
Dr. *Curles* advancement: but *Philip*, then Earl of *Pembroke*
(for *William* was lately dead) requested the King to bestow
it upon his kinsman *George Herbert*; and the King said,
Most willingly to Mr. Herbert, *if it be worth his acceptance*: and the Earl as willingly and suddenly sent it him,
without seeking; but though Mr. *Herbert* had formerly put
on a resolution for the Clergy: yet, at receiving this
presentation, the apprehension of the last great Account
that he was to make for the Cure of so many Souls, made
him fast and pray often, and consider, for not less than a
month: in which time he had some resolutions to decline
both the Priesthood, and that Living. And in this time of
considering, *He endur'd* (As he would often say) *such spiritual Conflicts, as none can think, but only those that
have endur'd them.*
In the midst of these Conflicts, his old and dear
friend Mr. *Arthur Woodnot*, took a journey to salute him at
Bainton (where he then was with his Wives Friends and
Relations) and was joyful to be an Eye-witness of his
Health, and happy Marriage. And after they had rejoyc'd
together some few days, they took a Journey to *Wilton*, the
famous Seat of the Earls of *Pembroke*; at which time, the
King, the Earl, and the whole Court were there, or at
Salisbury, which is near to it. And at this time Mr. *Herbert* presented his Thanks to the Earl, for his presentation to *Bemerton*, but had not yet resolv'd to accept it,
and told him the reason why; but that Night, the Earl
acquainted Dr. *Laud*, then Bishop of *London*, and after
Archbishop of *Canterbury*, with his Kinsmans irresolution.
And the Bishop did the next day so convince Mr. *Herbert,
That the refusal of it was a sin;* that a Taylor was sent
for to some speedily from *Salisbury* to *Wilton*, to take
measure, and make him Canonical Cloaths, against next day:
which the Taylor did; and Mr. *Herbert* being so habited,
went with his presentation to the learned Dr. *Davenant*,
who was then Bishop of *Salisbury*, and he gave him Institution immediately (for Mr. *Herbert* had been made Deacon
some years before) and he was also the same day (which was
April 26. 1630) inducted into the good, and more pleasant,
than healthful Parsonage of *Bemerton*: which is a Mile from
Salisbury.
I have now Brought him to the Parsonage of Bemerton,
and to the thirty sixth Year of his Age, and must stop

here, and bespeak the Reader to prepare for an almost in-
credible story, of the great sanctity of the short remain-
der of his holy life; a life so full of Charity, Humility,
and all Christian vertues, that it deserves the eloquence
of St. Chrysostom *to commend and declare it! A life, that*
if it were related by a Pen like his, there would then be
no need for this Age to look back into times past for the
examples of primitive piety: for they might be all found
in the life of George Herbert. *But now, alas! who is fit*
to undertake it! I confess I am not: and am not pleas'd
with my self that I must; and profess my self amaz'd, when
I consider how few of the Clergy liv'd like him then, and
how many live so unlike him now: But, it becomes not me to
censure: my design is rather to assure the Reader, that I
have used very great diligence to inform my self, that I
might inform him of the truth of what follows; and though
I cannot adorn it with eloquence, yet I will do it with
sincerity.

When at his Induction he was shut into *Bemerton* Church,
being left there alone to Toll the Bell, (as the Law requires him:) he staid so much longer than an ordinary
time, before he return'd to those Friends that staid
expecting him at the Church-door, that his Friend, Mr.
Woodnot, look'd in at the Church-window, and saw him lie
prostrate on the ground before the Altar: at which time
and place (as he after told Mr. *Woodnot*) he set some Rules
to himself, for the future manage of his life; and then
and there made a vow, to labour to keep them.

And the same night that he had his Induction, he said
to Mr. *Woodnot, I now look back upon my aspiring thoughts,*
and think my self more happy than if I had attain'd what
then I so ambitiously thirsted for: And, I can now behold
the Court with an impartial Eye, and see plainly, that it
is made up of Fraud, *and* Titles, *and* Flattery, *and many*
other such empty, imaginary painted Pleasures: Pleasures,
that are so empty, as not to satisfy when they are
enjoy'd; but in God and his service, is a fulness of all
joy *and* pleasure, *and no satiety: And I will now use all*
my endeavours to bring my Relations and Dependants to a
love and relyance on him, who never fails those that trust
him. *But above all, I will be sure to live well, because*
the vertuous life of a Clergyman, is the most powerful
eloquence to perswade all that see it, to reverence and
love, and at least, to desire to live like him. And this
I will do, because I know we live in an Age that hath more
need of good examples, than precepts. *And I beseech that*
God, who hath honour'd me so much as to call me to serve
him at his Altar: that as by his special grace he hath put
into my heart these good desires, and resolutions: so, he

will by his assisting grace give me ghostly strength to bring
the same to good effect: and I beseech him that my humble
and charitable life may so win upon others, as to bring
glory to my JESUS, whom I have this day taken to be my
Master and Governour; *and I am so proud of his service,*
that I will alwaies observe, and obey, and do his Will;
and alwaies call him Jesus my Master, *and I will always*
contemn my birth, or any title or dignity that can be
conferr'd upon me, when I shall compare them with my title
of being a Priest, *and serving at the* Altar *of* Jesus my
Master.

And that he did so, may appear in many parts of his
Book of *Sacred Poems*; especially, in that which he calls
the Odour.   In which he seems to rejoyce in the thoughts
of that word *Jesus*, and say that the adding these words *my*
Master to it, and the often repetition of them, seem'd to
perfume his mind, and leave an oriental fragrancy in his
very breath.   And for his unforc'd choice to serve at Gods
Altar, he seems in another place of his Poems ('The Pearl',
Matth. 13.) to rejoyce and say - *He knew the waies of*
Learning: knew, what nature does willingly; and what, when
'tis forc'd by fire: knew the waies of honour, and when
glory inclines the Soul to noble expressions: knew the
Court: knew the waies of pleasure, of love, of wit, of
musick, and upon what terms he declined all these for the
service of his Master JESUS, and then concludes, saying,

That, through these Labyrinths, not my groveling Wit,
But thy Silk-twist, let down from Heaven to me;
Did both conduct, and teach me, how by it,
                              To climb to thee.
                    ['The Pearl', 11. 37-48]

The third day after he was made Rector of *Bemerton,* and
had chang'd his sword and silk Cloaths into a Canonical
Coat; he return'd so habited with his friend Mr. *Woodnot*
to *Bainton*: And, immediately after he had seen and saluted
his Wife, he said to her - *You are now a Ministers Wife,*
and must now so far forget your fathers house, as not to
claim a precedence of any of your Parishioners; for you
are to know, that a Priests Wife can challenge no pre-
cedence or place, but that which she purchases by her
obliging humility; and, I am sure, places so purchased, do
best become them.   And let me tell you, *That I am so good*
a Herald, as to assure you that this is truth.   And she
was so meek a Wife, *as to assure him it was no vexing News*
to her, and that he should see her observe it with a
chearful willingness.   And indeed her unforc'd humility,
that humility that was in her so original, as to be born

with her, made her so happy as to do so; and her doing so,
begot her an unfeigned love, and a serviceable respect
from all that converst with her; and this love followed
her in all places, as inseparably, as shadows follow sub-
stances in Sunshine.

It was not many days before he return'd back to *Bemerton*, to view the Church, and repair the Chancel; and
indeed, to rebuild almost three parts of his house which
was fall'n down, or decayed by reason of his Predecessors
living at a better Parsonage-house; namely, at *Minal*, 16
or 20 miles from this place. At which time of Mr. *Herberts* coming alone to *Bemerton*, there came to him a poor
old Woman, with an intent to acquaint him with her neces-
sitous condition, as also, with some troubles of her mind;
but after she had spoke some few words to him, she was
surpriz'd with a fear, and that begot a shortness of
breath, so that her spirits and speech fail'd her; which
he, perceiving, did so compassionate her, and was so
humble, that he took her by the hand, and said, *Speak good
Mother, be not afraid to speak to me; for I am a man that
will hear you with patience; and will relieve your necessities too, if I be able: and this I will do willingly,
and therefore,* Mother, *be not afraid to acquaint me with
what you desire*. After which comfortable speech, he again
took her by the hand, made her sit down by him, & understanding she was of his Parish, he told her, *He would be
acquainted with her, and take her into his care:* And
having with patience heard and understood her wants (and
it is some relief for a poor body to be but hear'd with
patience) he like a Christian Clergyman comforted her by
his meek behaviour and counsel; but because that cost him
nothing, he reliev'd her with money too, and so sent her
home with a chearful heart, praising God, and praying for
him. *Thus worthy, and* (like *Davids* blessed man) *thus
lowly, was* Mr. George Herbert *in his own eyes*: and thus
lovely in the eyes of others.

At his return that Night to his Wife at *Bainton*, he
gave her an account of the passages 'twixt him and the
poor Woman: with which she was so affected, that she went
next day to *Salisbury*, and there bought a pair of Blankets
and sent them as a Token of her love to the poor Woman:
and with them a Message, *That she would see and be
acquainted with her, when her house was built at* Bemerton.

There be many such passages both of him and his Wife,
of which some few will be related; but I shall first tell,
that he hasted to get the Parish-Church repair'd; then, to
beautifie the Chappel (which stands near his House) and
that at his own great charge. He then proceeded to re-
build the greatest part of the Parsonage-house, which he

did also very compleatly, and at his own charge; and
having done this good work, he caus'd these Verses to be
writ upon, or ingraven in the Mantle of the Chimney in his
Hall.

        To my Successor.

     If thou chance for to find
     A new House to thy mind,
   And built without thy Cost:
     Be good to the Poor,
     As Good gives thee store,
   And then my Labour's not lost.

    We will now by the Readers favour suppose him fixt at
Bemerton, and grant him to have seen the Church repair'd,
and the Chappel belonging to it very decently adorn'd, at
his own great charge (which is a real Truth) and having
now fixt him there, I shall proceed to give an account of
the rest of his behaviour both to his Parishioners, and
those many others that knew and convers'd with him.
    Doubtless Mr. *Herbert* had consider'd and given Rules
to himself for his Christian carriage both to God and
man before he enter'd into *Holy Orders*. And 'tis not
unlike, but that he renewed those resolutions at his prostration before the *Holy Altar*, at his Induction into the
Church of *Bemerton*; but as yet he was but a *Deacon*, and
therefore long'd for the next *Ember-week*, that he might be
ordain'd *Priest*, and made capable of Administring both the
Sacraments. At which time, the Reverend Dr. *Humphrey
Hinchman*, now Lord Bishop of *London* (who does not mention
him, but with some veneration for his life and excellent
learning) tells me, *He laid his hand on Mr.* Herberts *Head,
and (alas!) within less then three Years, lent his Shoulder to carry his dear Friend to his Grave.*
    And that Mr. *Herbert* might the better preserve those
holy Rules which such a *Priest* as he intended to be, ought
to observe; and that time might not insensibly blot them
out of his memory, but that the next year might shew him
his variations from this years resolutions; he therefore
did set down his Rules, then resolv'd upon, in that order,
as the World now sees them printed in a little Book,
call'd, 'The Country Parson', in which some of his Rules
are:

The Parsons Knowledge.   The Parson Condescend-
The Parson on Sundays.   ing.
The Parson Praying.   The Parson in his Journey.
The Parson Preaching.   The Parson in his Mirth.
The Parsons Charity.   The Parson with his Church-
The Parson comforting   wardens.
   the Sick.   The Parson Blessing the
The Parson Arguing.   People.

And his behaviour toward God and man, may be said to be a
practical Comment on these, and the other holy Rules set
down in that useful Book. A Book, so full of plain, prudent and useful Rules, that that *Country Parson*, that can
spare 12 *d*. and yet wants it, is scarce excusable; because
it will both direct him what he ought to do, and convince
him for not having done it.

At the Death of Mr. *Herbert*, this Book fell into the
hands of his friend Mr. *Woodnot*; and he commended it into
the trusty hands of Mr. *Barnabas Oly*, who publish it with
a most conscientious, and excellent Preface; from which I
have had some of those Truths, that are related in this
life of Mr. *Herbert*. The Text for his first Sermon was
taken out of *Solomons Proverbs*, and the words were, *Keep
thy heart with all diligence*. (14) In which first Sermon,
he gave his Parishioners many necessary, holy, safe Rules
for the discharge of a good Conscience, both to God and
man. And deliver'd his Sermon after a most florid manner;
both with great learning and eloquence. But at the close
of this Sermon, told them, *That should not be his constant way of Preaching, for, since Almighty God does not
intend to lead men to heaven by hard Questions, he would
not therefore fill their heads with unnecessary Notions;
but that for their sakes, his language and his expressions
should be more plain and practical in his future Sermons.*
And he then made it his humble request, *That they would be
constant to the Afternoons Service, and Catechising.* And
shewed them convincing reasons why he desir'd it; and his
obliging example and perswasions brought them to a willing
conformity to his desires.

The Texts for all his future Sermons (which God knows
were not many) were constantly taken out of the Gospel for
the day; and, he did as constantly declare why the Church
did appoint that portion of Scripture to be that day read;
And in what manner the *Collect* for every Sunday does refer
to the *Gospel*, or to the *Epistle* then read to them; and
that they might pray with understanding, he did usually
take occasion to explain, not only the *Collect* for every
particular Sunday, but the reasons of all the other *Collects* and *Responses* in our Church-Service; and, made it

appear to them, that *the whole Service of the Church*, was
a reasonable, and therefore an acceptable Sacrifice to
God; as namely, that we begin with *Confession of our
selves to be vile, miserable sinners:* and that we begin
so, because till we have confess'd our selves to be such,
we are not capable of that mercy which we acknowledge we
need, and pray for; but having in the prayer of our Lord,
begg'd pardon for those sins which we have confest: And
hoping, that as the *Priest* hath declar'd our Absolution,
so by our publick Confession, and real Repentance, we
have obtain'd that pardon: Then we dare and do proceed to
beg of the Lord, *to open our lips, that our mouths may
shew forth his praise*, for, till then, we are neither
able, nor worthy to praise him. But this being suppos'd,
we are then fit to say, *Glory be to the Father, and to the
Son, and to the Holy Ghost*; and fit to proceed to a fur--
ther service of our God, in the *Collects*, and *Psalms*, and
Lauds that follow in the Service.

And as to these *Psalms* and *Lauds*, he proceeded to
inform them, why they were so often, and some of them
daily repeated in our *Church-service:* namely, the *Psalms*
every Month, because they be an *Historical* and thankful
repetition of mercies past; and such a composition of
prayers and praises, as ought to be repeated often, and
publickly; for *with such Sacrifices, God is honour'd,
and well-pleased.* This, for the *Psalms.*

And for the *Hymns* and *Lauds*, appointed to be daily
repeated or sung after the first and second Lessons are
read to the Congregation: he proceeded to inform them,
that it was most reasonable, after they have heard the
will and goodness of God declar'd or preach't by the
Priest in his reading the two Chapters, that it was then a
seasonable duty to rise up and express their gratitude to
Almighty God for those his mercies to them, and to all
Mankind; and then to say with the *blessed Virgin, That*
their *Souls do magnifie the Lord, and that* their *spirits
do also rejoyce in God their Saviour*; And that it was
their Duty also to rejoice with *Simeon* in his Song, and
say with him, *That their eyes have* also *seen their salvation*; for they have seen that salvation which was but
prophesied till his time: and he then broke out into those
expressions of joy that he did see it: but they live to
see it daily, in the History of it, and therefore ought
daily to rejoice, and daily to offer up their Sacrifices
of praise to their God, for that particular mercy. A service, which is now the constant employment of that *blessed
Virgin*, and *Simeon*, and all those blessed Saints that are
possest of Heaven: and where they are at this time inter-
changeably and constantly singing, *Holy, Holy, Holy Lord*

God, Glory be to God on High, and on Earth peace. — And
he taught them, that to do this, was an acceptable service
to God, because the Prophet *David* says in his Psalms, *He
that praiseth the Lord, honoureth him.*

He made them to understand, how happy they be that are
freed from the incumbrances of that Law which our Fore-
fathers groan'd under: namely, from the *Legal Sacrifices*:
and from the many *Ceremonies of the Levitical Law:* freed
from *Circumcision*, and from the strict observation of the
Jewish Sabbath, and the like: And he made them know that
having receiv'd so many, and so great blessings, by being
born since the days of our Saviour, it must be an acceptable Sacrifice to Almighty God, for them to acknowledge
those blessings daily, and stand up and worship, and say
as *Zacharias* did, *Blessed be the Lord God of* Israel, *for
he hath* (in our days) *visited and redeemed his people; and*
(he hath in our days) *remembred, and shewed that mercy
which by the mouth of the Prophets, he promised to our
Fore-fathers*: and this he hath done, *according to his holy
Covenant made with them*: And he made them to understand
that we live to see and enjoy the benefit of it, in his
Birth, in his *Life*, his *Passion*, his *Resurrection* and
Ascension into Heaven, where he now sits sensible of all
our temptations and infirmities: and, where he is at this
present time making intercession for us, to his and our
Father: and therefore they ought daily to express their
publick gratulations, and say daily with *Zacharias,
Blessed be that Lord God of* Israel, *that hath thus visited,
and thus redeemed his people.* — These were some of the
reasons by which Mr. *Herbert* instructed his Congregation
for the use of the *Psalms*, and the *Hymns* appointed to be
daily sung or said in the Church-service.

He inform'd them also, when the *Priest* did pray only
for the Congregation, and not for himself; and when they
did only pray for him, as namely, after the repetition of
the *Creed*, before he proceeds to pray the Lords prayer,
or any of the appointed Collects, the Priest is directed
to kneel down, and pray for them, saying — *The Lord be
with you* — And when they pray for him, saying — *And
with thy spirit*; and then they join together in the following Collects, and he assur'd them, that when there is
such mutual love, and such joint prayers offer'd for each
other, then the holy Angels look down from Heaven, and
are ready to carry such charitable desires to God Almighty;
and he as ready to receive them; and that a Christian
Congregation calling thus upon God, with one heart, and
once voice, and in one reverend and humble posture, look
as beautifully as *Jerusalem*, that is at peace with it
self.

He instructed them also, why the prayer of our Lord was pray'd often in every full service of the Church: namely, at the conclusion of the several parts of that Service; and pray'd then, not only because it was compos'd and commanded by our *Jesus* that made it, but as a perfect pattern for our less perfect Forms of prayer, and therefore fittest to sum up and conclude all our imperfect Petitions.

He instructed them also, that as by the second Commandment we are requir'd not to bow down, or worship an *Idol*, or *false God*; so, by the contrary Rule, we are to bow down and kneel, or stand up and *worship* the true God. And he instructed them, why the Church requir'd the Congregation to stand up, at the repetition of the Creeds; namely, because they did thereby declare both their obedience to the Church, and an assent to that faith into which they had been baptiz'd. And he taught them, that in that shorter Creed, or Doxology so often repeated daily; they also stood up to testify their belief to be, that, *the God that they trusted in was one God, and three persons; the Father, the Son, and the Holy Ghost, to whom they & the Priest gave glory*: And because there had been Hereticks that had deny'd some of these three persons to be God; therefore the Congregation stood up and honour'd him, by confessing and saying, *It was so in the beginning, is now so, and shall ever be so World without end*. And all gave their assent to this belief, by standing up and saying, *Amen*.

He instructed them also, what benefit they had, by the Churches appointing the Celebration of Holy-dayes, and the excellent use of them; namely, that they were set apart for particular Commemorations of particular mercies received from Almighty God; and (as Reverend Mr. *Hooker* (15) saies) to be the *Landmarks* to distinguish times; for by them we are taught to take notice how time passes by us; and that we ought not to let the Years pass without a Celebration of praise for those mercies which those days give us occasion to remember; & therefore they were to note that the Year is appointed to begin the 25*th* day of *March*; a day in which we commemorate the *Angels* appearing to the *B. Virgin*, with the joyful tidings that *she should conceive and bear a Son, that should be the redeemer of Mankind*; and she did so Forty weeks after this joyful salutation; namely, at our *Christmas*: a day in which we commemorate his Birth, with joy and praise; and that eight days after this happy Birth, we celebrate his *Circumcision*; namely, in that which we call *New-years day*. And that upon that day which we call *Twelfth-day*, we commemorate the manifestation of the unsearchable riches of Jesus to the Gentiles: And that that day we also celebrate the

memory of his goodness in sending a *Star* to guide the
three wise men from the *East* to *Bethlem*, that they might
there *worship*, and present him with their oblations of
Gold, Frankincense, and *Myrrhe*. And he (Mr. *Herbert*)
instructed them, that *Jesus* was Forty days after his
Birth, presented by his blessed mother in the *Temple*;
namely, on that day which we call, *the Purification of
the blessed Virgin, Saint* Mary. And he instructed them,
that by the *Lent-fast*, we imitate and commemorate our
Saviours humiliation in fasting Forty days; and, that we
ought to endeavour to be like him in purity. And, that
on *Good-friday* we commemorate and condole his *Crucifixion*.
And at *Easter*, commemorate his *glorious Resurrection*.
And he taught them, that after Jesus had manifested himself to his Disciples, to be *that Christ that was crucified, dead and buried*; and by his appearing and conversing
with his Disciples for the space of Forty days after his
Resurrection, he then, and not till then, *ascended into
Heaven*, in the sight of those Disciples; namely, on that
day which we call the *Ascension*, or *Holy Thursday*. And
that we then celebrate the performance of the promise
which he made to his Disciples, at or before his Ascension: namely, *that though he left them, yet he would send
them the Holy Ghost to be their Comforter*; and that he
did so on that day which the Church calls *Whitsunday*. —
Thus the Church keeps an Historical and circular Commemo-
ration of times, as they pass by us; of such times, as
ought to incline us to occasional praises, for the particular blessings which we do, or might receive by those
holy Commemorations.

He made them know also, why the Church hath appointed
Ember-weeks; and to know the reason why the *Commandments*,
and the *Epistles* and *Gospels* were to be read at the *Altar*,
or *Communion Table*: why the Priest was to pray the *Litany*
kneeling; and, why to pray some *Collects* standing; and he
gave them many other observations, fit for his plain Congregation, but not fit for me now to mention; for I must
set limits to my Pen, and not make that a Treatise, which
I intended to be a much shorter account than I have made
it; - but I have done, when I have told the Reader, that
he was constant in *Catechising* every *Sunday* in the Afternoon, and that his Catechising was after his second lesson, and in the Pulpit, and that he never exceeded his
half hour, and was always so happy as to have an obedient,
and a full Congregation.

And to this I must add, That if he were at any time too
zealous in his Sermons, it was in reproving the indecen-
cies of the peoples behaviour, in the time of Divine Service; and of those Ministers that hudled up the Church-

prayers, without a visible reverence and affection; namely
*such as seem'd to say the Lords prayer or a Collect in a
breath*; but for himself, his custom was, to stop betwixt
every Collect, and give the people time to consider what
they had pray'd, and to force their desires affectionately
to God, before he engag'd them into new Petitions.

And by this account of his diligence, to make his
Parishioners understand what they pray'd, and why they
prais'd, and ador'd their Creator: I hope I shall the
more easily obtain the Readers belief to the following
account of Mr. *Herberts* own practice; which was, to appear
constantly with his Wife, and three Neeces (the daughters
of a deceased Sister) and his whole Family, twice every
day at the Church-prayers, in the Chappel which does
almost joyn to his Parsonage-house. And for the time of
his appearing, it was strictly at the Canonical hours of
10 and 4; and then and there, he lifted up pure and
charitable hands to God in the midst of the Congregation.
And he would joy to have spent that time in that place,
where the honour of his *Master Jesus* dwelleth; and there,
by that inward devotion which he testified constantly by
an humble behaviour, and visible adoration, he, like *Josua*
brought not only *his own Houshold thus to serve the Lord*;
but brought most of his Parishioners, and many Gentlemen
in the Neighbourhood, constantly to make a part of his
Congregation twice a day; and some of the meaner sort of
his Parish, did so love and reverence Mr. *Herbert*, that
they would let their Plow rest when Mr. *Herberts Saints-
Bell* rung to Prayers, that they might also offer their
devotions to God with him: and would then return back to
their Plow. And his most holy life was such, that it
begot such reverence to God, and to him, that they thought
themselves the happier, when they carried Mr. *Herberts*
blessing back with them to their labour.— Thus powerful
was his reason, and example, to perswade others to a practical piety, and devotion.

And his constant publick prayers did never make him to
neglect his own private devotions, nor those prayers that
he thought himself bound to perform with his Family, which
alwaies were a Set-form, and not long; and he did alwaies
conclude them with that Collect which the Church hath
appointed for the day or week. — *Thus he made every days
sanctity a step towards that Kingdom where Impurity cannot
enter*.

His chiefest recreation was Musick, in which heavenly
Art he was a most excellent Master, and did himself compose many *divine Hymns* and *Anthems*, which he set and sung
to his *Lute* or *Viol*; and, though he was a lover of
retiredness, yet his love to *Musick* was such, that he went
usually twice every week on certain appointed days, to the

Cathedral Church in *Salisbury*; and at his return would
say, *That his time spent in Prayer, and Cathedral Musick,
elevated his Soul, and was his Heaven upon Earth:* But
before his return thence to *Bemerton*, he would usually
sing and play his part, at an appointed private Musick-
meeting; and, to justifie this practice, he would often
say, *Religion does not banish mirth, but only moderates,
and sets rules to it.*

And as his desire to enjoy *his Heaven upon Earth*, drew
him twice every week to *Salisbury*, so his walks thither,
were the occasion of many happy accidents to others: of
which, I will mention some few.

In one of his walks to *Salisbury*, he overtook a Gentleman that is still living in that City, and in their walk
together, Mr. *Herbert* took a fair occasion to talk with
him, and humbly begg'd to be excus'd, if he ask'd him some
account of his faith, and said, *I do this the rather,
because though you are not of my Parish, yet I receive
Tythe from you by the hand of your Tenant; and, Sir, I am
the bolder to do it, because I know there be some Sermon-
hearers, that be like those Fishes, that always live in
salt water, and yet are always fresh.*

After which expressions, Mr. *Herbert* asked him some
needful Questions, and having received his answer, gave
him such Rules for the trial of his sincerity, and for a
practical piety, and in so loving and meek a manner, that
the Gentleman did so fall in love with him, and his discourse, that he would often contrive to meet him in his
walk to *Salisbury*, or to attend him back to *Bemerton*; and
still mentions the name of Mr. *George Herbert* with veneration, and still praiseth God for the occasion of knowing
him.

In another of his *Salisbury* walks, he met with a Neighbour Minister, and after some friendly Discourse betwixt
them, and some Condolement for the decay of Piety, and too
general Contempt of the Clergy, Mr. *Herbert* took occasion
to say,

*One Cure for these Distempers would be for the Clergy
themselves to keep the* Ember-Weeks *strictly, and beg of
their Parishioners to joyn with them in* Fasting *and* Prayers, *for a more Religious Clergy.*

And another *Cure would be, for themselves to restore
the great and neglected duty of* Catechising, *on which the
salvation of so many of the poor and ignorant Lay-people
does depend; but principally, that the Clergy themselves
would be sure to live umblameably; and that the dignifi'd
Clergy especially, which preach Temperance, would avoid
Surfeiting, and take all occasions to express a visible
humility and charity in their lives; for this would force*

*a love & an imitation, and an unfeigned reverence from all
that knew them to be such.* (And for proof of this, we
need no other Testimony, than the life and death of Dr.
Lake, late Lord Bishop of *Bath* and *Wells*) *This* (said Mr.
Herbert) *would be a cure for the wickedness and growing
Atheism of our Age. And,* my dear *Brother, till this be
done by us, and done in earnest, let no man expect a reformation of the manners of the* Laity: *for 'tis not learning, but this, this only, that must do it; and till then,
the fault must lye at our doors.*

In another walk to *Salisbury,* he saw a poor man, with a
poorer horse, that was fall'n under his Load; they were
both in distress, and needed present help; which Mr. *Herbert* perceiving, put off his Canonical Coat, and help'd
the poor man to unload, and after, to load his horse: The
poor man blest him for it: and he blest the poor man; and
was so like the *good Samaritan,* that he gave him money to
refresh both himself and his horse; and told him, *That if
he lov'd himself, he should be merciful to his Beast.* —
Thus he left the poor man, and at his coming to his musical friends at *Salisbury,* they began to wonder that Mr.
George Herbert which us'd to be so trim and clean, came
into that company so soyl'd and discompos'd; but he told
them the occasion: And when one of the company told him,
He had disparag'd himself by so dirty an employment; his
answer was, *That the thought of what he had done, would
prove Musick to him at Midnight; and that the omission of
it, would have upbraided and made discord in his Conscience, whensoever he should pass by that place; for, if
I be bound to pray for all that be in distress, I am sure
that I am bound so far as it is in my power to practise what
I pray for. And though I do not wish for the like occasion every day, yet let me tell you, I would not willingly
pass one day of my life without comforting a sad soul, or
shewing mercy; and I praise God for this occasion*: And
now let's tune our Instruments.

Thus, as our blessed Saviour after his Resurrection did
take occasion to interpret the Scripture to *Cleopas,* and
that other Disciple which he met with and accompanied in
their journey to *Emmaus*; so Mr. *Herbert,* in his path toward Heaven, did daily take any fair occasion to instruct
the ignorant, or comfort any that were in affliction; and
did alwaies confirm his precepts, by shewing humility and
mercy, and ministring grace to the hearers.

And he was most happy in his Wifes unforc'd compliance
with his acts of Charity, whom he made his *Almoner,* and
paid constantly into her hand, *a tenth penny* of what he
receiv'd for Tythe, and gave her power to dispose that to
the poor of his Parish, and with it a power to dispose a

tenth part of the Corn that came yearly into his Barn;
which trust she did most faithfully perform, and would
often offer to him *an account of her stewardship*, and as
often beg an inlargement of his bounty, for she rejoyc'd
in the employment; and this was usually laid out by her in
Blankets and *Shooes*, for some such poor people as she knew
to stand in most need of them.   This, as to her Charity.
- And for his own, he set no limits to it; nor did ever
turn his face from any that he saw in want, but would
relieve them; especially his poor Neighbours; to the meanest of whose Houses, he would go and inform himself of
their wants, and relieve them chearfully if they were in
distress; and would alwaies praise God, as much for being
willing, as for being able to do it. - And when he was
advis'd by a friend to be more frugal, because he might
have Children, his answer was, *He would not see the danger
of want so far off; but, being the Scripture does so commend Charity, as to tell us, that* Charity *is the top of
Christian* vertues, *the covering of sins, the fulfilling of
the* Law, *the life of* Faith: *And that* Charity *hath a promise of the blessings of this life, and of a reward in
that life which is to come, being these, and more excellent things are in Scripture spoken of thee O* Charity, *and
that, being all my Tythes, and Church-dues, are a* Deodate
(16) *from thee O my God! make me, O my God, so far to
trust thy promise, as to return them back to thee; and, by
thy grace, I will do so, in distributing them to any of thy
poor members that are in distress, or do but bear the
image of* Jesus my Master.   *Sir* (said he to his friend) *my
Wife hath a competent maintenance secur'd her after my
death, and therefore as this is my prayer, so this my
resolution shall by God's grace be unalterable.*

This may be some account of the excellencies of the
active part of his life; and thus he continued, till a
Consumption so weakened him, as to confine him to his
House, or to the Chappel, which does almost joyn to it; in
which he continued to read Prayers constantly twice every
day, though he were very weak; in one of which times of
his reading, his Wife observ'd him to read in pain, and
told him so, and that it wasted his spirits, and weakned
him: and he confess'd it did, but said, *His life could not
be better spent, than in the service of his* Master Jesus,
who had done and suffered so much for him: But, said he,
*I will not be wilful: for though my spirit be willing, yet
I find my flesh is weak; and therefore Mr.* Bostock *shall
be appointed to read Prayers for me to morrow, and I will
now be only a hearer of them, till this mortal shall put
on immortality.*   And Mr. *Bostock* did the next day undertake and continue this happy employment, till Mr. *Herberts*

death. - This Mr. *Bostock* was a learned and vertuous man,
an old friend of Mr. *Herberts*, and then his Curate to the
Church of *Fulston*, which is a mile from *Bemerton*, to which
Church, *Bemerton* is but a *Chappel of ease*. - And, this Mr.
Bostock did also constantly supply the *Church-service* for
Mr. *Herbert* in that Chappel, when the Musick-meeting at
Salisbury caus'd his absence from it.

About one month before his death, his friend Mr. *Farrer*
(for an account of whom I am by promise indebted to the
Reader, and intend to make him sudden payment) hearing of
Mr. *Herberts* sickness, sent Mr. *Edmund Duncon* (who is now
Rector of *Fryer Barnet* in the County of *Middlesex*) from his
House of *Gidden Hall*, which is near to *Huntington*, to see
Mr. *Herbert*, and to assure him, he wanted not his daily
prayers for his recovery; and Mr. *Duncon* was to return
back to *Gidden*, with an account of Mr. *Herberts* condition.
Mr. *Duncon* found him weak, and at that time lying on his
Bed, or on a Pallat; but at his seeing Mr. *Duncon*, he
rais'd himself vigorously, saluted him, and with some
earnestness *inquir'd the health of his brother* Farrer? of
which Mr. *Duncon* satisfied him; and after some discourse
of Mr. *Farrers* holy life, and the manner of his constant
serving God, he said to Mr. *Duncon* - *Sir, I see by your
habit that you are a Priest, and I desire you to pray with
me*; which being granted, Mr. *Duncon* ask'd him, *what
Prayers?* to which, Mr. *Herberts* answer was, *O Sir, the
Prayers of my Mother, the Church of* England, *no other
Prayers are equal to them! but, at this time, I beg of
you to pray only the* Litany, *for I am weak and faint*;
and Mr. *Duncon* did so. After which, and some other discourse of Mr. *Farrer*, Mrs. *Herbert* provided Mr. *Duncon* a
plain Supper, and a clean Lodging, and he betook himself
to rest. - *This Mr.* Duncon *tells me*; and tells me, that at
his first view of Mr. *Herbert*, he saw *majesty* and *humility*
so reconcil'd in his looks and behaviour, as begot in him
an awful reverence for his person: and saies, *his discourse
was so pious, and his motion so gentile and meek, that
after almost forty years, yet they remain still fresh in
his memory*.

The next morning Mr. *Duncon* left him, and betook himself to a Journey to *Bath*, but with a promise to return
back to him within five days, and he did so; but before I
shall say any thing of what discourse then fell betwist
them two, I will pay my promis'd account of Mr. *Farrer*.

Mr. *Nicholas Farrer* (who got the reputation of being
call'd Saint *Nicholas*, at the age of six years) was born
in *London*: and doubtless had good education in his youth;
but certainly was at an early age made Fellow of *Clare-
Hall* in *Cambridge*, where he continued to be eminent for

his *piety, temperance,* and *learning.* - About the 26*th* year
of his Age, he betook himself to Travel: in which he added
to his *Latin* and *Greek*, a perfect knowledge of all the
Languages spoken in the Western parts of our Christian
world; and understood well the principles of their Religion, and of their manner, and the reasons of their worship. - In this is Travel he met with many perswasions to
come into a communion with that Church which calls it self
Catholick: but he return'd from his Travels as he went,
eminent for his obedience to his Mother, *the Church of
England.* In his absence from *England*, Mr. *Farrers* father
(who was a Merchant) allow'd him a liberal maintenance;
and, not long after his return into *England*, Mr. *Farrer*
had by the death of his father, or an elder brother, or
both, an Estate left him, that enabled him to purchase
Land to the value of 4 or 500 *l.* a year; the greatest part
of which Land was at *Little Gidden*, (17) 4 or 6 miles from
Huntington, and about 18 miles from *Cambridge*: which place,
he chose for the privacy of it, and for the Hall, which
had the Parish-Church, or Chappel belonging, and adjoining
near to it; for Mr. *Farrer* having seen the manners and
vanities of the World, and found them to be, as Mr. *Herbert*
says, *A nothing between two Dishes;* (18) did so contemn
it, that he resolv'd to spend the remainder of his life in
mortifications, and in devotion, and charity, and to be
alwaies prepar'd for Death: - And his life was spent thus.
     He, and his Family, which were like a little Colledge,
and about Thirty in number, did most of them keep *Lent*,
and all *Ember-weeks* strictly, both in fasting, and using
all those mortifications and prayers that the Church hath
appointed to be then used: and, he and they, did the like
constantly on *Fridays*, and on the *Vigils*, or Eves appointed
to be fasted before the Saints-days; and this frugality and
abstinence, turn'd to the relief of the Poor: but this was
but a part of his charity, none but God and he knew the
rest.
     This Family, which I have said to be in number about
Thirty, were a part of them his Kindred, and the rest
chosen to be of a temper fit to be moulded into a devout
life; and all of them were for their dispositions *serviceable* and *quiet*, and *humble*, and *free from scandal*. Having
thus fitted himself for his Family, he did about the year
1630, betake himself to a constant and methodical service
of God, and it was in this manner. - He being accompanied
with most of his Family, did himself use to read the Common prayers (for he was a Deacon) every day, at the
appointed hours of Ten and Four, in the Parish Church
which was very near his House, and which he had both
repair'd and adorn'd; for it was fallen into a great ruine,

by reason of a depopulation of the Village before Mr.
Farrer bought the Mannor: And he did also constantly
read the *Mattins* every Morning at the hour of six, either
in the Church, or in an Oratory, which was within his own
House: And many of the Family did there continue with him
after the Prayers were ended, and there they spent some
hours in singing *Hymns*, or *Anthems*, sometimes in the
Church, and often to an Organ in the Oratory. And there
they sometimes betook themselves to meditate, or to pray
privately, or to read a part of the New Testament to themselves, or to continue their praying or reading the
Psalms: and, in case the Psalms were not all alwaies read
in the day, then Mr. *Farrer*, and others of the Congregation, did at Night, at the ring of a Watch-bell, repair
to the Church or Oratory, and there betake themselves to
prayers, and lauding God, and reading the Psalms that had
not been read in the day; and, when these, or any part of
the Congregation grew weary, or faint, the Watch-bell was
Rung, sometimes before, and sometimes after Midnight:
and then another part of the Family rose, and maintain'd
the Watch, sometimes by praying, or singing Lauds to God,
or reading the Psalms: and when after some hours they also
grew weary or faint, then they rung the Watch-bell, and
were also reliev'd by some of the former, or by a new part
of the Society, which continued their devotions (as hath
been mentioned) until morning. - And it is to be noted,
that in this continued serving of God, the Psalter, or
whole Book of Psalms, was in every four and twenty hours,
sung or read over, from the first to the last verse: and
this was done as constantly, as the Sun runs his Circle
every day about the World, and then begins again the same
instant that it ended.

Thus did Mr. *Farrer*, and his happy Family, serve God
day and night: Thus did they alwaies behave themselves,
as in his presence. And they did alwaies eat and drink by
the strictest rules of Temperance; eat and drink so, as to
be ready to rise at Midnight, or at the call of a Watch-
bell, and perform their devotions to God. - And 'tis fit
to tell the Reader, that many of the Clergy that were more
inclin'd to *practical piety*, and *devotion*, then to doubt-
ful and needless Disputations, did often come to *Gidden
Hall*, and make themselves a part of that happy Society,
and stay a week or more, and then join with Mr. *Farrer* and
the Family in these Devotions, and assist and ease him or
them in their Watch by Night; and these various Devotions,
had never less than two of the Domestick Family in the
Night; and the Watch was alwaies kept in the Church or
Oratory, unless in extream cold Winter nights, and then it
was maintain'd in a Parlour which had a fire in it: and

the Parlour was fitted for that purpose; and this course
of Piety, and great liberality to his poor Neighbours, Mr.
Farrer maintain'd till his death, which was in the year
1639.

Mr. *Farrers*, and Mr. *Herberts* devout lives, were both
so noted, that the general report of their sanctity gave
them occasion to renew that slight acquaintance which was
begun at their being Contemporaries in *Cambridge*; and this
new holy friendship was long maintain'd without any interview, but only by loving and endearing Letters. And one
testimony of their friendship, and pious designs, may
appear by Mr. *Farrers* commending the considerations of
John Valdesso (a Book which he had met with in his Travels,
and Translated out of *Spanish* into *English*) to be examin'd
and censur'd by Mr. *Herbert* before it was made publick;
which excellent Book, Mr. *Herbert* did read, and return
back with many marginal Notes, as they be now printed
with it: And with them, Mr. *Herberts* affectionate Letter
to Mr. *Farrer*.

This *John Valdesso* was a *Spaniard*, and was for his
Learning and Vertue, much valued and lov'd by the great
Emperor *Charles the fifth*, whom *Valdesso* had followed as
a *Cavalier* all the time of his long and dangerous Wars;
and when *Valdesso* grew old, and grew weary both of War and
the World, he took his fair opportunity to declare to the
Emperour, that his resolution was to decline His Majesties Service, and betake himself to a quiet and contemplative life, *because there ought to be a vacancy of time,
betwixt fighting and dying.* - The Emperour had himself,
for the same, or other like reasons, put on the same resolution: but, God and himself did till then, only consider
them; and he did therefore desire *Valdesso* to consider
well of what he had said, and to keep his purpose within
his own breast, till they two might have a second opportunity of a friendly Discourse: which *Valdesso* promis'd to
do.

In the mean time, the Emperour appoints privately a day
for him and *Valdesso* to meet again, and, after a pious and
free discourse they both agreed on a certain day to
receive the blessed Sacrament publickly: and, appointed an
eloquent and devout Fryer, to preach a Sermon of *contempt
of the World*, and of the happiness and benefit of a quiet
and contemplative life; which the Fryer did most affectionately. - After which Sermon, the Emperour took occasion to declare openly, *That the Preacher had begot in him
a resolution to lay down his Dignities, and to forsake the
World, and betake himself to a Monastical life.* And he
pretended, he had perswaded *John Valdesso* to do the like;
but this is most certain, that after the Emperour had

called his son *Philip* out of *England*, and resign'd to him
all his Kingdoms, that then the Emperour, and *John Valdesso*, did perform their resolutions.

This account of *John Valdesso*, I receiv'd from a
Friend, that had it from the mouth of Mr. *Farrer*: and the
Reader may note, that in this retirement, *John Valdesso*
writ his 110 considerations, and many other Treatises of
worth, which want a second Mr. *Farrer* to procure, and
translate them.

After this account of Mr. *Farrer*, and *John Valdesso*, I
proceed to my account of Mr. *Herbert*, and Mr. *Duncon*,
who, according to his promise, return'd from the Bath the
fifth day, and then found Mr. *Herbert* much weaker than he
left him: and therefore their Discourse could not be long;
but at Mr. *Duncons* parting with him, Mr. *Herbert* spoke to
this purpose - *Sir, I pray give my brother* Farrer *an
account of the decaying condition of my body, and tell
him, I beg him to continue his daily prayers for me: and
let him know that I have consider'd,* That God only is
what he would bee; *and that I am by his grace become now
so like him, as to be pleas'd with what pleaseth him; and
tell him, that I do not repine but am pleas'd with my want
of health; and tell him, my heart is fixed on that place
where true joy is only to be found; and that I long to be
there, and do wait for my appointed change with* hope *and*
patience. Having said this, he did with so sweet a humility as seem'd to exalt him, bow down to Mr. *Duncon*, and
with a thoughtful and contented look, say to him, - *Sir, I
pray deliver this little Book to my dear brother* Farrer,
*and tell him, he shall find in it a picture of the many
spiritual Conflicts that have past betwixt God and my
Soul, before I could subject mine to the will of* Jesus my
Master: *in whose service I have now found perfect freedom; desire him to read it: and then, if he can think it
may turn to the advantage of any dejected poor Soul, let
it be made publick: if not, let him burn it: for* I and it,
are less than the least of God's mercies. - Thus meanly
did this humble man think of this excellent Book, which
now bears the name of 'The TEMPLE: Or, Sacred Poems, and
Private Ejaculations'; of which, Mr. *Farrer* would say,
*There was in it the picture of a divine Soul in every
page; and that the whole Book was such a harmony of holy
passions, as would enrich the World with pleasure and
piety.* And it appears to have done so: for there have
been more than Twenty thousand of them sold since the
first Impression. (19)

And this ought to be noted, that when Mr. *Farrer* sent
this Book to *Cambridge* to be Licensed for the Press, the
Vice-Chancellor would by no means allow the two so much
noted Verses,

Religion stands a Tip-toe in our Land,
Ready to pass to the American Strand.

['The Church Militant', 11. 235-6]

to be printed; and Mr. *Farrer* would by no means allow the
Book to be printed, and want them: But after some time,
and some arguments, for and against their being made publick, the *Vice-Chancellor* said, *I knew Mr.* Herbert *well,*
and know that he had many heavenly Speculations, and was a
Divine Poet; but I hope the World will not take him to be
an inspired Prophet, and therefore I License the whole
Book: So that it came to be printed, without the diminu-
tion or addition of a syllable, since it was deliver'd
into the hands of Mr. *Duncon*, save only, that Mr. *Farrer*
hath added that excellent Preface that is printed before
it. (20)

At the time of Mr. *Duncons* leaving Mr. *Herbert*, (which
was about three weeks before his death) his old and dear
friend Mr. *Woodnot*, came from *London* to *Bemerton*, and
never left him, till he had seen him draw his last breath,
and clos'd his Eyes on his Death-bed. In this time of his
decay, he was often visited and pray'd for by all the
Clergy that liv'd near to him, especially by his friends
the Bishop and Prebends of the Cathedral Church in *Salis-*
bury; but by none more devoutly, that his Wife, his three
Neeces (then a part of his Family) and Mr. *Woodnot*, who
were the sad Witnesses of his daily decay; to whom he
would often speak to this purpose. - *I now look back upon*
the pleasures of my life past, and see the content I have
taken in beauty, *in* wit, *in* musick, *and* pleasant Conversation, *are now all past by me, like a dream, or as a*
shadow that returns not, and are now all become dead to
me, or I to them; and I see that as my father and genera-
tion hath done before me, so I also shall now suddenly
(with Job) make my *Bed also in the dark; and I praise God*
I am prepared for it; and I praise him, that I am not to
learn patience, now I stand in such need of it; and that
I have practised Mortification, and endeavour'd to dye
daily, that I might not dye eternally; and my hope is,
that I shall shortly leave this valley of tears, and be
free from all fevers and pain: and which will be a more
happy condition, I shall be free from sin, and all the
temptations and anxieties that attend it; and this being
past, I shall dwell in the new Jerusalem, *dwell there with*
men made perfect; dwell, where these eyes shall see my
Master and Saviour Jesus; *and with him see my dear Mother,*
and all my Relations and Friends: - But I must dye, or not
come to that happy place: And this is my content, that I
am going daily towards it; and that every day which I have

*liv'd, hath taken a part of my appointed time from me, and
that I shall live the less time, for having liv'd this,
and the day past.* - These, and the like expressions, which
he utter'd often, may be said to *be his* enjoyment of
Heaven, before he enjoy'd it. - The *Sunday* before his
death, he rose suddenly from his Bed or Couch, call'd for
one of his Instruments, took it into hand, and said -

> My God, My God,
> My Musick shall find thee, and every string
> Shall have his attribute to sing.
> ['Thanksgiving', 11. 39-40]

And having tun'd it, he play'd and sung:

> The Sundays of Mans life,
> Thredded together on times string,
> Make Bracelets, to adorn the Wife
> Of the eternal glorious King:
> On Sundays, Heavens dore stands ope;
> Blessings are plentiful and rife,
> More plentiful than hope.
> ['Sunday', 11. 29-35]

Thus he sung on Earth such Hymns and Anthems, as the
Angels and he, and Mr. *Farrer*, now sing in Heaven.
Thus he continued meditating and praying, and rejoicing,
till the day of his death; and on that day, said to Mr.
*Woodnot, My dear Friend, I am sorry I have nothing to pre-
sent to my merciful God but sin and misery; but the first
is pardoned: and a few hours will now put a period to the
latter*; for I shall suddenly go hence and be no more seen.
Upon which expression, Mr. *Woodnot* took occasion to remember him of the Re-edifying *Layton* Church, and his many
Acts of mercy; to which he made answer, saying, *They be
good works, if they be sprinkled with the blood of Christ,
and not otherwise.* After this Discourse he became more
restless, and his Soul seem'd to be weary of her earthly
Tabernacle; and this uneasiness became so visible, that
his Wife, his three Neeces, and Mr. *Woodnot*, stood constantly about his bed, beholding him with sorrow, and an
unwillingness to lose the sight of him whom they could not
hope to see much longer. - As they stood thus beholding
him, his Wife observ'd him to breath faintly, and with
much trouble: and observ'd him to fall into a sudden
Agony; which so surpriz'd her, that she fell into a sudden
passion, and requir'd of him to know, *how he did?* to which
his answer was, *That he had past a Conflict with his last*

*Enemy, and had overcome him, by the merits of his Master
Jesus.* After which answer, he look'd up, and saw his Wife
and Neeces weeping to an extremity, and charg'd them, *If
they lov'd him, to withdraw into the next Room, and there
pray every one alone for him, for nothing but their lamen-
tations could make his death uncomfortable.* To which request, their sighs and tears would not suffer them to
make any reply: but they yielded him a sad obedience,
leaving only with him Mr. *Woodnot*, and Mr. *Bostock*.
Immediately after they had left him, he said to Mr. *Bostock, Pray Sir open that door, then look into that Cabi-
net, in which you may easily find my last Will, and give
it into my hand*; which being done Mr. *Herbert* deliver'd it
into the hand of Mr. *Woodnot*, and said, *My old Friend, I
here deliver you my last Will, in which you will find that
I have made you my sole Executor for the good of my Wife
and Neeces; and I desire you to shew kindness to them, as
they shall need it; I do not desire you to be just: for I
know you will be so for your own sake; but I charge you,
by the Religion of our friendship, to be careful of them.*
And having obtain'd Mr. *Woodnots* promise to be so; he said,
I am now ready to dye: after which words he said, *Lord,
forsake me not now my strength faileth me: but grant me
mercy for the merits of my Jesus; and now Lord, Lord now
receive my Soul.* And, with those words he breath'd forth
his Divine Soul, without any apparent disturbance: Mr.
Woodnot, and Mr. *Bostock*, attending his last breath, and
closing his eyes.

Thus he liv'd, and thus he dy'd like a Saint, unspotted
of the World, full of Alms-deeds, full of Humility, and
all the examples of a vertuous life; which I cannot conclude better, than with this borrowed observation:

> *All must to their cold Graves;*
> *But the religious actions of the just,*
> *Smell sweet in death, and blossom in the dust.* (21)

Mr. *George Herberts* have done so to this, and will
doubtless do so to succeeding Generations. – I have but
this to say more of him: That if *Andrew Melvin* dyed before
him, then *George Herbert* dyed without an enemy. – I wish
(if God shall be so pleased) that I may be so happy as to
dye like him.

*There is a debt justly due to the memory of Mr. Herberts
vertuous Wife; a part of which I will endeavour to pay, by
a very short account of the remainder of her life, which
shall follow.*
She continu'd his disconsolate Widow, about six years,

bemoaning her self, and complaining, That she had lost the
delight of her eyes; *but more*, that she had lost the
spiritual guide for her poor soul; *and would often say*, O
that I had like holy *Mary*, the Mother of Jesus, treasur'd
up all his sayings in my heart; but since I have not been
able to do that, I will labour to live like him, that
where he now is, I may be also. *And she would often say
(as the Prophet* David *for his son* Absolon) O that I had
dyed for him! *Thus she continued mourning, till time and
conversation had so moderated her sorrows, that she became
the happy Wife of Sir* Robert Cook *of* Highnam *in the County
of* Gloucester *Knight: And though he put a high value on
the excellent accomplishments of her mind and body; and
was so like Mr.* Herbert, *as not to govern like a Master,
but as an affectionate Husband; yet she would even to him
often take occasion to mention the name of Mr.* George Herbert, *and say*, That name must live in her memory, till she
put off mortality. - *By Sir* Robert, *she had only one Child,
a Daughter, whose parts and plentiful estate make her
happy in this world, and her well using of them, gives a
fair testimony, that she will be so in that which is to
come.*
    Mrs. Herbert *was the Wife of Sir* Robert *eight years,
and liv'd his Widow about fifteen; all which time, she took
a pleasure in mentioning, and commending the excellencies
of Mr.* George Herbert. *She dyed in the year* 1663. *and lies
buried at* Highnam; *Mr.* Herbert *in his own Church, under the
Altar, and cover'd with a Grave-stone without any inscription.*
    This Lady Cook, *had preserv'd many of Mr.* Herberts *pri-
vate Writings, which she intended to make publick; but
they, and* Highnam *house, were burnt together, by the late
Rebels, and so lost to posterity.*

Notes

1 Above, pp. 94 ff.
2 'De veritate' (1633); 'The Life and Reigne of King
   Henry the Eighth' (1649).
3 I.e. Elegy IX. The passages quoted are 11. 1-2 and
   23-4.
4 They constitute, in fact, the sequence of seven sonnets
   comprising 'La Corona'.
5 'Why mention "Vatican" and "Bodleian", O friend? / One
   single book a library is to us' (as below, p. 135).
6 Hereafter the 1670 edition of the 'Lives' reads: '...
   Melvin, a Gentleman of *Scotland*, who was in his own
   Country possest with an aversness, if not a hatred of

Church-government by Bishops: and, he seem'd to have a
like aversness to our manner of *Publick Worship*, and of
Church-prayers and *Ceremonies*. This Gentleman had travail'd *France*, nad resided so long in *Geneva*, as to
have his opinions the more confirm's in him by the
practice of that place; from which he return'd into
England some short time before, or immediately after
Mr. *Herbert* was made *Orator*. This Mr. *Melvin* was a
man of learning, and was the Master of a great wit, a
wit full of *knots* and *clenches*: a wit sharp and satyrical; exceeded, I think, by none of that Nation, but
their *Bucanen* [i.e. George Buchanan (1506–82)]. At Mr.
Melvins return hither, he writ and scattered in Latin,
many pieces of his wit against our *Altars*, our *Prayers*,
and our *Publick Worship* of God; in which, Mr. *Herbert*
took himself to be so much concern'd, that as fast as
Melvin writ and scatter'd them, Mr. *Herbert* writ and
scatter'd answers, and reflections of the same sharp-
ness, upon him and them; I think, to the satisfaction
of all un-ingaged persons. But, this Mr. *Melvin*, was
not only so busie against the *Church*, but at last so
bold with the *King* and *State*, that he rayl'd, and writ
himself into the *Tower*; at which time, the Lady *Arabella* was an innocent prisoner there;...'

7   'The cause that we're in prison we've in common, Ara-
      Bella; the fair cause is thine, the sacred Altar mine.'
      The lines depend on the pun on 'ara' (altar) and
      'bella' (beautiful; also, wars).
8   See headnote to No. 27.
9   See No. 2.
10   The letter is no longer extant; only a Latin one is
      (see Hutchinson, pp. 471–3). 'Andrews' is the saintly
      Lancelot Andrewes, one of the period's foremost
      scholars.
11   Translated expansively in Donne's poem to Herbert
      (No. 1).
12   Above, pp. 123 ff.
13   'Psal, 55[.22]. I Pet. 5.7.' (Walton's marginal note.)
14   Proverbs 4.23.
15   Richard Hooker, the great apologist of the Church of
      England.
16   Gift from God.
17   I.e. Little Gidding.
18   In 'Dotage', 1. 5.
19   The 1670 edition of the 'Lives' specifies the number of
      copies sold by that date as 'Ten thousand'.
20   See No. 4.
21   A rather garbled version of James Shirley's 'The Con-
      tention of Ajax and Ulysses' (1659), III, 22–4.

25.   CHARLES COTTON, FROM 'TO MY OLD, AND MOST WORTHY
FRIEND MR. IZAAC WALTON'

1675

Cotton's commendatory verses on Walton, prefixed to the
'Lives' of 1675, encompass a tribute to Herbert that is
tantamount to an interpretation of the poet's career.
See also above, p. 10.
   Source: Walton, 'Lives', sig. A8.

...*Herbert*: he, whose education,
Manners, and parts, by high applauses blown,
Was deeply tainted with Ambition;

And fitted for a Court, made that his aim:
At last, without regard to Birth or Name,
For a poor Country-Cure, does all disclaim.

Where, with a soul compos'd of Harmonies,
Like a sweet *Swan*, he warbles, as he dies
His makers praise, and, his own obsequies.

26.   EDWARD PHILLIPS, FROM 'THEATRUM POETARUM'

1675

Phillips, Milton's nephew, was the accomplished author of
a number of books addressed to a variety of subjects. His
'Theatrum Poetarum' is comprised of brief entries, among
them the following one on Herbert. See also above, p. 12.
   Source: Phillips, 'Theatrum Poetarum, or A Compleat
Collection of the Poets' (1675), p. 54.

George Herbert, a Younger Brother of the Noble Family of
the *Herberts* of *Montgomery*, whose florid Wit, obliging
Humour in Conversation, fluent Elocution, and great pro-
ficience in the Arts, gain'd him that Reputation at *Oxford*,
(1) where he spent his more Youthful age, that he was
chosen University Oratour; at last taking upon him Holy
Orders, not without special incouragement from the King,
who took notice of his parts; he was made Parson of

Bemerton near *Salisbury*; in this state his affection to
Poetry being converted to serious and Divine Subjects, produc'd those so generally known and approved Poems Entitled
the Temple.

Note

1 Actually, Cambridge.

27. JAMES DUPORT, 'IN DIVINUM POEMA (CUI TITULUS TEMPLUM)
GEORGII HERBERTI'

1676

Duport was, like Herbert, educated at Trinity College,
Cambridge, where he eventually became Fellow and Vice-
Master. His 'Ecclesiastes Solomonis' (1662) made available
for the first time Herbert's Latin epigrams against Andrew
Melville, the 'Musae responsoriae'. But it was Duport's
'Musae subcesivae' (1676) that provided the learned tribute
to Herbert, here reproduced with a translation by Ralph
Williams. See also above, p. 10.
    Source: Duport, 'Musae subsecivae, seu Poetica stromata'
(Cambridge, 1676), pp. 357-8.

In divinum Poema (cui titulus Templum) Georgii Herberti,
*Ingeniosissimi juxta ac Pientissimi Poetae, necnon Oratoris
publici Academiae* Cantabrigiensis & *Collegii* SS. Trinitatis
ibidem aliquando Socii.

    Zelus & ingenium, Pietas & acumen, in uno,
        Par insigne, unquam si coiêre Libro;
    Hic tuus, *Herberte*, est: & tu *punctum omne tulisti*,
        Qui tam dulce potes *sanctificare* melos.
    Quae cecinit sacros aequè ac tua suaviter hymnos,
        Haec vel *Davidis*, vel Lyra nulla fuit
    Ergo quid huc nostras juvat invitare Camoenas,
        Ut *tenuent parvis* Cantica magna modis?
    Frustra ego nam tantas conarer carmine laudes,
        Aut *pedibus Templi* scribere *metra* tui;
    Ni mihi vel *Sanctae* calamum daret ala *Columbae,*
        Prunáve ab *altari* tangeret ora tuo: (1)

Denique ni sacros sentirem corde calores,
  Enthea queis tecum par mihi vena foret.
Sit mihi fas igitur proprias tibi reddere voces,
  Hortos éque tuo fonte rigare meos:
Nam meliùs laudare duum, divina Poeta,
  Non potero, quàm tu Nobile Regis Opus. (2)
Quid Vaticanam Bodleianámque objicis, hospes?
  Vnicus est nobis Bibliotheca Liber.
De proprio tamen hoc addam; Nec sanctior alter,
  Nec melior mihi, post Biblia Sacra, Liber.
Quando ergo in terris non est divínior Hymnus,
  Cantio nec *Templo* par similísve tuo;
Restat ut in coelis aeterna poemata pangas,
  Angelicóque canas carmina digna Choro.

On the divine Poem (entitled 'The Temple') of George Herbert, at once the Most Ingenious and Most Pious Poet, and,
besides, Public Orator of Cambridge University and sometime Fellow of that Institution's College of the Most Holy
Trinity.

If zeal and genius, Piety and wit in like
  Pre-em'nence in one Book have ever joined,
'Tis, Herbert, this of thine: thou'st borne off every
                                        prize,
  Who melody so sweet canst sanctify.
No Lyre sang sacred hymns so graciously as thine,
  Save David's only - his, or none's.
What profit, then, to bid my Muses hither come
  To lessen thy great Songs with measures slight?
For I in vain should try to sing such lofty praise,
  Or in thy *Temple*'s feet my measures write,
Unless thy holy Dove's own wing provide my pen,
  Or coal from off thine altar touch my lips;
Unless, in fine, my heart should feel those holy flames
  Through which I too might have that sacred vein.
Permit me then thy proper phrases to return
  And mine own gardens water from thy fount.
For better, god-like Poet, I cannot praise thy work
  Than thou the Noble Royal Book didst laud:
'Why mention "Vatican" and "Bodleian", O friend?
  One single book a library is to us'.
For my part this I'll add: to me no other Book,
  God's Word apart, so sacred is or good.
Since, then, on earth no Hymn is so divine, nor like
  And equal to thy 'Temple' any Song,
This yet remains for thee: in heaven eternal poems
  To sound, and verses fit for angels' Choirs.

Notes

1 Alluding to Herbert's 'Easter-wings' and 'The Altar'.
2 Βασιλικὸν Δῶρον ('Royal Gift', by King James (1599)).

28. SAMUEL SPEED, FROM 'PRISON-PIETIE'

1677

Speed was a stationer and bookseller given to occasional
outbursts of doggerel verse. He remarked on Herbert in the
prefatory address To the Devout given below.
   Source: Speed, 'Prison-Pietie: or, Meditations Divine
and Moral. Digested into Poetical Heads' (1677), sig. A5v.

...such is the looseness of this Age, that many are of the
opinion, that Divinity in verse is unpleasant to the ear
and to the heart: let such be convinced by the Psalms of
David, or the Song of his son *Solomon*. Divine Verse hath
these two operations: it is pleasant, and makes an impression in the memory of the Reader; so true is that of the
excellent Mr. *Geo. Herbert*, University-Oratour of *Cambridge*.

>   A Verse may take him who a Sermon flies,
>   And turn delight into a Sacrifice.
>   ['The Church-porch', 11. 5-6]

29. RICHARD BAXTER, FROM HIS PREFACE TO 'POETICAL
FRAGMENTS'

1681

Baxter was a highly respected nonconformist clergyman,
best known for 'The Saints Everlasting Rest' (1650) and
'The Holy Commonwealth' (1659). These remarks on Herbert
occur in his address to the reader of his 'Poetical Fragments', within the context of an expeditious survey of
some of his favourite literary works. See further above,
p. 11.

Source: Baxter, 'Poetical Fragments' (1681), sigs
A7-A7v.

I must confess, after all that next the Scripture Poems,
there are none so savoury to me, as Mr. *George Herbert*'s,
and Mr. *George Sandys*'s. (1) I know that *Cooley* (2) and
others far excel *Herbert* in Wit and accurate composure.
But (as *Seneca* takes with me above all his Contemporaries,
because he speaketh *Things* by *words*, *feelingly* and *seriously*, like a man that is past jest, so) *Herbert* speaks
to God like one that *really believeth a God*, and whose
business in the world is most *with God*. *Heart-work* and
Heaven-work make up his Books.

Notes

1   Sandys's poetical labours include in particular a trans-
    lation of Ovid's 'Metamorphoses' (1626). But Baxter is
    alluding to Sandys's versification of the Psalms (1636)
    and other biblical books (1638).
2   I.e. Abraham Cowley.

30.   JOHN DRYDEN, FROM 'MAC FLECKNOE'

1682

Dryden's 'Mac Flecknoe', first published in 1682 but probably written some four years earlier, terminates its counsel to his rival Shadwell with an unmistakable allusion to
Herbert's poetry. The relevant lines (203-10) confirm the
advent of the novel attitudes already intimated by Hobbes
(No. 15). See also above, pp. 12-13.

Thy Genius calls thee not to purchase fame
In keen Iambicks, but mild Anagram:
Leave writing Plays, and chuse for thy command
Some peacefull Province in Acrostick Land.
There thou maist wings display, and Altars raise,
And torture one poor word Ten thousand ways.
Or if thou would'st thy diff'rent talents suit,
Set thy own Songs, and sing them to thy lute.

31. WILLIAM WINSTANLEY, FROM 'THE LIVES OF THE MOST
FAMOUS ENGLISH POETS'

1687

The compiler Winstanley was essentially a journalist - 'of
the lower classes of our biographers', it has been said.
The brief entries in his 'Lives of the most Famous English
Poets' are largely derivative. His account of Herbert was
copied - 'as usual', says Nethercot (I, p. 187) - from
Edward Phillips (No. 26); yet it is reprinted here since
it contributed much to the dissemination of Herbert's
reputation. See also above, p. 12.
    Source: Winstanley, 'The Lives of the most Famous Eng-
lish Poets' (1687), pp. 160-1.

Mr. GEORGE HERBERT.

    This divine Poet and person was a younger brother of
the Noble Family of the *Herberts* of *Montgomery*, whose florid wit, obliging humour in conversation, fluent Elocution, and great proficiency in the Arts, gained him that
reputation at *Oxford*, (1) where he spent his more youthful
Age, that he was chosen University Orator, a place which
required one of able parts to Mannage it; at last, taking
upon him Holy Orders, not without special Encouragement
from the King, who took notice of his Extraordinary Parts,
he was made Parson of *Bemerton* near *Salisbury,* where he
led a Seraphick life, converting his Studies altogether to
serious and Divine Subjects; which in time produced those
his so generally known and approved Poems entituled, 'The
Temple'.

    Whose Vocal notes tun'd to a heavenly Lyre,
    Both learned and unlearned all admire.

    I shall only add out of his Book an Anagram, which he
made on the name of the Virgin *Mary*.

            M A R Y.
            A R M Y.
    And well her name an Army doth present,
    In whom the Lord of Hosts did pitch his Tent.

Note

1 Actually, Cambridge.

32. JOHN DUNTON (?), FROM THE 'ATHENIAN MERCURY'

1694

The 'Athenian Mercury', a journal of the last decade of
the seventeenth century, tended to praise Herbert as a
matter of course. Its editor, John Dunton, is known to
have admired Herbert and may have been the author of
nearly all the encomiastic references to the poet. The ensuing remarks are in response to a reader who noticed the
journal's partiality for Herbert ('You have on several
Occasions, and sometimes I think without any, commended
Herbert's Poetry') and who quoted a few lines from Christopher Harvey's 'The Synagogue' in order to protest
'whether you have not notoriously betray'd your want of
Judgment in commending such Stuff as this to the Perusal
of your Reader'.
     Source: the 'Athenian Mercury', vol. 12, no. 22, 6 Janu-
ary 1694.

Mr. *Herbert*'s Reputation is so firmly and so justly establish'd among all Persons of *Piety* and *Ingenuity*, his Sense
so good, and most of his Poetry so fine, that those who
Censure him will be in more danger of having their Judgments question'd, than such as with good reason Admire
him. Nor can the Time he writ in, when Poetry was not near
so refin'd as 'tis now, be justly objected against him, so
as to make his Works of small or no Value, any more than
the *oddness* or *flatness* of some Expressions and Phrases,
since something of these are to be found in all other
Compositions that have yet appear'd in our Language; and
besides this, they were probably many of 'em made to
Tunes, Mr. *Herbert* being so great a Musitian, which every
one knows will often weaken the Sense. For 'The Synagogue',
all know 'tis none of his, tho' there are many fine
Thoughts, and not a few good Lines in't, carrying all thro'
in an Air and Spirit of great *Sense, Piety* and *Devotion*,
much more Valuable than all the foolish Wit that has so
often directed the World at so dear a Rate.

33.   DANIEL BAKER, 'ON MR. GEORGE HERBERT'S SACRED POEMS,
CALLED, THE TEMPLE'

1697

Baker's lengthy tribute to Herbert demonstrates, it has
been said, 'how far separated the reputation and actual
influence of Herbert could be' (Summers, p. 16; the poem
is also quoted by Leach, pp. 62-3). See also above, p. 13.
   Source: Baker, 'Poems upon Several Occasions' (1697),
pp. 83-9.

On Mr. George Herbert's *Sacred Poems, called, The Temple.*

I.

So long had Poetry possessed been
By Pagans, that a Right in her they claim'd,
   Pleaded Prescription for their Sin,
And Laws they made, and Arguments they fram'd,
Nor thought it Wit, if God therein was nam'd:
The true GOD; for of false ones they had store,
   Whom Devils we may better call,
   And ev'ry thing they deifi'd,
And to a Stone, Arise and help they cri'd.
   And Woman-kind they fell before;
Ev'n Woman-kind, which caus'd at first their Fall,
Were almost the sole Subject of their Pen,
And the chief Deities ador'd by fond and sottish Men.

II.

   Herbert at last arose,
   Herbert inspir'd with holy Zeal,
Their Arguments he solv'd, their Laws he did repeal,
   And Spight of all th'enraged Foes
That with their utmost Malice did oppose,
He rescu'd the poor Captive, Poetry,
Whole her vile Masters had before decreed
All her immortal Spirit to employ
   In painting out the Lip or Eye
Of some fantastick Dame, whose Pride Incentives did not
                                                   need.

This mighty *Herbert* could not brook;
It griev'd his pious Soul to see

        The best and noblest Gift,
          That God to Man has left,
Abus'd to serve vile Lust, and sordid Flattery:
So, glorious Arms in her Defence he took;
And when with great Success he'd set her free,
He rais'd her fancy on a stronger Wing,
Taught her of God above, and Things Divine to sing.

                    III.

Th' infernal Powers that held her fast before
And great Advantage of their Pris'ner made,
          And drove of Souls a gainful Trade,
          Began to mutiny and roar.
So when *Demetrius* and his Partners (1) view'd
Their Goddess, and with her, their dearer Gains to fall,
They draw together a confus'd Multitude,
          And into th' Theater they crowd,
And great *Diana*, great, they loudly call.
          Up into th' Air their Voices flie,
          Some one thing, some another crie,
          And most of them they know not why.
They crie aloud, 'till the Earth ring again,
          Aloud they crie; but all in vain.
Diana down must go; They can no more
Their sinking Idol help, than she could them before.
Down she must go with all her Pomp and Train:
The glorious Gospel-Sun her horned Pride doth stain,
No more to be renew'd, but ever in the Wane;
And Poetry, now grown Divine above must ever reign.

                    IV.

    A Mon'ment of this Victory
Our *David*, our Sweet Psalmist, rais'd on high,
When he this Giant under foot did tread,
And with Verse, his own Sword, cut off the Monster's
                                          Head.
For as a Sling and Heav'n-directed Stone
Laid flat the *Gathite* Champion, who alone
Made Thousands tremble, while he proudly stood
Bidding Defiance to the Hosts of God:
So fell th' infernal Pow'rs before the Face
Of mighty *Herbert*, who upon the Place
          A Temple built, that does outdo
          Both *Solomon*'s, and *Herod*'s too,
And all the Temples of the Gods by far;
So costly the Materials, and the Workmanship so rare

A Temple built, as God did once ordain
    Without the Saw's harsh Noise
Or the untuneful Hammer's Voice, (2)
But built with sacred Musick's sweetest strain,
Like *Theban* Walls of old, as witty Poets feign.

V.

Hail, heav'nly Bard, to whom great LOVE has giv'n
    (His mighty Kindness to express)
To bear his Three mysterious Offices;
Prophet, and Priest on Earth thou wast, and now a King
                                         in Heav'n.
        There thou dost reign, and there
        Thy Bus'ness is the same 'twas here,
And thine old Songs thou singest o'er agen:
    The Angels and the Heav'nly Quire
        Gaze on thee, and admire
To hear such Anthems from an earthly Lyre,
Their own Hymns almost equall'd by an human Pen.
    We foolish Poets hope in vain
    Our Works Eternity shall gain:
    But sure those Poems needs must die
    Whose Theme is but Mortality.
Thy wiser and more noble Muse
    The best, the only way did chuse
To grow Immortal: For what Chance can wrong,
    What Teeth of Time devour that Song
Which to a Heav'nly Tune is set for glorifi'd Saints to
                                         use?
O may some Portion of thy Spirit on me
(Thy poor Admirer) light, whose Breast
By wretched mortal Loves hath been too long possest!
When, Oh! when will the joyful Day arise
    That rescu'd from these Vanities,
    These painted Follies I shall be,
If not an inspir'd Poet, yet an holy Priest like thee.

Notes

1 'Acts 19.24 ff.' (author's marginal note).
2 '1 Kings 6.7' (author's marginal note).

34.   ANONYMOUS, FROM THE PREFACE TO 'SELECT HYMNS, TAKEN
OUT OF MR. HERBERT'S TEMPLE'

1697

Thirty-two poems from 'The Temple' were collected in 1697
as congregational hymns appropriate to the services of the
nonconformists known as Dissenters. If liberties had to
be taken with the metrics of each poem, the amendments to
Herbert's diction are not nearly as pronounced as they
were to be in the subsequent adaptations by Wesley and
others. Thematically, however, the very choice of some
poems at the expense of others transformed Herbert into a
hymnographer whom nonconformists could regard - in the
words of the preface to the collection - as 'Our Divine
Poet'. See further above, p. 14.
     Source: from 'Select Hymns, Taken out of Mr. Herbert's
Temple, And Turn'd into the Common Metre. To be Sung in
the Tunes Ordinarily us'd in Churches' (1697), sigs A2-A3;
reproduced from the facsimile of the Augustan Reprint
Soviety, with an introduction by William E. Stephenson
(Los Angeles, 1962).

Mr. Herbert's *Poems* have met with so general and deserv'd
Acceptance, that they have undergone Eleven Impressions
near Twenty Years ago: He hath obtain'd by way of Emi-
nency, the Name of *Our Divine Poet*, and his Verses have
been frequently quoted in Sermons and other Discourses;
yet, I fear, few of them have been Sung since his Death,
the Tunes not being at the Command of ordinary Readers.
     This attempt therefore, (such as it is) is to bring so
many of them as I well could, which I judg'd suited to the
Capacity and Devotion of Private Christians, into the
Common Metre to be Sung in their Closets or Families....
     How much more fit is *Herbert's 'Temple'* to be set to
the Lute, than *Cowley's 'Mistress'*! It is hard that no
one can be taught Musick, but in such wanton Songs as fill
the Hearts of many Learners with Lust and Vanity all their
Days. Why should it be thought a greater Prophaning of
Spiritual Songs to use them in a Musick-Scool, than it is
of the New Testament, to teach Children to spell; yet what
Christian would not rather have his Child taught to read
in a Bible than in a Play-Book? Especially, when they who
learn Musick as generally more apt to receive Impressions
from the Matter of the Song, than Children are from the
Books in which they first learn to Spell. My attempt hath
been easie, only to alter the measures of some Hymns,

keeping strictly to the Sence of the Author; But how noble
an undertaking were it, if any one could and would rescue
the high flights, and lofty strains found in the most
Celebrated Poets, from their sacrilegious Applications to
Carnal Love, and restore them to the *Divine Love*! When
the Devil drew off the Nations from the True God, He
caus'd the same Institutions with which God was honoured,
to be used in the Idol Service, *Temple*, *Priests*, *Sacrifices*, &c. and amongst the rest *Psalmody*: And it is
strange, that when we have so long been emerg'd out of
Heathenism, that such a Remnant of it should be amongst
us, wherein the most devotional Part of Religion doth consist.

Almost all Phrases and Expressions of Worship due only
to God, are continu'd in these artificial Composures in
the Heathenish use of them even from the *inspirations* that
they invoke in their beginning, to the *Raptures*, *Flames*,
Adorations, &c. That they pretend to in the Progress: Nor
are these meer empty Names with them, but their Hearts are
more fervently carried out in the musical use of them,
than they would be if their Knees were bow'd to *Baal* and
Astaroth: Few Holy Souls are more affected with the
Praises of a Redeemer, than they are of the wanton Object
that they profess to adore. Oh for some to write *Parodies*,
by which Name I find one Poem in *Herbert* call'd, which
begins, *Souls Joy, where art thou gone*, and was, I doubt
not, a light Love-song turn'd into a Spiritual Hymn.
Παρωδία, *Est quum alterius Poetae Versus in aliud Argumen-
tum transferuntur*. (1) I do not find it hath been made a
Matter of scruple to turn the Temples built for Idols into
Churches: And as to this Case, it is to be consider'd that
the Musick and Poetry was an excellent Gift of God, which
ought to have been us'd for Him; and that their high
strains of Love, Joy, &c. Suit none but the adorable
Saviour; and all their most warm and affecting Expressions
are stollen from the Churches Adoration of Christ; and who
can doubt but the Church may take her own, whereever she
finds it, whether in an Idolatrous Mass-Book or Prophane
Love-song? It was a noble Resolution of him (2) that
said,

I'll Consecrate my Magdalene *to Thee* -

The *Eyes, Mouth, Hair*, which had been abus'd to Lust
and Vanity were us'd to *Wash, Kiss, Wipe* the feet of a
Saviour: May Man and Angels Praise him for ever and ever!
Amen.

Notes

1 '*Parodia* is when the verses of one poet are applied to
   another theme.' This was the standard definition of
   the term, as by Camerarius.
2 I.e. Crashaw.

35. THOMAS WHITE, 'YOUTH'S ALPHABET: OR, HERBERT'S
MORALS'

ante 1702

The first edition of White's 'Little Book for Little
Children' (1671?) was, sometime on its way to a twelfth
edition (1702), expanded to include the following recita-
tion of Herbert's 'morals'. The oddest invocation of the
poet on record, it is a collection of doggerel verses that
occasionally resort to Herbert - as in the oft-quoted
opening verses (from 'The Church-porch', ll. 5-6) and
again under 'T' (ibid., ll. 35-6) - but habitually provide
the author's own attempts at poetry. As early editions
of White's labours are not extant, the present text is
reproduced from the edition of 1702. See also above,
p. 12.
   Source: White, 'A Little Book for Little Children:
Wherein are set down Several Directions for Little Children', 12th edn (1702), pp. 91-3.

Youth's Alphabet: or, Herbert's Morals.

A Verse may find him who a Sermon flies,
And turn delight into a Sacrifice.

A

Awful Revere is unto Kings most due,
For they're our Fathers, and our Country's too.

B

Be well *advised*, and wary Counsel make,
E're thou dost *any* action undertake.

C

Children that make their Parents hearts to Bleed,
May live t'have Children to revenge that deed.

D

Dare to be true, nothing can need a lie;
A fault which needs it most, grows two thereby.

E

Eclips'd the Sun! Earth quakes! Vail rents! dark sky!
Nature must needs be sick, when God can die.

F

First worship God; he that forgets to *Pray*,
Bids not himself *Good morrow*, nor *Good day*.

G

Great God I am thy Tabor, (1) thou my Sun,
From thee, the spring of light my Light begin.

H

How dar'st thou sin in *secret*? *God* doth *see*,
And will alone thy Judge and Jury be.

I

I never yet could read, nor hear of any
Undone by Hearing, but by Speaking many.

K

Kneeling ne're spoil'd silk stocking: quite thy State,
All equal are within the Churches Gate.

L

Live Jesus live, and let it ever be,
My *Life* to live, yea *die*, for love of thee.

M

Make not thy sport abuses; for the Fly
That feeds on Dirt is coloured thereby.

N

None is so wasteful as the scraping dame,
She loseth three for one, her Soul, Rest, Fame.

O

O my dear God, tho I am clean forgot,
Let me not love thee if I love thee not.

P

Premediate (2) your speeches, words once flown,
Are in the hearers power, not your own.

Q

Quaint wits, with words, my Posie windows fill;
Less than least mercies is my Posie still.

R

Reach Heav'n thou canst not here; how e're aspire,
And climb, if not in deed, yet in desire.

S

Swear not: An *Oath* is like a dangerous *Dart*
Which shot, rebounds to strike the shooters heart.

T

The *Drunkard* forfeits Man; and doth *divest*
All worldly *Right*, save what he hath by *Beast*.

U

Under that Stone, where Christ once laid his head,
The *Grave* it self doth now lie *buried*.

W

Worst Preachers speak *some* good; if all want sence,
God takes a Text, and preaches *Patience*.

X

Xerxes forbare to last the *Seas*; for *they*
Thy *proud* commands, and threats scorn to obey.

Y

Your *prudent* workmen never do refuse
The *meanest* Tool that they may chance to use.

Z

Zeal, thou shalt be my *Charrot*, (3) Whilest I ride,
Elijah like, with Word and Spirit, my Guide.

To get and fix these Rules of Memory,
There needs no art but this, mind ABC.

Notes

1 Drum. The reference may also be to Mount Tabor.
2 Consider in advance.
3 Chariot (as in 2 Kings 2.11).

Herbert in the Eighteenth Century

36. JOSEPH ADDISON, FROM THE 'SPECTATOR'

1711

Addison's celebrated discourse on wit extended over a
week's issues of the 'Spectator' ('I dare promise my self,
if my Readers will give me a week's Attention, that this
great City will be very much changed for the better by
next *Saturday* Night'). The mention of Herbert in the
first issue, which was devoted to false wit, confirmed
the gathering disapprobation of the poet that would linger
throughout the eighteenth century. See also above, p. 14.
Source: 'Spectator', no. LVIII (7 May 1711).

The first Species of false Wit which I have met with is
very venerable for its Antiquity, and has produced several
Pieces which have lived very near as long as the 'Iliad'
it self: I mean those short Poems printed among the minor
Greek Poets, which resemble the Figure of an Egg, a Pair
of Wings, an Ax, a Shephard's Pipe, and an Altar. (1) As
for the first, it is a little oval Poem, and may not improperly be called a Scholar's Egg. I would endeavour to
hatch it, or, in more intelligible language, to translate
it into *English*, did not I find the Interpretation of it
very difficult; for the Author seems to have been more
intent upon the Figure of his Poem, than upon the Sense
of it....
    It was impossible for a Man to succeed in these Per-
formances that was not a kind of Painter, or at least a
Designer: He was first of all to draw the Out-line of the
Subject which he intended to write upon, and afterwards
conform the Description to the Figure of his Subject. The

149

Poetry was to contract or dilate itself according to the
Mould in which it was cast. In a Word, the Verses were to
be cramped or extended to the Dimensions of the Frame that
was prepared for them; and to undergo the Fate of those
Persons whom the Tyrant *Procrustes* used to lodge in his
Iron Bed; if they were too short he stretched them on a
Rack, and if they were too long chopped off a Part of
their Legs, till they fitted the Couch which he had pre-
pared for them....
    This fashion of false Wit was revived by several Poets
of the last Age, and in particular may be met with among
Mr. *Herbert*'s Poems; and if I am not mistaken, in the
Translation of *Du Bartas*.... (2)

Notes

1   The practice was even more widespread than Addison sug-
    gests. Thomas Parnell in 'An Essay on the Different
    Stiles of Poetry' (1713), p. 3, generalised more
    accurately about the numerous poems

        Where *Wings* by *Fancy* never feather'd fly,
        Where *Lines* by measure form'd in *Hatchets* lie;
        Where *Altars* stand, erected *Porches* gape
        And Sense is cramp'd while Words are par'd to shape.

    As he added in a note, 'These and the like Conceits of
    putting Poems into several Shapes by the different
    Lengths of Lines, are frequent in old Poets of most
    Languages.'
2   Guillaume de Salluste du Bartas's 'Deuine Weekes and
    Workes', translated by Joshua Sylvester (1605 ff.).

37. GEORGE RYLEY, FROM 'MR HERBERT'S TEMPLE ... EXPLAINED
& IMPROVED'

1714/15

While the attitudes represented by Addison were hardening
into dogma, lesser figures continued to read Herbert even
as they articulated their increasing disquiet over his
'obscurity'. The best evidence in this respect is provided by George Ryley, about whom nothing is known beyond
the elaborate annotations he compiled on 'The Temple'

midway through the second decade of the eighteenth century. As the ensuing representative selections from his
considerable manuscript attest, Herbert's ethical aspects
were not questioned but his actual meaning was deemed to
require explication in depth. See further above, p. 18.

Source: Ryley, 'Mr Herbert's Temple & Church Militant
Explained & Improved By A Discourse upon Each Poem Critical & Practical', in Bodleian MS Rawlinson D.199, fols 22-3,
33-4, 69, 71-2, 164-5, 187-9, 244-6; selections reprinted
(with minor adjustments) from Köppl, pp. 85, 104-6,
114-15, 128, 129-31, 140-1, 148-9.

The Church

We Now Come to the Body of the Church. This is the
Title given to all the Rest of the Poems, Except two.
In the generall we have in these Poems a description of the
Disposition of a Sound Member of the Church; which is the
Body of Christ. there does not appear Any Exact Method in
the Poems; But a Variety of Contemplations, & private
Ejaculations.

He contemplates 1. on the *Altar*.

The altar A Broken ALTAR &c - to the End

As we [Christians] have Sacrifices to offer to god, of
Prayer, & praise, so we have Each of us an *altar*, of Gods
appointment, upon which we are to offer. This *altar* is
the heart: of which that, whose pattern was given to Moses
in the Mount, Exod. 20.24.24.26 was a *Shaddow*, or type:
which was Not to be of Hewn Stone, nor raised high: which
Intimates that the heart must be a *Broken heart*, & a
humble heart: & Such an Altar Most holy. Exod. 29.37.
Now Such a one is here Dedicated to god. it is 1. *A Broken
Altar*. Broken for Sin. &c by the Power of God. *Nothing
but thy power can Cut*. 2. It is a Cemented heart. put
togeather that Each part may Join to praise God. 3. the
Cement is *tears*. the tears of Repentance. a Contrite heart,
& Such a one may with boldness be offered to god: for Such
he will not despise. ps: 51.17 4. it is Unhewen heart. we
must disclaim any power of our own to frame a penitent
heart; for repentance is the *gift of God*. Act 5.31 *No
workmans tool has touched it*. Ministers may be Instrumental to cleanse, but Can never Modifie the heart of Man.

2. here is the Ground of this Dedication. That if our
tounges Should fail, att any time, to Express the praise
of God; his praise may Still be, like the Continual Burnt
offering, in the heart.

3. Here is the prayer upon the Dedication. *o let* &c
Solomon, Att the Dedication of the Temple; did pray: & a
christians dedication of himself to god, that first fruit
of Conversion, is allways attended with prayer. *behold he*
prayeth. Act: 9.11 He prays 1. for an interest in God
Sacrifice. the Lord Jes: Christ. 2. for the Sanctification of what he here Dedicates to god. I am Loath to
think he here Intimates that Justification allways pre-
cedes Sanctification. As Sanctification is a progressive
work, it's Certain Justification procedes Some Degrees of
it: But they allways go togeather, whom he Called, them he
also Justified. Rom. 8.30 (tho' it may be he does)....

Redemption.

Having been &c - *to the End* - Man is God's *Tenant*; as he
is his Creature, his Capacity, & Enjoyments, are his
Tenure. for as the *SS* (1) says, his *Talents.* for the
Product of which he is accountable to his Landlord. He is
also a Lease-Tenant for Life; oblidged to hold the tene-
ment, & account for the Profitts of it, as Long as he
lives. The 1st Lease this great Landlord gave to Man, his
Tenant; was the Covenant of works: by which man was bound
to yeild all the profitts of the Land to his Landlord's
use; the Condition being *he that doth them Shall live in*
them, & *the Soul that Sinneth Shall dye.* Man breaking the
Articles of this, once, rendered himself, for Ever, in-
Capable of retrieving that Loss; or of keeping them for
the future; so by these articles he could never *thrive*;
that is Never be *Justified.* *But what the Law* (that is
this Law of works) could not do God, Sending his own Son,
&c hath wrought for us: that is our Redemption: Making us
free from the Law of Sin, & death; & granting us a New
Lease *Small rented lease.* This was purchased for us by, &
granted us att, the Death of Christ. These premises will
lead us into the plain Sence of this Poem: in which the
Poet takes a Scope of tho't. putting himself into the
place of the 3^{d} tenant, & Supposing him Self, upon tryal,
to have found himself incapable of being Justified by the
deeds of the Law: Upon which he resolves to address his
Landlord, for Such a Lease, that is Such articles, by
which he may Attain a Righteousness before him. He goes,
& finds him, in the person of Christ, upon the Cross; &
there obtains his desire. Note. we Must Not hence Imagine that man had any hand in Contriving his Redemption: it
passed the Understanding of Angells; as well as men, & *in*
it God has abounded to us in all wisdom, & prudence, as
well as *grace.* Eph: 1.8. But this way of thinking, or

Supposing man, upon reflecting on his undone State.   By
Nature, & att a Loss to know how he may attain a Remedy,
is Justified from that of the Apostle Rom. 9.24. *when the
Commandment Came, Sin revived, & I dyed. o wretched Man!
who Shall deliver me?*....

Jordan.

There are 2 poems under this Title.... There is Some
Difficulty in Reconcileing the Titles with the Subject
matter of the Poems. Each Poem is an Invective against
Dark Poetry; which, by figure, &c., render the Sence of
the Poem, & the Drift of the Author obscure; & to Common
Ears Unintelligible. I am ready to Say the Author has, in
these, Lash't himself; by prefixing a title, that Either
is, or, att Least, is to me very obscure. to Attempt it –
It is the known property of Jordan to overflow it's Banks,
all the time of harvest. Josh: 3.15. thereby flooding
those Neibouring Lands, which should, att that time, be
cloathed with fruit: & making it Impossible to gather it.
so Dark poetry [or Any Dark Discourses] is A Jordan: that
is, flooded Sence: which we must Dive (it may be Deep)
for, before we can obtain it. Such as this our Author
here inveighs against.
   ...3 things are here reprov'd, as the common faults of
Poets. Falshood. obscurity. & Prophaneness; I have often
tho't it a pity that, Even in our Ages, in which we, so
Justly, boast of refined Invention, where in .all parts of
Literature are so much Improved; poëtry Should still be
fettered with the Awkward, fictitious, Historys of the
Heathens; & no one can be thot to write with the Air of a
poet, but he that Interlards his lines with Storys of
Jupiter, & mars, & Venus, & Cupid, &c, with the Roman
Hero's, or Trojan Exploits. Surely these Historys better
became those days of Ignorance. we, that have Such noble
Subjects, as Divine revealation affords, might look as
well, if we choose *these*, to Imploy our witt about. Are
they not full as Copious, nay I had allmost said much
more? For they are the Spring, these Prophane historys,
it's streams: as is well observed by *Dr Grew cosmol: Sacr:
Integr: of the Heb. Code)* (2) tis true the Strength of
fancy, & plenitude of tho't, in the old heathen writers,
such as Homer, Horace, Virgill, ovid, &c, is amasingly
fine; & deserves Imitation, in our Age: but we Should
think it a disparagement to our Litterati, not to allow
them, who have Stood upon their Shoulders, to be as polite
as they. We boast of the learning, & improvements, of the
present day; & say no age Ever produc't Such Virtuosi: &

I'm Sure no age could Ever boast more noble Subjects, than
the Divine in their Lustre att this day. but how few have
appeared in the Dress of Divine poëts, that are truely
qualified with a *Native genius* for it! Herbert, & Milton,
& a few Short handed ones, (3) have grac't the Stage; Such
as Reinolds, (4) &c, yet there is room Enough for more:
what might we have promised our Selves, if, Dryden,
Rochester, [Nahum] Tate, [Thomas?] Brown, & many more, that
have been, not only translaters, but Authors of the finest
tho'ts in another dress, had applyed themselves to Divine
Subjects, in Stead of either indifferent, or Immoral ones:
'tis indeed for a Lamentation. on the other hand, many have
appeared in the field of poësie, to treat of Divine Subjects, so wretchedly poor, & flatt, that it has allmost
Nauseated politer Genius with not only their performances,
but the Subjects themselves. Surely, when men are most in
Earnest, in professing respect to Christianity, they, who
are so happy as to be blest with a Genius for it, will
appear to do Justice, in this way, to the best, most
Authentick, & most usefull Historys....

The British-Church.

The Title is the object of the Following Poem. viz: the
English Diocesan Church. And it's orderly way of worship,
according to it's Liturgy, is the Subject of it. The Sum
of this Lyes towards the Close; that it hits the Mean between the 2 Extreams of the Romish Gaïty, & the Geneva
Plainness. *In medio Consistit Virtus* is A Maxim that
Generally holds Good: & tho' in Matters of Religion, It
may Seem to Some out ot the way to talk of Mean, &
Extreams, while we have a *Sure word of Prophesy*, to Direct;
yet, in Specifick Circumstantials, which are not distinctly
determined there, It is certainly Best to keep a Mean: that
we neither Slip into *Sylla*, nor *Charybdis*; that we neither
are guilty of Judaical Superstition, Evidently opposed in
the Scripture; nor of willfull Sloveness, under the Colour
of the Symplicity of Christianity: But do all things
Decently, & In order. This Every true Son of the British
Church Believes his Carefull Mother has wisely provided
for. The Preface to the Liturgy is well worth Reading
here....

Time.

In Hieroglyphicks Time is Drawn like a Raw, Meagre,
Man; with a Sythe in his hand. His thinness Expresses his

Hunger; like Pharaoh's Lean kine, that Eat up with the
others: therefore He is Call'd *Edax Rerum* or a Universal
Devourer. And his Sythe Expresses His office, which is to
Mow down Every thing; Man is as grass, or a flower of the
field; which Time, Like the Husband man, Mows down. Now,
tho' this office be Awfull, yet Its' Delays Are Tedious to
them, who are sensible of the Advantage of Its' Execution.
To me to Dye is Gain, therefore I Long to Depart, And have
time Execute his office is the Language of all Good men,
that are not Att Uncertainties as to their future State....

(*Meeting with Time* &c to the End)

This Poem is A Dialogue Between the *Poet, & Time*.
    1. The Poet Complains to Time of the Dullness of his
Sythe; that is that he Loiters so Long, Ere he Come to Cutt
him of. The whole Creation Growns Under the Burden of his
Delays, & Every good man Espeacially Longs for the End of
time: when their Bodys Shall be Redeemed, & their Bliss
Consummated. (*vid Rom 8. 22, 23*)
    2. Time Answers. 1. He has Mowed So long, that it were
no wonder if his work Should Slacken. this 5000, & More,
years has time been Mowing Down the Ages of the world; (5)
which, like the fabulous Story of the Hydra, Still has had
more heads Sprung up, as he Cut down Any. *No marvell if
his Sythe Deserve Some Blame* 2. Yet there are not Many of
this Poets Mind. not one in twenty, but Could be glad if
he were more Slow. They that Are with out God, or without
hope, in the world, as Nineteen in twenty, it is to be
feared, are, choose wisely when they Say it is good to be
here. 3. The Poet Replys. That Possibly in the Antechris-
tian Age of the world, before Life, & Immortallity, were
bro't to Light by Christ, Men Might Esteem this Life as
Best; because then the Sythe was, as a Hatchet, to Cut
down, & Destroy, att Least for Any thing they could Discover. But Now Heaven is Discover'd. & Death, as the way
to it: Man Esteems himself A Debtor, that is oblidged to
Death, for Conveying him thither; where he will be better,
because Blest by God, who Commands the Blessing. Besides
this Should, one would think, quicken Time's Activity;
Since Now he is not Terrible; his Hatchet appears to be
but a *pruning knife*: And Himself *A Gardiner*: which Mends
all he Meddles with. nay he is now an *Usher*, A *Transplan-
ter*, to Convey the Soul above the Starres. Upon this He
passionately Exclaims upon the Loiterer. Complaining that
as this Life is A place of Distance; Time is A Detainer
from God. And the Best Enjoyments of Time will never
Compensate for this Wrong. Complaining of the Unaccountable

length of time. *of what Strange Length must that needs be
which Even Eternity Excludes*? which the Most Extended
Measure Cannot Describe.   Eternity ItSelf, which Exceeds
the Limits of all Conception, will give us no Idea of the
Length of Time.

3. Time Rejoins, in a pet; That This Extravagant Tho't
is but begging time: which he Cannot favour: & rather hin-
ders his prosecution of his work; which he can't bear.
what do I here before his Door? why do I submit to be
Stop't in my Course by him, that att the Same time, pretended to Complain of my Slowness?...

It is A more proper use to be made of our Short Time to
fill it up with something that is good, than by useless,
Metaphysical, Harangues, to Trifle it away. for Time, tho
Tedious Enough, will not wait for Such Trifles....

The Collar.

The Title Lyes in the Last 2 lines. A Collar is a badge of
our obligation to Serve the Master that putts it on:
therefore the Negroes, & Such as are bound for life
to their Masters do ordinarily wear them.   A Christian is
bound to the Lord as Long as He Lives: And the Collar his
Lord putts on him is *my Child*: which Decyphers the Relation, in which he Stands to him. we Must Carry it to God
as Children to a father; Reverently; & Consult his honour,
& Interest, faithfully: must fear him with a *filial fear*,
for this He justly Claims.   And as it Decyphers the Relation so it proclaims the Protection of him that wears it.
He that is faithfull to God, as a Child to his Father,
will find God faithfull to him, as a father to his Child:
he will pity his weaknesses. *ps: 103:13* provide for his
wants.   *Jer:31.9. I will cause them to walk by the Rivers
of waters, - for I am a father to Israel* & give them a
portion.   *I will receive you, & be a father Unto you.
2. Cor: 6.17, 18.*   And He that is aware of this will admit
the Claim; & Echo Back his Sence of Duty. *My Lord!* whose
I am! & whom I will Serve! *however flesh Repine*!

(*I Struck the Board* &c to the End)

we have here a full Representation of the Ravings of a
Roving heart; weary, & Resolved to get Rid, of Christ's
Easy yoke.   He Represents Religion as a Dull, whining,
Confinement; which, while Attended upon, Debarres of that
Liberty, & Enjoyment, others take.   Thus he goes on, with-
out Interuption, in this Retreating soliloquy, 'till the
Last Line but one; where God by his Spirit, Interrupts, &

Claims a Right. which is Immediately Comply'd with.
observe here
   1. A Heavy Charge bro't against Religion's Exercises.
1. As Consisting only in Sighs, & groans, & pineing, &
fettering his feet; which would Naturally walk att
Large. *my Lines, that is the way Nature has described for
me, & Life are free*, &c that is open, without Interruption.
& Loose as the wind, which blows where it listeth, & gives
no account of it's Course to any one. *And Large as Store*;
that is full of Enjoyment, free to take it's fill of what
Ever it meets with which is Entertaining.   2. As only
filling with, never fulfilling our Expectation. *Shall I
be still in Suit*? that is pursuit? & never reach the Game?
3. As wounding the Spirit by its fruit. The Apostle says
the fruit of Righteousness is Sown in Peace. Jam: 3. ult
Here the Unsincere, or backsliding, wretch says *it's a
thorn to wound without Remedy*. Indeed Conscience will in
Such persons wound, not only as a Thorn, but as an Arrow.
   2. A Retreating Reflexion upon his Libertine Life. *Is
the year only lost to me?* q:d: 'Before I must turn Religi-
oso, I neither wanted wine, nor Corn; that is a heart to
take my fill of both: but now I must Look on the wind,
when it gives it's Colour *in the Cup. pro: 23:31. Now I
must Set a knife to my throat. v: 2. So is the year*, that
is the Product of the year, *Lost to me*. And is it quite
Lost? No. It is but fled, & is yet Recoverable. *There is
fruit, & thou has hands*; that is A naturall power to take
it: therefore take thy fill, *Recover all thy Sigh-blown
age on Double Pleasures*. Confine thy Mind no more to Gods
Law; *Despute No longer what is fit, & not fit*; break thro'
this poor, Confinement, & live att Large: break that
feeble, Incontinguous, *Rope of Sands*, that thy fance made
Able to bind thee, & lead thee blindfold. This is the Sad
advise he gives his Naughty heart. to which that as Readily
Replys *'I will abroad* I will carefully get loose, & take my
Liberty.' To this he Rejoins, to Confirm the former advice,
'Call in thy Death's head.' so basely is one of the Strongest Arguments for Religion Perverted to It's Damage.
Emblems of Mortallity Should be powerfull Enticements to a
preparation for Death; but here it is Improved to a quite
Contrary purpose. & Since Life is Short, I'll have a merry
one. *'Let us Eat, & drink*, without fear, or Care, *for to
Morrow we dye*. He that forbears to gratifie his Appetite
Deserves his Load; Deserves to be Still Confin'd to Sighs
& groans.'
   3. A Check to all this Raving. *As I grew more fierce,
& wild, at Every word, me thoughts, I heard one Calling
Child!* God Claims, & he Replys. *My Lord!* God Claims *my
Child*; not *my Slave*. his Service is no Drudgery, no

Melancholly work: & they that hear that, & are Convinced
of it's Truth, as they will be, who hearken to God Speaking by his Spirit, will Readily See all the former Cavils
Answer'd; And Embrace his work, which is perfect freedom.

Notes

1   I.e., the Holy Scriptures. See Matthew 25.14-30.
2   Nehemiah Grew, 'Cosmologia sacra' (1701), Bk IV, Ch. I,
    'Of the Integrity of the Hebrew Code'.
3   Possibly a reference to poets given to the epigrammatic
    style.
4   Possibly John Reynolds (d. 1614), author of a collec-
    tion of religious epigrams.
5   The length of time mentioned is dictated by the common
    belief that the world was created c. 4000 BC.

38.   GILES JACOB, FROM 'AN HISTORICAL ACCOUNT OF ...
ENGLISH POETS'

1720

Jacob's several compilations on literary and legal subjects
led Pope to hail him in 'The Dunciad' as 'the scourge of
Grammar' and the 'blunderbuss of Law' (III, 149-50). His
'Poetical Register' (1719), devoted in its entirety to
dramatic poets, was followed a year later by a companion
volume devoted to non-dramatic poets. The latter volume,
cast like its predecessor in the form of a comprehensive
biographical dictionary, encompasses Herbert under the ensuing entry. See also above, p. 15.
    Source: Jacob, from 'An Historical Account of the Lives
and Writings of our most Considerable English Poets'
(1720), pp. 73-4.

The Reverend Mr, GEORGE HERBERT

This Gentleman was a Younger Brother of the Noble Family
of the *Herberts* of *Montgomery*, now Earls of *Pembroke*. A
Family that has been blest with Men of Remarkable Wisdom.
He was born in the Year 1593. and Educated at *Westminster*
School, from whence he was Elected to *Trinity* College in
Cambridge; and being a Person of great Wit, Learning and

Eloquence, he was at length chosen University Orator. He
for some time followed the Court, and his great Abilities
and Polite Behaviour recommended him to the favour of King
James; but at last he entered into Orders, and had conferred on him the Living of *Bemerton* near *Salisbury* in
Wiltshire, wher he spent the remainder of his Life in
Retirement, and the Heavenly Studies of Divine Poetry.
His Works are printed in one Volume 12*mo*. Intitled, 'The
Temple: Sacred Poems, and Pious Ejaculations'. Which are
very much admired. And in the Year 1719. was Published
the Thirteenth Edition of them, they are Divided into
Three Parts 1. 'The Church-Porch'. 2. 'The Church'.
3. 'The Synagogue'. (1) And speaking of Poetry, in the
former he has this Couplet,

> A Verse may find him, who a Sermon flies,
> And turn Delight into a Sacrifice.
>> ['The Church-porch', 11. 5-6]

Note

1 This third 'part' of 'The Temple' is, in fact, the work
   of Christopher Harvey (see No. 8).

39. JOHN REYNOLDS, 'TO THE MEMORY OF THE DIVINE
MR. GEORGE HERBERT'

1725

Reynolds, a moderate dissenting minister, revised his
'Death's Vision' (1709) under the title 'A View of Death'
(1725), adding in particular the following lengthy tribute
to Herbert. A creditable if rather breathless poem, it is
an interpretation of Herbert in the light of distinctly
eighteenth-century premises (Summers, pp. 17-18). See
also above, p. 19.
    Source: Reynolds, from 'A View of Death' (1725), pp.
110-18. The volume also provides a Latin version of 'Mans
medley', 11. 19-24.

> To the Memory of the divine Mr. *George Herbert*,
> Author of the *Temple*.

SERAPHIC Singer! where's the fire
That did these lines and lays inspire?
B'ing dropt from heav'n, it scorn'd to dwell
Long upon earth, and near to hell!
The heart it purg'd, it did consume,
Exhal'd the sacrifice in fume,
And with it mounted, as of old
The angel, in the smoke enroll'd;
Return'd in haste, like thine own *Star*, (1)
Pleas'd with its prize, to native sphere.
But blest perfume, that here I find,
The sacrifice has left behind!
Strange! how each fellow-saint's surpris'd
To see himself anatomiz'd!
The *Sion*'s mourner breathes thy strains,
Sighs thee, and in thy notes complains;
Amaz'd, and yet refresh'd to see
His wounds, drawn to the life, in thee!
The warrior, just resolv'd to quit
The field, and all the toils of it,
Returns with vigour, will renew
The fight, with victory in view;
He stabbs his foes, and conquers harms,
With spear, and nails, and *Herbert*'s arms.
The racer, almost out of breath,
Marching through shades and vale of death,
Recruits, when he to thee is come,
And sighs for heav'n, and sings thy *Home*;
The tempted soul, whose thoughts are whirl'd,
About th' inchantments of the world,
Can o'er the snares and scandals skip,
Born up by *Frailty*, and the *Quip*;
The victor has reward paid down,
Has earnest here of life and crown;
The conscious priest is well releas'd
Of pain and fear, in *Aaron* drest;
The preaching envoy can proclaim
His pleasure in his *Master*'s name; (2)
A name, that like the grace in him,
Sends life and ease to ev'ry limb;
Rich magazine of health! where's found
Specific balm for ev'ry wound!

Hail rev'rend bard! hail thou, th' elected shrine
Of the great Sp'rit, and Shecinah (3) divine!
Who may speak thee! or aim at thy renown,
In lines less venerable than thy own!
Silent we must admire! upon no head
Has, since thy flight, been half thy unction shed.

What wit and grace thy lyric strains command!
Hail, great apostle of the muses land!
Scarce can I pardon the great *Cowley*'s claim,
He seems t' usurp the glories of thy fame; (4)
'Tis *Herbert*'s charms must chase (whate'er he boasts)
The fiends and idols from poetic coasts;
The *Mistress*, the *Anacreontic* lays, (5)
More demons will, and more disorders raise,
Than his fam'd hero's lyre, in modern play,
Or tun'd by Cowley's self, I fear, can lay;
'Tis *Herbert*'s notes must un-inchant the ear,
Make the deaf adder, and th' old serpent hear.

Soon had religion, with a gracious smile,
Vouchsaf'd to visit this selected isle;
The *British* emp'ror first her liv'ry wore,
And sacred cross with *Roman* eagles bore;
The sev'ral states, at last, her empire own,
And swear allegiance to her rightful throne;
Only the muses lands abjure her sway,
They heathen still, and unconverted lay.
Loth was the prince of darkness to resign
Such fertiliz'd dominions, and so fine,
Herbert arose! and sounds the trumpet there,
He makes the muses land the seat of war,
The forts he takes, the squadrons does pursue,
And with rich spoils erects a *Temple* too;
A structure, that shall roofs of gold survive,
Shall *Solomonic* and *Mosaic* work out-live,
Shall stay to see the universal fire,
And only, with the temple of the world, expire.

Strange, the late bard should his devotion rear
At *Synagogue*, (6) when, lo! the *Temple*'s near!
Such sacrilege it were of old, t' espouse
The wandring tent, before the wondrous house;
The house, in which a southern queen might be
A sacrifice to art and ecstasie.
Poor poets thus ingeniously can prove
Their sacred zeal misguided as their love!

Go forth, saint-bard! exert thy conqu'ring hand!
Set up thy Temple through the muses land!
Down with the stage, its wanton scenes cashier,
And all the demons wont to revel there!
Great *Pan* must dy, his oracles be dumb,
Where'er thy temple and its flames shall come;
Convert the *Muses*, teach them how to be
Ambitious of the *Graces* companie;

Purge *Helicon*, and make *Parnassus* still
To send his vicious streams to *Sion*'s hill!
Thence banish all th' unhallow'd, tuneful men,
From *Homer*, down to the phantastic *Ben*! (7)
Baptize the future poets, and infuse
A sacred flame in all belov'd by muse!
Teach them the efforts of great *Shiloh*'s love, (8)
The anthems, and the melodies above!
Tell them what matter, and what theam's in store,
For sacred past'ral, and divine amour;
Shiloh himself would condescend so low,
To be a shepherd, and a bridegroom too.
What myst'ries in church militant there to,
Teach them to look, and soar, and sing like thee.
Here poesy's high birth, and glory shine,
'Tis here, that it, like other grace, we see
From glory differs only in degree!

Whilst to thy temple proselytes repair,
And offer, and inflame devotion there.
Whilst, on its pillars deep inscrib'd, thy name
Stands consecrated to immortal fame,
Do thou enjoy the rich resolves of *Love*,
The pleasures, the society above!
No more thou'lt tune thy lute unto a strain
That may with thee all day complain; (9)
No more shall sense of ill, and *Griefs* of time
Dis-tune thy viol, and disturb thy rhyme;
No more shall *Sion*'s wrongs and sorrows sharp,
Upon the willows hang thy trembling harp;
The wish'd-for sight, the dear perfection's gain'd
The *Longing*, and the *Search*, have now obtain'd;
On Sion's mount, join thou the blisful throng,
That here were skill'd in sacred love and song;
Consort with *Heman*, *Asaph*, (10) and the rest,
Akin to thee, in Temple-service blest;
Who all rejoyce thy lov'd access to see,
And ply their harps, no doubt, to welcome thee;
Music and Love triumph! and *Herbert*'s lyre,
Serenely sounds amidst th' harmonious quire!
There still, on *Love* in his own person, gaze,
Drink in the beams flow from his radiant face,
Still to thy harp chant forth th' immortal verse
Does *Love*'s exploits in foreign land rehearse,
Move him to hasten his return below,
That church, now mil'tant, may triumphant grow,
And all thy pros'lyte-bands may mount, and see
The Temple there, and all the scenes of joy, with thee.

Notes

1 'See the ode entitled, *The Star*' (author's note).   The
   ensuing references are to other poems by Herbert:
   'Sion', 'Home', 'Frailtie', 'The Quip', 'Aaron',
   'Love' (I and III), 'Grief', 'Longing', and 'The
   Search'.
2 Cf. 'The Odour': 'How sweetly doth *My Master* sound!',
   etc.
3 The visible manifestation of the Divine Majesty; also
   applied to Christ.
4 'Cowley, in the beginning of his *Davideis*, says, "But
   thou, eternal word, has sent forth me, / Th'apostle,
   to convert those worlds to thee"' (author's note).
5 'The Mistress: or ... Love-Verses' and 'Anacreontiques'
   are clusters of poems by Cowley.
6 'Cowley, taking no notice of Mr. *Herbert* (an ornament
   of the *British* church) writes an elegy for Mr. *Crashaw*,
   author of the *Synagogue* (usually bound up with *Herbert's Temple*)...' (author's note).   It will be noted
   that Harvey's 'Synagogue' (No. 8) is already fathered
   upon Crashaw.
7 I.e. Jonson.
8 A reference to Christ, originally the site of a
   tabernacle (Joshua 18.1, 1 Samuel 3.21, etc.).
9 From Herbert's 'Ephes. 4.30', 11. 20-1.
10 Musical composers (2 Chronicles 5.12, 35.15, etc.)
   Psalms 50 and 73-83 are ascribed to Asaph.

40. WILLIAM COWPER, FROM HIS 'MEMOIR OF THE EARLY LIFE'

c. 1752

The memoir of his early life that the notable poet Cowper
wrote was not published until 1816, sixteen years after his
death.   The episode he mentions occurred c. 1752 when he
was twenty-one years old ('a critical season of my life').
See also above, p. 15.
     Source: 'Memoir of the Early Life of William Cooper,
Esq. written by himself' (1816), pp. 9-10; reproduced from
the more authoritative version in 'The Letters and Prose
Writings of William Cowper', ed. James King and Charles
Ryskamp (Oxford, 1979), I, 8-9.

Day and night I was upon the rack, lying down in horrors
and rising in despair. I presently lost all relish to
those studies I had been closely attached to; the classics
had no longer any charm for me; I had need of something
more salutary than mere amusement, but had none to direct
me where to find it. At length with Herbert's poems,
gothic and uncouth as they were, I yet found in them a
strain of piety which I could not but admire. This was
the only author I had any delight in reading. I pored
upon him all day long and though I found not there what I
might have found, a cure for my malady, yet it never
seemed so much alleviated as while I was reading him.
At length I was advised by a very near and dear relation
to lay him aside, for he thought such an author was more
likely to nourish my melancholy than to remove it.

41. HENRY HEADLEY, FROM 'SELECT BEAUTIES OF ANCIENT
ENGLISH POETRY'

1787

The important collection of 'Select Beauties of Ancient
English Poetry' by the poet and critic Henry Headley
reprints but one of Herbert's poems, 'Church monuments',
and provides the ensuing sketch of the poet's life. See
also above, p. 20.
    Source: from 'Select Beauties of Ancient English
Poetry', ed. Henry Headley (1787), I, lvi.

GEORGE HERBERT,

A writer of the same class, (1) though infinitely inferior
to both Quarles and Crashaw. His poetry is a compound of
enthusiasm without sublimity, and conceit without either
ingenuity or imagination. The piece I have selected (2)
is perhaps the best in his book. When a name is once
reduced to the impartial test of time, when partiality,
friendship, fashion, and party, have withdrawn their
influence, our surprise is frequently excited by past
subjects of admiration that now cease to strike. He who
takes up the poems of Herbert would little suspect that he
had been public orator of an University, and a favourite
of his Sovereign; that he had received flattery and praise
from Donne and from Bacon; and that the biographers of the

day had enrolled his name amongst the first names of his
country. He was born at Montgomery Castle, in Wales,
April 5, 1593; elected from Westminster to Trinity College,
Cambridge; and afterwards prebendary of Lincoln, according
to some verses called 'A Memorial,' prefixed to his
'Temple.' He died about 1635. The additional poems,
intituled 'The Synagogue,' are attributed by Granger (3)
to Crashaw. But they are unworthy of him. The title of
Crashaw's Poems (4) might have been borrowed from Herbert.
- Herbert's Life has been written, with his usual trifling
minuteness, by honest Isaac Walton.

Notes

1 I.e. the 'metaphysical' poets generally.
2 'Church monuments', reprinted in the edition cited
   (II, 31-2).
3 James Granger, 'A Biographical History of England'
   (1769), I (ii), 393.
4 'Steps to the Temple' (No. 11).

Herbert in the Nineteenth Century

42. SAMUEL TAYLOR COLERIDGE, FROM 'BIOGRAPHIA LITERARIA',
'THE FRIEND', ETC.

1817 ff.

Coleridge effected the revival of interest in Herbert
single-handedly. As the comments printed here attest, the
achievement is the more remarkable because he was the first
to commend Herbert primarily on literary grounds. See
further above, pp. 20-1.

From 'Biographia Literaria' (1817), II, 98-9 (Ch. XIX)

Another exquisite master of this species of style, where
the scholar and the poet supplies the material, but the
perfect well-bred gentleman the expressions and the
arrangement, is George Herbert. As from the nature of the
subject, and the too frequent quaintness of the thoughts,
his 'Temple; or Sacred Poems and Private Ejaculations' are
comparatively but little known, I shall extract two poems.
The first is a Sonnet, equally admirable for the weight,
number, and expression of the thoughts, and the simple dignity of the language. (Unless indeed a fastidious taste
should object to the latter half of the sixth line.) The
second is a poem of greater length, which I have chosen
not only for the present purpose, but likewise as a striking example and illustration of an assertion hazarded in a
former page of these sketches; namely, that the characteristic fault of our elder poets is the reverse of that,
which distinguishes too many of our more recent versifiers;
the one conveying the most fantastic thoughts in the most
correct and natural language; the other in the most fantastic language conveying the most trivial thoughts. The
latter is a riddle of words; the former an enigma of

thoughts. The one reminds me of an odd passage in
Drayton's IDEAS:

            SONNET IX.

  As other men, so I myself do muse,
  Why in this sort I wrest invention so;
  And why these *giddy metaphors* I use,
  Leaving the path the greater part to go!
  I will resolve: *I am lunatic!*

   The other recalls a still odder passage in the 'SYNA-
GOGUE: or the Shadow of the Temple', (1) a connected series
of poems in imitation of Herbert's 'TEMPLE,' and in some
editions annexed to it

            O how my mind
                Is gravell'd!
                    Not a thought,
            That I can find
                But's ravell'd
                    All to nought!
            Short ends of threds,
                And narrow shreds
                    Of lists,
                Knots snarled ruffs,
                    Loose broken tufts
                        Of twists;
        Are my torn meditation's ragged clothing,
        Which wound, and woven shape a sute for nothing:
        One while I think, and then I am in pain
        To think how to unthink that thought again!

   Immediately after these burlesque passages I cannot
proceed to the extracts promised, without changing the
ludicrous tone of feeling by the interposition of the
three following stanzas of Herbert's.

[Quotes the first three stanzas of 'Vertue', bypassing the
fourth; and quotes next 'Sinne' (I) and 'Love Unknown'.]

From 'The Friend: A Series of Essays', 2nd edn (1818),
I, 67n.

The best and most forcible sense of a word is often that,
which is contained in its Etymology. The Author of the
Poems ('The Synagogue') frequently affixed to Herbert's

'TEMPLE,' gives the original purport of the word Integrity, in the following lines (fourth stanza of the eighth Poem:)

Next to Sincerity, remember still,
Thou must resolve upon *Integrity.*
God will have *all* thou hast, thy mind, thy will,
Thy thoughts, thy words, thy works.

And again, after some verses on Constancy and Humility, the poem concludes with -

He that desires to see
The face of God, in his religion must
Sincere, *entire*, constant, and humble be.

Having mentioned the name of *Herbert*, that model of a man, a Gentleman, and a Clergyman, let me add, that the quaintness of some of his thoughts (not of his diction, than which nothing can be more pure, manly, and unaffected,) has blinded modern readers to the great general merit of his Poems, which are for the most part exquisite in their kind.

From a letter to William Collins, December 1818; in 'Letters of Samuel Taylor Coleride', ed. Ernest Hartley Coleridge (1895), II, 694-5.

I find more substantial comfort, now, in pious George Herbert's 'Temple,' which I used to read to amuse myself with his quaintness, in short, only to laugh at, than in all the poetry since the poems of Milton. If you have not read Herbert I can recommend the book to you confidently. The poem entitled 'The Flower' is especially affecting; and to me such a phrase as 'and relish versing' expresses a sincerity, a reality, which I would unwillingly exchange for the more dignified 'and once more love the Muse,' &c. And so with many other of Herbert's homely phrases.

From a letter to the Lady Beaumont, 18 March 1826; in 'Memorials of Coleorton', ed. William Knight (Edinburgh, 1887), II, 248-9.

My dear old friend Charles Lamb and I differ widely (and in point of taste and moral feeling this is a rare occurrence) in our estimation and liking of George Herbert's sacred poems. He greatly prefers Quarles, nay, he *dis*likes Herbert. (2) But if Herbert had only written the

two following stanzas - and there are a hundred other
that in one mood or other of my mind have impressed me -
I should be grateful for the possession of his works. The
stanzas are especially affecting to me; because the folly
of overvaluing myself in any reference to my future lot is
not the sin or danger that besets me, but a tendency to
self-contempt, a sense of the utter disproportionateness
of all I can call *me*, to the promises of the Gospel - *this*
is *my* sorest temptation: the promises, I say, not to the
threats. For in order to the fulfilment of these, it
needs only that I should be left to myself to sink into
the chaos and lawless productivity of my own still perishing yet imperishable nature.

[Herbert's two stanzas, and the conclusion of the letter,
have been cut away.]

From Notebook 26, fol. 81v-82; in British Library Add.
MSS 47524 (c. 1826).

   Prayer - A sort (3) of Tune which all things hear and
   fear. Herbert

   Every time I read Herbert anew, the more he grows in my
liking. I admire him greatly. - 14 June 1826.

                    Antiphon Men & Angels

a Chorus. Praīsĕd bē thē Gōd ŏf Lōve   - ᵥ - ᵥ - ᵥ -
b   M.   Here below   - ᵥ -
a   A.   And here above   ᵥ - ᵥ -
b Ch. Who hath dealt his mercies so   - ᵥ - ᵥ - ᵥ -
c   A.   To his Friend   - ᵥ -
b   M.   And to his foe.   ᵥ - ᵥ -

e   That both Grace & Glory tend   - ᵥ - ᵥ - ᵥ -
d   A.   Us of old   - ᵥ -
c   M.   And us in th' end   ᵥ - ᵥ -
d   ✴The great Shepherd of the Fold   - ᵥ - ᵥ - ᵥ -
e   A.   We (4) did make   - ᵥ -
d   M.   For us was sold.   ᵥ - ᵥ -
                         ['Antiphon' (II), 11. 1-12]

   The last syllable of the penultimate line of each stan-
stanza rhyming to the 1st & 3rd line of the following
stanza.
      ✴The licenses are hidden by the tune. Such must be
read tuning.

> He our foes in pieces brake. Him we touch
> And him we take. Wherefore since that he is such,
>   We adore And we do crutch [crouch]
>   [ibid., 11. 13-18]

Notes on 'The Temple', in 'The Complete Works of Samuel
Taylor Coleridge', ed. W.G.T. Sledd (1871), IV, 388-91;
also available in several editions of Herbert's 'Works':
1835-6, II, 379-82; 1857, pp. 345-7; and 1859, II, 379-84.
(The comments on Harvey's 'The Synagogue' are here
omitted.)

G. HERBERT is a true poet, but a poet *sui generis*, the
merits of whose poems will never be felt without a sympathy with the mind and character of the man. To appreciate this volume, it is not enough that the reader possesses a cultivated judgment, classical taste, or even
poetic sensibility, unless he be likewise a *Christian*,
and both a zealous and an orthodox, both a devout and a
devotional Christian. But even this will not quite
suffice. He must be an affectionate and dutiful child of
the Church, and from habit, conviction, and a constitu-
tional predisposition to ceremoniousness, in piety as in
manners, find her forms and ordinances aids of religion,
not sources of formality; for religion is the element
in which he lives, and the region in which he moves.
   The Church, say rather the Churchmen of England, under
the first two Stuarts, has been charged with a yearning
after the Romish fopperies, and even the Papistic usurpa-
tions, but we shall decide more correctly, as well as
more charitably, if for the Romish and papistic we sub-
stitute the patristic leaven. There even was (natural
enough from their distinguished learning, and knowledge of
ecclesiastical antiquities) an overrating of the Church
and of the Fathers, for the first five or even six centuries; the lines on the Egyptian monks, 'Holy *Macarius*
and great *Anthony*,' (5) supply a striking instance and
illustration of this.

> If thou be single, all thy goods and ground
> Submit to love; but yet not more than all.
> Give one estate as one life. None is bound
>
> To work for two, who brought himself to thrall.
>   God made me one man; love makes me no more.
>   Till labor come, and make my weakness score.
>   ['The Church-porch', 11. 283-8]

I do not understand this stanza.

> My flesh *began unto my soul* in pain,
>   Sicknesses clave my bones, &c.
>
> ['Affliction' (I), 1. 25-6]

Either a misprint, or a noticeable idiom of the word
'began'? Yes! and a very beautiful idiom it is: the first
colloquy or address of the flesh.

> What though my body run to dust?
> Faith cleaves unto it, counting every grain,
> *With an exact and most particular trust,*
>   Reserving all for flesh again.
>
> ['Faith', 11. 41-2]

I find few historical facts so difficult of solution as the
continuance, in Protestantism, of this anti-Scriptural
superstition.

> This verse marks that, and both do make a motion
>   Unto a third that ten Leaves off doth lie.
>
> ['The H. Scriptures' (II), 11. 5-6]

The spiritual unity of the Bible = the order and connexion
of organic forms in which the unity of life is shown,
though as widely dispersed in the world of sight as the
text.

> Then as dispersed herbs do *watch* a potion,
> These three make up some Christian's destiny.
>
> [ibid., 1. 7]

Some misprint.

> Sweet Spring, full of sweet days and roses,
> A *box* where sweets compacted lie.
>
> ['Vertue', 11. 9-10]

Nest.

> Each thing is full of duty:
> Waters united are our navigation:
> *Distinguished, our habitation;*
>   *Below, our drink; above, our meat:*
> *Both are our cleanliness.* Hath one such beauty?
>   Then how are all things neat!
>
> ['Man', 11. 37-42]

'Distinguished.' I understand this but imperfectly. Did they form an island? and the next lines refer perhaps to the then belief that all fruits grow and are nourished by water. But then how is the ascending sap 'our cleanliness'? Perhaps, therefore, the rains.

But he doth bid us take his blood for wine.
['Divinitie', 1. 21]

Nay, the contrary; take wine to be blood, and *the* blood of a man who died 1800 years ago. This is the faith which even the Church of England demands; for the consubstantiation only *adds* a mystery to that of transubstantiation, which it implies.

The Flower.

A delicious poem.

How fresh, O Lord, how sweet and clear (6)
Are thy returns! e'en as the flowers in the spring,
    To which, besides their own demean,
The late past frosts tributes of pleasure bring.
            Grief melts away
            Like snow in May,
As if there were no such cold thing.
['The Flower', ll. 1-7]

'The late past frosts tributes of pleasure bring.'

Epitritus primus + Dactyl + Trochee + a long word-syllable, which, together with the pause intervening between it and the word - trochee equals ⌣⌣⌣ - form a pleasing variety in the Pentameter Iambic with rhymes. Ex gr.

The late past frosts / tributes of pleasure / bring

N.B. First, the difference between -⌣|- and an amphimacer -⌣-| and this is not always or necessarily arising out of the latter being one word. It may even consist of three words, yet the effect be the same. It is the pause that makes the difference. Secondly, the expediency, if not necessity, that the first syllable both of the Dactyl and the Trochee should be short by quantity, and only =- by force of accent or position - the Epitrite being true *lengths*. - Whether the last syllable be - or = the force of the rhymes renders indifferent. Thus, ... 'As if there *were no such cold thing*.' Had been no such thing.

> Thou who condemnest Jewish hate, &c.
> Call home thine eye (that busy wanderer),
>   *That* choice may be thy story.
> ['Self-condemnation', ll. 1-6]

Their choice.

> Nay, thou dost make me sit and dine
> E'en in my *enemies*' sight.
> ['The 23rd Psalme', ll. 17-18]

Foemen's.

> Almighty Judge, how shall poor wretches brook
>   Thy dreadful look, &c.
> What others mean to do, I know not well;
>   Yet I here tell,
> That some will turn thee to some leaves therein
>   So void of sin,
> That they in merit shall excel.
> ['Judgement', ll. 1-10]

I should not have expected from Herbert so open an avowal of Romanism in the article of *merit*. In the same spirit is 'holy *Macarius* and great *Anthony*' [as above, p. 170].

Notes

1 By Christopher Harvey (No. 8).
2 Lamb's only surviving comment on Herbert is in a letter of 7 February 1826 to Bernard Barton, whose 'Devotional Verses' (1826), Lamb wrote, 'reminded me of Quarles, and Holy Mr. Herbert, as Izaac Walton calls him: the two best, if not only, of our devotional poets, tho' some prefer Watts, and some Tom Moore' (E.V. Lucas (ed.), 'The Works of Charles and Mary Lamb' (1905), VII, 698-9, and 'The Letters of Charles Lamb' (1935), III, 37-8).
3 Herbert in fact reads 'kinde'.
4 Herbert in fact reads 'Us'.
5 'The Church Militant', l. 41.
6 Herbert in fact reads 'clean'.

43.   RALPH WALDO EMERSON, FROM THE JOURNALS AND NOTEBOOKS,
A LECTURE, AND 'PARNASSUS'

1831 ff.

Coleridge's approbation of Herbert in England was matched
by Emerson's in the United States. The ensuing extracts
begin with an entry in Emerson's journals and notebooks,
continue with the relevant section of a lecture delivered
in 1835, and conclude with two more entries in the journals and notebooks as well as with part of the preface to
'Parnasses' (1874). See further above, pp. 21 f.
     Sources: 'The Journals and Miscellaneous Notebooks of
Ralph Waldo Emerson', ed. William H. Gilman, George P.
Clark, Alfred R. Ferguson, and Merrell R. Davis (Cambridge,
Mass., 1960 ff.), III, 284, VII, 316, and IX, 278; and –
for the 1835 lecture – 'The Early Lectures of Ralph Waldo
Emerson', ed. Stephen E. Whicher and Robert E. Spiller
(Cambridge, Mass., 1959), I, 349-53.

From an entry in the journals and notebooks, 15 September
1831.

I often make the criticism on my friend Herbert's diction
that his thought has that heat as actually to fuse the
words so that language is wholly flexible in his hands &
his rhyme never stops the progress of the sense. And, in
general, according to the elevation of the soul will the
power over language always be, & lively thoughts will
break out into spritely verse. No measure so difficult
but will be tractable so that you only get up the temperature of the thought. To this point I quote gladly my
old gossip Montaigne 'For my part I hold, & Socrates is
positive in it, That whoever has in his mind a spritely
& clear imagination, he will express it well enough in one
kind or another, & tho' he were dumb by signs.'

From a lecture on Ben Jonson, Herrick, Herbert, Wotton,
delivered 31 December 1835.

Another poet in that age was George Herbert, the author of
the Temple, a little book of Divine songs and poems which
ought to be on the shelf of every lover of religion and
poetry. It is a book which is apt to repel the reader on
his first acquaintance. It is written in the quaint epigrammatic style which was for a short time in vogue in

England, a style chiefly marked by the elaborate decom-
position to which every object is subjected. The writer
is not content with the obvious properties of natural
objects but delights in discovering abstruser relations
between them and the subject of his thought. This both by
Cowley and Donne is pushed to affectation. By Herbert it
is used with greater temperance and to such excellent ends
that it is easily forgiven if indeed it do not come to be
loved.

It has been justly said of Herbert that if his thought
is often recondite and far fetched yet the language is
always simple and chaste. (1) I should cite Herbert as a
striking example of the power of exalted thought to melt and
and bend language to its fit expression. Language is an
organ on which men play with unequal skill and each man
with different skill at different hours. The man who
stammers when he is afraid or when he is indifferent, will
be fluent when he is angry, and eloquent when his intellect is active. Some writers are of that frigid temperament that their sentences always seem to be made with
grammar and dictionary. To such the easy structure of
prose is laborious, and metre and rhyme, and especially
any difficult metre is an insurmountable bar to the expression of their meaning. Of these Byron says,

> Prose poets like blank verse
> Good workmen never quarrel with their tools.
>
> ['Don Juan', I, 201]

Those on the contrary who were born to write, have a self-
enkindling power of thought which never knows this obstruc-
tion but find words so rapidly that they seem coeval with
the thought. And in general according to the elevation of
the soul will be the power over language and lively
thoughts will break out into spritely verse. No metre so
difficult but will be tractable so that you only raise the
temperature of the thought.

'For my part,' says Montaigne, (2) 'I hold and Socrates
is positive in it, that whoever has in his mind a lively
and clear imagination, he will express it well enough in
one kind or another and though he were dumb by signs.'

Every reader is struck in George Herbert with the inimitable felicity of the diction. The thought has so much
heat as actually to fuse the words, so that language is
wholly flexible in his hands, and his rhyme never stops
the progress of the sense.

The little piece called Virtue beginning,

> Sweet day so cool so calm so bright
> The bridal of the earth and sky,

is well known. I will quote a few lines from 'The Confession':

[Quotes 11. 7-24.]

There is a little piece called 'The Elixir' of which a mutilated copy has crept into some of our hymn books:

[Quotes 'The Elixer' in full, followed by 'Providence', 11. 57-60, 89-92, and 125-8.]

What Herbert most excels in is in exciting that feeling which we call the moral sublime. The highest affections are touched by his muse. I know nothing finer than the turn with which his poem on affliction concludes. After complaining to his maker as if too much suffering had been put upon him he threatens that he will quit God's service for the world's:

> Well, I will change the service and go seek
>   Some other master out
> Ah, my dear God, though I be clean forgot
> Let me not love thee if I love thee not.
>   ['Affliction' (I), 11. 63-6]

Herbert's Poems are the breathings of a devout soul reading the riddle of the world with a poet's eye but with a saint's affections. Here poetry is turned to its noblest use. The sentiments are so exalted, the thought so wise, the piety so sincere that we cannot read this book without joy that our nature is capable of such emotions and criticism is silent in the exercise of higher faculties.

It is pleasant to reflect that a book that seemed formed for the devotion of angels, attained, immediately on its publication, great popularity. Isaac Walton informs us that 20,000 copies had been sold before 1670, within forty years. (3) After being neglected for a long period several new editions of it have appeared in England and one recently in America.

From an entry in the journals and notebooks, 28 September 1839.

It seems a matter of indifference what, & how, & how much, you write, if you write poetry. Poetry makes its own pertinence and a single stanza outweighs a book of prose.
One stanza is complete. But one sentence of prose is not.
    But it must be poetry.

I do not wish to read the verses of a poetic mind but
only of a poet. I do not wish to be shown early poems, or
any steps of progress. I wish my poet born adult. I do
not find youth or age in Shakspeare, Milton, Herbert; & I
dread minors.

From yet another entry, in 1845.

'Herbs gladly cure our flesh because that they
Find their acquaintance there'
['Man', 11. 23-4]

This is mystically true. The master can do his great
deed[,] the desire of the world, say to find his way between azote & oxygen, detect the secret of the new rock
superposition, find the law of the curves, because he has
just come out of nature or from being a part of that
thing. As if one went into the mesmeric state to find the
way of nature in some function & then[,] sharing it[,]
came out into the normal state & repeated the trick. He
knows the laws of azote because just now he was azote.
Man is only a piece of the universe made alive. Man
active can do what just now he suffered.

From the preface to 'Parnassus' (Boston, Mass., 1874),
pp. vi-vii.

Herbert is the psalmist dear to all who love religious
poetry with exquisite refinement of thought. So much
piety was never married to so much wit. Herbert identifies himself with Jewish genius, as Michael Angelo did
when carving or painting prophets and patriarchs, not
merely old men in robes and beards, but with the sanctity
and the character of the Pentateuch and the prophecy con-
spicuous in them. His wit and his piety are genuine, and
are to make a lifelong friend of a good reader.

Notes

1 Cf. Coleridge, in 'Biographia Literaria' (No. 42).
2 In the essay Of the Education of Children.
3 See above, p. 127.

44.   JOHN RUSKIN, FROM TWO LETTERS, 'MODERN PAINTERS',
AND 'PRAETERITA'

1840 ff.

Ruskin's earliest remark on Herbert was ventured in a
letter in 1840: 'I admire George Herbert', he wrote then,
'above everything' (see further above, p. 21). Thereafter to the end of his life he cited the poet repeatedly,
even as he attempted several eloquent judgments of which
these four may be regarded as representative.

From the introduction to 'Modern Painters' (1843 ff.); in
'The Works of John Ruskin', ed. E.T. Cook and Alexander
Wedderburn, Library Edition (1903 ff.), III, 82.

...neither their intrinsic excellence, nor the authority
of those who can judge of it, will ever make the poems of
Wordsworth or George Herbert popular, in the sense in which
Scott and Byron are popular, because it is to the vulgar a
labour instead of a pleasure to read them; and there are
parts in them which to such judges cannot but be vapid or
ridiculous.... Giotto, Orcagna, Angelico, Perugino, stand,
like George Herbert, only with the few.

From a letter to his mother, dated 13 April 1845, comparing
Herbert and Bunyan; in 'Ruskin in Italy: Letters to his
Parents 1845', ed. Harold I. Shapiro (Oxford, 1972),
pp. 17-18.

Now the imagination of George Herbert is just as vigourous
[as Bunyan's] and his communings with God as immediate,
but they are the imagination & the communings of a well
bridled & disciplined mind, and therefore though he feels
himself to have sold Christ over & over again for definite
pieces of silver, for pleasures or promises of this world,
he repents and does penance for such actual sin - he does
not plague himself about a singing in his ears. There is
as much difference between the writings & feelings of the
two men as between the high bred, keen, severe, thoughtful
countenance of the one - and the fat, vacant, vulgar,
boy's *face* of the other. Both are equally Christians,
equally taught of God, but taught through different channels, Herbert through his brains, Bunyan through his liver.

A week later, on 20 April, he added (ibid., pp. 33-4):

I have been more and more struck on rethinking and re-
reading with the singular differences between Bunyan &
Herbert. Bunyan humble & contrite enough, but always
dwelling painfully & exclusively on the relations of the
deity to his own little self - not contemplating God as
the God of all the earth, nor loving him as such, nor so
occupied with the consideration of his attributes as to
forget himself in an extended gratitude, but always looking to his own interests & his own state - loving or fearing or doubting, just as *he* happened to fancy God was
dealing with him. Herbert on the contrary, full of faith
& love, regardless of himself, outpouring his affection in
all circumstances & at all times, and never *fearing*,
though often weeping. Hear him speaking of such changes
of feeling as Bunyan complains of:

Whether I fly with angels, fall with dust,
Thy hands made both, & I am there.
Thy power & love, my love & trust
Make one place everywhere,
['The Temper' (I), 11. 25-8]

Vide the three last lovely stanzas of 'the temper'. I
think Bunyan's a most dangerous book, in many ways - first
because to people who do not allow for his ignorance, low
birth, & sinful & idle youth, the workings of his diseased
mind would give a most false impression of God's dealings
- secondly because it encourages in ill taught religious
people, such idle, fanciful, selfish, profitless modes of
employing the mind as not only bring discredit on religion
generally, but give rise to all sorts of schisms, here-
sies, insanities and animosities - and again, because to
people of a turn of mind like mine, but who have [no]
less stability of opinion, it would at once suggest the
idea of all religion being nothing more than a particular
phase of indigestion coupled with a good imagination & bad
conscience.

From his last work, 'Praeterita: Outlines of Scenes and
Thoughts perhaps worthy of memory in my past life' (1899),
II, 159-61 (sections 110-11); first published in 1885-9.
After acknowledging an early 'affection of trying to write
like Hooker and George Herbert' (see above, p. 21), Ruskin added that as a young man he was brought into a state
of 'religious temper':

I can scarcely yet call it religious thought; but the
steadily read chapters, morning and evening, with the continual comparison between the Protestant and Papal services every Sunday abroad, made me feel that all dogmatic
teaching was a matter of chance and habit; and that the
life of religion depended on the force of faith, not the
terms of it. In the sincerity and brightness of his
imagination, I saw that George Herbert represented the
theology of the Protestant Church in a perfectly central
and deeply spiritual manner: his 'Church Porch' I recognised to be blamelessly wise as a lesson to youth; and the
exquisitely faithful fancy of the other poems (in the
'Temple') drew me into learning most of them by heart, -
the 'Church Porch', the 'Dialogue', 'Employment', 'Submission', 'Gratefulness', and, chief favourite, 'The Bag',
- deliberately and carefully. The code of feeling and law
written in these verses may be always assigned as a standard of the purest unsectarian Christianity; and whatever
has been wisest in thought or happiest in the course of
my following life was founded at this time on the teaching
of Herbert. The reader will perhaps be glad to see the
poem that has been most useful to me, 'Submission', in
simpler spelling than in the grand editions:

[Quotes the poem.]

In these, and other favourite verses, George Herbert, as
aforesaid, was to me at this time, and has been since,
useful beyond every other teacher; not that I ever
attained to any likeness of feeling, but at least knew
where I was myself wrong, or cold, in comparison.

45. GEORGE ELIOT, FROM A LETTER

1841

An unexpected reader of Herbert's poetry at the outset of
the 1840s was George Eliot. Her solitary comment on the
poet occurs in a letter to Maria Lewis dated 1 October
1841. As a response to Herbert, it is distinctly and
meaningfully personal.
    Source: 'The George Eliot Letters', ed. Gordon S.
Haight (New Haven, Conn., 1954), I, 111-12.

Is not this a true autumn day? Just the still melancholy
that I love - that makes life and nature harmonize. The
birds are all consulting about their migrations, the trees
are putting on the hectic or the pallid hues of decay, and
begin to strew the ground that one's very footsteps may not
disturb the repose of earth and air, while they give us a
scent that is a perfect anodyne to the restless spirit.
Delicious Autumn! my very soul is wedded to it, and if I
were a bird I would fly about the earth seeking the successive autumns.

> Sweet day, so calm, so pure, so bright
> The bridal of the earth and sky
> The dew will weep thy fall tonight
> For thou alas! (1) must die!
>   ['Vertue', 11. 1-4]

Note

1 'alas!' is Eliot's interpolation.

46. ROBERT CHAMBERS, FROM 'CYCLOPAEDIA OF ENGLISH
LITERATURE'

1844

Coleridge's impact on the traditional view of Herbert was
far from immediate. Typical in this respect was the response in Chambers's 'Cyclopaedia of English Literature',
which reprinted six of Herbert's poems - the last given the
title 'Stanzas' since, we are told, it was 'oddly called
by Herbert "The Pulley"' - and a Waltonesque account of the
poet limited in its critical evaluation to the extract
reproduced here. See also above, p. 23.
    Source: George Herbert, in 'Cyclopaedia of English
Literature', ed. Robert Chalmers (Edinburgh, 1844), I,
131-3.

The lines on Virtue -

> Sweet day, so cool, so calm, so bright,

are the best in the collection; but even in them we find,

what mars all the poetry of Herbert, ridiculous conceits
or coarse unpleasant similes. His taste was very inferior
to his genius. The most sacred subject could not repress
his love of fantastic imagery, or keep him for half a
dozen verses in a serious and natural strain. Herbert
was a musician, and sang his own hymns to the lute or
viol; and indications of this may be found in his poems,
which have sometimes a musical flow and harmonious
cadence. It may be safely said, however, that Herbert's
poetry alone would not have preserved his name, and that
he is indebted for the reputation he enjoys, to his excellent and amiable character, embalmed in the pages of good
old Walton, to his prose work, the 'Country Parson', and
to the warm and fervent piety which gave a charm to his
life and breathes through all his writings.

47. MARGARET FULLER, THE TWO HERBERTS

1846

The most intriguing interpretation of Herbert - so far at
least as format is concerned - was ventured in an imaginary conversation between himself and his brother, Lord
Herbert of Chirbury. The author was Margaret Fuller, a
member of the Transcendental circle who was at once one
of the more fascinating personalities in mid-century
America and 'one of the best critics of her century'
(Margaret V. Allen, 'The Achievement of Margaret Fuller'
(University Park, Pa., 1979), p. 79). See also above,
p. 25.
    Source: Fuller, The Two Herberts, in 'Papers on Litera-
ture and Art' (1846), pp. 15-34.

The following sketch is meant merely to mark some prominent features in the minds of the two Herberts, under a
form less elaborate and more reverent than that of
criticism.
    A mind of penetrating and creative power could not find
a better subject for a masterly picture. The two figures
stand as representatives of natural religion, and of that
of the Son of Man, of the life of the philosophical man of
the world, and the secluded, contemplative, though beneficent existence.
    The present slight effort is not made with a view to

the great and dramatic results so possible to the plan.   It
is intended chiefly as a setting to the Latin poems of Lord
Herbert, which are known to few, - a year ago, seemingly,
were so to none in this part of the world.   The only desire
in translating them has been to do so literally, as any
paraphrase, or addition of words impairs their profound
meaning.   It is hoped that, even in their present repulsive
garb, without rhyme or rhythm, stripped, too, of the majestic Roman mantle, the greatness of the thoughts, and the
large lines of spiritual experience, will attract readers,
who will not find time misspent in reading them many times.
     George Herbert's heavenly strain is better, though far
from generally, known.
     There has been no attempt really to represent these per-
sons speaking their own dialect, or in their own individual
manners.   The writer loves too well to hope to imitate the
sprightly, fresh, and varied style of Lord Herbert, or the
quaintness and keen sweets of his brother's.   Neither have
accessories been given, such as might easily have been
taken from their works.   But the thoughts imputed to them
they might have spoken, only in better and more concise
terms, and the facts - are facts.   So let this be gently
received with the rest of the modern tapestries.   We can no
longer weave them of the precious materials princes once
furnished, but we can give, in our way, some notion of the
original design.

     It was an afternoon of one of the longest summer days.
The sun had showered down his amplest bounties, the earth
put on her richest garment to receive them.   The clear
heavens seemed to open themselves to the desire of mortals; the day had been long enough and bright enough to
satisfy an immortal.
     In a green lane leading from the town of Salisbury, in
England, the noble stranger was reclining beneath a tree.
His eye was bent in the direction of the town, as if upon
some figure approaching or receding; but its inward turned
expression showed that he was, in fact, no longer looking,
but lost in thought.
     'Happiness!' thus said his musing mind, 'it would seem
at such hours and in such places as if it not merely
hovered over the earth, a poetic presence to animate our
pulses and give us courage for what must be, but sometimes
alighted.   Such fulness of expression pervades these
fields, these trees, that it excites, not rapture, but a
blissful sense of peace.   Yet, even were this permanent in
the secluded lot, would I accept it in exchange for the
bitter sweet of a wider, freer life?   I could not if I
would; yet, methinks, I would not if I could.   But here

comes George, I will argue the point with him.'

He rose from his seat and went forward to meet his
brother, who at this moment entered the lane.

The two forms were faithful expressions of their several
lives. There was a family likeness between them, for they
shared in that beauty of the noble English blood, of
which, in these days, few types remain: the Norman tempered by the Saxon, the fire of conquest by integrity, and
a self-contained, inflexible habit of mind. In the times
of the Sydneys and Russells, the English body was a strong
and nobly-proportioned vase, in which shone a steady and
powerful, if not brilliant light.

The chains of convention, an external life grown out of
proportion with that of the heart and mind, have destroyed,
for the most part, this dignified beauty. There is no
longer, in fact, an aristocracy in England, because the
saplings are too puny to represent the old oak. But that
it once existed, and did stand for what is best in that
nation, any collection of portraits from the sixteenth
century will show.

The two men who now met had character enough to exhibit
in their persons not only the stock from which they
sprang, but what was special in themselves harmonized with
it. There were ten years betwixt them, but the younger
verged on middle age; and permanent habits, as well as tendencies of character, were stamped upon their persons.

Lord Edward Herbert was one of the handsomest men of
his day, of a beauty alike stately, chivalric and intellectual. His person and features were cultivated by all
the disciplines of a time when courtly graces were not
insignificant, because a monarch mind informed the court,
nor warlike customs, rude or mechanical, for individual
nature had free play in the field, except as restrained
by the laws of courtesy and honor. The steel glove became his hand, and the spur his heel; neither can we
fancy him out of his place, for any place he would have
made his own. But all this grace and dignity of the man of
the world was in him subordinated to that of the man, for
in his eye, and in the brooding sense of all his countenance, was felt the life of one who, while he deemed that
his present honour lay in playing well the part assigned
him by destiny, never forgot that it was but a part, and
fed steadily his forces on that within that passes show.

It has been said, with a deep wisdom, that the figure
we most need to see before us now is not that of a saint,
martyr, sage, poet, artist, preacher, or any other whose
vocation leads to a seclusion and partial use of faculty,
but 'a spiritual man of the world,' able to comprehend all
things, exclusively dedicate to none. Of this idea we

need a new expression, peculiarly adapted to our time; but
in the past it will be difficult to find one more adequate
than the life and person of Lord Herbert.

George Herbert, like his elder brother, was tall,
erect, and with the noble air of one sprung from a race
whose spirit has never been broken or bartered; but his
thin form contrasted with the full development which generous living, various exercise, and habits of enjoyment had
given his brother. Nor had his features that range and
depth of expression which tell of many-coloured experiences, and passions undergone or vanquished. The depth,
for there was depth, was of feeling rather than experience. A penetrating sweetness beamed from him on the
observer, who was rather raised and softened in himself
than drawn to think of the being who infused this heavenly
fire into his veins. Like the violet, the strong and
subtle odour of his mind was arrayed at its source with
such an air of meekness, that the receiver blessed rather
the liberal winds of heaven than any earth-born flower
for the gift.

Raphael has lifted the transfigured Saviour only a
little way from the ground; but in the forms and expression of the feet, you see that, though they may walk there
again, they would tread far more naturally a more delicate
element. This buoyant lightness, which, by seeking, seems
to tread the air, is indicated by the text: 'Beautiful
upon the mountains are the feet of those who come with
glad tidings.' (1) And such thoughts were suggested by
the gait and gesture of George Herbert, especially as he
approached you. Through the faces of most men, even of
geniuses, the soul shines as through a mask, or, at best,
a crystal; we look behind a shield for the heart. But,
with those of seraphic nature, or so filled with spirit
that translation may be near, it seems to hover before or
around, announcing or enfolding them like a luminous
atmosphere. Such an one advances like a vision, and the
eye must steady itself before a spiritual light, to recognize him as a reality.

Some such emotion was felt by Lord Herbert as he looked
on his brother, who, for a moment or two, approached without observing him, but absorbed and radiant in his own
happy thoughts. They had not met for long, and it seemed
that George had grown from an uncertain boy, often blush-
ing and shrinking either from himself or others, into an
angelic clearness, such as the noble seeker had not elsewhere found.

But when he was seen, the embrace was eager and affectionate as that of the brother and the child.

'Let us not return at once,' said Lord Herbert. 'I had

already waited for you long, and have seen all the
beauties of the parsonage and church.'

'Not many, I think, in the eyes of such a critic,' said
George, as they seated themselves in the spot his brother
had before chosen for the extent and loveliness of prospect.

'Enough to make me envious of you, if I had not early
seen enough to be envious of none. Indeed, I know not if
such a feeling can gain admittance to your little paradise, for I never heard such love and reverence expressed
as by your people for you.'

George looked upon his brother with a pleased and open
sweetness. Lord Herbert continued, with a little hesitation - 'To tell the truth, I wondered a little at the
boundless affection they declared. Our mother has long
and often told me of your pure and beneficent life, and I
know what you have done for this place and people, but, as
I remember, you were of a choleric temper.'

'And am so still!'

'Well, and do you not sometimes, by flashes of that,
lost all you may have gained?'

'It does not often now,' he replied, 'find open way.
My Master has been very good to me in suggestions of
restraining prayer, which come into my mind at the hour of
temptation.'

Lord H. - Why do you not say, rather, that your own
discerning mind and maturer will show you more and more
the folly and wrong of such outbreaks.

George H. - Because that would not be saying all that
I think. At such times I feel a higher power interposed,
as much as I see that yonder tree is distinct from myself.
Shall I repeat to you some poor verses in which I have
told, by means of various likenesses, in an imperfect
fashion, how it is with me in this matter?

Lord H. - Do so! I shall hear them gladly; for I, like
you, though with less time and learning to perfect it,
love the deliberate composition of the closet, and believe
we can better understand one another by thoughts expressed
so, than in the more glowing but hasty words of the moment.

George H. -

[Quotes 'Prayer' (I) in full.]

Lord H. - (who has listened attentively, after a
moment's thought.) - There is something in the spirit of
your lines which pleases me, and, in general, I know not
that I should differ; yet you have expressed yourself
nearest to mine own knowledge and feeling, where you have
left more room to consider our prayers as aspirations,

rather than the gifts of grace; as -

'Heart in pilgrimage;'
'A kind of tune, which all things hear and fear.'
'Something understood.'

In your likenesses, you sometimes appear to quibble in a
way unworthy the subject.

George H. - It is the nature of some minds, brother, to
play with what they love best. Yours is of a grander and
severer cast; it can only grasp and survey steadily what
interests it. My walk is different, and I have always
admired you in yours without expecting to keep pace with
you.

Lord H. - I hear your sweet words with the more pleasure, George, that I had supposed you were now too much
of the churchman to value the fruits of my thought.

George H. - God forbid that I should ever cease to
reverence the mind that was, to my own, so truly that of
an elder brother! I do lament that you will not accept the
banner of my Master, and drink at what I have found the
fountain of pure wisdom. But as I would not blot from the
book of life the prophets and priests that came before Him,
nor those antique sages who knew all

That Reason hath from Nature borrowed,
Or of itself, like a good housewife spun,
In laws and policy: what the stars conspire:
What willing Nature speaks; what, freed by fire:
Both th' old discoveries, and the new found seas:
The stock and surplus, cause and history, -
['The Pearl', 11. 3-8]

As I cannot resign and disparage these, because they have
not what I conceive to be the pearl of all knowledge, how
could I you?

Lord H. - You speak wisely, George, and let me add,
religiously. Were all churchmen as tolerant, I had never
assailed the basis of their belief. Did they not insist
and urge upon us their way as the one only way, not for
them alone, but for all, none would wish to put stumbling-
blocks before their feet.

George H. - Nay, my brother, do not misunderstand me.
None, more than I, can think there is but one way to
arrive finally at truth.

Lord H. - I do not misunderstand you; but feeling that
you are one who accept what you do from love of the best,
and not from fear of the worst, I am as much inclined to
tolerate your conclusions as you to tolerate mine.

George H. - I do not consider yours as conclusions, but
only as steps to such. The progress of the mind should be
from natural to revealed religion, as there must be a sky
for the sun to give light through its expanse.
Lord H. - The sky is - nothing!
George H. - Except room for a sun, and such there is in
you. Of your own need of such, did you not give convincing proof, when you prayed for a revelation to direct
whether you should publish a book against revelation? (2)
Lord H. - You borrow that objection from the crowd,
George; but I wonder you have not looked into the matter
more deeply. Is there any thing inconsistent with dis-
belief in a partial plan of salvation for the nations,
which, by its necessarily limited working, excludes the
majority of men up to our day, with belief that each individual soul, wherever born, however nurtured, may receive
immediate response, in an earnest hour, from the source of
truth.
George H. - But you believed the customary order of
nature to be deranged in your behalf. What miraculous
record does more?
Lord H. - It was at the expense of none other. A
spirit asked, a spirit answered, and its voice was thunder;
but, in this, there was nothing special, nothing partial
wrought in my behalf, more than if I had arrived at the
same conclusion by a process of reasoning.
George H. - I cannot but think, that if your mind were
allowed, by the nature of your life, its free force to
search, it would survey the subject in a different way,
and draw inferences more legitimate from a comparison of
its own experience with the gospel.
Lord H. - My brother does not think the mind is free to
act in courts and camps. To me it seems that the mind
takes its own course everywhere, and that, if men cannot
have outward, they can always mental seclusion. None is
so profoundly lonely, none so in need of constant self-
support, as he who, living in the crowd, thinks an inch
aside from, or in advance of it. The hermitage of such
an one is still and cold; its silence unbroken to a degree
of which these beautiful and fragrant solitudes give no
hint. These sunny sights and sounds, promoting reverie
rather than thought, are scarce more favourable to a great
advance in the intellect, than the distractions of the busy
street. Beside, we need the assaults of other minds to
quicken our powers, so easily hushed to sleep, and call it
peace. The mind takes a bias too easily, and does not ex-
amine whether from tradition or a native growth intended
by the heavens.
George H. - But you are no common man. You shine, you

charm, you win, and the world presses too eagerly on you
to leave many hours for meditation.

Lord H. - It is a common error to believe that the most
prosperous men love the world best. It may be hardest for
them to leave it, because they have been made effeminate
and slothful by want of that exercise which difficulty
brings. But this is not the case with me; for, while the
common boons of life's game have been too easily attained,
to hold high value in my eyes, the goal which my secret
mind, from earliest infancy, prescribed, has been high
enough to task all my energies. Every year has helped to
make that, and that alone, of value in my eyes; and did I
believe that life, in scenes like this would lead me to it
more speedily than in my accustomed broader way, I would
seek it to-morrow - nay, to-day. But is it worthy of a
man to make him a cell, in which alone he can worship?
Give me rather the always open temple of the universe! To
me, it seems that the only course for a man is that
pointed out by birth and fortune. Let him take that and
pursue it with clear eyes and head erect, secure that it
must point at last to those truths which are central to
us, wherever we stand; and if my road, leading through the
busy crowd of men, amid the clang and bustle of conflict-
ing interests and passions, detain me longer than would the
still path through the groves, the chosen haunt of contemplation, yet I incline to think that progress so, though
slower, is surer. Owing no safety, no clearness to my
position, but so far as it is attained to mine own effort,
encountering what temptations, doubts and lures may beset
a man, what I do possess is more surely mine, and less a
prey to contingencies. It is a well-tempered wine that
has been carried over many seas, and escaped many ship-
wrecks.

George H. - I can the less gainsay you, my lord and
brother, that your course would have been mine could I
have chosen.

Lord H. - Yes; I remember thy verse:-

> Whereas my birth and spirits rather took
>   The way that takes the town;
> Thou didst betray me to a lingering book,
>   And wrap me in a gown.
>   ['Affliction' (I), ll. 37-40]

It was not my fault, George, that it so chanced.

George H. - I have long learnt to feel that it noway
chanced; that thus, and no other, was it well for me. But
how I view these matters you are, or may be well aware,
through a little book I have writ. Of you I would fain

learn more than can be shown me by the display of your
skill in controversy in your printed works, or the rumours
of your feats at arms, or success with the circles of fair
ladies, which reach even this quiet nook. Rather let us,
in this hour of intimate converse, such as we have not had
for years, and may not have again, draw near in what is
nearest; and do you, my dear Lord, vouchsafe your friend
and brother some clear tokens as to that goal you say has
from childhood been mentally prescribed you, and the way
you have taken to gain it.

   Lord H. - I will do this willingly, and the rather that
I have with me a leaf, in which I have lately recorded what
appeared to me in glimpse or flash in my young years, and
now shines upon my life with steady ray. I brought it,
with some thought that I might impart it to you, which confidence I have not shown to any yet; though if, as I purpose, some memoir of my life and times should fall from my
pen, these poems may be interwoven there as cause and comment for all I felt, and knew, and was. The first contains my thought of the beginning and progress of life:-

[Quotes - in translation - 'De vita humana' and 'De vita
coelesti'.] (3)

   George H. - (who, during his brother's reading, has
listened, with head bowed down, leaned on his arm, looks
up after a few moments' silence) - Pardon, my lord, if I
have not fit words to answer you. The flood of your
thought has swept over me like music, and like that, for
the time, at least, it fills and satisfies. I am conscious of many feelings which are not touched upon there,
- of the depths of love and sorrow made known to men,
through One whom you as yet know not. But of these I will
not speak now, except to ask, borne on this strong pinion,
have you never faltered till you felt the need of a
friend? strong in this clear vision, have you never sighed
for a more homefelt assurance to your faith? steady in
your demand of what the soul requires, have you never
known fear lest you want purity to receive the boon if
granted?

   Lord H. - I do not count those weak moments, George;
they are not my true life.

   George H. - It suffices that you know them, for, in
time, I doubt not that every conviction which a human
being needs to be reconciled to the Parent of all, will be
granted to a nature so ample, so open, and so aspiring.
Let me answer in a strain which bespeaks my heart as truly,
if not as nobly as yours answers to your great mind, -

[Quotes 'A true Hymne' in full.]

Lord H. - I cannot say to you truly that my mind
replies to this, although I discern a beauty in it.   You
will say I lack humility to understand yours.
George H. - I will say nothing, but leave you to time
and the care of a greater than I.   We have exchanged our
verse, let us now change our subject too, and walk homeward; for I trust you, this night, intend to make my
roof happy in your presence, and the sun is sinking.
Lord H. - Yes, you know I am there to be introduced to
my new sister, whom I hope to love, and win from her a
sisterly regard in turn.
George H. - You, none can fail to regard; and for her,
even as you love me, you must her, for we are one.
Lord H. - (smiling) - Indeed; two years wed, and say
that.
George H. - Will your lordship doubt it?   From your
muse I took my first lesson.

> With a look, it seem'd denied
>   All earthly powers but hers, yet so
> As if to her breath he did owe
>   This borrow'd life, he thus replied -
>
> And shall our love, so far beyond
>   That low and dying appetite,
> And which so chaste desires unite,
>   Not hold in an eternal bond?
>
> O no, belov'd! I am most sure
>   Those virtuous habits we acquire,
> As being with the soul entire,
>   Must with it evermore endure.
>
> Else should our souls in vain elect;
>   And vainer yet were heaven's laws
> When to an everlasting cause
>   They gave a perishing effect. (4)

Lord H. - (sighing) - You recall a happy season, when
my thoughts were as delicate of hue, and of as heavenly a
perfume as the flowers of May.
George H. - Have those flowers borne no fruit?
Lord H. - My experience of the world and men had made
me believe that they did not indeed bloom in vain, but
that the fruit would be ripened in some future sphere of
our existence.   What my own marriage was you know, - a
family arrangement made for me in my childhood.   Such

obligations as such a marriage could imply, I have fulfilled, and it has not failed to bring me some benefits of
good-will and esteem, and far more, in the happiness of
being a parent. But my observation of the ties formed, by
those whose choice was left free, has not taught me that
a higher happiness than mine was the destined portion of
men. They are too immature to form permanent relations;
all that they do seems experiment, and mostly fails for
the present. Thus I had postponed all hopes except of
fleeting joys or ideal pictures. Will you tell me that
you are possessed already of so much more?

George H. - I am indeed united in a bond, whose reality
I cannot doubt, with one whose thoughts, affections, and
objects everyway correspond with mine, and in whose life I
see a purpose so pure that, if we are ever separated, the
fault must be mine. I believe God, in his exceeding
grace, gave us to one another, for we met almost at a
glance, without doubt before, jar or repentance after, the
vow which bound our lives together.

Lord H. - Then there is indeed one circumstance of your
lot I could wish to share with you. (After some moments'
silence on both sides) - They told me at the house, that,
with all your engagements, you go twice a-week to Salisbury. How is that? How can you leave your business and
your happy home, so much and often.

George H. - I go to hear the music; the great solemn
church music. This is, at once, the luxury and the necessity of my life. I know not how it is with others, but,
with me, there is a frequent drooping of the wings, a
smouldering of the inward fires, a languor, almost a
loathing of corporeal existence. Of this visible diurnal
sphere I am, by turns, the master, the interpreter, and
the victim; an ever burning lamp, to warm again the embers
of the altar; a skiff, that cannot be becalmed, to bear me
again on the ocean of hope; an elixir, that fills the dul-
lest fibre with ethereal energy; such, music is to me. It
stands in relation to speech, even to the speech of poets,
as the angelic choir, who, in their subtler being, may
inform the space around us, unseen but felt, do to men,
even to prophetic men. It answers to the soul's presage,
and, in its fluent life, embodies all I yet know how to
desire. As all the thoughts and hopes of human souls are
blended by the organs to a stream of prayer and praise, I
tune at it my separate breast, and return to my little
home, cheered and ready for my day's work, as the lark
does to her nest after her morning visit to the sun.

Lord H. - The ancients held that the spheres made
music to those who had risen into a state which enabled
them to hear it. Pythagoras, who prepared different kinds

of melody to guide and expand the differing natures of his
pupils, needed himself to hear none on instruments made by
human art, for the universal harmony which comprehends all
these was audible to him. Man feels in all his higher
moments, the need of traversing a subtler element, of a
winged existence. Artists have recognised wings as the
symbol of the state next above ours; but they have not been
able so to attach them to the forms of gods and angels as
to make them agree with the anatomy of the human frame.
Perhaps music gives this instruction, and supplies the
deficiency. Although I see that I do not feel it as
habitually or as profoundly as you do, I have experienced
such impressions from it.

   George H. - That is truly what I mean. It introduces me
into that winged nature, and not as by way of supplement,
but of inevitable transition. All that has budded in me,
bursts into bloom, under this influence. As I sit in our
noble cathedral, in itself one of the holiest thoughts
ever embodied by the power of man, the great tides of song
come rushing through its aisles; they pervade all the
space, and my soul within it, perfuming me like incense,
bearing me on like the wind, and on and on to regions of
unutterable joy, and freedom, and certainty. As their
triumph rises, I rise with them, and learn to comprehend
by living them, till at last a calm rapture seizes me, and
holds me poised. The same life you have attained in your
description of the celestial choirs. It is the music of
the soul, when centred in the will of God, thrilled by the
love, expanded by the energy, with which it is fulfilled
through all the ranges of active life. From such hours, I
return through these green lanes, to hear the same tones
from the slightest flower, to long for a life of purity
and praise, such as is manifested by the flowers.

   At this moment they reached the door, and there paused
to look back. George Herbert bent upon the scene a half-
abstracted look, yet which had a celestial tearfulness in
it, a pensiveness beyond joy. His brother looked on *him*,
and, beneath that fading twilight, it seemed to him a
farewell look. It was so. Soon George Herbert soared into
the purer state, for which his soul had long been ready,
though not impatient.

   The brothers met no more; but they had enjoyed together
one hour of true friendship, when mind drew near to mind by
the light of faith, and heart mingled with heart in the
atmosphere of Divine love. It was a great boon to be
granted two mortals.

Notes

1   Adapted from Isaiah 52.7.
2   Lord Herbert in 'De veritate' (1624) relates that he
    prayed on whether to publish it, and was promptly
    answered by 'a loud, though yet gentle noise' from
    heaven. Margaret Fuller quotes the account as 'a speci-
    men of absolute truth and frankness'.
3   The Latin texts are available in 'The Poems English and
    Latin of Edward Lord Herbert of Cherbury', ed. G.C.
    Moore Smith (Oxford, 1923), pp. 99-106.
4   Lord Herbert, 'An Ode upon a Question moved, Whether
    Love should continue for ever?', 11. 61-4, 69-72,
    89-92, 101-4.

48.   ARTHUR HUGH CLOUGH, FROM A LECTURE

c. 1850

In the following extract from a lecture of late 1850 or
early 1851, the poet Clough appears less than enthusiastic
about Herbert or, for that matter, Donne. In his own
poetry, however, Clough betrays the opposite attitude in
that Herbert's influence upon him may be said to have been
restricted but not negligible (see above, p. 25).
    Source: Clough, from the second of his lectures on
Dryden and His Times, in Harvard University's Houghton
Library MS bMS Eng 1036 (8), fol. 7; as printed in Walter
E. Houghton, 'The Poetry of Clough: An Essay in Revolution'
(New Haven, Conn., 1963), p. 49.

During the 50 years before the Restoration, the style
called by Dr Johnson, not very correctly perhaps, the
metaphysical, was prevalent, I may say virulent. George
Herbert is a great example, Donne the satirist another.
Shakespeare was too facile not to let himself be carried
away by the taste of his age, there is only too much of
it found defacing his inspirations. I take it to consist
mainly in the thinking of the words rather than of the
thought, & running off upon the casualties of the form of
an expression instead of moving on with the essential tendency of the thought. You are led on per saltum from word
to word, & word again after that, instead of continuously
gliding along the stream of reflection. You get into

conceits, as they are called, & all but into puns.   By
way of a pleasing digression you turn aside to a simile,
& you hunt it to death before you resume your proper road.

49.   WILLIAM JERDAN, FROM HIS INTRODUCTION TO 'THE WORKS
OF THE REV. GEORGE HERBERT'

1853

Of three major editions of Herbert's poetry published
halfway through the nineteenth century, none deviated from
a Waltonesque emphasis on Herbert's didactic aspects.   The
first of these editions, prepared by the journalist William
Jerdan, proclaims the common thrust in its opening sentence.   But Herbert's literary merit, it will be observed,
is being increasingly commended too.   See also above,
p. 24.
     Source: Jerdan, from the Introduction to 'The Works of
the Rev. George Herbert' (1853), pp. iii-iv and ix-xxx.

The Mission of Poetry is refining, pure and holy.   If it be
not, it will not last, descend the stream of time, and be
cherished from generation to generation through succeeding ages.
     It is only as the heroic partakes of this influence, in
the form of noble sentiment, that it enjoys a similar immortality: whilst wit, humour, and description are doomed,
however admirable in their way, to a much more limited
existence.
     Upon the truth of these great laws and canons of criti-
cism rests the claim of George Herbert to be evermore
revived and perpetuated in the poetic literature of England.   In his lifetime, and immediately after his death,
above two hundred years ago, his popular fame was almost
unparalleled: and that it was founded on a solid basis has
been proven by its vitality and palmy bloom during two
centuries, and the numerous editions through which his
productions, in prose and verse, have gone.
     On adding another to the list, it behoves us to lay a
few observations on the subject before our readers,
together with a brief preliminary biographical sketch of
the author, whose life was first written by Barnabas Oley,
and then by Isaak Walton as a suitable example of virtue,
to complete an illustrious trio with the metaphysical

Dr. Donne and the accomplished Sir Henry Wotton....

[After a florid biographical account of Herbert. Jerdan
provides a telling interpretation of the age before
attending to the poetry.]

   Having given this outline of the Poet, it is incumbent
upon us to offer some observations upon the period in
which he flourished, and that which succeeded it, and endeavour to suggest the reason why, when all other contemporaneous stars have paled their ineffectual fires, his
orb has beamed more brightly through the shade of so many
years, and still commands the admiration and worship of
the devout and pious. The beginning of the seventeenth
century was unsettled in religious principle, and we
regret to add, that a considerable portion of the Clergy
might, from their latitudinarian lives and conduct, be
deemed not only remiss, but absolutely irreligious. A
natural consequence of this laxity was to raise up a class
of zealous and holy men, who beheld with grief the profana-
tion of the Sanctuary, and adopted the opposite course with
a degree of sacred fervour which could hardly have been
excited by any ordinary cause. The eternal laws of nature
tend to extremes in re-action, and so it happened here; and
the functions of the priest were either neglected and
abused, or performed with an intensity of devotedness too
much for the endurance of the human frame. Vigils, abstinence, and mortifications, cut short the useful and exemplary lives of such as George Herbert: whilst, perhaps,
the lives of their opposites were, in some cases, abridged
by recklessness, indulgence, and intemperance.
   The civil war brought these conditions, involving the
laity in their vortex, into collision; and the era which
immediately succeeded, saw religion almost banished from
the realm, and perishing of disgust at its violences,
hypocrisies, and crimes: the whole crowned by the Popish
struggle of the infatuated James the Second, when men
changed their religion as indifferently as their garments.
   These three phases occupied nearly a century. The first
exhibited the contrast of loose manners and almost ascetic
prostration. The second was religion in arms, and revel-
ling in tyranny and bloodshed. The last was not only
scorn of the cruel and vile violators of God's holy name,
but apathy towards his Divine precepts, without obedience
to which, profligacy and infidenlity must stamp the earth
with innumerable curses.
   In the midst of this chaotic darkness and confusion, we
see, and from the circumstances can account for the lamp
of Herbert shining so brightly. His deep aspiration and

earnest effort to walk in the footsteps of his 'Master,'
made himself a pattern for all time. If there might be an
excess, it was on the side of heaven, to the utter disregard of every worldly object, and so glorious as to render comparatively feeble and effete the later admired
praise of a good Priest, that

Even his failings leant to Virtue's side.

The poetic standard of the Herbert period was not so
high as to eclipse the lesser luminaries; and in our day
there is no general acquaintance with their productions.
Yet, doing what must always be done in just and correct
criticism, allowing for the taste and cultivation of their
time, there are very many and great beauties to be found
in his fellow-illustrators of Mount Parnassus, or from the
nature of their compositions we ought, perhaps, rather to
say of Mount Carmel. Withers, till lost in polemics and
politics, gave more than promise of sweetness and power.
Quarles, with his Emblems, and his conceits bearing much
resemblance to Herbert's own, is redolent of charming
thoughts. Crashaw, a few years later, is fine, in spite of
his strange inequalities; and Carew delights us with many a
pleasing verse; whilst the gay, light, and lively Suckling
shone the prototype of the troubadours, whose songs gilded
the Restoration. True it is, the latter were often objectionable on the score of licentiousness; but, after all,
polished vice is less obnoxious and injurious than coarse
and vulgar profligacy in word or deed. We are not the
apologists for either; and only note the fact, to show the
validity of the immutable rule with which we set out, that
without goodness and purity, no poetic talent, however
brilliant, can hope to transmit its creations to a late
posterity.
    In the converse of this lay the secret of Herbert's
immense popularity, and his descent to our day with a halo
of rightous glory about him, which will not fail so long
as true and genuine Christianity has votaries in the land.
On a minor scale, Dr. Watts's Hymns may be mentioned as an
example of a similar kind, and serving to confirm the argument we have laid down.
    Before entering into a more particular review of Her-
bert's works, we shall only add to these general remarks
that he was a passionate lover of Music, as his chiefest
recreation and an adjunct to Piety and Poetry; and that,
whilst he kept his own practical devotions within strict
limits, observing Fasts, and serving (it might be said) at
the Altar, and in his domestic household, night and day,
with unintermitting vigilance, he did not carry them to

the utter extreme of some of his dearest friends. Of
these, the most loved and honoured was Mr. Nicholas Ferrar,
'who got the reputation of being called Saint Nicholas at
the age of six years,' and after finishing his education
as a Fellow of Clare Hall, Cambridge, travelled much, and
returned home to a good estate, deeply imbued with the
principles of an anchorite or founder of a new sect of
rigid puritanism, - 'For he, having seen the manners and
vanities of the World, and found them to be as Mr. Herbert
said, "a nothing between two dishes," did so contemn it
that he resolved to spend the remainder of his life in
mortifications and in devotion, and charity, and to be
always prepared for death.' (1) To this end, with his
family, about thirty in number, he converted his residence
into a little college, kept Lent and all Ember-weeks, and
every Friday, strictly with fastings and mortifications,
read the Common Prayers every day between the appointed
hours of ten and four in the Parish Church (he being a
Deacon), read the Matins also daily at the hour of six,
either in the Church or an Oratory within the house, and
after prayers spent some hours in singing hymns and
anthems; and then betaking them to private prayers and
meditations. But even these observances did not suffice,
for at night, at the ringing of a watch-bell, the Church
or Oratory was again peopled for prayers, lauding God,
and reading the Psalms; and when these, or any part of the
congregation grew weary or faint, the watch-bell was rung
sometimes before and sometimes after midnight, and then
another part of the family rose, and maintained the watch;
and when, after some hours, they also grew weary and faint,
then they rung the watch-bell, and were relieved by some
of the former, or by a new part of the Society, which
continued their devotions till morning. And this was
done as constantly as the Sun runs his circle every day
about the world, and then begins again the same instant
it is ended.
    Such is the remarkable description of Gidden Hall, and
peculiarly interesting, not only in forming an estimate of
Herbert, but in considering the best means by which the
cause of Gospel religion can be promoted.
    Herbert is warm in his eulogy upon Mr. Ferrar and his
establishment, but did not carry his own practice to similar extremes. Such extremes, indeed, must always be exceptional, for the business of life must stop if they were
universal. In a world of Trappists, the human species
would be extinct in one generation; and so near an approach
to Trappism is rather calculated to repress than inspire
inclinations and feelings towards Christianity. Mark,
accordingly, the results. There are no traces of such

austerities as those of Gidden Hall now in social existence; but the example and teaching of the Rector of
Bemerton have diffused a vast amount of holiness throughout the British Empire and the Universe, during the suc-
cession of seven generations of the people! Moderation
and temperance in all things tend to usefulness and virtue: excess, even in good, prevents imitation, and leads
to apathy, if not to opposition. Had there not been a
Herbert, it is probable there might never have been a
Wesley; for in the founder of the Methodists, it is impossible not to recognise almost every impulse and emotion he
expressed, every doctrine he preached, and every duty he
practised.

In this light, it will be seen that the providence of
Herbert's Court-life and opportunities for acute observation of mankind, contributed essentially to his eminent
position of a minister of the Church of England, an author,
and a poet. Commingling the wisdom of Solomon with the
inspiration of David, he became effective for previous
benefits, and not the mere admirable executionist on the
timbrel or the harp. His prose and his verse abound with
maxims, precepts, and aphorisms of high morality and
sterling sense - worthy of the utmost consideration of the
worldling; - and over the whole is shed that divine Spirit
which transports us to another sphere far beyond the cares
and afflictions of our present sojourn -

> Where the wicked cease from troubling, and the
> weary are at rest.

The Jacula Prudentum is a valuable and ample selection of
of proverbs and pregnant sayings made by Mr. Herbert,
whilst Public Orator at Cambridge; but his own original
brief comments, scattered over his writings, are equally
instructive and pithy, and these were the fruits of his
acquaintance with actual life.

> I have always observed the thread of life to be like
> other threads or skeins of silk, full of snarls and
> incumbrances.
> Religion does not banish mirth, but only moderates
> and sets rules to it.
> If I be bound to pray for all that be in distress, I
> am sure I am bound, so far as is in my power, to prac-
> tise what I pray for.

Such as the axioms which grace his prose: in his poetry
we shall find more, and all in unison with his fervent
humility and liberal charity.

Of 'The Country Parson' we will say nothing farther than
that the more the lessons are taken to heart and the advice
followed, the better will it be for the Church of Christ,
its consecrated apostles, and the laity who are its commu-
nicants. From this topic, therefore, which would draw us
into statements foreign to our purpose in this Essay, we
pass with pleasure to a cursory examination of the Poems
before us.

They are prefaced, as usual at that time, with commendatory verses, which are chiefly characterised by the
poverty of such compositions, full of common-place compliments and strained comparisons, and exaggerated laudation
in unpoetic language. Their defects, however, serve as a
foil to demonstrate how superior Herbert was to the rhyming
herd; though we confess it is no lofty merit to surpass
such poetry as this -

What father of a Church can you rehearse,
That gained more souls to God 'twist prose and verse?
                    ...Show me the man
That sang more sweetly than this dying swan,
This bird of Paradise, this glow-worm bright,
This Philomel, this glory of the night.

Or, as sung another commendator -

He was the wonder of a better age,
The eclipse of this, of empty heads the rage.
Phoenix of Wales, of his great name the glory.
A theme above all verse, beyond all story.
A plant of Paradise; which, in a word,
Worms ne'er shall wither, as they did the gourd....
Go, thaw your hearts at his celestial fire;
And what you cannot comprehend, admire!

We quote these morsels of the ordinary train, level with
the mass of the age whose attributes they indicate and
exemplify; and their contrast with the productions they
have the rashness to bepraise, is about as irresistible a
testimony to the merits of these productions as the
admirers of their author could desire. And as

A verse may find him who a sermon flies,
                    ['The Church-porch', 1. 5]

So much are mankind indebted to the man who penned that
line, and embalmed so many other consolatory and ennobling
sentiments in verse, in his ceaseless and pious endeavour
to produce the happy effects which he anticipated from

'rhyming to good, and making a bait of pleasure' [ibid.,
1. 4].

This line is, indeed, the key to his labours, and the
touchstone to the writings of Herbert. His whole nature
is developed in its nine words! The love and service of
God: the love and use of Poetry! In his most abject
humiliations and his most exalted adorations, the means to
the end are still the poetic. Nothing dissevers the twin-
union. The glow or the tremblings, the exulting confidence or the racking doubts of religion, are ever combined
with the naturally inspired element; and it is difficult
to conceive that the mind of the bard was so constituted
as to hold the flame more sacred than the other. Like
the Psalmist, his outpourings must be in verse, or they
would be beneath his aspirations. His prose appeared to
him as if it were the effort of a stammerer: he only
reached a fulness of expression when he sung –

>   And now in age I bud again,
>   After so many deaths I live and write;
>   I once more smell the dew and rain,
>   And relish versing: O, my only light,
>   It cannot be,
>   That I am he
>   On whom thy tempests fell at Night.
>   ['The Flower', 11. 36–41]

And yet even poetry fails to satisfy his longings:

>   Verses, ye are too fine a thing, too wise
>   For my rough sorrows; cease, be dumb and mute,
>   Give up your feet, and running to mine eyes,
>   And keep your measures for some lover's lute,
>   Whose grief allows him music and a rhyme:
>   For mine excludes both measure, tune, and time.
>   Alas, my God!
>   ['Grief', 11. 13–19]

The foregoing lines, particularly the third of them,
may prepare readers for one of the prominent characteristics of the author, namely that of sprinkling strange and
quaint conceits over all, even his most serious compositions. It was the taste of the times, and endured for
above a hundred and fifty years, with admiration and
applause. Nor was it confined to secular works or versification. It revelled in the pulpit, and our eldest and
greatest divines afford the most extraordinary instance of
its prevalence and permanency. And usage made the illustrations tell. People did not laugh at the oddest and

merriest of them. On the contrary, they pointed the moral
to the habits and intellect of those days, and are not to
be judged by our changed habits and opinions now. And it
must be observed that Herbert is rarely extravagant, but
generally very demonstrative and fortunate in this style of
writing, though occasionally we have such specimens as the
following:

[Quotes 'The Pulley' in full.]

The familiarity of expression and play on words in this
example have much the air of profanity to modern apprehension; but there is no doubt that such a composition was, in
its own day, reckoned one of the most successful and persuasive of the Author's appeals to all classes, including
the simple and uninformed, to induce them to put their
trust in the Almighty, who had bestowed so much upon them,
and only reserved a blessing likely to prove a curse and
keep them from seeking refuge with him.
    In the first edition of Herbert's Works, published in
1633, the year after his death, the effect of a number of
the poems was enhanced by the fanciful devices in which
they were typographically moulded into the shapes of
angels' wings, hour-glasses, altar-pieces, and other forms
analogically connected with their matter. This accounts,
in some measure, for the endless variety of his versification; which, in these cases, despising dactyls or spondees,
adjusted itself, long and short, to the model set for its
external appearance. How different are our book embellish-
ments now, to attract and delight the eye; yet, after all,
the substance is in the Poet, and only the ornament and
decoration in the artist.
    Yet we are free to own that Fancy combines more har-
moniously with sweet or pathetic ideas than with sacred
exhortations and mysteries; and Herbert overflows with
charms of this description, both familiar and touching.
They occur at every page; as, for example, of the first:

    For sure, when Adam did not know
        To sin, or sin to smother;
    He might to Heaven from Paradise go,
        As from one room to another.
                        ['The H. Communion', ll. 33-6]

And -

        Death is still working like a mole,
        And digs my grave at each remove;

Let grace work too, and on my soul
                    Drop from above.
                              ['Grace', 11. 13-16]

And -

O, raise me then, poor bees, that work all day
        Sting my delay,
    Who had a work, as well as they
        And much, much more.
                              ['Praise' (I), 11. 17-20]

Again -

O, that I were an Orange tree,
    That busy plant!
Then should I ever laden be,
    And never want
Some fruit for him that dresseth me.
                              ['Employment' (II), 11. 21-5]

How the quaintnesses spring!

My thoughts are all a case of knives,
    Wounding my heart
    With scattered smart;
As watering-pots give flowers their lives.
    Nothing their fury can control
    While they do wound and prick my soul.
                              ['Affliction' (IV), 11. 7-12]

On man -

Nothing wears clothes, but man; nothing doth need
But he to wear them. Nothing useth fire,
But man alone, to show his heavenly breed:
And only he hath fuel in desire.
                              ['Providence', 11. 109-12]

With an obnoxious problem which, if true, would dissolve
society, we close these specimens of the far-fetched
'humours' of the past age -

Surely, if each one saw another's heart,
    There would be no commerce,
No sale or bargain pass: all would disperse,
    And live apart.
                              ['Giddinesse', 11. 21-4]

Besides illustrating the poetical tastes of our ancestors,
and Herbert's ministration to them, as well as some of his
figures without their extrinsic linear representations;
these quotations, nevertheless, convey fine moral and
religious thoughts in a manner impressive upon their own
contemporaneous date, though liable to be lost on our fastidious era, when partial education is more widely extended, and minute criticism more largely indulged.

But these which we may view as blemishes, must not be
taken as fair and candid specimens of the saintly muse of
Herbert. They are rather the exceptions which establish
the rule of his beauty and excellence. In 'The Church
Porch,' which opens the Poems of 'The Temple,' there is,
if we may allegorize the theme, an attractive series of
niches filled with delightful images: and through all the
sequel, no less happily conceived and executed ideas
abound. The admonitions of the Church against lust,
drunkenness, lying, idleness, and other vices, are of singular force; and the more so because they are delivered
with gentleness, and a sympathy for erring humanity. Even
the slight quaintnesses which occur, impart to them something of a friendly tone. Herbert

Allures to brighter worlds, and points the way.

He is a man like his readers, and assuming no dogmatism
on account of his self-sacrifice and almost superhuman
devotedness, to the well-being of his fellow-creatures
here and hereafter, and the service of his adored Creator.
In him there is nothing polemic or antagonistic; nothing of
the Pharisee, everything of the benevolent Samaritan.
From his pen we have no threats, no anathemas, no bigotry,
no damning, of those who differ from him, though strongly
attached to the Protestant Church of his fathers. All is
done in kindliness, earnestness, and love; and it is this
which has preserved his writings through such a lapse of
time, so mutable and wonderful that thousands of other
worthy ventures have sunk and perished, and renders them,
at this hour, when the Spirit of Religion is so vividly
renewed, more than ever deserving of the deepest study by
every member of the thinking world. A most edifying lesson for all; it will require small painstaking to extract
from the Volume of Herbert's works. We hope it will be a
pleasure to go a little way along with us, snatching a
glance at his fair flowers and medicinal herbs as we pass
on our way to his 'Church:'

[Quotes 'The Church-porch', ll. 25-6, 31-3, 55-9.]

Herbert is equally energetic against falsehood, and
the neglect of education of children and examination of
self; and the next stanza is replete with that common
sense we have noticed as so valuable an ingredient in his
spiritual admonitions:

[Quotes 11. 151-60, 175-8, 181, 271-2, 347, 451-6.]

If the mere 'Church Porch' yields such wisdom, morality,
and poetry as these quotations, hastily taken from many of
equal claim, it may readily be believed that (let us put
poetry statistically in this utilitarian age) as thirteen
is to one, so must the rest of Herbert's beauties be to
the sample, we have quoted and indicated, inasmuch as they
conform to that proportion in the entire body of his
Poetry.

Of this major division, however, we are bound to take
some notice, and designate some, though (to avoid the pro-
lixity objectionable in the introduction to an established
author, a very scanty illustration of its manifold, powerful, and pathetic attractions. Even personal affliction is
made touchingly poetical:

        I had my wish, my way:
    My days were strew'd with flowers and happiness:
            There was no month but May!
    But with my years sorrow did twist and grow,
    And made a party unawares for woe.

    My flesh began unto my soul in pain,
            Sickness clave my bones,
    Consuming agues dwelt in every vein,
            And tuned my breath to groans:
    Sorrow was all my soul; I scarce believed,
    Till grief did tell me roundly, that I lived.
                        ['Affliction' (I), 11. 20-30]

Some slight exuberance of imagery follows this; but
nothing can obliterate the Job-like poetry of the exquisite
description passing from the joys of youth and health,
when there was no month but May, to the bleak December of
disease and sorrow.

The short poems, 'Frailty,' 'Peace,' and 'The World,'
are altogether pleasing specimens of Herbert's genius and
turn of mind: but we can only refer to them, and adopt even
shorter pieces to substantiate our observations on the
Author. An exhortation to the faithful observance of Lent
is thus nobly improved and applied:

[Quotes, 'Lent', 11. 43-8.]

The very next poem, entitled 'Virtue,' begins with a
most affecting verse:

>Sweet day, so cool, so calm, so bright,
>The bridal of the earth and sky,
>The dew shall weep thy fall to-night;
>>For thou must die.

This piece has been imitated by many succeeding poets,
but not one has excelled the original; nor can the English
tongue produce a more exquisite passage than the few lines
we have just quoted. There is one termination only equal,
and, perhaps, superior, to this fine passage, which readers
will find in the lines entitled 'The Collar,' wherein the
Christian repines and asserts his determination to enjoy
the pleasures of life, and throw off the bondage of religion. Can anything be more sublime than this conclusion?

[Quotes the poem's last nine lines.]

To the immortal simplicity of this, we should be ashamed to
add either comment or farther quotation. We have attempted
to bring Herbert justly and honestly before the reader;
convinced that the example of his humility, piety, and
passionate faith must produce good fruits now and for
ever. To show that his Poetry is not to be judged by or
censured for the peculiarities of his age, but to be tried
by and cherished for merits which fit it for the improvement and blessing of all ages. In fine, to invite the
British Public to a treat it seldom or never enjoys - to
forget the present moment for awhile, and cast a retro-
spect on the past - and thence to learn much that is most
desirable to know. Living flowers are, no doubt, sweet
and agreeable: but they are mostly mere temporary pleasures
addressed to the sense. The precious plants of Christian
growth and efficacy, which have been crushed under the
weight of years, when revived, yield odours which not only
refresh the body but the soul. So may it be with Herbert's
Godly works!

Note

1 Walton, above, pp. 123-4.

50.   GEORGE GILFILLAN, FROM HIS INTRODUCTION TO 'THE
POETICAL WORKS OF GEORGE HERBERT'

1853

The second edition of Herbert's poetry within 1853 was the
labour of the Reverend George Gilfillan, a writer of considerable range. As his introduction clearly attests,
Walton's influence persists - but so does the commendation
of Herbert's literary merit ('of a very rare, lofty, and
original order'). See also above, p. 24.
    Source: Gilfillan, from On the Life and Poetical Works
of George Herbert, in 'The Poetical Works of George Herbert' (Edinburgh, 1853), pp. v, xviii-xix, xxi-xxiv, xxvi.

'Life,' it has been said, 'is a Poem.' This is true, probably, of the life of the human race as a whole, if we
could see its beginning and end, as well as its middle.
But it is not true of all lives. It is only a life here
and there, which equals the dignity and aspires to the
completeness of a genuine and great Poem. Most lives are
fragmentary, even when they are not foul - they disappoint,
even when they do not disgust - they are volumes without
a preface, an index, or a moral. It is delightful to turn
from such apologies for life to the rare but real lives
which God-gifted men, like Milton or Herbert, have been
enabled to spend even on this dark and melancholy foot-
breadth for immortal spirits, called the earth.
    We class Milton and Herbert together, for this, among
other reasons, that in both, the life and the poems were
thoroughly correspondent and commensurate with each other.
Milton lived the 'Paradise Lost' and the 'Paradise Regained,' as well as wrote them. Herbert was, as well as
built, 'The Temple.' Not only did the intellectual arche-
type of its structure exist in his mind, but he had been
able, in a great measure, to realise it in life, before
expressing it in poetry....

[After a biographical account of Herbert - in matter
Waltonesque and in manner florid - Gilfillan attends to
the poetry.]

    We come not to criticise 'The Temple,' although the
term criticism applied to what is a bosom companion rather
than a book may seem cold and out of place. We come,
then, we shall rather say, to announce our profound love
for the work, and to assign certain reasons for that love.

We may first, however, allude to the faults with which
it has been justly charged. These are, however, venial,
and are those not of the author so much as of his day.
He is often quaint, and has not a few conceits, which are
rather ingenious than tasteful. Anagrams, acrostics,
verbal quibbles, and a hundred other formulae, cold in
themselves, although indigenous to the age, and greatly
redeemed by the fervour his genius throws into them,
abound in 'The Temple,' and so far suit the theme, that
they remind us of the curious figures and devices which
add their Arabesque border to the grandeur of old
Abbeys and Cathedrals. It was the wild, crude rhythm of
the period, and had Herbert not conformed himself to it,
he had either been a far less or a far greater poet than
he was. Yet, though bound in chains, he became even in
durance an alchymist, and turned his chains into gold.

Herbert has, besides, what may be considered more
formidable faults than these. He is often obscure, and
his allegorising vein is opened too often, and explored
too far; so much so, that had we added a commentary or
extended notes on 'The Temple,' it would have necessarily
filled another volume nearly as large as the present.
This the plan of our publication, of course, entirely for-
bids. We may merely premise these advices to those who
would care to understand as well as read the succeeding
poem: - 1*st*, Let them regard it as in many portions a
piece of picture-writing; 2*dly*, Let them seek the secret
of this, partly by a careful study of the book itself,
and partly by reading the similar works of Donne, Quarles,
Giles Fletcher, and John Bunyan; 3*dly*, Let them believe
in Herbert, even when they do not understand him; and
4*thly*, Let them rejoice that the great proportion of the
book is perfectly clear and plain, to Christians by experience, to poets by imaginative sympathy, to all men in
general by the power of conscience, the sense of guilt,
and that fear of the terrors and that hope of the joys of
a future state of being, by which all hearts at times are
moved....

[Two effusive pages later, Gilfillan continues:]

'The Temple,' looking at it more narrowly, may be
viewed in its devotional, in its poetical, and in its
philosophical aspects, which we may figure as its altar,
its painted window, and its floor and foundation. First,
as a piece of devotion it is a Prayer-book in verse. We
find in it all the various parts of prayer. Now like a
seraph he casts his crown at God's feet, and covers his
face with his wings, in awful adoration. Now he looks up

in His face, with the happy gratitude of a child, and murmurs out his thanksgiving. Now he seems David the penitent, although fallen from an inferior height, and into
pits not nearly so deep and darksome, confessing his sins
and shortcomings to his Heavenly Father. And now he asks,
and prays, and besieges heaven for mercy, pardon, peace,
grace, and joy, as with 'groanings that cannot be uttered.'
We find in it, too, a perpetual undersong of praise. It
is a Psalter, no less than a Prayer-book. And how different its bright sparks of worship going up without effort,
without noise, by mere necessity of nature, to heaven, from
the majority of hymns which have since appeared! No
namby-pambyism, no false unction, no nonsensical raptures,
are to be found in them; their very faults and mannerisms
serve to attest their sincerity, and to shew that the whole
man is reflected in them. Even although the poem had
possessed far less poetic merit, its mere devotion, in its
depth and truth, would have commended it to Christians,
as, next to the Psalms, the finest collection of ardent
and holy breathings to be found in the world.

But its poetical merit is of a very rare, lofty, and
original order. It is full of that subtle perception of
analogies which is competent only to high poetical genius.
All things, to Herbert, appear marvellously alike to each
other. The differences, small or great, whether they be
the interspaces between leaves, or the gulfs between
galaxies, shrivel up and disappear. The ALL becomes one
vast congeries of mirrors - of similitudes - of dupli-
cates -

Star nods to star, each system has its brother,
And half the universe reflects the other. (1)

This principle, or perception, which is the real spring
of all fancy and imagination, was very strong in Herbert's
mind, and hence the marvellous richness, freedom, and
variety of his images. He hangs upon his 'Temple' now
flowers and now stars, now blossoms and now full-grown
fruit. He gathers glories from all regions of thought -
from all gardens of beauty - from all the history, and
art, and science then accessible to him, - and he wreathes
them in a garland around the bleeding brow of Immanuel.
Sometimes his style exhibits a clear massiveness like one
of the Temple pillars, sometimes a dim richness like one of
the Temple windows; and never is there wanting the Temple
music, now wailing melodiously, now moving in brisk,
lively, and bird-like measures, and now uttering loud
paeans and crashes of victorious sound. It has been truly
said of him, that he is 'inspired by the Bible, as its

vaticinators were inspired by God.' It is to him not only
the 'Book of God, but the God of Books.' He has hung and
brooded over its pages, like a bird for ever dipping her
wing in the sea; he has imbibed its inmost spirit - he has
made its divine words 'the men of his counsel, and his
song in the house of his pilgrimage,' till they are in his
verse less imitated than reproduced. In this, as in other
qualities, such as high imagination, burning zeal, quaint
fancy, and deep simplicity of character he resembles that
'Child-Angel,' John Bunyan, who was proud to be a babe of
the Bible, although his genius might have made him without
it a gigantic original.

We might have quoted many passages corroborating our
impressions of the surpassing artistic merit of George
Herbert's poem. But the book, as well as the criticism,
is now in the reader's hands, and he is called upon to
judge for himself. We may merely recommend to his attention, as especially beautiful and rich, 'The Church-Porch,'
'The Agony,' 'Redemption,' 'Easter,' 'Sin,' 'Prayer,'
'Whitsunday,' 'Affliction,' 'Humility,' 'To all Angels
and Saints,' 'Vanity,' 'Virtue' (which contains the stanza
so often quoted, 'Sweet Day,' &c.), 'The British Church,'
'The Quip,' and 'Peace.' Many more will detain and fas-
cinate him as he goes along, - some by their ingenious
oddity, some by their tremulous pathos, some by the peculiar profundity of their devotional spirit; and the rest
by the sincerity and truth which burn in every line.

We have spoken of the philosophy of 'The Temple.' We
do not mean by this, that it contains any elaborately constructed, distinctly defined, or logically defended system, but simply that it abounds in glimpses of philosophic
thought of a very profound and searching cast. The singular earnestness of Herbert's temperament was connected with
- perhaps we should rather say *created* in him - an eye
which penetrated below the surface, and looked right into
the secrets of things. In his peculiarly happy and blessed
constitution, piety and the philosophic genius were united
and reconciled; and from those awful depths of man's mysterious nature, which few have more thoroughly, although
incidentally, explored than he, he lifts up, not a howl of
despair, nor a curse of misanthropy, nor a cry of mere
astonishment, but a hymn of worship. We refer especially
to those two striking portions of the poem entitled 'Man'
and 'Providence.' The first is a fine comment on the
Psalmist's words, 'I am fearfully and wonderfully made.'
Herbert first saw, or at least first expressed in poetry,
the central position of man to the universe - the fact that
all its various lines find a focus in him - that he is a
microcosm to the All, and that every part of man is, in

its turn, a little microcosm of him. The germ of some of
the abstruse theories propounded by Swedenborg, and since
enlarged and illustrated by the author of 'The Human Body,
Considered in its Relation to Man' (a treatise written
with a true Elizabethan richness of style and thought,
and which often seems to approach, at least, great abysses
of discovery), may be found in Herbert's verses. 'Man,'
Herbert says, 'is everything and more.' He is 'a beast,
yet is or should be more.' He is 'all symmetry - full of
*proportions, one limb to another, and all to all the world
besides.*'

> Head with foot hath private amity,
> And both with moons and tides.
>
> His eyes dismount the highest star:
> *He is in little all the sphere.*
> Herbs gladly cure our flesh, *because that they*
>   *Find their acquaintance there.*
>
> *Each thing is full of duty.*
>
> More servants wait on Man,
> Than he'll take notice of: in every path
>   He treads down that which doth befriend him,
>   When sickness makes him pale and wan.
> Oh, mighty love! Man is *one world*, and hath
>   *Another to attend him.*

How strikingly do these words bring before us the
thought of Man the Mystery! 'What a piece of workmanship'
verily he is! He is formed as of a thousand lights and
shadows. He is compacted out of all contradictions. While
his feet touch the dust, and are of miry clay, his head is
of gold, and strikes the Empyrean....

[The paean continues for two pages of the same order, and
Gilfillan finally concludes:]

Altogether, there are few places on earth nearer Heaven,
filled with a richer and holier light, adorned with
chaster and nobler ornaments, or where our souls can worship with a more entire forgetfulness of self, and a more
thorough realisation of the things unseen and eternal,
than in 'The Temple' of George Herbert. You say, as you
stand breathless below its solemn arches, 'This is none
other than the house of God, it is the gate of Heaven.
How dreadful, yet how dear is this place!'

Note

1   Adapted from Pope.'s 'Epistle to Burlington', 11. 117-18:
    'Grove nods at grove, each Alley has a brother, / And
    half the platform just reflects the other'. The allu-
    sion was identified by Mr Anthony W. Shipps.

51. ROBERT ARIS WILLMOTT, FROM HIS INTRODUCTION TO 'THE
WORKS OF GEORGE HERBERT'

1854

The third major edition of Herbert's poetry in the 1850s
was prepared by the widely-read Reverend R.A. Willmott,
replete with annotation and a number of tellingly pious
plates. Reprinted several times thereafter, the edition
includes an introduction where the biographical account of
Herbert was shaped under the influence of Walton. The
extract concerns the poetry, significantly commended for
its 'creative playfulness'. See also above, p. 24.
    Source: Willmott, from the introduction to 'The Works
of George Herbert' (1854), pp. xxi-xxx.

Herbert belongs to that third Italian school, which was to
occupy a chapter in Gray's history of poetry, as he commu-
nicated the plan to Warton. (1) It was a school, in his
opinion, full of conceit, beginning in the reign of Elizabeth; continued under James and Charles the First, by
Donne, Crashaw, and Cleveland; carried to its height by
Cowley, and ending with Sprat. Herbert was certainly a
disciple. Complicated metaphors abound. The poems of
that age recall the mechanical contrivances of the eccentric Mr. Winstanley, the first architect of the Eddystone
Lighthouse. In his strange abode nothing was what it
seemed to be. An old slipper upon the floor started into
a spectral figure; a visitor resting in a chair, was suddenly embraced by two muscular arms; or sauntering into a
summer-house, straightway found himself floating away into
the middle of a Canal. The poetic surprises of Herbert
are sometimes equally unexpected, and it must be confessed,
not less ingenious. The reader's eye is perpetually struck
with a transformation, or a grotesque invention.
    Even the friendly taste of Mr. Keble (2) was offended
by the constant flutter of his fancy, for ever hovering

round and round the theme. But this was a peculiarity
which the most gifted writers admired. Dryden openly
avowed that nothing appeared more beautiful to him than the
the imagery in Cowley, which some readers condemned. It
must, at least, be said in praise of this creative playfulness, that it is a quality of the intellect singularly
sprightly and buoyant; it ranges over a boundless landscape, pierces into every corner, and, by the light of
its own fire - to adopt a phrase of Temple - discovers a
thousand little bodies, or images in the world, unseen by
common eyes, and only manifested by the rays of that poetic
sun.

There is in Herbert another sort of quaintness, which is
neither the fruit of his age, nor of his own understanding,
but of the authors whom he studied. 'He that reads Mr.
Herbert's poems attendingly, shall find the excellence of
Scripture Divinity, and choice passages of the Fathers
bound up in metre.' If James Montgomery had considered
this remark of Barnabas Oley; he would have hesitated *to
see 'devotion itself turned into masquerade'* by the poet.
(3) Herbert did not forget to consult, for his outpourings of heart-praise and love, that commonplace book of
Greek and Latin theology which the Country Parson is recommended to collect and ponder. Many of his curiosities
of fancy have a Patristic, rather than a poetic ancestry,
and are to be sought in Chrysostom or Cyprian, instead of
in Donne, or Marini.

Every true work of art, whether it be of the pencil,
the chisel, or the pen, addresses itself to particular sympathies. Of course, there will be a certain outward
excellence which the universal taste cannot fail to understand and admire. I speak of the inner and the hidden
charm. The beauty of Raffaelle's Madonna reveals itself
very differently to the critic and the worshipper. Milton
may be admired by the common reader, for his grandeur of
sentiment; but it is only through the spectacles of books
that the splendour and the loveliness of his visions are
clearly discerned. Now, Herbert has, according to his
degree, the distinctive peculiarities of Raffaelle and
Milton. His sweetness of fancy, his vigorous sense, and
his happiness of idiom may be appreciated by all people;
just as the grace and the dignity of the picture and the
epic come home to the least refined observer. But there is
a remoter and a delightfuller quality, that requires a
kindred heart to comprehend it. Herbert is pre-eminently
a poet of the Church; his similes are drawn from her
ceremonial; his most solemn thoughts are born of her
mysteries; his tenderest lessons are taught by her
prayers. To a reader without a deep Catholic devotion, he

is only the ingenious or the fantastic rhymer; to one
who has that feeling, his verses are the strings of a
musical instrument, making melody in themselves, and
awaking sweet sounds in the hearts of those who hear it.

There is a passage in one of Southey's letters that
seems very forcibly to illustrate this view. Speaking of
Wordsworth, he asks, 'Does he not associate more feeling
with particular phrases, and you also with him, than those
phrases convey to any one else? This I suspect. Who would
part with a ring of a dead friend's hair? And yet a jew-
eller will give for it only the value of the gold.' (4)
This is just the case with Herbert. His verses are not to
be tossed into the scale, and weighed. There is the hair
of the dead Friend in the gold. The Gospel consecrates
every rhyme. The Liturgy is reflected in nearly every
devout sentiment. The poem on 'SIN' is almost a Collect
in its majestic harmony, and simpleness of language. The
'Sacrifice' has quite a Scriptural solemnity of grouping
and representation.

A remarkable charm of Herbert's poetry is seen in what
may be named - the proverbial philosophy of common sense.
All the famous writers of that, and the former century,
abounded in it; whether we take up the Apologies and
Defences of Jewell; the Essays of Bacon; or the exhortations of Taylor. The quantity of plain, practical wisdom,
for every-day life, treasured up in the verses of Herbert,
has scarcely been considered. The Church Porch is a little
hand-book of rules for the management of temper, and conversation, and business. Every child ought to get it by
heart. It recalls the comparison by which Plato characterised Socrates. The outside of the vase is scrawled over
with odd shapes and writing, but within are precious
liquors, and healing medicines, and rare mixtures of far-
gathered herbs and flowers. It connection with this
moralising disposition may be mentioned a certain familiar
humour, suddenly shooting gleams across a serious passage,
(5) and very strongly reminding us of the pleasantry of
Cowper. In the following pages the reader will be struck
by a playfulness, that looks like a thoughtful smile from
Weston.

The masculine sense of Herbert has drawn eyes that were
skilful enough to avoid his faults. 'From the dregs of
Crashaw, of Carew, of Herbert, and others (for it is well
known he was a great reader of all those poets), Pope has
judiciously collected gold.' So writes Dr. Warton. (6)
From Crashaw Pope might gather some fuel to feed that
devotional flame which burns so vehemently in his Eloisa;
but in Herbert he obtained, what he knew better than any
of his contemporaries how to use, an ample store of

practical wisdom tersely uttered. His discoveries were
not confined to loose gold in the rubbish; he found pieces
of it worked up into an elegance of form, which he himself
could not improve. Many lines in the Temple have the
polish and the glitter of the Moral Essays; and not seldom
the structure of his own couplet, and the identical pause
of the caesura are anticipated.

The characteristic of Herbert's fancy is fruitfulness.
The poetry, like the theology of that age, put all learning into an abridgment. A course of lectures flowed into
the rich essence of a single sermon. A month's seed
bloomed in an ode. The 17th was the contradiction of the
19th century, the object being then to give the most
thought in the smallest space, as now to sow the widest
field with the frugallest corn. Herbert's 'Pilgrimage'
is an example. Written, probably, before Bunyan was
born, - certainly while he was an infant, - it contains all
the Progress of the Pilgrim in outline. We are shewn the
gloomy Cave of Desperation, the Rock of Pride, the Mead
of Fancy, the Copse of Care, the Wild Heath where the
Traveller is robbed of his fold, and the gladsome Hill
that promises a fair prospect, but only yields a lake of
brackish water on the top. Such a composition would
scarcely escape the notice of that Spenser of the people,
who afterwards gave breadth and animation, and figures to
the scene.

The language of Herbert cannot be too highly praised -
however distant the thought may be, the expression of it
is, with very few exceptions, pure, racy, and idiomatic.
He had evidently been a living and a constant hearer, or
reader of Shakespere, whose Plays appeared in his childhood, and were, doubtless, the delight of his eyes during
the short summer-day of his courtly hopes, and the frequent subject of talk at Wilton. Many passages might be
quoted; but the Shakesperian tone will be recognized in
the following:

        How neatly do we give one only name
        To parent's issue, and the Sun's bright star!
        A son is light and fruit; a fruitful flame
        Chasing the father's dimness.
                            ['The Sonne', 11. 5-8]

And still more distinctly in the next,

        My comforts drop and melt away like snow;
        I shake my head, and all the thoughts and ends
        Which my fierce youth did bandy, fall and flow

Like leaves about me, or like summer friends,
Flies of estate and sunshine.
['The Answer', 11. 1-5]

The beautiful phrase - 'Summer Friends' - was introduced by Gray into his Hymn on Adversity. (7) Once more:

[Quotes 'The Church-porch', 11. 85-9.]

Pages might easily be filled with instances of felicitous words and phrases. In the Poem on Providence we have
the 'leaning' elephant [1. 140] afterwards exhibited by
Thomson in his magnificent landscape:

Peaceful, beneath primeval trees that cast
Their ample shade o'er Niger's yellow stream,
And where the Ganges rolls his sacred wave,
High-raised in solemn theatre around,
Leans the huge elephant.
['The Seasons: Summer', 11. 716-20]

Herbert's versification is frequently affected by his
manner of thinking. The compression of thought causes
harshness. Sometimes the rhythm drags with a slow, jolting, uneven step, making the reader to remember Walpole's
criticism of an Ode, amended by Mason, which, he told him,
had a sudden sink, like a man with one leg shorter than
the other. (8) But not seldom the harmony is soft and
flowing, and lovely fancies are chanted to their own music.
The 'Flower,' 'Virtue,' and 'Gratefulness,' are exquisite
specimens of this class.
The poetry and the prose of Herbert differ as much as
Cowley's. He has not, indeed, left any composition to be
compared with the delightful Essays; but he possessed a
large share of the same freshness, gaiety, and ease. If
we had the manuscripts that perished in the flames of
Highnam House, (9) we might propose a nearer parallel.
But Fuller justly pronounced even his remains to be shav-
ings of gold. 'The Country Parson' is destined to live.
Among the few English writings of a practical class, between 1600 and 1650, and yet retaining a reputation, Mr.
Hallam places this treatise of Herbert; which he judges to
be 'on the whole, a pleasing little book,' but, 'with the
precepts sometimes so overstrained, as to give an air of
affectation.' (10) This is faint praise; and the censure
is refuted by the Work itself. The author informs us,
that he wrote it with a view to his own spiritual improvement, drawing the form and character of a true Pastor,
that he might have a mark to aim at; and setting it as

high as he could, since 'he shoots higher that threatens
the moon, than he that aims at a tree.'
    Herbert must be considered to have fulfilled his design.
The epidemics of one age require a different treatment
from those of another. The cure of the past fails in the
present. The popular disease, in the former half of the
17th century, was the degraded condition of the country
Clergy. It had almost become chronic. There could be no
instruction where there was no respect. Such shepherds
neither guided nor fed their flocks. Herbert's object was
two-fold; to raise the teacher and to win the people; the
former lesson he shewed by precept, the second by example.
He painted the portrait of the Good Parson, and was himself the original. His views of the pastoral office,
even in the rudest country hamlet, were lofty and glowing;
and he recommended the study of Plato for the sake of
acquiring the desterity of Socrates, and applying it to
the common intercourse and teaching of a Parish. He was a
burning and a shining light in his own time, and he still
sheds a softened lustre over ours. Such men ennoble their
brethren, by their beautiful union of all that is practical, with whatever is graceful in life. In them nothing
is harsh or repulsive. The austere raiment is bound with
a fair girdle. Sanderson sings psalms to his own music;
Ken warbles hymns before he sleeps; Herbert delights to
set anthems to his lute; and Wotton bequeaths his viol to
a friend. (11)

    O could we copy their mild virtues, then
    What joy to live, what blessedness to die!
    Methinks their very names shine still and bright;
    Apart - like glow-worms on a summer night:
    Or lonely tapers, when from far they fling
    A guiding-ray; or seem, like stars on high,
    Satellites burning in a lucid ring. (12)

Notes

1 The poet and critic Joseph Warton was also the recipient
   of a communication from Pope involving Herbert (see
   above, p. 15).
2 See No. 52.
3 Quoted more fully above, pp. 22-3. On Oley's remark,
   see above, p. 76.
4 Charles C. Southey, 'The Life and Correspondence of
   Robert Southey' (1850), II, 191.
5 Cf. Coleridge on the way that, in Sir Thomas Browne,
   'the Humorist [is] constantly mingling with & flashing

across the Philosopher' ('Coleridge on the Seventeenth
Century', ed. Roberta F. Brinkley (Durham, NC, 1955),
p. 448).
6 Above, p. 15.
7 Thomas Gray, 'Ode to Adversity', 1. 22.
8 Letter to William Mason, 19 March 1774; in 'The Letters
   of Horace Walpole', ed. Mrs Paget Toynbee (Oxford,
   1904), VIII, 431.
9 See below, p. 257 (note 2).
10 Henry Hallam, 'Introduction to the Literature of
   Europe in the 15th, 16th, and 17th Centuries' (repr.
   1970), II, 364.
11 Bishop Robert Sanderson (1587-1663); Thomas Ken
   (1637-1711); Sir Henry Wotton (1568-1639).
12 Wordsworth, 'Ecclesiastical Sonnets', III, v, 7-13.

52. JOHN KEBLE, FROM A LECTURE

1854

Herbert and Keble were often juxtaposed during the nineteenth century, but Keble himself mentioned his greater
predecessor only once (see also above, p. 26). The occasion was a lecture on poetry, in the course of which he
remarked on the assumption of a shepherd's guise by pastoral poets. He continued as shown below.
     Source: 'Keble's Lectures on Poetry 1832-1841', trans.
Edward K. Francis (Oxford, 1912), p. 99. The translation
is from the original text in Latin (Oxford, 1854),
pp. 471-2.

...the whole tribe of lyrical poets (if that is the right
name for them) cannot avail itself of this expedient of
shifted responsibility, since in this species of poetry
everything is uttered in the poet's own person. Consequently, the art and skill of the writer had to effect
that which could not be effected by the nature of the
poem: and let us see whether there are not two chief
methods which enable lyrical poets to maintain the true
dignity of poetic reserve, and to protect their inmost
thoughts and enthusiasms and emotions from being exposed
to the full blaze of daylight. I suggest that this is
effected, first, by the tact or judgement of the writers,
in choosing subjects somewhat remote from those which in

truth hold their affection.   Thus it comes about that,
even if perchance they touch on these deepest subjects,
they appear rather to fall in with them incidentally, than
to have sought them purposely.   But in the main they, as
it were, trifle with and play round their dearest delights.
Such is, to a great extent, the method of our own Herbert,
who hides the deep love of God which consumed him behind a
cloud of precious conceits: the result appears to most
readers inappropriate, not to say chilling and repellent.
Fair-minded critics are wont to excuse him on the score of
the taste and tone of the age in which he lived: still,
granting as much weight as you choose to this cause, it
will still be open to us to contend that it was Herbert's
modest reserve which made him veil under these refinements
his deep piety.

But the end which Herbert and many others effected
mainly by choice of subject, some, unless I err, have
attempted to gain by elaborate metrical devices....

53.   ANONYMOUS, FROM A REVIEW IN THE 'BRITISH QUARTERLY REVIEW'

1854

A hostile anonymous essay - nominally a review of the editions by Gilfillan and Willmott (Nos 50 and 51) - commenced
innocently enough with a florid 'sketch', generally subservient to Walton, of Herbert's life ('Herbert's ... last
three years were soothed and brightened by the watchful
care and beaming smiles of his devoted Jane').   Its hos-
tility surfaced especially in this extract, which follows
and extends an attempted evaluation of Herbert's poems in
the light of seventeenth-century practice together with an
'estimate of their respective merits'.   See also above,
p. 26.
   Source: from an untitled article in the 'British Quarterly Review', XIX (1854), 393-8 and 407.

In what rank shall we place Herbert as a poet?   If some
critics have passed him over what that faint praise which
is almost blame, others have claimed for him high place
even among our foremost poets.   That Herbert has been a
favourite writer, and that twenty thousand copies of his
'Temple' had been sold when Walton published his life, has
little to do with his poetical merits, for political

reasons alone might account for it. It was just when
episcopalian and puritan were about to gird themselves
for mortal conflict, that these poems first appeared; and
during the long strife, members of the English church,
indifferent to the light poems of Carew, and Randolph,
and Lovelace; scandalized at the ribaldry of Suckling and
Cleveland, must have hailed a book not only so unexcep-
tionable but so pious. And then, when that church was
proscribed, with still warmer feelings would they cherish
the poems of one, who, with almost idolatrous affection,
celebrated that 'dear mother' who then sat lone and desolate. Thus Herbert's 'Temple' became a hand-book to the
devout episcopalian; and Christopher Harvey's extravagant
rhapsodies actually obtained wide circulation, because
they were tagged on as a supplement - a most needless one -
to 'Master Herbert's divine poems.'

Let us not be misunderstood in these remarks, as though
we denied Herbert's poetical merit; we only show how far
political feeling can aid in bringing a work into wide
circulation; after that is done, if it have merit it will
live, if not, like that far more popular book, 'Eikon
Basilike,' (1) it will sink into oblivion, and be nowhere
found save on the shelf of the book collector. Now, that
Herbert has merit, his continued popularity proves - not
transcendant merit, for *that* the popular mind does not
appreciate, as is proved in its estimate of the various
works of our greatest poets, but among the minor poets of
a most poetical age, Herbert, in right of some true gems,
may be placed.

The chief fault of Herbert is his great inequality.
This, it is true, was the characteristic of many contemporary poems, but then they were long ones; and while we
feel vexed, almost repelled, as we turn these over, we
are sure to be compensated when we come to the shorter.
Now although Herbert cannot be charged with diffuseness,
his fault is, to use an old proverb, that 'he cannot let
well alone.' Thus some of his poems, short as they are,
would still admirably bear curtailment. Here is one,
'The Elixir;' it consists of six verses, reduce it to
three, and what a fine poem it becomes, - weighty with
solemn wisdom, and pointed with noble thought: -

[Quotes stanzas 1, 4, and 6.]

Many others might be shortened in the same way, and
much to their improvement. The extravagant quaintnesses
that abound in Herbert's poems, and which Mr. Gilfillan
strangely asserts are 'not of the author so much as of his
day,' Mr. Willmott assigns more correctly to the influence

of Donne. Where, indeed, save in Donne and the few writers
who followed him, shall we find those strange conceits, and
far-fetched, or ludicrous figures? Shakespeare and Milton
were of that day, but do we meet with such vagaries in
their poems? Even courtly Jonson, writing for a pedant
king, rarely in his exquisite verses ventures upon a
quibble. And Herrick, Sylvester, Wither, even Quarles, -
how graceful is their imagery, how unmatched, too, in
sweetness is their very diction! We should, therefore,
like to know what Mr. Gilfillan means by 'the wild crude
rhythm of the period' - a period distinguished far beyond
every other for the delicious melody and variety of versification. That Herbert's verse is harsh, in many
instances, his admirers must allow; and when we remember
his passionate love for music, we cannot account for it.
But there seems a labour in many of his poems which is
fatal to rhythmical excellence. Here is a specimen from
the poem entitled 'Praise,' which will illustrate his overstrained use of metaphor and his harsh numbers:-

> When Thou dost favour any action,
>   It runs - it flies:
> All things concurre to give it a perfection.
>   That which had but two legs before,
> When Thou didst blesse hath twelve; one wheel doth rise
>   To twentie then, or more.
>
> But when Thou dost on businesse blow,
>   It hangs - it clogs:
> Not all the teams of Albion in a row,
>   Can hale or drawe it out of doore.
> Legs are but stumps, and Pharaoh's wheels but logs,
>   And struggling hinders more.
>   ['Praise' (III), 11. 7-18]

Now, take a similar illustration, though differently
applied, from that fine old writer Quarles:-

> Whene'er the old exchange of profit rings,
>   Her silver saint's bell of uncertain gains;
> My merchant soul can stretch both legs and wings,
>   Now I can run, and take unwearied pains, -
> The charms of profit are so strong, that I,
> Who wanted legs to go, find wings to flie.
>
> But when I come to Thee, my God, that art
>   The royal mine of everlasting treasure,
> The real honor of my better part,
>   And living fountain of eternal pleasure, -

How nerveless are my limbs! how faint, and slow!
I have no wings to flie, nor feet to go.

So when the streams of swift-foot Rhine convey,
    Her upland riches to the Belgick shore,
The idle vessel slides the watery way
    Without the blast or tug of wind or oar, -
Her slippery keel divides the silver foam
With ease, so facile is the way from home.

But when the home-bound vessel turns her sails
    Against the breast of the resisting stream,
O, then she slugs; nor sail or oar prevails,
    The stream is sturdy, and her tides extream,
Each stroke is loss, and every tug is vain,
A boat's length purchase is a league of pain.

How beautifully is this figure wrought out! - each epithet,
even the very rhythm, adding finish to the picture.
Quarles has often been censured for his quaintnesses, but
he has none so extravagant as Herbert's, while there are
heights of noble poetry in his despised 'Emblems,' which
the former could never reach. Take this:-

The still commandress of the silent night,
    Borrows her beams from her bright brother's eye;
His fair aspect fills her sharp horns with light, -
    If he withdraw, her flames are quenched, and die;

Even so the beams of Thy enlight'ning spirit,
    Infused, and shot into my dark desire,
Inflame my strength, and fill my soul with fire,
    That I am ravish'd with a new delight; -
    But if Thou shroud thy face, my glory fades,
And I remain a nothing, all composed of shades.

The following verses, which form the conclusion of the
poem on 'Let your light so shine before men,' resemble
Herbert's, but there is greater finish:-

Art thou afraid to trust thine easy flame,
    To the injurious waste of fortune's puff?
Ah, coward! rouse, and quit thyself for shame,
    Who dies in service, hath lived long enough,
Who shines, and makes no eye partaker,
    Usurps himself, and closely robs his Maker.

Make not thyself a prisoner, thou art free;
    Why dost thou turn thy palace to a jail?

> Thou art an eagle, and befits it thee
>   To live immured like the cloister'd snail? -
> Let toys seek corners; things of cost
>   Gain worth by view: hid jewels are but lost.

For ourselves, we are greatly inclined to prefer Herbert's homelier poems to those on which he lavished so
much ingenuity. Many of these latter have, indeed, fine
passages; but the lofty thought too often is followed by
one actually ludicrous, and the beautiful figure by another
its very reverse. With the exception of the two poems
referred to in our remarks on his life, we scarcely find
one free from this. Even those exquisite lines, - 'Sweet
day, so cool, so calm, so bright,' - how are they spoilt by
the next verse, where the very flower of beauty is
addressed as:-

> Sweet rose, whose hue, angry and brave,
> Bids the bold (2) gazer wipe his eye.
>
> ['Vertue', ll. 5-6]

The rose angry! - the soft, rich colouring of its folded
leaves painful to the sight! What but the strangest love
of paradox could have imagined such a figure. Sometimes
the illustrations are really ludicrous, however solemn the
subject, as this:-

> Christ left his grave-clothes, that we might, when grief
> Draws tears, or blood, not want a handkerchief.
>
> ['Dawning', ll. 15-16]

But when Herbert sits down simply to write for others,
as in his 'Church Porch,' and in some few of his smaller
poems, 'the proverbial philosophy of common sense,' as Mr.
Willmott truly says, gives his poetry a powerful charm.
How fine and sententious is 'Business' - how appallingly
forcible his 'Domesday'! -

> Come away,
> Make no delay,
> Summon all the dust to rise, -
> *Till it stir, and rub the eyes.*
>
> ['Dooms-day', ll. 1-4]

That a 'vision of dry bones' is this! But, above all, how
powerful and how winning are his counsels in that noble
'Church Porch'! Truly Shakespearean are many stanzas: -

> Art thou a magistrate? then be severe;

If studious, copy fair what time hath blurred;
Redeem truth from his jawes; if soldier,
    Chase brave employments with a naked sword
Throughout the world. Fool not; for all may have
If they dare try, a glorious life, or grave....

Slight those who say amid their sickly healths,
    Thou livest by rule. What doth not so but man?
Houses are built by rule, and commonwealths;
    Entice the trustie sum, if that you can,
From his ecliptic line; beckon the skie,
Who lives by rule then, keeps good company.
                                    [ll. 85-90, 133-8]

The chief cause of Herbert's wide celebrity has arisen,
we think, from the notion that he and Milton - some would
perhaps add Quarles - were the only writers of religious
poetry of that day. So effectually indeed did the pretended taste of 'the Augustan age' complete the work of
the Restoration by ignoring all our earlier poetry, that
when Percy, Dalrymple, and Sir Egerton Brydges, first
brought out their specimens, (3) the public were almost as
surprised as if parchments from Pompeii had been unrolled
before them. They knew that the field of English poetry
had lain fallow and bare beneath the blight of the Restoration, but were all unconscious of the glorious harvest - a
scanty handful of which was now brought them - that had
been reaped by earlier hands. Still less were they aware -
even the present generation is not yet aware - of the
stores of magnificent sacred poetry with which that era
abounds. Few, indeed, were the poets of the two earlier
schools who did not sometimes tune their harps to 'a
higher mood.' Spenser, Lady Pembroke, Sydney, Sir John
Davies, Secretary Davison, all wrote fine sacred poetry.
Later, Ben Jonson could turn aside from masque and drama
to write religious verse. Donne, too, whom we can scarcely
forgive for spoiling Herbert's style, - even Herrick, the
English Anacreon, who with richer imagination sang of
spring, and spring-tide blossoms, and the blue sunny skies,
as though life were but one long holiday, in his old age -
sent forth a volume of hymns, forgotten now, but never can
his exquisite 'Letany' be forgotten, with its earnest,
touching refrain, 'Sweet Spirit comfort me!' To Quarles we
have already referred. Herrick's 'Noble Numbers' are all
unworthy his fame; but there are two other religious poets
to whom the age has yet to do justice, - one already holding high place among our secular poets, - George Wither;
the other a writer popular in his day, but who has sunk
into oblivion from being viewed as a mere translator; but

whose fine 'Letanies on the Lord's Prayer', we have never seen even noticed - Joshua Sylvester....

[After nine pages in praise of Wither and Sylvester, the article concludes:]

Did our space allow, we might add much more, - for volumes might be written on our early poets, and yet much remain unsaid. It is, however, to the religious poems of Herbert's contemporaries alone, that we have now confined our attention, since as Herbert only takes rank as a sacred poet, it is with similar compositions that his own must be compared. And if in making that comparison it may be thought we have scarcely done justice to his merits, be it remembered that those were no common poets with whom he has been measured. Very beautiful are many portions of the 'Temple,' and very beautiful the fine christian feeling diffused over all. Nor do we wonder, that during the long dearth of all that was suggestive and ennobling, - when our old poets were forgotten, and our later had not begun their song, - George Herbert, with all his quaintnesses, was loved, and read, and got by heart; and on the shelf that had no place for 'Paradise Lost,' his little volume might often be found. Everything is great or small by contrast. Side by side with the glorious writers of our earlier days, George Herbert takes a lower place; but compared with those of a later period, his station is deservedly high. The fair spreading tree, the landmark of the plain, looks dwarfed beside the giants of the forest; the star, whose soft gleam attracts the eye, while sparkling alone in the blue heaven, shines with paler lustre, as the hosts of night come forth in their burning splendour.

Notes

1 The work of John Gauden, though often attributed to the martyred Charles I.
2 'rash' in 'The Temple'.
3 Thomas Percy, Sir David Dalrymple, and Sir Egerton Bridges were alike editors of the 'earlier poetry' mentioned.

54. JAMES THOMSON, 'ON GEORGE HERBERT'S POEMS'

1862

The oddest poetic tribute was ventured by Thomson. It may
represent an effort to emulate Herbert's mode of articulation; if so, the mode was in all essentials misconstrued.
    Source: 'Poems and Some Letters of James Thomson',
ed. Anne Ridler (Carbondale, Ill., 1963), p. 74.

ON GEORGE HERBERT'S POEMS

What are these leaves dark-spotted and acerb?
    'A very holy *herb*.'
To what good use may I this herb convert?
    'Press it on thy soul's *hurt*.'
When *herb* unto the *hurt* I thus apply?
    '*Herb-ert* is sanctity.'

55. ANONYMOUS, GEORGE HERBERT AND HIS TIMES, IN THE
'CHRISTIAN REMEMBRANCER'

1862

Occasioned by the publication of two editions of Herbert's
Works - the reissues of the Pickering text (1850) and the
Willmott edition (1859) - an anonymous review in 1862 was
swiftly transformed into a sustained study and, in effect,
a major effort to propagandise in Herbert's favour (see
also above, p. 26). The essay begins by commending the
proliferating editions of several poets - we are else, the
author states, 'in danger ... of neglecting the treasures
of the past' - and attends to Herbert in the ensuing
fashion.
    Source: from George Herbert and his Times, 'Christian
Remembrancer', n.s., XLIV (July 1862), pp. 105-31 and
133-7.

Most persons merely know [Herbert's] poetry by a few lines
culled here and there to provoke a smile at their quaintness and want of rhythm. Even among those who cherish
with loving reverence the memory of his holy and beautiful

life, few are aware - for it needs patient research, un-
discouraged by the archaisms of a style strangely dissonant to our modern ears - how high a place he is entitled
to, purely on the ground of intellectual ability. Among
the rich legacies of literature bequeathed to us from the
past, and fast being lost under the accumulating dust of
ages, Herbert's 'Remains' especially deserve to be rescued
from neglect and restored to a place on our bookshelves
and in our hearts. They are valuable, not merely or
chiefly to the archaeologist, but intrinsically; and, in
particular, at the present time, as containing the anti-
dote to many of the evils incidental to the tendencies of
our modern literature. But we must proceed to adduce our
reasons for claiming so high a niche in their gallery of
worthies for one, of whom probably our readers have hitherto formed a far lower estimate.
    In his own century Herbert's writings were popular
enough. It is characteristic of his modesty, or, more
strictly speaking, of the victory which he won over his
naturally eager and ambitious temperament, that they
were all posthumous in publication. The Poems seem to
have been written before the 'Country Parson.' His preface to the latter is dated 1632, the year of his death;
and its other name, by which it was more usually known at
first, 'A Priest to the Temple,' seems to indicate that
it was conceived in its author's mind as a companion volume to the already existing, though unpublished collection
of poems, entitled 'The Temple.' These poems were evidently not the work of any particular period in his life,
but the growth of years; kept under lock and key, according to the wise advice of Horace, until arrived at nonage.
'The Temple' was first given to the world in 1633, by
Nicholas Ferrar, Herbert's literary executor; under his
editorship it was printed by his daughters and other members of his household, or 'Protestant Nunnery' as it has
been called, at Little Gidden, (1) in Northamptonshire,
and then published at Cambridge, after being, of course,
formally licensed by the Vice-Chancellor's 'imprimatur.'
(2) In about forty years, so good Izaak Walton says in
1674, it passed through ten editions, more than 20,000
copies being sold; a success quite out of proportion to
that of the far greater poet, of whose 'Paradise Lost,'
shortly afterwards, only 1,300 copies were sold in the
first two years, and only 3,000 in the first eleven years
after its appearance. But the unpopularity of Milton's
politics and theology easily explains this disparity, to
say nothing of the inevitable repugnance, which even in
those laborious days a profoundly learned and recondite
epic, in twelve books, would have to encounter in the

majority of readers. The 'Country Parson' - it is not
plain for what cause - was not published till 1652. It
would naturally attract scarcely any but professional
readers, yet it went through three editions in twenty
years. We cannot trace the progress of either volume
through succeeding editions. The men of the eighteenth
century were not likely to admire George Herbert. His
style was too abrupt and unadorned for their elaborately
rounded periods, his religious aspirations too glowing for
their decorous conventionalities, his theology too patristic for their latitudinarianism, and, we may add, his
thoughts at once too profound and too rudely chiselled for
their polished but superficial philosophy. Till Pickering's costly and beautiful edition in 1840 - one among
many other instances of the good taste and too enterprising spirit of that publisher - there was no complete edition of George Herbert's works. But, as we begun by
saying, they were honoured among their contemporaries.
Valeat quantum. (3) Let us try to estimate the worth of
that popularity.

    The Elizabethan era, towards the close of which George
Herbert was born, has been called by some, who prefer its
sturdy masculine vigour to the superior refinement of
Pope and Addison, the Augustan age in English literature.
It resembles rather the last days of the Republic, when
the massive intellect of Rome was beginning to appropriate
to itself the treasures of Grecian civilization. With
equal avidity, and with equal inexperience and awkwardness
at first, the great minds of Elizabeth's age, and of that
which immediately succeeded it, seized the new stores of
intellectual wealth laid open to them by the revival of
classical learning, and by frequent intercourse with
Italy, then, even more emphatically than ever, the land of
art and song. That era may be compared to that delicious
season of the year, the 'jocund month of May,' of which
the poets of the time were never weary of singing the
praises, combining at once the freshness and transparency
of spring with something of the riper loveliness, without
the languor of summer. The ruggedness, too, of the
literature of those times finds its parallel in the sharp
winds of May, of which we, the less hardy descendants of
the men who repelled the Armada, are, with the exception
Mr. Kingsley, (4) as his 'Ode to the East Wind' shows, so
apt peevishly to complain. It was an age of mother wit,
as yet comparatively rude and unpolished, and of learning
pursued as yet with too indiscriminating a voracity. The
healthy appetite of the giants of those days, uncloyed by
modern profusion, delighted in whatever it found, and was
discouraged by no difficulties. We see in George Herbert

at times, and more often in Milton and other contemporaries, something which looks at first sight like a
pedantic ostentation of learning, but is really the mere
exuberance of delight at discovering a vein of hidden ore.
The great minds of that day were, after all, the masters,
not the slaves, of their learning. Their originality was
not stifled nor dwarfed beneath its weight. The very difficulties of the work gave an additional zest to it, and
stimulated their faculties to the utmost. The severity of
this discipline, for there was no 'royal road' to learning
then, and few of those appliances which facilitate our
journey, rendered whatever knowledge was acquired more real
and solid, more thoroughly assimilated to the mind of the
learner. To be a 'painful scholar' was great praise, and
synonymous with being a good one. Books were then scarce
and dear, and prized accordingly. When George Herbert
wished to buy a new book at College, he was obliged in
spite of his liberal allowance, to 'fast for it,' as he
writes to his father-in-law, Sir John Danvers, in order to
indulge himself in so great a luxury. In these days of
cheap paper and steam presses, we can hardly conceive the
reverence then felt for anything in the shape of a printed
book, almost as if a sacred thing. Nor is it easy for us,
living in the whirl of incessant communication by the
rail, the post-office and the telegraph, to throw ourselves
back even for a moment into the deliberate movements, not
in travelling only, but in speaking, writing, thinking, of
the men of those days. As we trace their faded manuscripts, we see in their strong, square penmanship, with
every single letter firmly and perfectly defined, the nervous and muscular grasp of the writers. It is the transcript of their character, of their energy, exactitude,
perseverance. The succinct and condensed sentences, formal
and stiff certainly, yet terser and racier than our comparatively loose and inarticulate style, express the per-
spicuity and reality, as well as the narrowness and slowness, of their conceptions. Hallam calls that age 'the
most learned, in the sense in which the word was then
taken, that Europe has ever seen.' (5) The limitation is
important, as reminding us that inductive philosophy was
yet in its infancy. The learned were more conversant with
the unchanging laws of mind, inherited through the school-
men from the Porch and the Academy, than with the fluctua-
ting sciences of the material world. In its own way the
learning of the Elizabethan and post-Elizabethan ages was
prodigious.
    But the peculiar characteristics of that age, which
essentially distinguish it from our own, were, as we have
already hinted, deliberation, earnestness, concentration

of purpose. Men had a more leisurely, and yet a more
painstaking way of thinking and acting, and a sense of
enjoyment and repose in their work, not easily attainable
in these days of high pressure. They could realise better
than we the beautiful thought with which Milton consoled
himself in the forced inactivity of his blindness –

They also serve, who only stand and wait.
                                  [Sonnet XIX, l. 14]

They could find hours, while we can scarcely spare
moments, for undisturbed meditation; a habit of mind as
much at variance with our mobile temperament, as the still-
ness of the old inns of court is unlike the din and tur-
moil of Fleet Street, which roars outside their gates. The
feverish spirit of speculation, which in commerce makes or
destroys a fortune in a day, and exercises the same per-
turbing influence even over our philosophy and literature,
was altogether alien to the orderly and scrupulous habits
of that age. The advantages of our own day are great, in
the triumphal march of physical science, in the vastness of
our intellectual horizon, in the richer complexity of our
acquirements, and, above all, because the critical faculty
is quickened and refined by long experience. But in this
very diffusiveness of aims there is a great danger. We
seem to want that closeness of concentration which stamps
the Elizabethan age.
    One among the best of our living poets, Mr. Matthew
Arnold, in the preface to his volume of poems, complains
of the want of 'sanity' in modern literature. There is an
unnatural straining after originality, and an impatience
of authority or control, which too often disfigure even
our greatest works. The clever and popular 'George
Eliot,' for example, may be taken as a typical instance in
many respects, though not, we may hope, in all, of modern
tendencies. The wonderfully graphic delineations of life
and character are spoilt by bad taste, an unevenly
balanced judgment, and a strange confusion in the ideas of
right and wrong. It is a great relief to turn from such
unwholesome exhalations of a false and unreal philosophy,
to the bright, clear, buoyant atmosphere which Shakespeare and his contemporaries breathed. No wonder that the
Elizabethan age attracts so powerfully the sympathies of
writers like Mr. Kingsley. They find there a hearty and
robust geniality, a manly common-sense, an emancipation
from modern subjectivity of thought, such as they delight
in, while they are lenient towards the coarseness of
speech into which that boyish exuberance of animal spirits
was apt to degenerate. It would be great injustice to set

down the age of Elizabeth and James as licentious and
immoral, on the score of the occasional *grossièreté* of its
drama.   True, that the continental fashions then being
imported from France and Italy, and by the Englishmen who
served in great numbers in the debauched camps of the Low
Countries, tended to corrupt the court.   If we may judge
from Howel's gossiping letters, Lord Dalgarno, in Scott's
'Nigel,' is no unfair sample of its profligacy.   But this
laxity of morals did not taint the great bulk of the
nation - the country gentry living at home on their own
estates, the stalwart yeomen of the country, the staid
citizens of the towns.   At no other period, perhaps, was
the 'middle-class' (using that vague term to embrace both
professions and trades), so generally sound at the core.
Never was our commerce at once so daringly enterprising
and so strictly honourable: never was the sanctity and
happiness of domestic life so fully realised.   Accustomed,
as we are, to the pert slang of 'governor' for father, and
accustomed, it must be owned, to relegate our religion too
exclusively to one day in seven, we of this century may
smile as we read of grown-up sons, high in office, making
lowly obeisance at meeting father or mother, and may wonder that the constant presence of a chaplain was almost a
matter of course in every large household.   We are so used
to see the common recreations of our working man of a low
and debasing kind, that we can hardly realise the fact,
that almost every family circle in those days in all
classes, from the highest to the lowest, could while away
the long bright summer evenings in the open air, or the
dull afternoons in winter round the hearth, with glee,
and round, and madrigal; each age and sex bearing its own
part in the manifold harmony of the strain.   There is
something lost in all this.   The Spartan-like deference
for old age, the sense of religion as interwoven with the
daily affairs of life, the love of music, with leisure to
enjoy its cheering and elevating influences, these are
habits which no nation can well afford to lose.

     But we must return to George Herbert.   We have dwelt at
length on the characteristics of his age, not merely to
show cause why the verdict of his contemporaries should not
be set aside as valueless, but also because the man and the
age cannot be separated.   He is, at the same time, a result
of his age in some degree, and one of the efficient causes
of it; being himself modified by its circumstances, while
contributing to make it what it is.   For this reason we
must pause for a few moments longer, to count the long list
of illustrious names which that age unrolls.

     It was an age fertile in great men.   Spenser was writ-
ing his 'Faery Queene' just about the time of George

Herbert's birth. Raleigh's brilliant but erratic career
reached its unhappy close while Herbert was public orator
at Cambridge. While holding that office, and dividing his
time as he did between the Court and the University, Herbert must have had frequent opportunities of seeing and
hearing on the stage the marvellous creations of Shakespeare's genius, then in all the freshness of their first
appearance. More exactly coëval with Herbert were Milton,
and a galaxy of stars in the poetic firmament of far
lesser magnitude and feebler lustre, of whom only a few
scattered rays penetrate to us through the intervening
mist of years, Daniel, Quarles, Wither, Drummond, Sandys,
Suckling, and others. In theology there were Usher,
Chillingworth, Hammond, Andrewes, Sanderson, and Hall, a
strong array; in philosophy Hobbes and Selden; in juris-
prudence Coke and Hale; in political life the Cecils,
and many other truly sagacious statesmen; and, last in
our enumeration, but foremost in philosophy, in law, and
in affairs of state, the great Lord Bacon. We may add
to the list Burton, whose 'Anatomy of Melancholy' is no
bad sample of the quaint and miscellaneous erudition then
in repute. But the drama was the distinguishing glory of
those days. Then flourished, in the words of Southey,
'a race of dramatic writers, which no age and no country
has ever equalled.' Ben Jonson, the founder of the
English 'comedy of manners,' and, inferior only to him,
in Hallam's judgment, Massinger; with Beaumont and
Fletcher, Ford, Shirley. Such were Herbert's contemporaries; some of them, as Bacon, (6) Andrewes, Sanderson,
his intimate personal friends; as were also Lord Pembroke,
his kinsman, one of the chief actors in the important work
of colonising Virginia, and governing the rising colony;
Donne, Cotton, Ferrar, and Sir Henry Wotton, all men of no
common ability, highly cultivated, and of a still more uncommon moral excellence. Certainly it was a rich soil,
prolific of a healthy and luxuriant vegetation, the age in
which George Herbert found himself.

   It is impossible to approach Herbert's writing in an
unprejudiced state of mind, unless we first form a just
conception of the writer. When the reader feels that he
is addressed by one who has a claim on his attention, he
is alive to beauties that might otherwise be unnoticed,
less on the look-out for faults, can afford to overlook a
few blemishes of style here and there - in a word, brings
himself into that conformity of feeling with his author,
which all artists exact by right as indispensable. Without
this *provisional* sympathy, and even deference, no one can
be a fair critic. We must divest ourselves at once of the
vulgar notion of George Herbert. Far from being a mere

devotee, planted on his solitary column in unnatural isola-
tion, inaccessible to his fellow-men, he was emphatically a
man of social sympathies, sustained and directed upwards by
the entire devotion of his heart to heaven, as the tendrils
of a vine are taught to ascend by the elm round which it
clings. He loved to watch the 'quidquid agunt' (7) of men,
their business and pleasures, not with the contemptuous
indifference of a Stoic or Epicurean, but as being all, if
duly regulated, component parts in the order and beauty of
the universe. Gifted himself with rare natural advantages,
he neither neglected nor misused them. Excepting good
health (for he was constitutionally delicate, and, in particular, subject to painful and weakening attacks of the
ague, then far more prevalent and serious than in our days
of good draining), hardly one of fortune's gifts was wanting. He was born of a family noble in the truest sense of
the word; for the name of Herbert was eminent then, as
now, for the high character of those who bore it, with the
difference that modern civilisation has elicited a more
peaceful application of the same high spirit which distinguished the 'fighting-men and men of renown,' of whom
Lord Herbert of Cherbury, with his usual complacency,
reckons not a few among his ancestors. Well born and well
bred, with a very prepossessing exterior, with accomplishments of many kinds, and a sweetness of disposition that
could not fail to win and retain friends, with abilities
that raised him to one of the highest posts in the University at the early age of twenty-five, he started in the
race of life with a bright prospect of success before him.
His only fault, according to his brother, Lord Herbert, was
that he was naturally quick-tempered, 'not exempt from
passion and choler;' and Walton tells us, that 'if in his
undergraduate life he expressed any error, it was that he
kept himself too much retired, and at too great a distance
from his inferiors; and his clothing seemed to prove that
he set too great a value on his parts and parentage.' (8)
His allowance at college, we gather from his letter, though
liberal, was not always sufficient for his rather expensive
habits. Certainly in his after-life, as the 'country parson,' denying himself in every way for his parishioners,
identifying himself with their homely lives, and lending a
patient ear to every poor old woman who came with a story
of distress, we see no traces of this reserve or exclusive-
ness, natural as it was to his fastidious delicacy of
taste. He was the youngest but one of seven brothers, all
men of note, and all apparently marked by a strong family
likeness in high spirit and ability. The eldest, who
raised himself to the rank of Lord Herbert of Cherbury, is
well known to this day for his versatile talents as

diplomatist and philosopher. The two next, Richard and
William, after receiving a liberal education, served with
distinction in the Low Countries, and were renowned according to the punctilious code of honour then in force, as
duellists, Richard carrying twenty-four wounds with him to
his grave at Bergenopzoom. Charles died young, a Fellow of
New College. These four were George Herbert's seniors.
But he seems to have been more closely drawn to the
brother next after himself in age, who afterwards became
Sir Henry, a favourite at court, at one time 'Master of the
Revels,' and of course, like all the fine gentlemen of the
day, famous in 'affairs of honour.' The youngest, Thomas,
was a brave sailor. The brother of such men was not likely
to be a bookworm.

George Herbert's naturally high spirits are evident in
the few letters which remain, mostly belonging to the early
part of his life. They are chiefly addressed from Cambridge to his brother Henry, and are very racy, considering
the stiffness of letter-writing then in vogue. It is an
instance of the chivalrous respect then paid to ladies,
that while signing himself to Henry, 'your loving brother,'
he is 'your loving brother *and servant*' to his poor sick
sister Elizabeth, wife of Sir Henry Jones. Writing to his
brother at Paris, he tells him, 'be covetous of all good,
which you see in Frenchmen, in knowledge, in fashion, in
words;' and particularly in that 'wittiness of speech'
which has always been a specialty of that nation. 'Let
there be no kind of excellency which it is possible for
you to attain to, which you seek not.'

About the same date he writes from Cambridge of having
'some forty businesses on hand,' and with equal relish of
'the gaynesses' incident to his office of public orator.
In those days the Universities were in close communication
with the Court, and to be distinguished at Oxford or Cambridge was a sure passport in political life. The office
of 'public orator' was especially valued as an introduction to the Court; and a bright vista in that direction
was opening itself to the young scholar-courtier. At first
he hailed it gladly. Looking back afterwards on those
sunny days from his quiet parsonage at Bemerton, he says:

> my birth and spirit rather took
> The way that takes the town.
> ['Affliction' (I), ll. 37-8]

But it is not in the tone of vain regret. He thanks the
guiding Providence which diverted him by his bad health
from the glittering prizes of that highway to greatness to
the 'fallentis semita vitae,' (9) in which he was to serve

God and his country. His intention of taking Holy Orders
was clearly an afterthought; but that of leading a strictly
religious life, even in the midst of secular avocations,
clearly was not. He was not one of those, who, as Carlyle
expresses it, 'go through a mud-bath in youth, in order to
come out clean.' The dedication of all his powers to their
highest use, whatever his way of life might be, at Court or
in the University, was his fixed purpose from first to
last, formed in very early life, and never laid aside for
a moment, even in his 'fierce' youth, 'eager, hot, and
undertaking,' as he himself describes it. In his first
year at Cambridge he complains, 'many love-poems are daily
writ and consecrated to Venus, few that look towards God
and Heaven.' His delicate health was, no doubt, one cause
that determined him to retire from the stirring scene of
the Court. But he was also moved by a strong longing to
raise the country clergy from the low estimation in which
they were generally held, as the coffee-house squibs of
that day show too plainly. Oley attributes this contempt
of the clergy partly to the too indiscriminate admission
of candidates first into the Universities, and thence into
Holy Orders - for, as perhaps sometimes happens now, testi-
monials were given too much as a mere form - and partly to
the general poverty of the country clergy, and the dearth
of men of high family among them. (10) It was a common
thing then for their children to be apprenticed to trades.
Herbert's 'Country Parson' is described as 'taking care not
to put his children into vain trades, nor unbefitting the
reverence of their father's calling, such as taverns for
men and lacemaking for women.' Elsewhere chaplains are
warned against being 'over-submissive and cringing,' and
the rural clergy against haunting alehouses and taverns.
Herbert resolved to set himself to rescue the high vocation of the clergy from this loss of caste and consequent
loss of influence.

   But it was not without a severe inward struggle that he
decided on that renunciation of pursuits, otherwise innocent, which the consecration of a man's life to the work
of the ministry demands. If he came late to the work, he
did not come empty-handed. Crowned with academical honours, and graced with the prestige of high social position, he brought his abilities, his reputation, his prospect of worldly success, and freely devoted them all to
the work. He could truly say in a short poem, called the
'The Pearl,' that he knew the ways of learning, the ways
of honour, the ways of pleasure, of love, of wit, of
music, and, as Walton adds, 'he knew on what terms he renounced all these for the service of his Master.' (11) In
another poem, 'The Quip,' he personifies 'Beauty, Money,

Glorie, and Wit,' as severely assailing him with raillery
for his neglect of their fascinations; to each and all he
replies by turning to his heavenly Master:

But Thou shalt answer, Lord, for me.

Not as one seeking in the cool shadow of the Church a
refuge from the glare of worldly disappointments, but with
humble thankfulness, as feeling unworthy of the office, he
undertook the responsibilities of the ministry. After
retiring for a year to his brother Henry's house in Kent,
there to pause before taking the irrevocable step, he was
ordained deacon in 1625; and after four years passed in
deacon's orders (for he imposed on himself this unusually
long period of probation, and his diffidence was hardly
overcome at last by the persuasions of Lord Pembroke and
Laud, then Bishop of London), he was ordained priest, and
appointed to the small rectory of Bemerton, in 1630, being
them in his thirty-seventh year. His resolutions, formed
on the eve of induction, and the rules which he then laid
down for himself, are recorded by Walton. We must extract
part of them. 'I beseech that God, who hath honoured me
so much as to call me to serve at His altar, that as by
His special grace He hath put into my mind these good
desires and resolutions, so He will by His assisting grace
give me ghostly strength to bring the same to good effect.
And I beseech Him that my humble and charitable life may
so win upon others as to bring glory to my Jesus, whom I
have this day taken to be my Master and Governor. And I
am so proud of His service, that I will always observe and
do His will; and will always call Him *Jesus my Master.*
And I will always contemn my birth or any title or dignity
that can be conferred on me, when I shall compare them
with my title of being a priest, and serving at the altar
of *Jesus my Master.*' In one of his poems he turns again
and again with fresh delight to these words:

How sweetly doth '*my Master*' sound '*my Master.*'
['The Odour', l. 1]

With all his self-discipline and devotion George Herbert
bert was not a man to be happy alone. Some little time
before this crisis in his life he married a daughter of
Mr. Danvers (a name well known in the county), of Bainton,
in Wilts, a member of the same family as Lord Danby. It
was a very short courtship. Walton naïvely says, 'she
changed her name into Herbert on the third day after this
first interview.'(12) But, to say nothing of love at first
sight, their families were already connected, and they

had heard so much of each other through friends, that they
met for the first time not as strangers, but as if long
acquainted. 'They wooed so like princes,' Walton explains,
'as to have select proxies, such as were true friends to
both parties.' (13) One is reminded for a moment of
Richard Hooker and his extraordinary marriage. But the
cases are quite different. That learned, but, for once,
*in*judicious divine, simply acquiesced in the choice of
the landlady of his lodgings, who took the opportunity of
nominating her own daughter. The proof of marriage is of
course in its consequences. Every one knows how poor
Hooker was found by a former pupil vainly endeavouring to
give his mind to the great treatise which he had on hand,
while rocking the cradle amid the objurgations of his
Xantippe. (14) But Herbert's married life was singularly
happy. His wife proved herself worthy of such a husband.

The rest of his life is soon told. For little more
than two years he lived and worked among his parishioners,
and then his short, but useful and happy life, was closed
by a deathbed in perfect unison with all that had preceded
it, serene and hopeful as a cloudless sunset. Two years
and three months may seem a disproportionate space of
time for his work in the ministry, after so long and so
careful preparation for it. But it is not for us to call
his death premature. To himself the old adage may safely
be applied - 'his wings were grown;' and, as for his work,
it was ended. 'Non diu sed multum vixit.' (15) His contemporaries complained that 'he lost himself in that
humble way,' while devoting his energies to that obscure
little parish. But his influence, in forming the highest
type of Christian character for laity as well as clergy,
has been extended, by his example and writings, far beyond
the narrow limits of that little parish on Salisbury Plain,
with its 'twenty cottages' and 'less than a hundred and
twenty souls' - far beyond the age in which he lived.

It is not difficult, from hints contained in Walton's
life, and in his own sketches of the ideal 'country parson,' to form a tolerably complete idea of Herbert's daily
life at Bemerton. The picture is a delightful one. His
little church has lately been restored at great cost by
the munificence of a lady worthy to bear the name, which
he and others like him have ennobled in the highest sense
of the word. As it stood in his day, with its low dove-
cote-like bell turret and narrow irregular windows, it must
have been very like the homely but picturesque little
churches which may still be seen often enough in Herefordshire, lingering amid other vestiges of the past in that
old-fashioned district, and bearing witness, by their contrast to the statelier structures of the eastern counties,

to the inferiority of western England in wealth and popu-
lation. The romantic hills and dingles of Herefordshire
are certainly as unlike as can be to the gently undulating
plain about Bemerton. But there is, perhaps, no county
which, at the present time, so nearly realises the truly
pastoral relation which subsisted two centuries ago between a country parson and his people. In spite of the
close vicinity of rampant Dissent in Wales, the old
traditional respect for the Church and the clergy is still
half-unconsciously cherished there among the peasantry and
farmers; while each little parish seems to constitute only
one large family, as described in Herbert's 'Country Parson,' with the parson himself acting *in propriâ personâ* -
not as in towns, through the mediation of curates and com-
mittees - the head and centre of everything that is going
on, not excepting even the lesser and more trivial affairs
of common life. In a little world of this sort we may
imagine the poet-rector, loving and beloved by his flock,
and reverenced by them not only for his office, but for
his rank, learning, and sanctity - holding much the same
position among them as the late Augustus Hare in his little
parish on another of the Wiltshire plains. Herbert
brought all the weight of his personal advantages to bear
on his work, incommensurate to his powers, as it may seem,
in worldly appreciation. He made his knowledge of the
Platonic dialogues useful in the public catechising of the
young people in church - a practice on which he set great
store - borrowing the method of the sage, 'who taught the
world as one would teach a child.' He used to entertain
all his parishioners in turn at his Sunday dinner-table,
welcoming the poorest with an especial share of that high-
bred courtesy for which he was eminent even in a day when
the etiquette of chivalry was still observed, and 'the
grand manner' was more common among gentlemen than it is
now. We may fancy him seated in his study, digesting his
omnigenous stores of learning into a large common-place
book - so he advises in 'The Country Parson' - but turning
at any moment from the congenial occupation to encourage
any poor applicant for relief, who came to unfold a simple
story of petty anxieties. His influence with the higher
classes, always less amenable to such an influence, was as
great as with the poor. 'There was not a man in his way,'
writes Oley, *be he of what rank he would*, that spoke awry
in order to God, but Herbert would wipe his mouth (!) with
a modest, grave, and Christian reproof.' (16) He had a
singular graciousness in reproving - always a disagreeable
task - 'a dexterity in sweetening this art;' a gentle yet
uncompromising manner; a delicate tact in guiding conversation, which is wanting in persons of equal zeal, but

less discretion. The eighteenth chapter of the 'Country
Parson' gives some idea of this suavity and tenderness
with unflinching firmness of manner; and, if such an art
can be imparted by any rules, it may be by those laid down
in the 'Church Porch.' Walton tells a story, illustrative
of Herbert's winning manner, of his gaining a lasting influence for good over a gentleman living in Salisbury, by
a short, casual conversation as they walked together,
being previously unacquainted, on the road to that city.
(17) There must have been an irresistible charm about
him, not the result of merely outward polish, but of in-
nate sweetness of disposition and unselfishness, disciplined by the 'self-reverence, self-knowledge, self-
distrust,' which were the results of his religion. It is
no wonder that his flock followed him willingly, instead
of being driven. 'When Mr. Herbert's Saints' bell
[Sanctus-bell?] rang to prayers,' his neighbours, rich and
poor, loved to resort to the little chapel adjoining his
house, where the Church-service was daily performed 'at
the canonical hours of ten and four.' Men 'would leave
their plough to rest awhile, that they might offer their
devotions to God with him, and then return to their work.'
(18) In our days of busy competition, even George Herbert
would find it difficult to collect a large congregation in
a small rural parish on a week-day. Herbert describes the
country parson as observing the stated times of fasting
and abstinence. The passage is characteristic of the man
and his age. 'As Sunday is his day of joy, so is Friday
his day of mortification, which he observes not only with
abstinence of diet, but also of company, recreation, and
all other outward contentments; and besides, with confession of sins and all acts of humiliation.' It was the
general practice then. Of late years many religious persons have been deterred by fear of an observance which,
more easily, perhaps, than any other, degenerates into
formalism; while persons less serious have been only too
glad to be freed from its restraint. Plainly, with George
Herbert, it was no mere 'opus operatum.' (19) His remarks
in the tenth chapter show that he felt the obligation in
the spirit rather than in the letter. 'If a piece of dry
flesh at my table be more unpleasant to me than some fish
there, certainly, to eat the flesh and not the fish, is to
keep the fast-day naturally.' He goes on to say that fasting must never interfere with health, the preservation of
sound mind in sound body being a paramount duty. We have
dwelt at some length on this point, because the idea of
Herbert and his contemporaries would be incomplete without
it.
    George Herbert was not one of those who sacrifice common

everyday duties to those of a more directly religious
kind, and who are so intent on the far distance as, in
their abstraction, to be unconscious of the ground under
their feet. The good parson is portrayed as exercising
a general supervision, even over those departments of the
household which do not usually belong to the 'pater-
familias' to regulate. The following passage is very
quaint. 'As he is just in all things, so he is to his
wife also, counting nothing so much his own as that he may
be unjust to it. Therefore he gives her respect both
afore her servants and others, and half, at least, of the
government of the house, reserving so much of the affairs
as [may] serve for a diversion for him; yet never so
giving over the reins but that he sometimes looks how
things go, demanding an account, *but not by the way of an
account.*'

His religion was not something distinct from the daily
routine of life; it penetrated and ruled every action. If
beggars, for example, come for alms, the parson takes the
opportunity, 'before giving, of making them say their prayers, or the Creed, or the Ten Commandments; and as he
finds them perfect, so rewards them the more.' His own
household was managed in the same spirit. The tie between master and servant was closer and more affectionate
then:- 'Besides the common prayers of the family, the
parson straitly requires of all to pray by themselves,
before they sleep at night and stir out in the morning,
and knows what prayers they say, and *till they have learned
them makes them kneel by him.*' Herbert knew well the truth
of Michael Angelo's great saying, 'These trifles make up
perfection; and perfection itself is no trifle.' His devotion, being sober and unfanatical, never obscured the
homelier duties of life. When some friend objected that
he was spending too much in alms-giving, he could answer
that 'a competent maintenance was secured to his wife after
his death.' His parish never made him forgetful of friends
or relatives.

> Meliorne amicus, sponsus, an pastor gregis
> Incertum est,

is the verdict of Dean Duport. (21)
To complete our sketch, inadequate at the best, of
George Herbert, at Bemerton, we must think of him as
gracefully unbending at times from the tension of work,
and joining in such social recreations as accorded with his
profession. Twice a week, after walking in to Salisbury
for the cathedral service, which it was 'his heaven upon
earth' to attend, he would spend part of the evening 'at

some private musical meeting, where he would usually sing
and play his part.' We may imagine him, as really happened
once, stopping on his walk, 'like the good Samaritan, and
putting off his canonical coat to help a poor man with a
poorer horse that was fallen under his load.' He arrived
in Salisbury in such a state that his musical friends
there 'began to wonder that Mr. George Herbert, who used
to be so trim and neat, came into that company so soiled
and discomposed.' We may fancy him, rod in hand, strolling
along the river side, one of the 'gentle anglers' whom his
friend Walton commemorates, shaping into verse his sacred
meditations. Certainly a life like this, in which work
and rest, self-discipline and natural impulse, secular
duties and heavenly aspirations, are blended into harmonious unity, as in one of those rich strains of music, now
grave, now joyous, but always duly measured, which he loved
to follow; a life in which the coarser threads of existence
are inextricably intertwined with, and transfigured by the
radiance of, the more etherial filaments; in which the
calmness and equanimity which the Roman poet vainly longed
for seems attained; is the highest and most complete
development of human nature possible on earth. Monastic
seclusion may secure peace by eliminating the elements of
discord. 'They make desolation and call it peace.' A life
like Herbert's calls into action all the component parts of
our organization, and consecrates them severally to their
appointed use.

It is his largeness of mind, quickness of sympathy, and
practical sense, that we have been especially endeavouring
to illustrate in George Herbert, for of his learning and
piety there can be no question. We commend his life and
works to the admirers of 'muscular Christianity.' True,
Herbert had no share in Mr. Kingsley's horror of anything
like asceticism, nor so unreserved a confidence in the un-
disciplined impulses of nature; still, they agree well in
the warm appreciation of whatever is noble and beautiful,
whether in the moral or material universe, and particularly in the great truth that the work and excellence of
man lies *in* the world and not *out* of it, and has a frui-
tion in this life, though not in this life only. We might
often fancy that we are reading the more didactic parts of
'Westward Ho!' or 'Two Years Ago,' in the genial, plain-
spoken, thoroughly fresh and real moralisings of Herbert.
Some few extracts we must give (for his condensed wisdom
loses much by dilution), chiefly those bearing on the
secular aspects of life. In the 'Parson's Survey,' not of
his own parish only, but of what is now called 'the spirit
of the times,' for the good parson is described as being
also a good citizen, Herbert speaks of idleness among the

young nobility as the 'great national sin of the times.'
It seems to have been one of the newest fashions imported
from France and Italy; as Shakespeare writes of a lacka-
daisacal youth -

> For I remember, when I was in France,
> Young gentlemen would be sad as night;
> And all for wantonness.
>
> ['King John', IV, i, 15-17]

To remedy this evil (one not peculiar to that century),
Herbert prescribes manly occupations. He recommends the
young nobility to learn farming; to act as magistrates; to
study civil law, the basis of international relations, and
therefore especially useful to statesmen and diplomatists;
to improve themselves by travelling abroad; 'to ride the
great horse' - that is, to acquire the accomplishments of
the tiltyard. No doubt, if alive now, he would add the
rifle corps to his list. His wisdom is not of a clois-
tered tone. On the other hand, it is far removed from the
sharp practice of mere worldlings. It is, like the pru-
dential maxims of the Book of Proverbs or Ecclesiasticus,
the identification of duty with expediency. The 'Church
Porch,' an introduction in verse to the other poems,
reminds the reader of the best parts of Horace's 'Satires,'
not less by its 'pedestrian muse,' than by its shrewd wit
and graceful pleasantry. It abounds in pithy sayings, such
as may give a man not the manners only, but the principles
and feelings of a true gentleman. Mr. Willmott well says,
'The "Church-Porch" is a little handbook of rules for the
management of temper, conversation, and business. Every
child [?] ought to get it by heart.' (22) Here is good
advice tersely given:

> Pitch thy behaviour low, thy projects high;
> So shalt thou humble and magnanimous be.
>
> [ll. 331-2]

Here is a word for the over-sensitive:

> Think not thy fame at every twitch will break.
> By great deeds show that thou canst little do:
> Then do them not.
>
> [ll. 219-21]

Beneath all the lighter raillery lies a profound vein
of sentiment, the utterances of which sound like the voice
of that great and wise king, who tried all things under the
sun, and found them vanity. It is this keen sense of the

ridiculous, as well as of the awful side of human life,
which Shakespeare so well pourtrays in the melancholy
Hamlet, and in the cheerier Pantagruelism of the young
prince, the future hero of Agincourt. Herbert, in the
same way, was one of the few who can realize at once the
utter nothingness of even the greatest affairs of this
life in one point of view, and the immeasurable importance
of even the most rivial as forming the moral destiny. It
is characteristic of him, that he translated the sensible
little treatise on 'Temperance and Sobriety' of Ludovicus
Cornarus, known to Italian scholars as Luigi Cornaro, of
Padua; a delightful sketch of a hale and hearty old age,
with rules for attaining it. Herbert seems to have had a
peculiar aptness, both by nature and education, for casuistry; not for hair-splitting and sophistries, but for the
'noble art,' as he rightly calls it, of solving the perplexing cases of conscience which occur every day. His
way of cutting these knots, or rather of disentangling
them, is thoroughly English. It is the evidence of a
healthy moral sense, practised in logic, but with its own
unerring instincts unblunted. A few examples must suffice.
He shows when it is wrong, and when not, to take usury –
to inform against a neighbour – to omit customary acts of
devotion; how far tears and other physical accompaniments
of contrition are really essential or only accidental to
it – how persons may test their motives in seeking preferment. On the question which often perplexes the benevolent, of giving relief to unworthy applicants, he advises
to give *most* to those of best character, but *something*
to any in distress; for evident miseries 'have a
natural privilege and exemption from all laws.' His
'proverbs,' some apparently his own, others merely
collected by him, which the reader will find among his
greater works under the title of 'Jacula Prudentum,'
leave hardly anything in life untouched. We quote at
hazard two of the pithiest:

'Marry your *son* when you *will*, your *daughter* when you
can.'
'Buy at a fair, sell at home.'

We refer our readers to the rest, if they value the
guidance of Herbert's aphorisms in the mazes of life.
The 'Country Parson' is, of course, the book by which
Herbert is best known. Though intended primarily for the
clergy, it is a book to delight readers of any profession
by the charming series of portraits which it unfolds of
the good pastor in almost every conceivable attitude and
grouping. Oley, in his day, feared only that an ideal so
faultless 'would make the laity discontented.' There can

be no danger of this, now that so many of the clergy
strive to raise themselves to Herbert's high standard.
The literary merits, too, of the book are great. There
is no fine writing in it; there are no grand passages.
But the language throughout is choice, scholarlike, and
equable; singularly simple, exact, and terse; above all,
it is in perfect keeping with the ideas to be conveyed.
If, indeed, the great thing in style is, as Aristotle
teaches, to be 'clear and pleasing,' if the language
ought to fit as closely yet easily to its ideas as a well-
made dress to the limbs, then Herbert's prose must be
ranked high. It is like a well-dressed person. The
reader is unconscious where its charm lies; but if he
change a word, or the place of a word, or add or take
away anything, he discovers how exquisite, yet to all
appearance, unstudied, is the composition. In this
'curiosa felicitas,' Herbert's style resembles that of his
friend, Lord Bacon. It is entirely free from the euphuism
then in fashion at court, and its graceful ease is the
more remarkable, considering the ponderous manner of the
learned men of the day. Hallam, in his 'History of
Literature,' passes by the 'Country Parson' too summarily.
While allowing to it the faint praise of being 'a pleasing
little book,' he objects that 'its precepts are sometimes
so overstrained according to our notions as to give an
appearance of affectation.' (23) So much the worse, then,
for us and 'our notions.' But a book on the life and
habits of a country parson was not much in Hallam's way;
nor was he likely, from the associations which environed
him, to free himself from an unintentional prejudice
against the theological school, in which, according to his
'notions,' Herbert would be classed. To the charge of
being 'overstrained,' it is enough to answer that the precepts in question were laid down by the author as 'rules
and resolutions' for his own guidance. 'He set the form
and character of a true pastor,' he says, 'as high as he
could, for himself to aim at;' and he practised what he
taught. Many useful manuals for the clergy have been
written lately, testifying to their revived earnestness in
their professional duties: Evans' 'Bishopric of Souls,'
Oxenden's 'Pastoral Office,' Monro's 'Parochial Work,'
Heygate's 'Ember Thoughts,' Bishop Wilberforce's 'Ordination Addresses,' and Blunt's admirable 'Lectures on the
Parish Priest.' But the 'Country Parson' can never be
superseded. Short as it is and unassuming, it is inex-
haustible in its suggestiveness. Walton sayd, 'He that
can spare 12*d*. and yet wants a book so full of plain,
prudent, and useful rules, is scarcely excusable.' (24)
It will never be obsolete. Here and there may occur

something inapplicable to modern usages. Now that the
ties of neighbourhood are less binding, it is not likely
that, 'in case of any calamity by fire or famine to a
parish,' all the inhabitants of an adjoining parish would
go in procession, with the parson at their head, 'to carry
their collection of alms themselves, to cheer the afflic-
ted.' Nor would it be generally practicable now, though
something similar is customary in some hotels, for the
'parson on journey' to assemble his fellow-travellers 'in
the hall of the inn' for family prayers, 'with a due
blessing of God for their safe arrival.' Still, in both
cases, the principle holds good. Generally, his advice
may be taken literally. His advice, for example, on the
way of reproving, is as true now as then, and much needed
by many zealous young clergymen. 'Those whom he finds
idle or ill employed, he chides *not at first*, for that
were neither civil nor profitable, but always *in the close*,
before he departs from them: yet in this he distinguish-
eth; for if it be a plain countryman, he reproveth him
plainly, for they are not sensible of fineness; if they
be of higher quality they commonly are quick and sensible,
and very tender of reproof, and therefore he lays his discourse so that he comes to the point very leisurely, and
oftentimes as Nathan did, in the person of another, making
them to reprove themselves.' Again, his remarks on reading the prayers in church are very seasonable, while complaints are heard continually of the bad elocution of the
clergy; of their 'gabbling' in one church, of their 'drawl-
ing' and 'mouthing' in another. The parson's manner is
thus described:- 'His voice is humble, the words treat-
able [*sic*] and slow; yet not so slow as to let the fer-
vency of the supplicant hang and die between speaking; but
with a grave earnestness between fear and zeal, *pausing,
yet pressing*, he performs his duty.' We would not, however, recommend our clerical readers to follow him implicitly, when he assigns no less than 'one full hour' as the
time not to be exceeded in preaching; for the diffusion of
books has changed the functions of the pulpit. There are
preachers who may profit by his advice against over-
analysing a text. The old story of 'let us *tap* this
"*but*"' finds its counterpart in some pulpits in our day.
On the difficulties of parochial work, there is much to
be learnt from the 'Country Parson;' for example, on avoiding the danger of bribing the poor into an unreal profession of religion, while rewarding the most deserving.
    One of the most beautiful and characteristic chapters
in the book is 'the parson on Sunday.' In the description
of Sunday as a joyous, as well as holy day, equally free
from the interruption of worldly cares, and from the dull

vacuity and gloom of ultra-sabbatarians, we see the cheerfulness of his religion. 'On the Sunday before his death,'
writes Walton, 'he rose suddenly from his couch, called
for one of his instruments, and having tuned it, he played
and sang -

    The Sundays of man's life,
      Threaded together on Time's string,
   Make bracelets to adorn the wife
     Of the eternal glorious King.'

[above, p. 129]

Very beautiful, again, is the chapter on 'the parson in
contempt.' Few, if any, clergymen can expect to go through
their pastoral duties without incurring some degree of
obloquy; too often in proportion to their fidelity to their
charge. Those who

          feel bowed to earth
   By thankless toil, and vile esteemed,

may gather strength from Herbert's picture of a man,
naturally sensitive like himself, raised above the suscep-
tibility of injuries or affronts, 'showing that reproaches
touch him no more than a stone thrown against heaven,
where he is and lives.' But it is endless to make
extracts. We must refer our readers to the book itself.
Only one word more for the younger clergy, and we have
done. They are in danger of becoming too much absorbed in
their secular duties, of growing shallow and fussy,
amid the countless distractions incidental to these days
of penny magazines and penny savings' banks. They may
learn from the 'Country Parson,' with his huge 'body of
divinity, a book digested by himself out of writers old
and new; the storehouse of his sermons,' that they must
rescue some portion of every day from such secular avocations, however laudable, as may be better discharged by
lay agency, in order, by patient study, to lay a solid
foundation of learning, especially in that great province
of knowledge which is peculiarly their own.
   Herbert's contributions to our controversial theology
are less than might be expected from so learned and profound a theologian. He was naturally averse to publishing;
and many of his manuscript papers were lost in the fire at
Highnam House: besides, his early death may have prevented
more. All that remains is gold, fine and unalloyed. In
his short preface to his friend Ferrar's edition of the
'Divine Considerations of John Valdesso' - the companion
of Charles V., first in his campaigns, afterwards in his

retirement from the world - he touches cursorily, but with
a master-hand, on several of the great questions now agi-
tating men's minds in England, his candour and comprehen-
siveness of intellect, and what may be called philosophical
intuition, qualifying him peculiarly to answer such doubts
and difficulties as are propounded in the 'Essays and Reviews,' so far as they came before him. He is so free
from the conventionalities of religious phraseology, so
philosophical, so calmly judicial, and, at the same time,
so thoroughly real and earnest in his convictions, that
whatever falls from him in defence of received truths carries no slight weight. Thus, while expressing the deepest
reverence for the written Word of God as unfathomable in
its meaning, or, to use its own words, 'ever teaching more
and more,' he does not shrink from using the plainest language about such actions there recorded even of eminent
saints, as would be censured in ordinary men. But he adds,
'it is one thing not to judge, another to defend them.'
It is not, however, by passages directly bearing on the
questions mooted in 'Essays and Reviews,' so much as by
his general characteristics as a theologian, that Herbert's
writings afford a solution of them. What especially marks
his theology is, that reverence and free thought go hand
in hand. He applies his consummate powers of reasoning to
the question discussed, not as if himself standing aloof
from it, or merely theorising on paper, but with intense
personal conviction, and as qualifying the laws of thought
by the plain dictates of common sense and common morality.
He seems capable of realizing a mystery, without its mysterious nature evanescing in his grasp. Whatever truth,
however abstruse, he handles, ceases to be a mere bodiless
abstraction, and becomes a living reality. Thus, with
him every article of the Creeds is a substantial unity,
incorporated into his very existence. Though well versed
in all the philosophy of the schools, there are no cobwebs
of idle speculation in his reasoning to be brushed aside,
before arriving at the truth. All is real, definite,
actual, so far as regards the knowledge attainable by man;
beyond that he does not presume to pronounce. His superiority to that habit of mind which wastes its energies in
objectless unsatisfying speculation, and his repugnance to
the intrusion of unauthorized definitions and dogmatisings
into the illimitable field of heavenly mysteries, are evi-
denced in these lines. He is speaking of

      Divinities' transcendent sky,
    Which with the edge of wit they cut and carve;
      Reason triumphs, and faith lies by.
    Could not that wisdome, which first broacht the wine,

      Have thickened it with definitions?
    And jagged His seamlesse coat, had that been fine,
      With curious questions and divisions?

    Love God, and love your neighbour. Watch and pray.
      Do as you would be done unto.
    O dark instructions, ev'n as dark as day!
      Who can these Gordian knots undo?
                              ['Divinitie', 11. 6-12, 17-20]

    It is the combination in Herbert's character of the
practical and imaginative elements which renders him so
eminently and thoroughly English.
    He was by no means a partisan in theology. His ortho-
doxy was not of a partial and exclusive cast. He was one
who would have symbolized heartily with the 'Evangelical'
party in the fulness of their assertion of justification
by faith: only, without losing sight of the other great
truths handed down from apostolic times. He assents
freely to Valdesso insisting on the supreme importance of
faith; only adding, that from real faith all other graces
are sure to spring. The words, 'I am less than the least
of Thy mercies,' were ever in his thoughts and prayers.
When his friends round his death-bed were reminding him of
some good deeds which he had done, he replied, 'Not good
unless sprinkled by the blood of Jesus.' He seems to have
been as far removed from Arminian self-righteousness as
from the licence of the Antinomians. Perhaps nothing
better, in small compass, has ever been written on the
great problem, how to reconcile free will and grace, than
his lines, which begin -

    Lord, Thou art mine, and I am Thine.
                              ['Clasping of hands']

    Again, on the vexed question of election, these few
words speak volumes:- 'The thrusting away of God's arm
doth alone (and nothing else) make us not loved by Him.'
It is a great loss that no copy remains of his 'Letter on
Predestination,' which Bishop Andrewes valued so highly,
that he always carried it 'in his bosom.' Herbert was one
of the few who can appreciate the manifold aspects of
every question as it may be regarded on this side or on
that. He resembles Pascal in many ways; in fine wit, in
profound, yet clear insight, in freedom from the narrowness of party spirit. His short poem against the invocation of saints is a remarkable instance of feeling duly
balanced by judgment. He protests, elsewhere also,
against Romanist errors, but always with temperance and

consideration. No one need be surprised to find George
Herbert identifying Papal Rome with Babylon, as if the
matter did not admit of question. It was the way of his
generation: a fact, which exposes the fallacy of an assertion, too often allowed to pass unchallenged, that the
Reformers clung to the old tenets, and would have made a
more sweeping reformation if living in these days. But
this is not the place to pursue these theological questions. It is enough to repeat what no student of George
Herbert's remains will deny, that it would not be easy to
find a more perfect representative than in him of the
spirit of our English theology as embodied in our English
Prayer-Book.

It remains to speak of Herbert's poetry. As might be
expected, we find it almost ignored by critics like Ellis
and Warton. 'Apage sus; non tibi spiro.' (25) The former,
in his 'Specimens of the Early English Poetry,' super-
ciliously dismisses Herbert with a laboured antithesis,
which betrays equal ignorance of the facts of Herbert's
life and of the most salient features in his character.
'Nature intended him for a knight-errant, but disappointed
ambition made him a saint!' (26) Any one less Quixotic
than George Herbert, or less like a man soured by worldly
disappointment, can hardly be conceived. Warton, in a
strange confusion of metaphors, speaks of Pope 'judiciously collecting *gold* from the *dregs* of Herbert,
Gashaw,' (27) &c. It would be nearer the mark to say,
that Pope had penetration to detect the rich unpolished
ore, strewn at random in Herbert's poems, and skill to
give it new lustre by the charm of his elaborate workmanship. Hallam passes by Herbert's poetry without a word.
Campbell, in his 'British Poets,' while devoting two or
three pages apiece to the merest poetasters, can only
spare the corner of a page, and half a dozen lines of preface, for George Herbert. But we must bear in mind the
prejudices which rendered Herbert's writings 'caviare to
the general' of late years. More surprising is it that
Southey, in his continuation of Ellis, should mention
Donne, Wither, and Quarles, without any notice of one
certainly their superior as a poet. (28) On the other
hand, as we have seen, Herbert's poems made a great impression on the minds of the seventeenth century. Henry
Vaughan bears witness to Herbert's influence as the ori-
ginator of a new school in poetry. Baxter, the nonconformist, a man of no common ability, was a warm admirer of
Herbert's poems. Even in our own day, the great poet-
philosopher, Coleridge, again and again extols George
Herbert, not as a man only, but as a poet. 'Let me add,'
he writes in 'The Friend', 'that the quaintness of some

of his thoughts, not of his diction, than which nothing
can be more pure, manly, and unaffected, has blinded
modern readers to the general merits of his poems, which
are for the most part *exquisite in their kind*.' In the
'Biographia Literaria' he speaks of the 'weight, number,
and compression of Herbert's thoughts, and the simple
dignity of the language.' He writes to his friend Mr.
Collins, the Academician, 'Read "The Temple," if you have
not read it.' (29) Certainly, this is high praise from a
great critic. Still, it must be owned that there is
much in Herbert's poems to account for distaste on a first
perusal. At first sight they seem, not here and there
only, but throughout, stiff, obscure, fantastic. Perhaps
the reader casts aside the 'Sunday-puzzle,' as the late
Bishop Blomfield nicknamed the 'Christian Year,' (30) in
utter perplexity, or with the exclamation which Plato pro-
voked from a despairing student, 'Si nonvis intelligi, non
debes legi. (31) But on a closer approach, and with
patience, the mist clears off; and what seemed to be un-
substantial and impalpable conceits, 'airy nothings,'
prove to have a form and substance well worth some trouble
in deciphering. Coleridge says, truly, that the difficulty
arises not from any fault in the expression, but from the
very nature of the thoughts to be expressed. 'The characteristic of our elder poets,' and he cites Herbert as an
instance, 'is the reverse of that which distinguishes more
recent versifiers; the one (Herbert and his school) conveying the most fantastic thoughts in the most correct and
natural language; the other, in the most fantastic language
conveying the most trivial thoughts. The latter is a
riddle of words, the former an enigma of thoughts.' (32)
Great allowance must be made for the influence of the
Italian poets, with that fondness for quaint fancies, which
may be seen in the frigid conceits and extravagant metaphors of Tasso and Ariosto - an influence from which
Shakespeare himself was not exempt, as his atrocious puns
show, and to which we may attribute the wretched acrostics
of that period, in which it was the fashion for a lover to
express his ardour, or a mourner his grief even on the
memorial stone. Something, too, is owing to his patristic
studies. As Oley says, 'You find in him the choicest passages of the fathers bound in metre.' (33) Mr. Keble,
again, characteristically traces much of this redundance
of imagery, 'and constant flutter of his fancy, for ever
hovering round his theme,' to an instinctive delicacy
which shrank from exposing his religious feelings too
openly before the eyes of the world. (34) It is evident,
also, that Herbert's neglect of poetical propriety was, in
part, a reaction from the smoothness and unreality of the

popular love songs of the day. In the last lines of a
short poem, entitled 'Grief,' he gives way to the feelings
of devotion struggling for a free utterance:

[Quotes the last seven lines of the poem.]

In the same spirit he describes himself as at first seeking out 'quaint words and trim invention,' as fitting
ornaments 'to deck the sense,' in speaking of 'heavenly
joyes,' but at last abandoning the vain attempt, and
resolving that he will, since

> There is in love a sweetness ready penned,
> Copy out only that.
>   ['Jordan' (II), 11. 17-18]

Elsewhere he seems to long to rescue all the flowers of
poetry, 'sweet phrases,' 'lovely metaphors,' 'lovely,
enchanting language,' from all lower purposes, for a
worthier use. We must remember, also, in criticising
'The Temple,' that it was not originally intended for
publication. It was the literal transcript, where he
found relief in recording his own religious experiences.
On his death-bed he left 'this little book' for the hands
of his friend Ferrar, adding, 'He shall find in it a
picture of the many spiritual conflicts that have passed
between God and my soul, before I could subject mine to
the will of Jesus, my Master. If he can think it may turn
to the advantage of any poor dejected soul, let it be made
public; if not, let him burn it.' The too frequent recurrence of anticlimax, and even downright bathos, at the end
of many of the poems, indicates that they were never properly revised by the 'last hand' of the author. All these
considerations tend to avert the hasty condemnation which
might otherwise fall on Herbert's poems as abrupt, rugged,
and enigmatical; at any rate, they excuse the poet, even
where they cannot alter our opinion of his poetry.
    After all, it cannot be denied that Herbert, as a poet,
never will and never can be a general favourite. The want
of poetic diction - and it must be remembered that in his
day the language of poetry was not yet recognised by tacit
consent as distinct in many points from that of prose -
the quaintness of his thoughts, and the homeliness of his
phrases, are grave faults in the eyes of most people.
Even the multiplicity and compression of his ideas make
him unpopular, though it may satisfy a more critical taste,
just as a thorough musician enjoys a closely compacted
fugue more than flowing airs and melodies. His subject,
too, is against him. The very names of his poems -

'Faith,' 'Prayer,' 'Virtue,' 'Obedience,' 'Conscience,' to
say nothing of other titles positively ludicrous to our
modern ears - are a stumbling-block on the threshold,
except to those who approach in a devout, or, as Coleridge
preferred to say, 'devotional' spirit. To all others, the
pervading sense of the unseen world in every line is as an
unknown tongue, an unintelligible rhapsody. His words
are, as the old Greek dramatist says, 'eloquent to those
who go along with them,' but to none else. They are not
likely to attract the uninitiated; their influence is
rather in deepening and quickening religious feelings
already existing. Like music in a minor key, his poetry
does not command attention by a full burst of sound, but
quietly instils congenial musings into the attentive ear.
All these causes are more than enough to relegate Herbert
into the class of poets whose lot it must be 'to find fit
audience, though few.' He would himself gladly acquiesce
in such retirement, in the same spirit as that in which
Wordsworth sings -

    Shine, poet, in thy place, and be content.
                        ['If thou indeed derive', 1. 16]

    Herbert's poetry can never be popular. But all true
lovers of poetry will find hidden treasure there, if they
have patience to search below the surface. There is the
difficulty. It must be read *leisurely* to be appreciated.
The eager, bustling spirit of our times is incapable,
without some self-constraint, of comprehending those com-
pressed utterances, the result of undisturbed meditation.
Just as in a dimly-lighted room any one, who gives only a
hurried glance, may turn away disappointed from a really
fine painting, so it is only after a mental effort of
fixed attention that the latent beauties of poetry like
Herbert's can be descried. Then, and not till then, what
seemed confused and meaningless comes out in light and
shadow, disclosing the significance of even the minutest
details. A short poem called 'Aaron' is an instance.
Herbert is pourtraying the Christian minister as unworthy
in himself, but as rendered worthy by the indwelling gifts
of the great High Priest:

[Quotes the poem in full.]

    On a hasty reading, these lines sound as the merest
extravagance. They are full of meaning to those who care
to find it. The metre, too, is characteristic. At first,
it seems cramped and inelastic; when grown more familiar
to the ear, it has a plaintive sweetness of its own.

Take, again, 'The Call':

[Quotes the poem in full.]

It only requires thought to see the deep connexion which
underlies this string of apparently disconnected images.
    Religious poetry is seldom of the highest order. The
subject transcends human capacity: and the religious poet
is liable to the danger of having his sensuous perceptions
dimmed by the superior brightness of the immaterial world.
Exceptions, indeed, there are few, but glorious. Among
our countrymen, Milton stands alone in this category;
Cowper, Keble, Trench, and some few others, occupying the
next places. Many persons, who would otherwise never have
dreamt of versifying, have published what is meant for
poetry, solely under the promptings of strong religious
feeling, as the prolific doggrel of our innumerable hymn-
books testifies. To compare Herbert with the colossal
genius of Milton would be preposterous. He is more nearly
on a par with the others whom we have mentioned. If he
wants their polished and musical diction, and is comparatively deficient in the variety of natural imagery and the
tenderness of domestic pathos which belong to the poets of
Olney and Hursley, he may be ranked above Keble in terseness and vigour, while his manly cheerfulness is a delightful contrast to the morbid gloom which throws its chilling
shade over many of Cowper's most beautiful passages. In
the general characteristics of profound and reflective
philosophy, Herbert and Trench may be classed together.
Between Herbert and Keble the resemblance is still more
striking. The influence of the older poet is very perceptible throughout the 'Christian Year' - here and there in
the very words of it.

[Several passages from the two poets are then juxtaposed.]

These parallel passages are interesting as marking the
similarity of character which subsists in great and good
men, even of very distinct individualities. The admirers
of the 'Christian Year' will find much in 'The Temple' to
remind them of their favourite passages. If 'The Temple'
is never likely to exercise the extraordinary influence of
the 'Christian Year' - an influence on the religious mind
of England greater than has ever been exercised by any
book of the kind, an influence extending itself im+percep-
tibly even to quarters seemingly most alien - still it is
a book to make a deep impression, where it impresses at
all; and its influence is of a kind to percolate through

the few to the many.

The resemblance between Herbert and Cowper is fainter; or rather a strong resemblance is qualified by equally strong traits of difference. Both poets have much in common with Horace, strange as any comparison may appear at first sight between them and the pagan poet of the licentious court of Augustus. They have no small share of his lyrical fervour, his adroitness in the choice of words, and in the adaptation of metres; and, in satire, the same light touch, the same suppressed humour, the same half-sportive, half-pensive strictures on the anomalies of life. Both Herbert and Cowper love to dwell on the transitoriness of earthly pleasures; but there is this difference: Herbert oftener adds that man may enjoy them in moderation while they last:

[Quotes 'Mans medley', 11. 19-24.]

Both poets complain alike of times of religious depression; but Herbert's lyre is more often tuned to joy and thankfulness for refreshment and relief. He was naturally of a more hopeful temperament. But there are other causes to account for the difference. That distrustful dread of alienation from the favour of heaven, which, in religious minds of Cowper's school, seems even to overcloud the sense of reconciliation through the cross, was no part of Herbert's creed. On the contrary, it was the very essence of his faith, a source of unfailing strength, to regard himself and his fellow-Christians as having all the privileges of adoption within reach freely to enjoy. Again, while poor Cowper's mental vision was for ever introverted on himself, and busied with that dissection of transient phrases of feeling which paralyses the healthy action of the soul, Herbert's glance was oftener turned to the great objective truths of Christianity, deriving from them support in the consciousness of infirmity. Here is the secret of the *cheerfulness* of his poetry. This vivid realization of the great external facts of Christianity is what distinguishes him from the 'erotic school' of Germany. But for this, he might be classed with many of the poets of the 'Lyra Germanica.' But his poetry, though instinct with the same glow of seraphic love, is more definite, more practical, less sentimental. There is in it more substance for the mind to take hold of, more suggestiveness of something beyond, less evaporation into mere transports of emotion. His expressions of devout love, however eager and impulsive, are always (as in a short poem called 'Artillerie') profoundly reverential. Love and obedience, faith and duty, are with him inseparable. This habitual

attitude of mind toward the Deity, this filial feeling of
love tempered by awe, is beautifully apparent in the
closing lines of another poem:

[Quotes the last four lines of 'The Collar'.]

   We have endeavoured to illustrate particular traits in
Herbert's character, rather than to select his finest
passages. Some few of these we feel that we ought to cite
before concluding, especially as our author is one not so
well known as he deserves to be. The beautiful lines on
'Virtue,' beginning 'Sweet day, so cool, so calm, so
bright...,' are perhaps the best known, being quoted in
Campbell's 'British Poets' and elsewhere. They are singularly applicable to Herbert's own life and character, and
are redolent of the sweetness and brightness of his disposition. The 'Sonnet,' if we may use the word out of its
strict signification, on 'Time,' and the lines on 'Love
Unknown,' were both favourites with Coleridge. The former has been well compared to a collect in the Prayer-
Book in its perfect rhythm, and in the fulness and
compactness of its meaning. The latter is a short allegory, highly imaginative, and rich in devotional feeling.
We subjoin a specimen of Herbert's more philosophic poetry,
not unworthy of Wordsworth:

[Quotes 'Providence,' 11. 13-16, 29-32.]

Again, in 'The Search:'

[Quotes 11. 29-44.]

   Our limits forbid any more extracts. We can assure our
readers that, if they care to look for themselves, they
will find many passages, not of a kind, perhaps, to make
an immediate impression, but such as will approve themselves gradually more and more to a thoughtful and sympa-
thising mind, and from which it may derive solace and
strength.
   Herbert's Greek and Latin poems need not detain us
long. They evince his mastery over the idioms and metres
of those languages; but like most classical compositions
of his day, they seem harsh and strained, from the effort
required to force the old languages to adapt themselves to
modern ideas, for which they have no equivalent. His
Latin letters are open to the same criticism. The redundance of flowery compliments in them is also a fault of
the period.
   In our quotations we have referred to Pickering's

edition of 1850, as being, in our opinion, the best
extant. It is, as may be expected from the publisher's
name, carefully and beautifully executed; in type and
general effect perfectly in keeping with the author's age.
The old spelling is retained, as in Mr. Keble's Hooker,
and for the same reason, as assisting the reader to carry
back his thoughts to the associations amid which the
author lived and wrote. Mr. Willmott's edition betrays
haste by its unpardonable inaccuracies both of spelling
and punctuation, especially in the Latin letters, without
even any list of the errata. In not a few poems the
sense is quite obscured by their not being printed in form
of dialogue. The notes, scanty and misplaced, are of
little service, being attached generally to words that
need no explanation, as, for instance, 'shrewd,' 'callow,'
'diurnall,' 'oblation,' 'glozing,' while passing by the
few phrases that really present any difficulty. Mr. Willmott deserves thanks for adding a few short Greek poems:
not that they are of any great value in themselves, but because they show the versatility of Herbert's genius, and
his proficinecy, not in Latin only (a common accomplishment in his day), but in the less trodden field of Greek
literature. Mr. Willmott has done well in omitting 'The
Synagogue,' (35) a poor imitation, almost a caricature, of
of 'The Temple.' The omission of Walton's inimitable life
is unaccountable; nor is it compensated for by the editor's
editor's own 'Introduction.' It might have been hoped,
from an editor like Mr. Willmott, that he would have
thrown some light on the connexion between the poet's life
and particular passages in his writings. These omissions
are the more to be regretted, as this edition is entitled
to the credit of introducing an undeservedly neglected
author in an attractive and popular form for general reading.

   We have prolonged these remarks, we fear, beyong the
patience of our readers. In truth, we have been reluctant
to quit a subject so fascinating. Men like George Herbert
are rare. It is not his wide learning, nor his refined
taste; not his high spirit, nor his amiability, nor even
his strictness of life; it is not any of these qualities
singly that distinguishes him: but the rare combination in
one person of qualities so diversely beautiful. He was
'master of all learning, human and divine.' So writes his
brother, Lord Herbert of Cherbury, (36) and his remains,
few as they are, confirm this eulogy; yet his learning is
not what strikes the reader most, it is so thoroughly controlled and subordinated by his lively wit and practical
wisdom. He was exemplary in the domestic relations of
life, 'tender and true' as son, husband, friend: yet he

257 George Herbert: The Critical Heritage

seems to have lived as a 'home-missionary' among his parishioners. He was a man of letters; yet ever condescending to
the petty concerns of his poor ignorant clients: an ambitious man; yet he relinquished all worldly objects for the
humble work of the ministry. He was, in a word, a man of
extraordinary endowments, both personal and such as belonged to his rank - not lost in indolence nor wasted on
trivialities, but all disciplined and cultivated to the
utmost, and then devoted to thè highest purposes. Men of
a less evenly-balanced genius may create a greater sensa-
tion in the world; as the eccentric course of a comet may
attract more notice than steadier and less startling luminaries. But it may be questioned whether the influence of
men like George Herbert is not wider and deeper, though
less perceptible, in the end. From them issue the hidden
watercourses of thought and action that irrigate the world
with ever fresh supplies of life and vigour by innumerable,
unnoticeable rills, preserving its morality from corruption
and stagnation. The influence of those who possess Herbert's natural ability, combined with his *solidity* of
character, cannot be measured by what we see. It is to
men of this metal that England owes her greatness - men,
like him, of high spirit, strict principle, genial, practical energy - men who, over and above other fine qualities, are strong in that reality and earnestness on which
we are apt to pride ourselves as peculiarly English. Such
a hero, in the truest sense, England has but lately lost
in Lord Herbert of Lea; such, in a different sphere of
life, was his kinsman, the country parson of Bemerton.
May the race of men like these never be extinct among our
statesmen and our clergy! There is said to be a dearth of
talent among the younger clergy now. The most promising
young men in the universities, it is asserted, draw back
from ordination, and prefer other professions. They may
learn, from the example of George Herbert, how to devote
their talents to a worthy end.

Notes

1 I.e. Little Gidding.
2 'Many private papers of George Herbert were lost in the
   fire at Highnam House, Gloucestershire, the seat of
   Sir Robert Cook, the second husband of George Herbert's
   widow' (author's note).
3 I.e. 'valeat quantum valere potest' (let it pass for
   what it is worth).
4 Charles Kingsley (1819-75).
5 Henry Hallam, in his 'Introduction to the Literature of

Europe' (as above, p. 218: note 10).

6 'Lord Bacon dedicated some metrical psalms to George
   Herbert; "and usually", says Walton, "desired his
   approbation, before he would expose any book of his to
   be printed"' (author's note; see above, pp. 57 and
   100).

7 Literally, 'whatever they do' - adapted from Juvenal,
   'Satires', I, 85-6.

8 Above, pp. 66 and 98.

9 The 'path of a retiring life', i.e. the course of an
   obscure life - adapted from Horace, 'Epistles', I,
   xviii, 103.

10 Above, p. 81.

11 Above, p. 111.

12 Above, p. 108.

13 Above, p. 108.

14 The ill-tempered wife of Socrates.

15 'He lived not long but much' - i.e. actively, richly.

16 Above, p. 79.

17 Above, p. 120.

18 Above, p. 119.

19 'Task to be performed'.

20 'relieving the particle of divine breath from the de-
   pressing burden of the body burdened' - adapted from
   Horace, 'Satires', II, ii, 77-9.

21 'It is uncertain whether a bridegroom or a shepherd is
   a better friend'. On Duport's tribute to Herbert, see
   No. 27.

22 In the edition cited, above, No. 51.

23 As above, note 5.

24 Above, p. 114.

25 'Away with you, swine; I don't favour you.'

26 George Ellis, 'Specimens of the Early English Poets',
   4th rev. edn (1811), III, 125; first published in
   1790.

27 'Gashaw' is, of course, Crashaw. See above, p. 15.

28 Thomas Campbell, 'Specimens of the British Poets'
   (1819), III, 81-2, and Robert Southey, 'Specimens of
   the Later English Poets' (1807), 3 vols.

29 Above p. 168.

30 By John Keble (1827).

31 'If you do not wish to understand, you should not
   read.'

32 Above, pp. 166-7.

33 Above, p. 76.

34 Adapted from Keble's lecture (No. 52).

35 By Christopher Harvey (see above, p. 5).

36 No. 10.

56.   JOHN NICHOL, FROM HIS INTRODUCTION TO 'THE POETICAL
WORKS OF GEORGE HERBERT'

1863

The first professional academic to attend to Herbert was
John Nichol, Professor of English Literature at the University of Glasgow (see also above, p. 27).   In his introduction to the 1863 edition of Herbert's poetry - its
text, one would wish to mark, edited by Keats's friend
Charles Cowden Clark - Nichol began with a brief but cosmic view of developments during the Elizabethan period and
continued in the manner shown below.
     Source: Nichol, from The Life and Poetry of George
Herbert, in 'The Poetical Works of George Herbert' (1863),
pp. vi-vii and xix-xxvi.

The first quarter of the seventeenth [century] saw a lull
between storms - comparative peace abroad and quiet at
home, when Church and State seemed to rest firmly on the
basis of a provisional settlement, and the smouldering
elements of discord only made themselves felt in the out-
break of an occasional and easily suppressed conspiracy.
If the literature belonging to this period is tamer than
that of the preceding era, there is an air of repose about
it which has a charm of its own, and which is seen alike
in the two opposite styles by which the poetry of the time
is mainly represented - in the graceful lyrics of Herrick,
and Lovelace, and Suckling, in the more sombre fancies of
Donne and Crashaw, and the psalmody of George Herbert.
Herbert, the first and the best of our purely religious
poets, belongs both by character and date to this era.
Five years after his birth, Shakspeare was an actor in one
of Ben Jonson's plays; in the year when Milton took his
degree at Cambridge, our author died.   He is still pre-
eminently the laureate of the Church of England, and he
was so at a time when she first began to feel herself
securely established, 'double-moated' between the valley
and the hills, and unsuspicious of the storms to come.
Before he lived, the divergence between the Anglo-Catholic
and Evangelical - the High and Low sections of the Church,
had begun to manifest itself in the first murmurs of the
strife that was, in the succeeding age, to rend her asun-
der; but during his life they had grown fainter, or he was
unconscious of them.   Next to Christianity itself, the
Church, the whole Church, and nothing but the Church is
his anchorage; round her service and doctrine his whole

thoughts circulate, to her advancement all his aspirations
tend, and the Puritanic purity of his morals is made to
fit in harmoniously with the Anglicanism of his creed.
Gentler than Milton, though not half so great, Herbert
differed in many ways from his immortal successor, and
most of all by the fact of his implicit faith in established forms....

[After a biographical account of Herbert, heavily dependent on Walton, Nichol attends to the poetry.]

'The Temple,' which Herbert had placed in Mr Duncan's
hands, was the repository of verses gradually accumulated
during his residence at Bemerton, the silent labour of his
life, a monument reared, as has been suggested, as quietly
as that other Temple of Jerusalem; we may rather say, it
grew up, like the fabled walls of Thebes, to the music of
his lyre. Mr Farrar superintended the publication of the
volume; and when Izaak Walton wrote the author's life,
20,000 copies had been already circulated.
     The collection of poems entitled 'The Temple,' which,
with the prose treatise, 'A Country Parson,' 'The Church
Militant,' (1) and a few minor verses in English and Latin,
completes the list of our author's works, embraces an
almost indefinite variety of theme and measure, from the
slender notes of the flute to the full tones of the organ
bass; yet it is pervaded by a unity of thought and purpose which justifies the single name. Those poems are a
series of hymns and meditations within the walls of an
English church. They are Church music crystallised.
There is a speciality about them which continually recalls
the circumstances of the writer. 'The Temple,' as
Coleridge remarked, will always be read with fullest
appreciation by those who share the poet's devotion to
the Dear Mother whose praises he has undertaken to celebrate. (2) The verses on 'Easter' and 'Lent,' on 'Baptism' and 'Communion,' on 'Church Monuments' and 'Music,'
seem most directly to address the worshippers in that
flock of which he was so good a shepherd, whose affections
are entwined around his Church, who love to linger on the
associations of her festivals, the rubrics of her creed,
and the formularies of her service - to feel themselves
under the shadow of the old cathedrals - to draw allegories
from the fantasies of their fretted stone - to watch the
light flicker through the painted glass on marble tombs,
and listen to the anthems throbbing through the choir. Yet
there is in the author and in his work catholicity enough
to give his volume a universal interest, and make his
prayer and praise a fit expression of Christian faith under

all varieties of form. The defects of the book - those
which remove it, as a whole, from the first class of
poetry - are those which are peculiar to the writer and
his Church and time; its excellences, which raise it to
the front of the second rank result from an exercise of
those qualities which Herbert shares with all great religious poets. Those defects are serious, and have em-
boldened depreciatory critics to say that the author of
'The Temple' has been handed down to us more by his life
than his work. Foremost among them is a want of condensation, which has led the poet into frequent repetition
of the same ideas under slightly altered phraseology.
Sometimes, even within the limits of the same poem, he
turns a thought over till we are tired of it; and to read
through his book continuously is no easy task. It has
been said correctly that Herbert has more genius than
taste; and his deficiency in the latter quality, combined with a grotesque vein of allegory which belonged to
the time, has not unfrequently, as in the verse entitled
'Jesu,' led the most reverent of men into conceits which
seem to approach irreverence. The extremes of levity
and pious word-worship meet now and then in a devout pun.
There are many instances in which we cannot help complaining that too much is made of little things, as in a
pre-Raphaelite picture the whole effect is apt to be
sacrificed to microscopic detail; so that we think of 'The
Temple' rather in connexion with the mosaic-work of Wilton
Chapel, than the neighbouring and more stately grandeur of
the severe majestic Salisbury. Herbert is prone, by his
own admission, to overlay his matter with far-fetched, and
sometimes incongruous imagery. His

>   Thoughts begin to burnish, sprout, and swell,
>   Curling with metaphors a plain intention;
>   Decking the sense as if it were to sell;
>   ['Jordan' (II), ll. 4-6]

so that we are apt to think less of the lesson than of the
quaint mannerism of the words in which it is read to us.
Though in his higher flights he often succeeds in 'wedding
noble music unto noble words,' the poet-musician is not,
on the whole, a musical poet; he has certainly tried more
varieties of measure than he has mastered. If to this we
add that Herbert almost wholly wants the element of
humour, a defect which shews itself in such lines as

>   All Solomon's sea of brass and world of stone
>   Is not so dear to Thee as one good groan,
>   ['Sion', ll. 17-18]

we shall be at no loss to explain why the great and
deserved popularity of 'The Temple' is, comparatively
speaking, restricted to those masterpieces of its structure, with which all readers are or ought to be familiar.
      The best poems in the volume, as 'The Church Porch,'
'The Agony,' 'Sin,' 'Faith,' 'Love,' 'The Temper,'
'Employments,' 'Church Music,' 'Sunday,' 'The World,'
'Lent,' ' Virtue,' 'The Pearl,' 'Man,' 'Mortification,'
'The British Church,' 'The Quip,' 'The Size,' and many
more, in themselves make up a treasury of sacred song
whose price is beyond rubies. They are more like modern
psalms than any other poems we know. Like those older and
grander voices, they, too, have their place by the wayside
of the Christian life - rousing, warning; cheering, comforting, sorrowing and rejoicing with us as we go. Like
church windows they have a double aspect; we may look in
through them from without on the writer's heart, and see
him as a priest and man struggling like ourselves with
doubts and fears, but with 'a face not fearing light,' and
a will well bent to do his Master's work; we may look out
through them from within on the world as seen with the
poet's eye - a fair round world of light and shade, over-
arched by clouds and stars.
      The asceticism of Herbert's character appears in his
verse. He does not think, with Glaucon, (3) that we can
'make the best of both worlds.' To him it seems that to
be full in both 'is more than God was, who was hungry
here.' He constantly opposes to passion the laws of temperance and authority. With him

        Life is a business, not good cheer,
                  Ever in wars.
                          ['Employment' (II), ll. 16-17]

He is fond of dwelling on the dangers of good company, and
the folly that lurks in a disdain of rule. Three lines
in 'The Church Porch,' so full of that good strong sense
which is seen even in his collection of Proverbs, are the
refrain of his leading counsels:

        Chase brave employments with a naked sword
        Throughout the world. Fool not, for all may have,
        If they dare choose, a glorious life or grave.
                          [ll. 88-90]

Almost the only thing of which he is intolerant is frivo-
lity:

        Laugh not too much; the witty man laughs least,

For wit is news only to ignorance.

[ll. 229-30]

And indifference -

Who say 'I care not' - those I give for lost.

[l. 347]

Yet he was no sour ascetic - witness his love of music and
the tender grace of some of his verses, as 'Peace' or
'Virtue,' which Shelley might have written. He loved the
beauty as much as he revered the solemnity of his religion,
and was wont to wander about 'the fruitful beds and bor-
ders in God's rich garden,' as well as to kneel in awe
beneath the thunders of Sinai.
    The commencement of the lines entitled 'Man's Medley,'
shews how thoroughly he was alive to the sweet influences,
the pleasant sights and sounds of nature. He always wished
to have a 'pleasing presence,' and held

            All worldly joys go less
    To the one joy of doing kindnesses.

[ll. 329-30]

This love of practical benevolence was one side of his
nature; another was the deep spirit of devotion and
evangelical piety which comes out in those pieces which
are more properly prayers set to music, and in the doctrinal part of his poetry.
    Herbert was altogether greater as a man than as an
artist; but some of his lines seemed inspired by a deeper
flow of imagination than the rest, and will bear comparison with the best of all but our greatest poets. What
could be more suggestive than this image?

    Successive nights, like rolling waves,
    Convey them quickly who are bound for death.
                    ['Mortification', ll. 11-12]

What summary of man's ideal more complete than this? -

    A grain of glory mix'd with humbleness
                    ['The Church-porch', l. 335]

Or what better express his relation to God than?

    I am but finite, yet Thine infinitely.
                    ['Artillerie', l. 32]

Or where have we more gracefully condensed the duty of submission than here?

> Yet take thy way; for sure thy way is best,
>   Stretch or contract me thy poor debtor.
> This is but tuning of my breast
>   To make the music better.
>   ['The Temper' (I), ll. 21-4]

Herbert's poem on 'Man' is his masterpiece. The most philosophic as well as the most comprehensive of his writings, it stands by itself, and has enlisted the admiration even of those furthest removed from him in creed, and cast, and time. Embodying his recognition of the mysterious relationship of the chief of created beings to his Creator and to the universe, it seems to anticipate centuries of discovery. The faculty which can range from heaven to earth, from earth to heaven, discerns the hidden links by which the world is woven together, and poetry prophesies what science proves. In the microcosm of man –

> East and west touch, – the poles do kiss,
>   And parallels meet.
>   ['The Search', ll. 43-4]

Man, with Herbert, is everything, 'a tree,' 'a beast, yet is, is, or should be more;' he is

>   all symmetry,
> Full of proportions, one limb to another,
>   And all to all the world besides.
>   ['Man', ll, 13-15]

Claiming brotherhood with moons and tides, 'in little, all the sphere,' everything ministers to his service:

>   For us the winds do blow
> The earth doth rest, heaven move and fountains flow.
>   [ibid., ll. 25-6]

Clenching the whole into one grand line the poet exclaims:

> Man is one world, and hath
>   Another to attend him.
>   [ibid., ll. 47-8]

And then from the open vault of day he turns again reverently towards the temple, crying,

> Since, then, my God, thou hast
> So brave a palace built, oh, dwell in it.
>
> [ibid., 11. 49-50]

This, which was the prayer and effort of his life, was
surely in full measure granted to George Herbert. Nothing
arrests us more than his perfect honesty. There is no
writing for effect in his pages; as we turn them we feel
ourselves in the presence of a man speaking out of the
fulness of his heart and carried away into a higher air by
the sustaining power of his own incessant aspirations.

Herbert can scarcely be called a lesser Milton. His
Gothic temple has nothing of the classic grace and grandeur of the hand that reared the great dome of our English
Epic on smooth pillars of everlasting verse. He breathes
rather the spirit of the author of the 'Olney Hymns'; (4)
but Herbert's was a more cheerful faith than Cowper's,
and the brightness of God's countenance seemed ever to
shine upon him as he went on his way singing to the gates
of the celestial city.

Notes

1 Nichol clearly assumes that 'The Church Militant' does
   not form part of 'The Temple'.
2 Above, p. 170.
3 The son of Minos and Pasiphaë, master of the art of
   divination following his resurrection from the dead by
   the seer Polyidos.
4 William Cowper, whose 'Olney Hymns' were published in
   1779.

57. GEORGE MACDONALD, GEORGE HERBERT, IN 'ENGLAND'S
ANTIPHON'

1868

'Antiphon', the title of two poems by Herbert, was in
1868 borrowed by the poet and novelist George Macdonald
for his collection of essays, 'England's Antiphon'. It
was a symbolic gesture, in that Macdonald's chapter on
Herbert within the collection is a distinctly enthusiastic
evaluation of the poet - an evaluation, moreover, accompanied by a sustained plea for the recognition of Herbert's

'exquisite art', significantly intimated to be superior to Donne's. See also above, p. 27.
    Source: Macdonald, George Herbert, in 'England's Antiphon' (1868), Ch. XII (pp. 174-93).

But, with my hand on the lock, I shrink from opening the door. Here comes a poet indeed! and how am I to show him due honour? With his book humbly, doubtfully offered, with the ashes of the poems of his youth fluttering in the wind of his priestly garments, he crosses the threshold. Or rather, for I had forgotten the symbol of my book, (1) let us all go from our chapel to the choir, and humbly ask him to sing that he may make us worthy of his song.
    In George Herbert there is poetry enough and to spare: it is the household bread of his being. If I begin with that which first in the nature of things ought to be demanded of a poet, namely, Truth, Revelation - George Herbert offers us measure pressed down and running over. But let me speak first of that which first in time or order of appearance we demand of a poet, namely music. For inasmuch as verse is for the ear, not for the eye, we demand a good hearing first. Let no one undervalue it. The heart of poetry is indeed truth, but its garments are music, and the garments come first in the process of revelation. The music of a poem is its meaning in sound as distinguished from word - its meaning in solution, as it were, uncrystallized by articulation. The music goes before the fuller revelation, preparing its way. The sound of a verse is the harbinger of the truth contained therein. If it be a right poem, this will be true. Herein Herbert excels. It will be found impossible to separate the music of his words from the music of the thought which takes shape in their sound.

        I got me flowers to strow thy way,
            I got me boughs off many a tree;
        But thou wast up by break of day,
            And brought'st thy sweets along with thee.
                                    ['Easter', 11. 19-22]

    And the gift it enwraps at once and reveals is, I have said, truth of the deepest. Hear this song of divine service. In every song he sings a spiritual fact will be found its fundamental life, although I may quote this or that merely to illustrate some peculiarity of mode.
    The Elixir was an imagined liquid sought by the old physical investigators, in order that by its means they might turn every common metal into gold, a pursuit not

quite so absurd as it has since appeared. They called this something, when regarded as a solid, *the Philosopher's Stone*. In the poem it is also called a *tincture*.

[Quotes 'The Elixer' in full.]

With a conscience tender as a child's, almost diseased in its tenderness, and a heart loving as a woman's, his intellect is none the less powerful. Its movements are as the sword-play of an alert, poised, well-knit, strong-wristed fencer with the rapier, in which the skill impresses one more than the force, while without the force the skill would be valueless, even hurtful, to its possessor. There is a graceful humour with it occasionally, even in his most serious poems adding much to their charm. To illustrate all this, take the following, the title of which means *The Retort*.

[Quotes 'The Quip' in full.]

Here is another instance of his humour. It is the first stanza of a poem to 'Death.' He is glorying over Death as personified in a skeleton.

Death, thou wast once an uncouth, hideous thing –
      Nothing but bones,
   The sad effect of sadder groans:
Thy mouth was open, but thou couldst not sing.

No writer before him has shown such a love to God, such a childlike confidence in him. The love is like the love of those whose verses came first in my volume. (2) But the nation had learned to think more, and new difficulties had consequently arisen. These, again, had to be undermined by deeper thought, and the discovery of yet deeper truth had been the reward. Hence, the love itself, if it had not strengthened, had at least grown deeper. And George Herbert had had difficulty enough in himself; for, born of high family, by nature fitted to shine in that society where elegance of mind, person, carriage, and utterance is most appreciated, and having indeed enjoyed something of the life of a courtier, he had forsaken all in obedience to the voice of his higher nature. Hence the struggle between his tastes and his duties would come and come again, augmented probably by such austere notions as every conscientious man must entertain in proportion to his inability to find God in that in which he might find him. From this inability, inseparable in its varying degrees from the very nature of growth, springs all the

asceticism of good men, whose love to God will be the
greater as their growing insight reveals him in his world,
and their growing faith approaches to the giving of thanks
in everything.

When we have discovered the truth that whatsoever is
not of faith is sin, the way to meet it is not to forsake
the human law, but so to obey it as to thank God for it.
To leave the world and go into the desert is not thus to
give thanks: it may have been the only way for this or
that man, in his blameless blindness, to take. The divine
mind of George Herbert, however, was in the main bent upon
discovering God everywhere.

The poem I give next, powerfully sets forth the struggle
between liking and duty of which I have spoken. It is at
the same time an instance of wonderful art in construction,
all the force of the germinal thought kept in reserve, to
burst forth at the last. He calls it - meaning by the
word, *God's Restraint* - 'The Collar.'

[Quotes 'The Collar' in full.]

Coming now to speak of his art, let me say something
first about his use of homeliest imagery for highest
thought. This, I think, is in itself enough to class him
with the highest *kind* of poets. If my reader will refer
to 'The Elixir,' he will see an instance in the third
stanza, 'You may look at the glass, or at the sky:' 'You
may regard your action only, or that action as the will of
God.' Again, let him listen to the pathos and simplicity
of this one stanza, from a poem he calls 'The Flower.'
He has been in trouble; his times have been evil; he has
felt a spiritual old age creeping upon him; but he is once
more awake.

> And now in age (3) I bud again;
> After so many deaths I live and write;
> I once more smell the dew and rain,
> And relish versing. O my only light,
>   It cannot be
>   That I am he
> On whom thy tempests fell all night!

[11. 36-42]

Again:

> Some may dream merrily, but when they wake
>   They dress themselves and come to thee.

['Home,' 11. 51-2]

He has an exquisite feeling of lyrical art. Not only
does he keep to one idea in it, but he finishes the poem
like a cameo. Here is an instance wherein he outdoes the
elaboration of a Norman trouvère; for not merely does each
line in each stanza end with the same sound as the corresponding line in every other stanza, but it ends with the
very same word. I shall hardly care to defend this if my
reader chooses to call it a whim; but I do say that a
large degree of the peculiar musical effect of the poem -
subservient to the thought, keeping it dimly chiming in
the head until it breaks out clear and triumphant like a
silver bell in the last - is owing to this use of the same
column of words at the line-ends of every stanza. Let him
who doubts it, read the poem aloud.

[Quotes 'Aaron' in full.]

Note the flow and the ebb of the lines of each stanza -
from six to eight to ten syllables, and back through eight
to six, the number of stanzas corresponding to the number
of lines in each; only the poem itself begins with the
ebb, and ends with a full spring-flow of energy. Note also
the perfect antithesis in their parts between the first
and second stanzas, and how the last line of the poem
clenches the whole in revealing its idea - that for the
sake of which it was written. In a word, note the *unity*.
Born in 1593, notwithstanding his exquisite art, he
could not escape being influenced by the faulty tendencies
of his age, borne in upon his youth by the example of his
mother's friend, Dr. Donne. A man must be a giant like
Shakspere or Milton to cast off his age's faults. Indeed
no man has more of the 'quips and cranks and wanton wiles'
of the poetic spirit of his time than George Herbert, but
with this difference from the rest of Dr. Donne's school,
that such is the indwelling potency that it causes even
these to shine with a radiance such that we wish them
still to burn and not be consumed. His muse is seldom
other than graceful, even when her motions are grotesque,
and he is always a gentleman, which cannot be said of his
master. We could not bear to part with his most fantastic
oddities, they are so interpenetrated with his genius as
well as his art.
In relation to the use he makes of these faulty forms,
and to show that even herein he has exercised a refraining
judgment, though indeed fancying he has quite discarded in
only somewhat reforming it, I recommend the study of two
poems, each of which he calls 'Jordan,' though why I have
not yet with certainty discovered.
It is possible that not many of his readers have

observed the following instances of the freakish in his
rhyming art, which however result well. When I say so,
I would not be supposed to approve of the freak, but only
to acknowledge the success of the poet in his immediate
intent. They are related to a certain tendency to
mechanical contrivance not seldom associated with a love
of art: it is art operating in the physical understanding.
In the poem called 'Home,' every stanza is perfectly
finished till the last: in it, with an access of art or
artfulness, he destroys the rhyme. I shall not quarrel
with my reader if he calls it the latter, and regards it
as art run to seed. And yet - and yet - I confess I have
a latent liking for the trick. I shall give one or two
stanzas out of the rather long poem, to lead up to the
change in the last.

[Quotes the poem's last three stanzas, ending with:]

> Come, dearest Lord, pass not this holy season,
>   My flesh and bones and joints do pray;
> And even my verse, when by the rhyme and reason
>   The word is *stay*, (4) says ever *come*.
>   O Show thyself to me,
>   Or take me up to thee.

Balancing this, my second instance is of the converse.
In all the stanzas but the last, the last line in each
hangs unrhymed: in the last the rhyming is fulfilled.
The poem is called 'Denial.' I give only a part of it.

[Quotes the poem's last three stanzas.]

It had been hardly worth the space to point out these,
were not the matter itself precious.
    Before making further remark on George Herbert, let me
present one of his poems in which the oddity of the visual
fancy is only equalled by the beauty of the result.

[Quotes 'The Pulley' in full.]

    Is it not the story of the world written with the point
of a diamond?
    There can hardly be a doubt that his tendency to un-
natural forms was encouraged by the increase of respect to
symbol and ceremony shown at this period by some of the
external powers of the church - Bishop Laud in particular.
Had all, however, who delight in symbols, a power, like
George Herbert's, of setting even within the horn-lanterns
of the more arbitrary of them, such a light of poetry and

devotion that their dull sides vanish in its piercing
shine, and we forget the symbol utterly in the truth which
it cannot obscure, then indeed our part would be to take
and be thankful. But there never has been even a living
true symbol which the dulness of those who will see the
truth only in the symbol has not degraded into the very
cockatrice-egg of sectarianism. The symbol is by such
always more or less idolized, and the light within more or
less patronized. If the truth, for the sake of which all
symbols exist, were indeed the delight of those who claim
it, the sectarianism of the church would vanish. But men
on all sides call that *the truth* which is but its form or
outward sign - material or verbal, true or arbitrary, it
matters not which - and hence come strifes and divisions.

Although George Herbert, however, could thus illumine
all with his divine inspiration, we cannot help wondering
whether, if he had betaken himself yet more to vital and
less to half artificial symbols, the change would not have
been a breaking of the pitcher and an outshining of the
lamp. For a symbol may remind us of the truth, and at the
same time obscure it - present it, and dull its effect.
It is the temple of nature and not the temple of the
church, the things made by the hands of God and not the
things made by the hands of man, that afford the truest
symbols of truth.

I am anxious to be understood. The chief symbol of
our faith, *the Cross*, it may be said, is not one of these
natural symbols. I answer - No; but neither is it an
arbitrary symbol. It is not a symbol of *a truth* at all,
but of *a fact*, of the infinitely grandest fact in the
universe, which is itself the outcome and symbol of the
grandest Truth. *The Cross* is an historical *sign*, not
properly *a symbol*, except through the facts it reminds us
of. On the other hand, *baptism* and the *eucharist* are symbols of the loftiest and profoundest kind, true to nature
and all its meanings, as well as to the facts of which they
remind us. They are in themselves symbols of the truths
involved in the facts they commemorate.

Of Nature's symbols George Herbert has made large use;
but he would have been yet a greater poet if he had made
a larger use of them still. Then at least we might have
got rid of such oddities as the stanzas for steps up to
the church-door, the first at the bottom of the page; of
the lines shaped into ugly altar-form; and of the absurd
Easter wings, made of ever lengthening lines. This would
not have been much, I confess, nor the gain by their loss
great; but not to mention the larger supply of images
graceful with the grace of God, who when he had made them
said they were good, it would have led to the further

purification of his taste, perhaps even to the casting out
of all that could untimely move our mirth; until possibly
(for illustration), instead of this lovely stanza, he
would have given us even a lovelier:

> Listen, sweet dove, unto my song,
>   And spread thy golden wings on me;
> Hatching my tender heart so long,
>   Till it get wing, and fly away with thee.

> ['Whitsunday', 11. 1-4]

The stanza is indeed lovely, and true and tender and
clever as well; yet who can help smiling at the notion of
the incubation of the heart-egg, although what the poet
means is so good that smile almost vanishes in a sigh?

There is no doubt that the works of man's hands will
also afford many true symbols; but I do think that, in
proportion as a man gives himself to those instead of
studying Truth's wardrobe of forms in nature, so will he
decline from the high calling of the poet. George Herbert
was too great to be himself much injured by the narrowness
of the field whence he gathered his symbols; but his song
will be the worse for it in the ears of all but those who,
having lost sight of or having never beheld the oneness of
the God whose creation exists in virtue of his redemption,
feel safer in a low-browed crypt than under 'the high
embowed roof.'

When the desire after system or order degenerates from
a need into a passion, or ruling idea, it closes, as may
be seen in many women who are especial housekeepers, like
an unyielding skin over the mind, to the death of all
development from impulse and aspiration. The same thing
holds in the church: anxiety about order and system will
kill the life. This did not go near to being the result
with George Herbert: his life was hid with Christ in God;
but the influence of his *profession*, as distinguished from
his work, was hurtful to his calling as a poet. He of all
men would scorn to claim social rank for spiritual service; he of all men would not commit the blunder of supposing that prayer and praise are that service of God:
they are *prayer* and *praise*, not *service*; he knew that God
can be served only through loving ministration to his sons
and daughters, all needy of commonest human help: but, as
the most devout of clergymen will be the readiest to confess, there is even a danger to their souls in the unvary-
ing recurrence of the outward obligations of their service; and, in like manner, the poet will fare ill if the
conventions from which the holiest system is not free send
him soaring with sealed eyes. George Herbert's were but a

little blinded thus; yet something, we must allow, [of]
his poetry was injured by his profession. All that I say
on this point, however, so far from diminishing his
praise, adds thereto, setting forth only that he was such
a poet as might have been greater yet, had the divine
gift had free course. But again I rebuke myself and say,
'Thank God for George Herbert.'

To rid our spiritual palates of the clinging flavour of
criticism, let me choose another song from his precious
legacy - one less read, I presume, than many. It shows
his tendency to asceticism - the fancy of forsaking God's
world in order to serve him; it has besides many of the
faults of the age, even to that of punning; yet it is a
lovely bit of art as well as a rich embodiment of tenderness.

[Quotes 'The Thanksgiving' in full.]

With the preceding must be taken the following, which
comes immediately after it.

[Quotes 'The Reprisall' in full.]

Even embracing the feet of Jesus, Mary Magdalene or
George Herbert must rise and go forth to do his will.

It will be observed how much George Herbert goes beyond
all that have preceded him, in the expression of feeling
as it flows from individual conditions, in the analysis of
his own moods, in the logic of worship, if I may say so.
His utterance is not merely of personal love and grief,
but of the peculiar love and grief in the heart of George
Herbert. There may be disease in such a mind; but, if
there be, it is a disease that will burn itself out.
Such disease is, for men constituted like him, the only
path to health. By health I mean that simple regard to
the truth, to the will of God, which will turn away a
man's eyes from his own conditions, and leave God free to
work his perfection in him - free, that is, of the inter-
ference of the man's self-consciousness and anxiety. To
this perfection St. Paul had come when he no longer cried
out against the body of his death, no more judged his own
self, but left all to the Father, caring only to do his
will. It was enough to him then that God should judge
him, for his will is the one good thing securing all good
things. Amongst the keener delights of the life which is
at the door, I look for the face of George Herbert, with
whom to talk humbly would be in bliss a higher bliss.

Notes

1 I.e. the title of Macdonald's book, borrowed from
   'Antiphon'.
2 I.e. the thirteenth-century religious poets discussed
   in Macdonald's first chapter.
3 'He was but thirty-nine when he died' (author's note).
4 'To rhyme with *pray* in the second line' (author's note).

58. GERARD MANLEY HOPKINS, FROM A LETTER TO R.W. DIXON

1879

Hopkins's respect for Herbert was evidently far more substantial than the ensuing brief remark might suggest (see
above, pp. 27-8). The remark, from a letter to Canon R.W.
Dixon dated 27 February 1879, is limited to a comparative
evaluation of Herbert and Vaughan.
     Source: 'The Correspondence of Gerard Manley Hopkins
and Richard Watson Dixon', ed. Claude C. Abbott, 2nd rev.
impr. (1955), pp. 23-4.

[Vaughan] was a follower of Herbert both in life and
style: he was in fact converted from worldly courses by
reading Herbert's poems on a sickbed and even his muse
underwent a conversion (for he had written before). He has
more glow and freedom than Herbert but less fragrant
sweetness. Somewhere he speaks of some spot 'primrosed
and hung with shade' and one piece ends

     And here in dust and dirt, O here
     The lilies of his love appear. (1)

(I am assuming that you have not got the book.)   Still I
do not think him Herbert's equal.

Note

1 From 'Regeneration', l. 4 (in 'Silex Scintillans',
   1650), and 'The Revival', ll. 13-14 (in 'Thalia
   Rediviva', 1678), respectively.

59.   A.C. BENSON, FROM 'ESSAYS'

1896

The scholar and occasional poet A.C. Benson was one of
those who by the end of the nineteenth century felt that
the reiterated comparison of Herbert and Keble - often in
the latter's favour - should be arrested. Such a comparison, he maintained in his evaluation of Keble, is entirely
'inapt'. The succinct reasons he offered are given in the
following extract. See also above, p. 26.
    Source: Benson, from The Poetry of Keble, in 'Essays'
(1896), pp. 196-7.

...as to technical treatment and form, it would be difficult to select to poets so utterly and radically unlike as
George Herbert and Keble. The only point of resemblance
is that they are both sometimes unnecessarily obscure; but
in George Herbert's case this arises from a curious elaboration of expression, an intensity of compression, an omission of logical steps, a tendency to cram a sentence into
a word; while in Keble's case, his obscurity arises from a
kind of indefinite garrulity, a tendency to diverge on side
issues, a vapid displacement of language.

60.   GEORGE SAINTSBURY, FROM 'A SHORT HISTORY OF ENGLISH
LITERATURE'

1898

The Professor of Rhetoric and Belles Lettres at the Uni-
versity of Edinburgh should have been heard with respect
when in his frequently reprinted 'Short History of English
Literature' he ventured the ensuing remarks on Herbert.
But his reservations - like the indifference of a later
successor to his chair (No. 71) - were slowly becoming
irrelevant and would eventually be bypassed altogether.
See also above, pp. 29-30.
    Source: Saintsbury, from The Metaphysicals - The Lyric
Poets - The Miscellanists, etc., in 'A Short History of
English Literature' (1898), pp. 414-16.

An infinitely more popular poet than Crashaw, and certainly a more equable, though at the best of both Crashaw
towers over him, was George Herbert, a member of the noble
Norman-Welsh family of that name, and brother of Lord Herbert of Cherbury. He was born at Montgomery Castle on
13th April 1593, went to Cambridge, became Fellow of Trinity in 1615, and Public Orator four years later, at the
early age of twenty-six. He held the place for eight
years with great distinction, though he was charged with
the fault of haughtiness, and seems to have looked forward
to a political career. But something led him to the course
of saintly life as a country clergyman, latterly at Bemerton, near Salisbury, which he pursued for six years, till
his early death in 1632. His verse (almost entirely
included in the well-known collection called 'The Temple,'
which made Crashaw call his 'Steps to the Temple') was not
published till after his death, but very soon after, for
though the date of the first edition is 1633, there are un-
dated copies which seem to have been distributed in the
previous year. 'The Temple' consists of 160 pieces,
arranged partly with a fancy of reference to the structural
arrangement of a church, beginning with 'The Porch'; partly
under the heads of the great festivals and services; often
under quite fantastic titles, 'The Quip,' 'The Pulley,'
and so forth. There is no prevailing metre - couplets,
stanzas, and regular and irregular lyrical forms being
chosen as may best suit the poet's purpose, while occasionally he will even condescend, as in 'Easter Wings,' to
that device of adjusting his verse lengths to artificial
patterns which excited almost more horror than ridicule in
the eighteenth century.
    And the note of fantasy is at least as much present in
idea and in diction, though Herbert seldom pushes either to
very extravagant lengths. In the 'Church Porch,' which is
a string of ethical and religious maxims, this fantasy does
not often pass beyond the almost proverbial imagery to
which we are accustomed in such connections. But in the
more abstract and doctrinal poems Herbert gives himself a
much wider range, and ransacks art and nature for quaint
similes, sometimes worked out in the fashion of the emblem-
poetry then so popular. The Game of Bowls; the real or
fancied properties of the orange tree; the Palace of the
World, with Wisdom sweeping away its cobwebs, Pleasure
adorning it with balconies, Sin splitting the walls with
stealthy fig-tree growth, Grace shoring them, and Death
throwing them down; the imaginary peculiarities of the
crocodile and elephant - Herbert presses all these and a
myriad more into his service. Yet the unaffected piety,
and perhaps still more the perfect charity, of his tone,

his abstinence from anything like strife and crying, the
heavenly peace that pervades him, have made his work
tolerated by many who are not as a rule very tolerant of
conceits.

As a poet he is certainly not the equal of either
Crashaw or Vaughan, and in his own quiet fashion he has
in the present century been equalled by Keble and surpassed by Miss Christina Rossetti. He very seldom transports: the throb of response to the highest and happiest
thoughts and expressions of the poets is very uncommon
in reading him; his is an equable merit, a soothing and
healthful pleasure, rather than the dazzling excellence,
the contagious rapture, of the great ones. But he can
never be mentioned with contempt by any one who loves
poetry, and he undoubtedly holds a high place among those
who have attempted the exceedingly difficult task of sacred verse. If his successes are never so great as those
of some others, it is hardly too much to say that he never
fails with the maddening failure too common in religious
poets, and this is in itself a great thing.

Herbert in the Twentieth Century

61. EDWARD DOWDEN, FROM 'PURITAN AND ANGLICAN'

1900

Professor of English Literature at the University of
Dublin, Edward Dowden included in his widely read 'Puritan
and Anglican' a brief but refreshing interpretation of
Herbert's life and poetry. The terms of reference commonly deployed to this time are seen to recede still further as Dowden searches 'below the surface'. See also
above, p. 30.

Source: Dowden, from Anglo-Catholic Poets: Herbert,
Vaughan, in 'Puritan and Anglican': Studies in Literature' (1900), pp. 104-6.

To become part of a great and Divine Order, to regulate
his life by rules, to perform a round of duties exactly,
reverently, gracefully, gladly, and at the same time to
express in song the tides, the fluctuations, the in-
cursions, the ebb and flow of the spirit, made up the life
of George Herbert. He could not wholly shape his course
by rule. Still the passionate temperament of his race remained with him; but his ardour was in great measure regulated, and served before all else to quicken his fidelity
in duty and to prevent his observance of forms from sinking into formalism. Still he was subject to swift alter-
ations of mood:

How should I praise Thee, Lord! how should my rhymes
    Gladly engrave Thy love in steel,
If what my soul doth feel sometimes
    My soul might ever feel!

> Although there were some forty heavens, or more,
>   Sometimes I peer above them all;
> Sometimes I hardly reach a score,
>   Sometimes to hell I fall.
>
> O rack me not to such a vast extent.
>   ['The Temper' (I), 11. 1-9]

In the poem entitled 'Misery,' Herbert reviews the infirmities and follies of the race of men; at the close, by a
sudden return upon himself, he gives the whole a personal
application. What is man, wavering on the billows of the
world and flung upon the sands or rocky shelves? What is
he but 'a sick tossed vessel'

>   dashing on each thing;
> Nay, his own shelf:
> My God, I mean myself.
>   [11. 76-8]

Yet beneath all fluctuations of mood now lay steadfast-
ness; beneath all restlessness of desire lay a deep content.
    He knew that he was a tiny wheel or cog in the divine
machinery, a machinery which had its pulse and movement in
the spirit. A lover of beauty, he carried his sense of
beauty into his realisation of a sacred order. He still
could smell the dew and rain and relish versing. What are
the songs that celebrate with ingenious praise a girdle or
a glove but 'dust blown by wit'? All his inventions he
would seriously lay upon the altar. He had nobler
beauties to sing than the red and white of a woman's cheek
or the trammels of golden hair. He could wittily play
with fancies and twist his metaphors, if the mood took
him; for God does not disdain the pretty, pious sports of
His children. He could spread his Easter wings, or build
his visible altar of verse, upon the page, or labour his
devout anagram, or tangle his wreath of rhymes; it was
the fashion of the day, and why should not fashion itself
be sanctified? But he could also be plain and bid farewell to sweet phrases, curled metaphors, trim inventions,
honey of roses, winding stairs of subtle meaning:

> Shepherds are honest people; let them sing:
> Riddle who list for me, and pull for prime:
> I envy no man's nightingale or spring.
>   ['Jordan' (I), 11. 11-13]

And in truth Herbert's range as a poet was considerable.

He could wind himself into the daintiest conceits. He could be gravely majestic:

>   This heap of dust,
>   To which the blast of death's incessant motion,
>   Fed with the exhalation of our crimes,
>   Drives all at last.
>   ['Church monuments', 11. 3-6]

He could write in a strain of genuine simplicity:

>   Teach me, my God and King,
>   In all things Thee to see,
>   And what I do in any thing,
>   To do it as for Thee.
>   ['The Elixer', 11. 1-4]

And whatever was within him, ornament or simplicity, seriousness or innocent play, belonged to God and to God's Church.

62. WILLIAM ALEXANDER, FROM HIS INTRODUCTION TO 'POEMS OF GEORGE HERBERT'

1903

William Alexander, Archbishop of Armagh, in a foreword to Herbert's poems in 1903 argued in a manner reminiscent rather of the obsolete past than of the increasingly promising future. His boundless admiration for Keble may have been a factor that conditioned his judgement on Herbert. See also above, p. 30.

Source: Alexander, from the foreword to 'Poems of George Herbert' (1903), pp. vii-ix, x-xi, xiii.

It is useless to disguise the fact that the admiration and even the patience of some modern readers of 'The Temple' may be somewhat severely taxed. If we turn to the structure of the verse, the occasional magnificence or sweetness of the lines, printed sometimes so as to form altars or wings, scarcely redeems whole poems from contempt. Identical rhymes try the ear attuned to poetical music again and again. Metaphors of almost inconceivable meanness or unpleasant repugnance are too often found. Thus in 'Banquet':

> Oh what sweetnesse from the bowl
> >   Fills my soul,
> >   Such as is, and makes divine!
> Is some starre (fled from the sphere)
> >   Melted there,
> >   *As we sugar melt in wine.*
>
> >   [ll. 7-12]

Occasionally our poet carries a beautiful image into details of almost audacious littleness. For instance:

> Listen, sweet dove! unto my song,
> And spread thy golden wings in me,
> *Hatching* my tender heart so long
> Till it get wing.
>
> >   ['Whitsunday', ll. 1-4]

Herbert is in a special sense the poet of the rose among
the flowers. The rose is the recognizance of his genius.
In one of his poems the words

> What is fairer than a rose,
> What is sweeter?
>
> >   ['The Rose', ll, 18-19]

makes us anticipate something of a piece with that strain
of poetic enchantment which begins:

> Sweet day, so calm, so cool, so bright,
> Sweet rose, whose hue angry and brave,
>
> >   ['Vertue']

But the strangely and very unpleasantly 'medical' conclusion almost makes one angry.
    Our great English sacred poet, John Keble, restrains his
admiration for Herbert within bounds somewhat suprisingly
narrow. There is nothing of rapture in the solitary mention of Herbert in his once famous 'Prælections'. (1)
One single line of Herbert's is said, upon the best authority, to have been a great favourite with the poet-priest of
Hursley:

> Love is a present for a mighty king.
> >   ['The Church-porch', l. 350]

Once, and once only, Keble, who culls ideas and expressions
far and wide from Homer and Aschylus, from Gray and Scott,
even from Burns and Byron, has a direct echo of Herbert.
The truth seems to be that Keble was in one respect

separated from Herbert, whose way of dealing with the Holy Communion was, we may be sure, repugnant to the great professor of poetry....

[Yet] 'The Temple' contains twelve or thirteen pieces, some of which are almost perfect in their way, and all of which will thoroughly requite 'studious regard with opportune delight'. I note them down for the reader's use:

'Sin'.
'Prayer'.
'The Windows'.
'Constancy'.
'Sunday'.
'To all Angels and Saints'.
'Virtue'.
'Life'.
'The British Church'. (A wonderful, almost prophetic concentration of the whole genius and history of Anglican theology.)
'Business'.
'The Call'.
'Aaron'.

Herbert's verse, no less than Keble's, has been accused by many of being what Archbishop Whately called the 'Christian Year', 'my Sunday puzzle', but Sir John Coleridge's saying will be always found true by those who will give themselves a little time to think - 'If Herbert's words are sometimes hard, you may at least be sure that they always *have a meaning*'....

[The foreword eventually concludes on a characteristic note:]

Yet, after all, a tribute more precious, if it could be made known to the psalmists of successive ages, would be the assurance that the thoughts which they had invested with the music of their utterance had soothed desponding souls, or raised mortal spirits to immortal hope.

Note

1 See above, No. 52.

63. H.C. BEECHING, FROM 'LYRA SACRA'

1903

H.C. Beeching, canon of Westminster and editor notably of
Milton, allotted in his anthology of religious poems considerable space to Herbert. He also summarised in a note
the common disapprobation of Herbert's obscurity and conceits, marking, too, the ever-increasing awareness of his
technical brilliance. See also above, p. 30.
    Source: 'Lyra Sacra: A Book of Religious Verse', ed.
H.C. Beeching (1903), pp. 81-2.

Herbert's poems are, if not the high-water mark of English
devotional verse, yet its most characteristic expression,
being the work of a scholar and a gentleman as well as a
divine. His sense of rhythm was faultless, and his style
exquisite. Observe on the one hand the skill with which he
develops such an elaborate ode as 'The Collar,' and on the
other his fine use of the regular metres. His fault was a
too great fondness for conceits, by which some of his best
poems are marred. A few passages are introduced at the
close of the selection from poems which for this or other
reasons could not be printed entire. (1)
    No poet is in such need of a commentator. Edition fol-
lows upon edition, but with no effort to clear up for the
general reader Herbert's obscurities.

Note

1   After providing twelve stanzas from 'The Church-porch'
    and sixteen poems in full, Beeching concludes with six
    poems drastically reduced and, in three cases, re-
    titled - e.g. the two of the seven stanzas of 'Giddinesse'
    are christened 'Regeneration'.

64. W.J. COURTHOPE, FROM 'A HISTORY OF ENGLISH POETRY'

1903

Professor of Poetry at Oxford, W.J. Courthope provided in
his widely consulted 'History of English Poetry' an account

of Herbert that interprets his life in terms of his poetry.
Herbert's 'quaintness' lingers, and so does his 'clumsy'
imagery. But the poet's strengths are also noted, firmly.
See also above, p. 30.

Source: Courthope, 'A History of English Poetry'
(1903), III, 208-19.

Taken in connection with the spiritual utterances of his
poetry, the outward facts of George Herbert's life reveal
clearly the course of inward feeling which led him away
from the business of the world into the bosom of the
Church. In the interesting autobiographical glimpses he
gives us in his poem called 'Affliction,' we see that he
had always been disposed towards religion; but he holds
that he had been constantly checked by the will of God from
surrendering himself to his own 'bias.' Of his time at
Cambridge he says:

[Quotes 'Affliction' (I), ll. 37-48.]

When his ambitious hopes were disappointed, and his outlook
on the external world darkened, he turned, with the fervour
of a religious nature, to the alternative of self-
examination:

[Quotes 'Content', ll. 33-6.]

But he did not seek this self-knowledge by the same philosophic road as the author of 'Nosce Teipsum.' (1) To reach
the calm necessary for heavenly contemplation, it was necessary for him to feel directly the presence of God, and
from this he was hindered by the intensity of his sense of
sin:

[Quotes 'The Reprisall', ll. 9-16.]

The goal of self-knowledge was to be reached by self-
immolation through the teaching and discipline of the
Church. Hence, on his arrival at Bemerton, he seems to
have resolved to shut out all distracting views of the
world:

When at his induction (says Walton) he was shut into
Bemerton Church, being left there alone to toll the bell
as the law required him, he stayed so much longer than
an ordinary time before he returned to his friends that
stayed expecting him at the church door, that his
friend Mr. Woodnot looked in at the church window, and

> saw him lying prostrate on the ground before the altar:
> at which time and place (as he afterwards told Mr.
> Woodnot) he set some rules to himself for the future
> manage of his life, and then and there made a vow to
> labour to keep them.   [above, p. 110]

Nature, in Herbert's view, was no longer to be contemplated
directly, but as she was seen through the interpretation of
the Scripture. Of the Bible he says:

[Quotes 'The H. Scriptures' (II) in full.]

In the opening portion of 'The Temple' he seems to deliver a farewell address, full of the secular wisdom
gathered from his own experience, to hearers who assemble
in the 'Church Porch' to look for a moment into the sacred
edifice, and then disperse to mingle in the business and
amusements of the world. From these he himself turns away,
to find, in the lights that stream through the 'Church
Windows' on to the 'Church Pavement,' in the 'Church Monuments,' and even in the 'Church Door and Lock,' ideas that
may lift his soul out of her fleshly prison-house into a
heavenly atmosphere. Or he seeks, by means of the sacraments of the Church, to bring his own nature into close and
actual communion with God, as he says in one of his most
subtly characteristic poems:

[Quotes 'The H. Communion', ll. 1-24.]

This habit of self-conscious introspection, and the submission of the intellect to ecclesiastical authority, determine the character of Herbert's poetry, both in respect
of its conception of Nature and of its modes of expression.
There is no attempt in him to represent the Christian
scheme as an imaginative whole in any form of epic action,
such as we find in Phineas Fletcher's 'Purple Island' or
Giles Fletcher's 'Christ's Death and Victory.' The didactic form is common in his poetry, but here Herbert's treatment of external Nature compares unfavourably with the
large and vigorous reasoning power displayed by the author
of 'Nosce Teipsum.' One of his longest poems is written
on the subject of 'Providence,' and is intended to illustrate the Divine government of the world. Each stanza
contains an isolated conceit; and in his examples of
God's wisdom the poet never advances beyond the scholastic
knowledge provided for him in Pliny's 'Natural History.'
Streams are supposed to move in a circular course through
the ocean back to their own springs: antidotes are believed always to grow by poisons. Exceptional phenomena,

incorrectly observed, are cited as proofs of the existence
of Providence:

> Most things move th' under-jaw; the crocodile not:
> Most things sleep lying; th' elephant leans or stands.
> ['Providence', ll. 139-40]

And the mere enumeration of commonplace facts is supposed
to illustrate design:

> Thy cupboard serves the world: the meat is set
> Where all may reach; no beast but knows his feed:
> Birds teach us hawking; fishes have their net;
> The great prey on the less, they on some weed.
>
> Nothing ingendered does prevent his meat;
> These have their tables spread ere they appear;
> Some creatures have in winter what to eat,
> Others to sleep, and envy not their cheer.
> [ibid., ll. 49-56]

Herbert's strength of poetical conception lies in vivid,
and often sublime, renderings of the spiritual aspects of
human nature, such as are found in the verses curiously
called 'The Pulley':

[Quotes the poem in full.]

By his power of intense meditation, he often seems either
to penetrate into the farthest regions of abstract
thought, or to assure his soul of the inward presence of
God. In a poem called 'The Search' he asks:

[Quotes ll. 30-60.]

As a poetical vehicle for his religiously metaphysical
mood, he found a convenient model in the 'wit' of Donne,
using, like Plato, the imagery of the physical, to suggest
the invisible movements of the intellectual, Eros. Herbert
begins his spiritual voyage where Donne (at least in his
early poems) ends. The latter found inspiration for his
metaphysical fancy in the strange paradoxes of sensual
love: Herbert pursued conceits equally remote into the
paradoxes of religion. Donne opens one of his love-poems
on the pains of absence from the beloved object with the
following stanza:

> Soul's joy, when thou art gone,
>   And I alone

> Which cannot be,
> Because thou dost abide with me,
> And I depend on thee:
>
> ['Song' (attr.)]

Herbert, in a poem called 'A Parody,' makes this stanza
the starting-point for a meditation on the spiritual intercourse of the soul with God. Concentrating all his imaginative energy on the meditations of his own soul, he
sought, by means of the imagery of metaphysical 'wit,' applied to the doctrines, festivals, and ceremonies of the
Catholic Church, to express these meditations in a series
of spiritual epigrams. Viewed simply in its poetical aspect, this principle of composition had its strength and
weakness. Its strength lay in the intensity and simplicity with which the poet was able to realise and express
each mood while it lasted. When, for example, the action
of his soul is exalted by partaking of the Holy Communion,
he feels himself to be like Adam before his fall:

> For such when Adam did not know
>   To sin, or sin to smother,
> He might to heaven from Paradise go,
>   As from one room t' another.
>
> ['The H. Communion', ll. 33-6]

But when the mood passes, depression sinks him almost as
deep as he had been raised by enthusiasm:

[Quotes 'The Temper' (I), ll. 1-8.]

And then, since he has deliberately severed himself from
the world of life and action, he is reduced by introspection to childish and impotent longings that his nature
were of a more perfect, even if of a lower, order:

> O that I were an orange-tree,
>   That busy plant!
> Then should I ever laden be,
>   And never want
> Some fruit for Him that dressèd me!
>
> ['Employment' (II), ll. 21-5]

As the epigram was the mould which Herbert naturally
chose for the expression of his varying spiritual moods,
so (and in this too he followed the footsteps of Donne) the
elaboration of metaphor was the main device by which he
sought to give point to his spiritual epigrams. Success
attended him in proportion as the thought which he strove

to express was simple and natural. His imagery is often
beautiful: nothing, for example, can surpass in exquisite
propriety the simile by which he likens the shrinking of
religious feelings in his soul to the hibernation of
flowers:

> Who would have thought my shrivell'd heart
> Could have recover'd greenness? It was gone
>   Quite underground; as flowers depart
> To see their mother root, when they have blown,
>   Where they together
>   All the hard weather,
> Dead to the world, keep house unknown.

['The Flower', ll. 8-14]

On the other hand, his habit of expressing the abstract
by the concrete led him into temptations to which he constantly yielded. He cultivated quaintness for its own
sake. Sometimes he makes a whole sonnet consist of nothing but metaphors, as, for example, when he strives to
depict the manifold spiritual aspects of prayer:

[Quotes 'Prayer' (I) in full.]

This conscious artificiality impaired the fineness of his
judgement and taste. He did not perceive when an image,
naturally beautiful, was spoiled by over-elaboration, so
that he constantly wrote stanzas like the following:

> Listen, sweet Dove, unto my song,
>   And spread Thy golden wings in me,
>   *Hatching my tender heart so long,*
> *Till it get wing, and fly away with Thee.*

['Whitsunday', ll. 1-4]

Nor did he understand how great would be the feeling of
artistic disappointment in the reader to find a poem on
'Virtue' opening with the perfect stanza:

> Sweet day, so cool, so calm, so bright,
> The bridal of the earth and sky,
> The dew shall weep they fall to-night;
>   For thou must die;

and concluding with this:

> Only a sweet and virtuous soul,
> Like seasoned timber, never gives,
> And though the whole world turn to coal,
>   Then chiefly lives.

I fear it is only too evident that Herbert was content to
write 'coal,' where he meant 'ash,' because the latter
word would not rhyme with 'soul.' Nor did he care whether
his images were ugly and clumsy in themselves, so long as
they sufficiently allegorised his meaning. When he wishes
to describe the condition of the soul incapable of rising
into acts of 'Praise,' he writes:

> But when Thou dost on business blow,
>   It hangs, it clogs;
> Not all the teams in Albion, in a row,
>   Can hale or draw it out of door;
> Legs are but stumps and Pharaoh's wheels but logs,
>   And struggling hinders more.
>   ['Praise' (III), 11. 13-18]

He often offends by the materialism and familiarity of the
images under which he describes the most sacred acts of
religion. Thus he represents the Holy Communion as a
'Banquet':

[Quotes 'The Banquet', 11. 7-30.]

From the character of these lines it will readily be di-
vined that there was something in the religious instincts
of many Englishmen which would hardly find its full satisfaction within the Anglican channels marked out for it by
George Herbert. For himself, his metaphysical intellect
and his power of abstract thought found sufficient scope
in the sober doctrine and ritual of that Communion, as it
was being developed under the influence of Laud's principle of the Beauty of Holiness. But men of a purely emotional temperament were carried irresistibly by their
aesthetic needs towards the more splendid ceremonial of
the Church of Rome. We have already had an illustration,
in the poetry of Southwell, of the effects produced on
metrical composition by religious mysticism; and this
movement of the imagination reached a fuller development
in the genius of one of the most remarkable poets of the
reign of Charles I.

[The ensuing discourse concerns Crashaw.]

Note

1 Sir John Davies (1599).

65. GEORGE HERBERT PALMER, FROM 'FORMATIVE TYPES IN
ENGLISH POETRY'

1905/18

In the evolving critical attitudes toward Herbert,
Palmer's formidable edition of 'The English Works of
George Herbert' (Boston, Mass., 1905) is a major signpost
by any standards. To have represented it here through an
extract of a few pages, however, would grossly have de-
tracted from its achievement; and it might have been es-
chewed altogether - strictly by default - but for Palmer's
felicitous summary of his critical stance thirteen years
later, in his 'Formative Types in English Poetry', which
devotes one chapter each to Chaucer, Spenser, Herbert,
Pope, Wordsworth, Tennyson, and Browning. Herbert's presence in such a company is eloquent in itself; yet even
more pertinent is Palmer's reiteration of three salient
aspects of his great edition: the renunciation of
Walton's 'charming romance' as a viable interpretation,
the division of Herbert's life into four periods, and the
emphatic assertion of structure or form. See further
above, pp. 30 f.
     Source: Palmer, from George Herbert, in 'Formative
Types in English Poetry' (Boston, Mass., 1918), pp. 15-31.

We are apt to think of Herbert as an aged saint, who
spent a lifetime in the courts of the Lord, and came to
find every wordly thought repulsive. This absurd estimate has largely been induced by Walton's charming romance. (1) Biography was at that time in its infancy, and
the few examples of it that occur aim at eulogy and stimu-
lus rather than description. To comprehend the man
Herbert, all these romantic notions must be dismissed.
He died comparatively young, just under forty. Most of
his life was spent in courts, universities, and among the
most eminent and fashionable of his time. During only
three years was he a priest. Unfortunatly the romantic
view of him has gained currency, too, through an adjec-
tive which early became attached to his name, 'holy
George Herbert.' That is exactly what Herbert was not.
A holy man is a whole man, one who is altogether in harmony with himself and God. Herbert's was a divided
nature. Opposing impulses tore him. It is these which
bring him near to us and make him a true representative
of psychological poetry. When he was dying, he handed
over the meagre roll of his poems to a friend - for none

were published during his life. All are private poems,
stamped with that genuine sincerity which can be had only
in writings not intended for the public eye - and said,
'Here is a record of the many spiritual conflicts that
have passed betwixt God and my soul. Let my friend Mr.
Ferrar read it; and then if he can think it may turn to
the advantage of any dejected poor soul, let it be made
public; if not, let him burn it.' Mr. Ferrar fortunately
published it immediately, and it so exactly hit the taste
of its time that a dozen editions were called for in half
a century. We shall do it and its author much injustice
if we withdraw our attention from those 'Conflicts.'
    The life of Herbert is most significantly divided into
four periods: that of education, of hesitation, of crisis,
and of consecration. (2) The period of education covers
the first twenty-six years of his life, from his birth in
1593 to his acceptance of the Oratorship at Cambridge in
1619. The second, the period of hesitation, covers his
Oratorship; that is, eight years, up to the death of his
mother in 1627. A crisis period follows, in which Herbert
was surveying himself and asking whether his life was to
be wasted. This continued for three years, from 1627 to
1630. Then comes at last the glorious period of his consecration, his period as a priest. Obviously these
periods are very unequal, yet each makes its special contribution to our understanding of him.
    His family was one of the noblest in England. Three
earldoms were in it, the head of the whole clan being that
William Herbert, Earl of Pembroke, who was one of the most
influential nobles at the close of the reign of Elizabeth
and during the reign of James. Herbert always prided himself on his aristocratic birth. The exquisite gentleman
appears in him everywhere, both for strength and weakness.
His father, belonging to the branch of the Herbert family
which lived at Montgomery Castle in Wales, died when George
was but four years old, and Lady Herbert became both
father and mother to him. She was one of the masterful
women of that age and one of the most admired. A dozen
years after the death of her husband, though she already
had ten children, she married Sir John Danvers, a man
twenty years her junior. Nor was the marriage unhappy.
Sir John Danvers was accordingly the only father Herbert
ever knew, except his spiritual father, Donne. Donne and
his large family had been assisted by Lady Herbert at a
critical period of his life. Gratitude and kindred tastes
drew him to her subsequently, and at least three poems of
his addressed to her have come down to us. Her poetic
son thus early felt Donne's influence. To George Herbert
Donne bequeathed his seal ring.

Herbert's position in life put him in the way of meeting many others who were then eminent in literature and
the State. William Herbert, the head of his house, has
been believed by many to be the mysterious 'Mr. W.H.' to
whom Shakspere's Sonnets are inscribed. Certainly it is
to him that the first folio of Shakspere's plays is dedicated. Possibly, therefore, Herbert may have seen Shakspere. While he was Orator at the University Milton was a
student there. When Lord Bacon in 1625 published certain
Psalms which he had translated into verse, he dedicated
them to Herbert as the first of his time 'in respect of
divinity and poesy met.'

Leaving Westminster School in London in 1610, Herbert
entered Trinity College, Cambridge. The same year, he
being at the time seventeen, he addressed two sonnets to
his mother which are of extreme significance. (3) In them
and an accompanying letter he lays down a programme for his
life. He will become a poet, a poet of love. That is the
only worthy theme, he declares. But he will be nothing
like the fashionable poets. They have degraded the sacred
passion, 'parcelling it out' to one and another person.
That is to empty love of all meaning. The only way in
which it can be understood is to view it in full scale,
drawing God and the human soul together. Herbert will
therefore write nothing but religious verse and so will
manifest love unlimited. With this purpose Herbert went up
to the University. To that purpose he remained true, becoming - if we except Robert Southwell - our first purely
religious poet.

One other aim Herbert had for shaping his life, and long
was the shaping deferred. From birth he was physically
weak, with a tendency to consumption. His brothers were
martial men, and this was the general inheritance of the
family. His eldest brother, Edward, was that Lord Herbert
of Cherbury, the founder of English deism, the eccentric
soldier, ambassador, duellist, egotist, who wrote one of
the most entertaining autobiographies. Two other brothers
were officers in the army and navy; Henry, nearest in age
to George, and perhaps his favorite, was Master of Revels
at the Court. One born in such station found few employments open. He could not engage in trade. He must enter
either the army, the Church, or the Civil Service. Herbert's mother early saw that he was of too feeble a
frame to serve in the army or probably in the State. She
dedicated him, therefore, to the Church. Herbert accepted
the proposed career without question, and soon an association of ideas became fixed in his mind, uniting the
thought of being a priest with that of being an upright
man. Whenever secular affairs interested him, as they

naturally did through most of his life, he counted himself
cut off from God. Whenever higher moods were on, he was
all eager for the priesthood.

He took his Bachelor's degree when he was twenty and
remained at the University to study divinity. Being, however, already noted as something of a connoisseur in words,
and skilled in Latin and Greek as well as English, he
undertook also some teaching in rhetoric. In these pleasant employments and agreeable surroundings year by year
went by and brought him no nearer to the priesthood.
Finally the Oratorship of the University fell vacant. In
it Herbert saw something much to his liking. He aspired
to it. Fortunately we have a letter from him replying to
a question a friend had asked, whether the Oratorship was
quite compatible with aiming at the priesthood. He thinks
it is, for it only defers that purpose a little; and besides, the Oratorship is the finest post in the University.
The Orator sits above everybody at table, receives all distinguished visitors, writes the letters of the University,
and has in addition a very pretty salary.

He received the appointment in 1619 and held the office
for eight years. The suspended section of Herbert's life
which follows I have called his period of hesitation. In
it his doublemindedness is striking. Certainly he will be
a priest. He has never intended anything else, a priest
and a poet. But hurry? Why should one hasten such a
career? There are many good things by the way. Even Walton records that during his oratorship 'he was seldom at
Cambridge unless the King was there, and then he never
missed.' Herbert loves stately ceremonials, fine clothes
and manners, whatever of beauty the world can show. That
is one side of him. He is a man of the Renaissance, sensitive to all the glories of earth and exulting in them.
But there is another side, just as genuine. When we notice the strength of one of these two sides of Herbert,
we are apt to imagine the other feeble or unreal. That is
not the case. It is to misunderstand Herbert as a man, and
quite to miss the type of his poetry of the inner life, if
we fail to give credit to discordant elements in him. His
purpose of allegiance to God, taking the form of entering
the priesthood, is a positive passion, however long he
loiters by the way.

In 1625 King James died. Herbert had hoped to climb,
like the preceding Orator, into some public office. He
dreamed of becoming Assistant Secretary of State. The
King's death destroyed these hopes. A year later Bacon
died. Worse still, in 1627 died that mother who had never
ceased to guide him, who had fixed the plan of his life,
and had not seen that plan fulfilled. Herbert was

overwhelmed. His health was poor at the time, and mental
conflicts made it worse. He resigned the Oratorship, left
the University where he had lived for seventeen years, retired to his brother Henry's country home, and there passed
through what I have called his 'crisis.'

A record of this crisis he has left us. Life was slip-
ping away, with nothing accomplished. How was it all to
end? In a single section of my edition of his poems (4) I
have brought together the pathetic group of those that
paint this struggle. We hear him now expressing delight
in the world and asking how he can possibly leave it, now
pouring forth eager longings to be fully a child of God,
now doubting his fitness for that exalted life. After two
or three years of this self-scrutiny, search for health,
and efforts to reinstate his early resolve, he met Jane
Danvers and married her, Walton says, three days after
their first meeting. I question the tale, for she was a
near relative of Herbert's stepfather and lived but a few
miles from his brother's house. Yet even if the story is
inexact, it well illustrates Herbert's headlong temper. He
says himself that people 'think me eager, hot, and undertaking. But in my prosecutions slack and small.' We may
perhaps say that he was of so hesitating a disposition, so
prone to delay, that finally he would act on some small impulse, and suddenly important issues would be closed. It
was in this way that at last he entered the priesthood.
The Earl of Pembroke invited him to Wilton House to meet
Archbishop Laud, who was at the time a visitor there. Laud
remonstrated with him over his long delay. Walton says
Herbert sent for a tailor the next day and was measured for
his canonical clothes.

Herbert entered the priesthood in 1630, at the age of
thirty-seven, and spent in it the last three years of his
brief life. At first he found great happiness in it. He
had at length made a reality of a lifelong dream. There
could be no more discontent. He might now possess a united
mind. But the little parish which the Earl of Pembroke
gave him at Bemerton, between Wilton and Salisbury, contained only a hundred and twenty people, men, women and
children. For many years Herbert had been living in the
full tide of the bustling world, with the most intellectual men of that world as his companions. Now he found
himself shut up to a small group of illiterate rustics.
He tried to develop all the possibilities of his office,
and in his beautiful notebook, 'A Priest to the Temple,'
has left an elaborate study of what the country parson can
do and be. He kept his intellectual interests alive with
this book, with writing far more verse than formerly, and
with frequent visits to the organ in Salisbury Cathedral.

But after all, he could not help wondering whether such a
life was what God and he had intended. This disposition
to doubt was much increased as consumption pressed him
harder.   Of this disease he died in 1633. Had he died
three years earlier, we should never have known him, or at
most should have found his name mentioned somewhere as
that of an elegant dilettante from whom contemporaries expected much, but who left only a dozen or more Latin and
Greek pieces of slender merit and a few English verses on
ecclesiastical subjects. It is chiefly Bemerton with its
enforced loneliness, questionings, revolts, and visions of
completed love which made Herbert an example of all that is
best in the metaphysical poetry of the inner life.   In
three poems - the long 'Affliction' [I], 'Love Unknown,'
and 'The Pilgrimage' - Herbert traces at different periods
the course of his infirm and disappointed life. The shor-
test of them, and perhaps the obscurest, written near its
end, is the most fully confessional and poignant.

It will be seen how truly such a divided and introspective life typifies the age which produced it. Donne and
his followers (5) are no accident. They sum up in artistic form the questioning tendencies of their time. In few
other periods of English history has the English people
believed, acted, enjoyed and aspired so nearly like a
single person as during the first three quarters of the
reign of Elizabeth. Foreign dangers welded the nation together. The Queen, her great ministers, and the historical
plays of Shakspere, set forth its ideals of orderly government. Spenser's poem consummated its ideals of orderly
beauty, as did Hooker's 'Ecclesiastical Polity' those of an
orderly church. Men in those days marched together. Dissenters, either of a religious, political, or artistic sort,
were few and despised. But with the Stuart line a change,
long preparing, manifested itself. In science, Bacon questioned established authority and sent men to nature to observe for themselves. In government, the King's preroga-
tive was questioned, and Parliament became so rebellious
that they were often dismissed. A revolution in poetic
taste was under way. Spenser's smooth strains and blood-
less heroes were being replaced by the jolting and passionate realism of Donne. The field of human interest, in
short, was becoming more and more an internal one; the
individual soul and its analysis calling for much attention
from its anxious possessor.

In choosing Herbert to represent this introspective
poetry we must acknowledge that he stands outside his
school in one important respect, in orderliness and brevity.
No other member of his group has his artistic feeling.
Their poems are usually a tangled growth, developed rather

to ease the unrest of the writer than to convey objects of
beauty to a reader. Some promising situation attracts the
poet's attention and he begins to write, wandering wherever
thought or a good phrase leads, playing about his subject
till he and his readers have had enough. Beginning anywhere, he ends nowhere. Where, too, no plan controls,
there is likely to be excessive length. From such form-
less composition Herbert turns away. All his work has
structural unity. He knows when to stop. Each poem presents a single mood, relation, or problem of divine love,
and ends with its clear exposition. His poems are at once
short and adequate. Out of his hundred and sixty-nine
nearly a hundred have less than twenty-five lines each;
only four exceed one hundred and fifty. Within these narrow bounds the theme is fully and economically developed.
We feel it is not he who directs its course; he is merely
responsive to the shaping subject. Accordingly any set of
Herbert's verses conveys such singleness of impression as
is rarely found among his contemporaries.

But while he thus lacks one common, though undesirable,
trait of his school, he may well serve as its representative. Like the rest of them, he fixes his gaze on himself
alone and introspects the working of a single soul. Like
them he finds complications and paradoxes there and amuses
himself with them, while still retaining our belief in his
sincerity and earnestness. With him as with them energetic and unusual thought is a delight, and nothing pleases
him more than to stuff words with a little more meaning
than they can bear. And like them he surprises his reader
with sudden turns of sweet and tender simplicity, imbedded
in a crabbed context.

In technical matters, too, he is substantially in accord
with them. While all his lines are rhymed, he employs imperfect rhymes freely, alliteration and vowel color rarely.
His working foot is the iambic, in which rhythm all but
eleven of his poems are written, these eleven being tro-
chaic. He has no blank verse, Alexandrine, or 'four-
teener.' He has seventeen sonnets, but confines himself to
the Shaksperean form or to one peculiar to himself. He
does not use Spenser's stanza nor Chaucer's Rhyme Royal.
His feeling for the texture of a line is much finer than
that of his master, of whom Ben Jonson said to Drummond
that 'for not keeping of accent Donne deserved hanging.'
(6) For each lyrical situation he invents exactly the
rhythmic setting which befits it. Each set of emotions he
clothes in individual garb, and only when what is beneath
is similar is the same clothing used a second time. One
hundred and sixteen of his poems are written in metres
which are not repeated. In his verse matter and form are

bound together with exceptional closeness.

So much has been said in this chapter about Herbert as
a poet of the personal life and of his agreement with his
group in analyzing individual experience, that perhaps in
closing a few words of caution are needed. These subtle
longings, dejections, and vacillations of the lover of God,
like similar moods reported by the poets of human love,
are not mere statements of autobiographic fact. Undoubtedly they start with fact, and how large is the measure of
that fact in Herbert's verse I have shown in my account of
his life. But though seven eighths of his poems employ the
word 'I,' they do not confine themselves to personal
record. What Herbert gives us of inner experience, no less
that what Chaucer gave of outer, is colored by the temperament through which it passes. Starting with a veritable
fact, Herbert allows this to dictate congenial circumstances, to color all details with its influence, to elimi-
nate the belittlements of reality, and so to exhibit an
emotional completeness which may not have been found in his
actual life. This is the work of the artist everywhere, to
idealize reality. Herbert thus idealizes. But he is no
mere sentimentalist, living in shifting feelings, and fancying that to-day God has withdrawn his love from him whom
he yesterday favored. Nor yet are the poems fictitious
which so declare him. Herbert's own experience warrants
fears which he knows are not peculiar to himself. They belong to love everywhere. In them he finds subjects of sad
pleasure which his empty days, disciplined mind, and artistic skill fashioned into forms of permanent beauty.

Notes

1 Cf. Palmer's earlier comment on Walton, quoted above,
   p. 31.
2 Detailed by Palmer in his edition of 'The English Works
   of George Herbert' (Boston, Mass., 1905), I, 19 ff.
3 First printed by Walton (above, p. 97).
4 In the edition cited (note 2): II, 321-401.
5 Later in this essay twice described as a 'school', and
   earlier said to include 'Donne, Herbert, Vaughan,
   Crashaw, Quarles, Traherne, perhaps Cowley'.
6 'Ben Jonson', ed. C.H. Herford and Percy Simpson
   (Oxford, 1925), I, 133.

66. PAUL ELMER MORE, FROM GEORGE HERBERT, IN 'SHELBURNE
ESSAYS'

1906

The American scholar and critic Paul Elmer More, a leader
of the New Humanist movement, was among the first to respond to Palmer's edition of Herbert (No. 65). Militantly
indisposed to Palmer's efforts to qualify Walton's view of
the 'holy' Herbert, More so defended the traditional interpretation that he stands last in the honourable line
that heard through the poet 'the tinkling purity of a silver sacring bell'. See also above, p. 31.
    Source: More, from George Herbert, in 'Shelburne
Essays', 4th series (1906), pp. 66-9, 74-8, 86-98.

No other or our lesser poets has received the same long
and detailed study which Prof. George Herbert Palmer has
lavished on the Rector of Bemerton. As he lay in his
cradle, he says, a devotee of Herbert gave him the old
poet's name, dedicating his life by that act to the service of so venerable a godfather. And the fruit of this
devotion of fifty years is now before us in an elaborate
edition of Herbert, that is learned without being pedantic,
and full without being replete - the kind of work of which
our universities might well be more prodigal. In estab-
lishing the text he has, I presume, left nothing for the
future to correct. He has discriminated, as no one before
him had thought of doing, between the earlier and the later
poems. And he has gone further than that: by separating
the poems into homogeneous groups, he has thrown the development and inner changes of the writer into sharp relief; a caviller might even say that the relief is here
too high, and that a certain injustice results from rais-
ing the wavering moods of a man into contradictions of
character. To all this he has added a series of essays on
the life and writings of Herbert which form a proper
introduction to the editorial part of the volumes. In particular the chapter on The Type of Religious Poetry displays exemplary knowledge of a great and complicated
movement.
    It might seem as if little were left for the gleaner in
this field, as if, indeed, any further writing on this
subject would be superfluous or presumptuous; and yet I
trust this is not entirely the case. It is even possible
that the minute analysis of Professor Palmer's method has
hindered him in seeing the real significance of his theme

as a whole; otherwise it is hard to understand how he
could wave aside so cavalierly the character which Herbert
bore to his contemporaries, and has since borne to all the
world. 'My brother George,' wrote the baron of Cherbury,
'was so excellent a scholar, that he was made the public
orator of the University of Cambridge, some of whose English works are extant, which, though they be rare in their
kind, yet are far short of expressing those perfections he
had in the Greek and Latin tongue, and all divine and human literature; his life was *holy and exemplary*, in so
much that about Salisbury, where he lived beneficed for
many years, he was *little less than sainted*: he was not
exempt from passion and choler, being infirmities to which
all our race is subject, but that excepted, without reproach in his actions.' (1) Holy and little less than
sainted Herbert appeared not only to his brother, but to
all who walked beside him; nevertheless in his latest
editor's mind than holy 'a more misleading epithet could
not have been devised.' It requires a certain temerity
thus to run counter to the verdict of tradition, and the
scholar who so ventures needs to be well fortified. The
fact is, Professor Palmer, despite the long absorption in
his theme, brings to it still some alienation of mind.
Now lack of sympathy, I know, is a dubious phrase in
criticism; it is a bludgeon too often raised by the indiscriminating against any who condemn the lower and false
delights of literature in favour of what is high and true.
But in the present case it would seem to be connected with
a more serious failure of the historic sense. That sense
has a double function; it points out the differences that
creep in from age to age, the changes of manners and forms
that come with time and make the generations of men like
foreigners to one another. And here the training of the
day will keep any scholar from error. But we are also
justified in demanding that clearer faculty of vision
which pierces beneath those transient modes and discovers
what each age has attained of essential and permanent
truth. This is a high faculty of scholarship which is
growing daily rarer among us since we have become en-
slaved by the philosophy of progress, and one may suspect
that Professor Palmer has not altogether avoided bowing
the knee to the Idol of the Present. But for this, I do
not see why there should be in his essays so continued a
note of apology, as if Herbert's religious emotion were
something outworn and outgrown, something incomprehensible
to the man of to-day only by deliberately narrowing his
larger spiritual interests to a lesser sphere. At least
there is room to doubt whether the religious instinct has
deepened with the broadening of our sympathies, and I

should like, with all deference to Professor Palmer's
authority, and with a frank use of the material his volumes afford, to look at Herbert again for a little while
as he appeared to his own age.

    And I feel a certain confidence in attempting this, be-
cause that great lover of fish and men, Izaak Walton, has
left a life of Herbert which is as clear in purpose as it
is beautiful in execution....

[Five Waltonesque pages later, More considers Donne's influence on Herbert.]

There is nothing of the eagle in Herbert, nothing of the
soaring quality which lifted Donne out of the common
sphere, into his own supreme dominion, nothing of that originality which makes of Donne one of the few real turning-
points in our literature. Herbert was content to look up
at that dizzy flight and follow with humbler wing. How
much his poems took their style and manner from Donne's
might be shown by a hundred points. Donne, apparently,
had found the great conventions of the Elizabethan school
tiresome and unreal, and he had broken through them as
resolutely as Wordsworth was to rebel against those of the
eighteenth century. He swept away not only the frigid
platitudes of the sonnet, but also the flowing ease of the
lyric and the larger liberty of the drama. With him the
language must be fresh and immediate; sharp, unusual words
must cut through the crust of convention; the mind must
be surprised out of its equilibrium by novel juxta-
positions; the soul must be stirred in its most secret
recess by the sudden shock of unexpected emotions. Like
Socrates, he would rouse men from their apathy by the
jingling of pots and pans and all common things. It is
not the highest form of poetry, for that, like manners,
must rest on a noble convention and avoid the whim and license of the impertinent individual; but it was new and
stimulating, exquisite at times and again merely grotesque.
In all these things Herbert followed his master, only
softening the cruder asperities and exercising a gentlemanly taste which his model never possessed. With the
other poets of the Jacobean and Caroline age he adopted
Donne's use of 'conceits'; he even directly imitated what
is perhaps the most curious extravagance in that Museum of
Wit. Donne had thought proper to introduce an Epithala-
mium with a startling description of the morning that
ushers in the happy day - and he succeeds. All the 'chirp-
ing choristers' greet the dawn in his verse, and then -

> The husband cock looks out, and straight is sped,
> And meets his wife, which brings her feather-bed,
> ['An Epithalamion ... on the Lady Elizabeth', 11. 11-12]

Herbert kept the metaphor, but applied it to a different
kind of creature, with no decrease of absurdity in this
case, it must be confessed:

> God gave thy soul brave wings; put not those feathers
> Into a bed, to sleep out all ill weathers.
>   ['The Church-porch', 11. 83-4]

But the influence of Donne goes deeper than style and
manner. It is probable that Herbert's very desire to temper religion with poetry was sustained, if not created, by
the example of his friend, and certainly, I think, his ambition to be the lyric poet of divine love is derived from
that source. Donne's life had suffered a division such as
was regular enough in those days, however suspicious it
may appear to us. In youth and early manhood he had given
himself up to wanton intrigues and had written a series of
poems which betray only too frankly his irregular passions.
Afterwards he turned to religion, disavowed his earlier
pursuits, and sought to make poetry the handmaid of his
new faith. It was a course quite familiar to his contemporaries, corresponding to the sharp cleavage in their
minds between secular and sacred things. So Joseph Hall
indited scurrilous satires before taking orders and devoting his pen to Christian meditations; and a little
later Vaughan, to name no others, was to repent his youthful servitude to the profane Muse. Now Herbert began his
poetical preludings just about the time when Donne was
passing from his first to his second career. We have a
letter, dated exactly July 11, 1607, which Donne sent to
Lady Magdalen with a copy of 'Holy Hymns and Sonnets,' and
a sonnet addressed personally to the recipient. They were
no doubt read by Lady Magdalen's son, who was then fourteen; and if there was any wavering his mind between profane and religious verse, these lines may have weighed in
his decision:

> O! might those sighs and tears return again
> Into my breast and eyes, which I have spent,
> That I might in this holy discontent
> Mourn with some fruit, as I have mourned in vain.
>   ['Holy Sonnets', IV, 1-4]

Again, three years later, Donne, writing to Sir Henry
Goodyere, promised a copy of his stanzas called 'A Litany'

which he compares with the poems canonised by Pope Nicholas
and commanded for public service in the churches; but mine,
he adds, 'is for the lesser chapels, which are my friends.'
It is a pleasant fancy to think that Herbert, then at Cambridge, was one of these lesser chapels, and may have received the 'Litany' from Donne; if so, he would have
paused at the twenty-seventh stanza:

> That learning, Thine ambassador,
> From Thine allegiance we never tempt;
> That beauty, paradise's flower
> For physic made, from poison be exempt;
> That wit - born apt high good to do -
> By dwelling lazily
> On nature's nothing be not nothing too;
> That our affections kill us not, nor die;
> Hear us, weak echoes, O, Thou Ear and Eye.

It is dangerously easy, I know, to dwell on these possible
coincidences, but at any rate Donne's stanza expresses the
kind of influence that was at work upon Herbert when he
wrote those two sonnets to his mother. For him there
should be no such division as that which made two different
poets of Donne; he would clothe his verse in the 'Venus
livery' of the early Donne and the other Elizabethans, but
it should be the Venus Urania; he would be the love-poet
of religion. As others had written out their sighs and
groans to a deaf mistress, so would he lament when his
prayers to Heaven fell back unheard; so would he exult
when grace descended into his heart from above. But, and
the point needs emphasis, there is nothing to be rebuked in
Herbert's marriage of sacred and profane ideas, nothing of
the sensuousness that clings to the ardours of Crashaw;
above all, no taint of decay such as repels a clean mind in
Verlaine's sickly fusion of the flesh and the spirit. It
is more in Herbert the close personal relation of the human
soul to God and the soul's fluctuations of joy and despon-
dency than any dubious use of amorous metaphor that gives
him his position.

[Eight more Waltonesque pages later, More paused to
summarise.]

There was no convulsion in Herbert's inner experience,
no wrenching conversion from the world, but rather a growth
in assurance, passing through seasons of doubt. His latest
verse is merely a development and deepening of what he had
set himself to sing at the age of seventeen. In all lives
there is a certain period which stamps itself on the

popular memory as expressive of the man's essential nature;
it is not measured by duration, but by significance. The
consummation of this inner tendency had been delayed in
Herbert by other modes fulfilling his ideal, by a hesitancy
of will, by the feeling of his friends that the calling of
a minister was not worthy of his high birth and talents, by
worldly allurements, if you please; but it came as surely
as the tropic vine struggles up to freedom, and in the sun-
light spreads its blossoms. After all, he had just turned
thirty-seven when he accepted his charge, and should it be
weighed against him that he did not live to complete his
fortieth year?

   Of those three years of priesthood we have a picture of
singular beauty and winsomeness. To the humblest of duties
of his office he gave himself with unreserved devotion, and
in his prose treatise of 'The Country Parson' he has left a
manual of conduct whose sincerity of aim and fine simplicity make it still attractive to-day to the lay reader.
About the ordinances of worship, which he carried out with
extreme regularity, his fancy played with a kind of cher-
ishing wit, as when he wrote of the communion cup:

> O what sweetness from the bowl
>   Fills my soul,
> Such as is and makes divine!
> Is some starre (fled from the sphere)
>   Melted there,
> As we sugar melt in wine?

['The Banquet', ll. 7-12]

   His chief diversion now, as it had always been, was
music. 'He was a most excellent master,' says Walton,
'and he did himself compose many divine hymns and anthems,
which he set and sung to his lute or viol. And, though he
was a lover of retiredness, yet his love to music was such
that he went usually twice every week, on certain appointed
days, to the cathedral church in Salisbury; and at his return would say that his time spent in prayer and cathedral
music elevated his soul, and was his heaven upon earth.
But before his return thence to Bemerton he would usually
sing and play his part at an appointed private music-
meeting; and, to justify this practice, he would often
say, Religion does not banish mirth, but only moderates
and sets rules to it.' (2) It was but a walk of a mile
across pleasant meadows from Bemerton to Salisbury, whose
spire is visible from the rectory windows. Many times he
made this brief journey the occasion of good works, and
once he appeared before his hosts well spattered with mud
from assisting a poor stalled carter. When he was twitted

by his friends for disparaging himself with so dirty an employment, his answer was 'that the thought of what he had
done would prove music to him at midnight'; and added, 'I
would not willingly pass one day of my life without comforting a sad soul or showing mercy.'

There were indeed times of depression, almost of agony;
seasons when he regretted the sacrifice of courtly ameni-
ties. Often he found grief 'a cunning guest'; (3) often
his high pretensions to faith appeared to him a mockery,
and to many readers the poems in which he expresses these
fluctuations of joy and sorrow will seem the richest in
human experience of the collection. But I cannot see that
for this reason he should be denied the epithet of holy
which those who knew him best were quickest to ascribe to
him. His was not the spirit of the triumphant hero, perhaps
not even that of the martyr....

And withal the dominant tone in Herbert is one of quiet
joy and peace. From the very doubts and hesitations that
beset him he wrung a submissive victory, as may be read in
that most characteristic of his poems, 'The Pulley':

[Quotes the poem in full.]

Will you pardon me a fancy? As often as I read these
stanzas the picture rises before me of the Salisbury fields.
It is an afternoon of the early autumn, when the grey sun-
light shimmers in the air and scarcely touches the earth,
brooding over all things with a kind of transient peace.
A country parson, after a day of music in the cathedral and
at the house of a friend, is walking homeward. In his heart
is the quiet afterglow of rapture, not unlike the subdued
light upon the meadows, and he knows that both are but for
a little while. Memory is awake as she is apt to be in the
trail of exultation, and he recalls the earlier scenes of
his life - the peculiar consecration of his youth, the
half-hearted ambitions of the scholar and courtier, the invisible guidance that had brought him at last to the shel-
tered haven whereto he was even now returning. Providence
and the world had dealt kindly with him as with few others,
yet one thing was still lacking - he had not found rest.
He was aware, keenly aware, that this moment of perfect
calm lay between an hour of enthusiasm and an hour of de-
jection. He was not like some he knew who laid violent
hands on the kingdom of peace; he must suffer his moods.
And then came the recollection of the Greek Hesiod whom he
had studied at Cambridge, and of the story of Pandora.
The quaint contrast of that myth with the certainty of his
own faith teased him into reflection. Hope, indeed, the
new dispensation had released from the box and had poured

out blessings instead of ills; but one thing still remained shut up - *rest in the bottom lay*. And straightway
he began to remould the Greek fable to his own experience.
    All this consonant with the tone which in the beginning
he adopted as the lyric poet of divine love and which remained with him in his Bemerton study:

[Quotes 'Dulnesse', ll. 1-12, 17-20, 25-8.]

    To some this peculiarly individual note in religion,
this anxiety over his personal beatitude, will be a
stumbling-block. 'For the most part,' says Professor
Palmer in disdain, 'he is concerned with the small needs of
his own soul.' It is like a taunt thrown ungraciously at
the ideals of a great and serious age. My dear sir, even
to-day in the face of our magnified concerns, are the needs
of a man's soul so small that we dare speak of them with
contempt? I am not holding a brief from the human soul.
Let it be, if you choose, a mere name for certain hopes and
fears which separate from the world and project themselves
into eternity; but let us recognise the fact that those
hopes and fears have been of tremendous force in the past,
and are still worthy of reverence. It is one of the glories
of Herbert's age that it introduced into poetry that quick
and tremulous sense of the individual soul. Religion came
to those men with the shock of a sudden and strange reality, and we who read the report of their experience are
ourselves stirred, willingly or rebelliously, to unused
emotions. Do you know, in fact, what most of all is lacking in the devotional poetry of recent times? It is just
this direct personal appeal. Take, for example, the better
stanzas of Keble's 'Whitsunday':

    So, when the Spirit of our God
        Came down His flock to find,
    A voice from Heaven was heard abroad,
        A rushing, mighty wind.

    Nor doth the outward ear alone
        At that high warning start;
    Conscience gives back the appalling tone;
        'Tis echoed in the heart.

    It fills the Church of God; it fills
        The sinful world around;
    Only in stubborn hearts and wills
        No place for it is found.

That is Keble's version of the coming of the Holy Ghost at

Pentecost; set it beside a single stanza of Herbert's poem
of the same name:

> Listen, sweet Dove, unto my song
>   And spread thy golden wings in me;
>   Hatching my tender heart so long,
>   Till it get wing and flie away with thee.

[ll. 1-4]

Is the advantage all in favour of the modern faith? Or
rather, is not the response to the descending spirit in
Keble dulled by the intrusion of foreign interests, by the
sense that he is writing for the Church and imparting a
moral lesson, whereas in Herbert you feel the ecstatic up-
lift that springs from the immediate contact of the poet's
imagination with its object? Religion has changed from
the soul's intimate discovery of beatitude to the dull convention of sermons. 'He speaks of God like a man that
really believeth in God,' said Baxter of Herbert; (4) is
this altogether a small matter?
    Nor is it quite true that his personal concern with re-
ligion is a selfish withdrawal from men or that 'any notion
of dedicating himself to their welfare is foreign to him.'
Such a statement would have been unintelligible to Herbert's
contemporaries; it forgets the sacramental nature of the
priesthood as it was then conceived. His days, indeed,
were given to the humblest duties and charities, yet to his
friends it would have seemed that the example of so saintly
a life was a still more perfect beneficence than any mini-
strations of the body. Such, too, was the more difficult
ideal that Herbert set before himself:

[Quotes 'Aaron', ll. 1-5.]

And, beyond the mere force of example, it was supposed that
worship in itself was an excellent thing, and that some
grace was poured out upon the people through the daily
intercessions of their priest:

[Quotes 'Providence', ll. 5-16, 25-8.]

And it was in this sense that elsewhere he likened the
priest to a window in the temple wall, 'a brittle crazy
glass,' (5) through which, nevertheless, the light fell
upon the people stained with holy images. His poems he
called *window-songs*. Certainly to Walton the concern 'with
the small needs of his own soul' did not appear to be an
abuse of precious talents. Says the Life: 'And there, by
that inward devotion which he testified constantly by an

humble behaviour and visible adoration, he, like Joshua,
brought not only his own household thus to serve the Lord,
but brought most of his parishioners, and many gentlemen
in the neighbourhood, constantly to make a part of his congregation twice a day. And some of the meaner sort of his
parish did so love and reverence Mr. Herbert that they
would let their plough rest when Mr. Herbert's saints-bell
rung to prayers, that they might also offer their devotions to God with him; and would then return back to their
plough. And his most holy life was such that it begot such
reverence to God, and to him, that they thought themselves
the happier when they carried Mr. Herbert's blessing back
with them to their labour.' (6)

A part of the intense individualism of Herbert's religion during these last years was no doubt due to the increasing burden of ill health. Occasionally a note of pure
bodily pain breaks through his song, and the thought of the
inevitable end grew daily more insistent. Death is a thing
of which we have become ashamed. We huddle it up and speak
of it with averted glance. But it was not always so; men
of Herbert's day looked upon it as the solemn consummation
of life and prepared for it as for a public ceremony.
Read Sir Thomas Browne's 'Letter to a Friend', and see how
he dwells on the 'deliberate and creeping progress into
the grave.' Or go not so far; stop in the eighteenth century and read the letters in which Cowper relates the passing of his brother. You will find nothing comparable to
this in the literature of to-day; the very word is almost
banished from our books. It may be that we have gained in
power by putting away from us the thought of this paralys-
ing necessity, yet sometimes I wonder if we have not suffered an equal loss. For with Herbert, at least, the
fairest of his poems were inspired by this ever-present
thought. A very thrill of joy leaps through such lines as
these:

What wonders shall we feel when we shall see
              Thy full-ey'd love!
When thou shalt look us out of pain.
                              ['The Glance', ll. 19-21]

Is the rapture of Dante, lifted from sphere to sphere at
the sight of Beatrice's eyes, finer than this *When thou
shalt look us out of pain?* And death is the theme of that
sweetest song, which no one who writes of Herbert can
afford to omit:

[Quotes 'Virtue' in full.]

Just before the end Herbert gave to a friend who was
visiting him a manuscript book, bidding him deliver it to
Nicholas Ferrar to be made public or burned as that gentleman thought good. It was, as he described it, a picture
of the many spiritual conflicts that had passed betwixt
God and his soul, being the small volume of verse which
was the labour and the fruit of his life. There is much to
censure critically in the work, much that is frigid and
fantastic; but at its best the note is rare and penetrating, with the tinkling purity of a silver sacring bell.
Many have loved the book as a companion of the closet, and
many still cherish it for its human comfort; all of us
may profit from its pages if we can learn from them to
wind ourselves out of the vicious fallacy of the present,
and to make our own some part of Herbert's intimacy with
divine things.

Notes

1 No. 10.
2 Above, pp. 119-20.
3 'Confession', 1. 1.
4 No. 29.
5 'The Windows', 1. 2.
6 Above, p. 119.

67. A.G. HYDE, FROM 'GEORGE HERBERT AND HIS TIMES'

1906

A.G. Hyde's biography of Herbert - the first in the twentieth century - paid tribute to Walton ('it must be frankly
admitted that the labours of a modern biographer of Herbert
are reduced to little more than a commentary on Walton's
narrative') yet advanced in novel directions particularly
by attending to the poetry qua poetry. Of the two chapters devoted to a discussion of 'The Temple', the first
centred on 'The Church-porch', and the second - reprinted
below - on the other poems. Hyde's view is summarily
stated in the very opening paragraph of his biography,
where his mention of poets like Crashaw, Vaughan, Herrick,
and Quarles terminates in the judgement that 'Herbert must
be allowed a very high, if not the highest, place'. See
also above, p. 32.

Source: Hyde, 'The Temple': The Shorter Poems, in
'George Herbert and his Times' (1906), Ch. XV.

If 'The Church Porch' is comparatively free from the metaphysical and other defects commonly charged on the poet,
the hundred and sixty shorter pieces to which it serves as
an introduction show them in full measure, though perhaps
not to the degree that some of his critics maintain. But
with his ascent to a higher plane of thought and experience he stumbles frequently, and now and then falls –
mountain summits have their perils for sacred as well as
other verse writers. His theme is essentially that of
Milton and St. Paul: man's first disobedience and its
fruits, the Christian Sacrifice, and the elemental travail
of the human soul to which they gave birth; but his treatment, as might be expected, is didactic rather than epic.
The metaphor suggested by his title is carried on; the
portico now passed, the Temple itself is entered:

[Quotes 'Superliminare' in full.]

   Though short individually, the poems taken together
form a considerable body of verse; and to say that their
merit varies is to affirm what is true of the work of almost every writer of force and originality – only medio-
crity seems capable of maintaining a uniform level. That
Herbert's poetry is seriously marred by the taste of his
age, an age that took delight in over-strained metaphors,
and an elaborate ingenuity of thought rather than its more
simple and obvious processes, is apparent at once; and
whether he drew the influence from its leading exponent,
Donne, or from the surrounding air, is hardly material,
though the fact is to be regretted. Had he been as
serenely impervious to the time-spirit in this respect as
his contemporary, Herrick, the world would have seen a
greater poet; but on the other hand, it might have lost
its George Herbert, for the Parable of the Tares is of
wide application. The line above quoted, from what might
be called the inscription over the Church door: 'Or that
which groaneth to be so,' marks him off from the majority
of his fellow-singers even in sacred things; and if by
any cause the intensity of his aspiration for holiness
had been abated, no mere literary perfection would have
atoned for the loss.
   The shorter 'Temple' poems, within their general scheme,
cover a wide range of subjects. They are by no means confined to the symbolism of the Church precincts and furni-
ture, or to its seasons and spiritual offices; on the

contrary, the greater number bear the names of abstract,
if they may not rather be called concrete, things: five
are entitle 'Affliction,' three 'Praise,' two 'Justice,'
two 'Love,' one 'Virtue,' and so on.   Many of the titles
give as little hint of their character as the names of
Ruskin's books: 'The Bag,' 'The Collar,' 'The Pulley,'
'The Size,' and others, are examples.   Nearly all are composed in a vein of spiritual egotism, if it may be so
called, and deal with individual experience.   The first
person predominates: chiefly it is man speaking with God;
but once, in 'The Sacrifice,' it is Christ who speaks to
man from the Cross;   and once, in the 'Dialogue,' Christ
and man speak to each other alternatively;   while again
elsewhere, men and angels converse together antiphon-wise.
In all the poems, however artificial the mechanism may be,
the feeling is strong and genuine - dulness of mind or
heart, indeed, is the one thing Herbert abhors, and will
not forgive in himself or in others.   Like most religious
poets of the time, he is deeply moved by the tragedy of
the Crucifixion: it is the subject of one of the earliest
and longest of the 'Temple' pieces - 'The Sacrifice' just
mentioned - in which Christ Himself is the speaker;   and
it is treated with a simplicity that suggests the old
miracle plays, yet with the profoundest feeling:

> O all ye who pass by, whose eyes and mind
> To worldly things are sharp, but to me blind,
> To me, who took eyes that I might you find;
> > Was ever grief like mine?
> > > [ll. 1-4]

The sixty-three stanzas, all but two ending with the same
refrain, recite in sad monody the story of the betrayal,
desertion, and other events of the Passion, and are almost
wholly free from conceits and kindred blemishes.   Unfortunately, in other instances, the solemnity of his theme
does not save him from gross lapses of the kind.   A species of unpleasant materialism, for realism it cannot be
called, infected the theologians of the age, as it infected many in later as well as in earlier times: neither
the mystery of the Incarnation nor of the Eucharist was
safe from what Wordsworth would have called their finger-
ing habits;   and even poets fell into the snare.   Herbert
is not a sinner more than others: he is, indeed, less
culpable in this respect than Crashaw;   but to our more
fastidious, if not better taste, his handling of such mo-
mentous topics is often repellent, despite the earnestness
of his aim.

But the poetry of 'The Temple' is not to be expressed

in negations; and if it has everywhere the note of suffering, it also overflows with joy. Where there is music
there is gladness; and, with all their defects, its lines
are full of music:

[Quotes 'Antiphon' (I), ll. 1-8.]

It may be in the higher symmetry of his thoughts that
his music chiefly abounds; for, according to Sir Thomas
Browne, music exists wherever there is harmony, order, and
proportion; and these are distinguishing qualities of Herbert's verse. In the well-known 'Elixir,' the magic
draught which has sweetened the hardest labours of house
and field for many generations, there is music of both
kinds, except perhaps in the second and third stanzas:

[Quotes the poem in full.]

That, with his profound knowledge and experience of
spiritual life, he should have dwelt much on the insidious
nature of evil, ever clouding the soul's best desires and
purposes, and creeping, serpent-like, through the barriers
of moral restraint, is entirely in keeping with his character. Two of his shorter poems are entitled 'Sin'; and
the longer one is unique in its curious blending of psychological truth with beauty and quaintness of language:

[Quotes 'Sinne' (I) in full.]

It is this martial note, this 'sound of glory' ever in
his ears, that makes Herbert's poetry so inspiring. However lowly his theme, however dark the Valley of Humiliation through which at the time he walks, he hears the
music of the celestial host, and it stirs his soul like a
trumpet. To quote, either wholly or in part, his more
familiar poems, may seem superfluous; but as a rule they
are his best and cannot well be omitted. It is interesting to observe how many are conceived in the spirit of the
Christian pilgrim: Herbert, in fact, anticipates Bunyan's
allegory; and Vanity Fair, not less than the Slough of
Despond, is one of his temptations by the way. He is especially beset with the allurements of what may be called
its popular stalls, the delights of the eye and other
gauds captivating to the natural man. In the oddly named
'Quip,' Beauty creeps into a rose, and scornfully flouts
him when he does not pluck the flower; Money jingles his
full purse at his ear; and 'brave Glory' puffs by in
whistling silks; but, as might be supposed, his most dangerous tempters are 'quick Wit and Conversation,' who

plausibly invite him to make a public speech - a reminis-
cence, doubtless, of his old academic office. In 'The
Pulley,' justly ranked as one of his finest poems, the
desirable gifts thus personified, and others, are freely
granted to mankind, only rest being withheld:

[Quotes the poem in full.]

   Profoundly philosophical as 'The Pulley' is, its seduc-
tive seventh line ('Then Beauty flowed, the Wisdom, Honour,
Pleasure') classes it, along with 'The Pearl' ('I know the
ways of Learning,' etc.), among what may be called Herbert's Vanity Fair poems; to which his courtier days must
have supplied valuable materials. More distinctively suggestive of Bunyan, however, is his own 'Pilgrimage,' a
metaphysical poem in the best sense, and, although not well
known, assuredly one of his best. It is in poems like this,
and a few others, that he enters the mystic's peculiar do-
main, and approaches most nearly to his own greatest disciple, Henry Vaughan. Bunyan, whose only books while im-
prisoned in Bedford gaol are said to have been the Bible
and Foxe's 'Book of Martyrs,' probably never read his pre-
deccessor's lines, which were published when he was about
five years old; but it is curious to see how closely he
follows the story, though not, it must be said, in its
ending:

[Quotes 'The Pilgrimage' in full.]

   This is, indeed, the Enchanted Ground; and the interpretation of the allegory, or dream, if such it be, is not
for the gay pilgrims of the Tabard Inn, who travel in large
companies, and repeat light tales by the way for each
other's entertainment.
   With the exception of 'The Church Porch,' the Church
fabric poems, if they may be so called, are hardly equal
to these. Yet there are lines in the 'Church Monuments'
which, despite the common defects of tombstone meditations,
have all the marks of the great style - the style of
Shakespeare and Wordsworth. Desiring his flesh to

   ...take acquaintance of this heap of dust,
   To which the blast of Death's incessant motion,
   Fed with the exhalation of our crimes,
   Drives all at last,

the poet sends his body

...to this school, that it may learn
To spell his elements, and find his birth
Written in dusty heraldry and lines,

[11. 3-6, 7-9]

as others have done, not always profitably. The poem entitled 'Church Music' ('Sweetest of sweets, I thank you!')
naturally strikes a cheerfuller note; the 'Church Lock and
Key' suggests the sins that close the ears of Heaven to
mortal suppliants; the materials of 'The Church Floor'
symbolise certain moral virtues, though as elsewhere,

Hither sometimes sin steals, and stains
The marble's neat and curious veins;

[11. 13-14]

but 'The Windows' happily lets in purifying light. 'The
Altar' belongs to the class of artificial poems censured by
Addison in his Papers on Wit, (1) in which the lines are
made to conform to the shape of material objects: in this
case it is an altar or a table, and the verse suffers from
the forcing process.

The seasons and offices of the Church should naturally
afford a wider scope; but on the whole it cannot be said
that Herbert is at his best in dealing with them in verse.
His 'Sunday' ('O Day most calm, most bright!') probably
deserves the highest place. 'Easter' begins with promise:
'Rise, heart, thy Lord is risen;' but is marred by fla-
grant conceits, though the last three stanzas atone, if
only by their music, for the fault:

I got me flowers to strew Thy way;
I got me boughs off many a tree;
But Thou wast up by break of day,
And brought'st Thy sweets along with Thee.

[11. 19-22]

'Whit-Sunday' supplies the critic with an egregious metaphor and other faults; 'Trinity Sunday' and 'Lent' are
somewhat conventional; and 'Christmas' is only relieved by
one of the poet's charming instances of child-like realism
- his meeting with his divine Lord at an inn. 'Holy
Baptism' shows again the vice of false ingenuity; 'Holy
Communion' is subtle and characteristic, but may be thought
inferior to 'The Banquet,' a poem overflowing with conceits, but of interest as showing Herbert's curiously familiar and affectionate treatment of the Eucharist. We are
now told that such endearing phrases are foreign to the
genius of Englishmen, and belong properly to the emotional

races of the South; but the Englishman of that time was a
different being from his phlegmatic offspring of to-day:

[Quotes 11. 1-12.]

   Herrick or Crashaw might possibly have written like
this, though hardly Vaughan. The second and last, however,
of Herbert's poems entitled 'Love,' that closing 'The
Temple' series, appears to refer to the same sacred Feast;
(2) and if so it must be considerably by far the best of
its kind which he has left us. It is also the most characteristic example of his child-like simplicity and tenderness in dealing with his favourite theme, human unworthi-
ness and the Divine Benignity.
   'Herbert's strength of poetical conception,' says Professor Courthope, 'lives in vivid, and often sublime, renderings of the spiritual aspects of human nature;' (3) and
to us this strength may seem oftenest shown in his poems
on what might be called the larger philosophical abstrac-
tions. Whatever their names, whether unambiguous titles
like 'Sin,' 'Affliction,' and 'Constancy,' or such cryptic
designations as 'The Pulley' or 'The Collar,' they appear
to afford his imagination more of kindling fire and sustained heat. His short and exquisite 'Virtue,' probably
the best known of all his verses, is one of this class;
though its beautiful imagery makes us too often forget the
moral propounded at the close....

[Quotes the poem in full.]

   It is of course an imperfect poem: some of the conceits
are distinctly unpoetical, and some of the words and
phrases now out of date; but of its kind it is an imperishable gem, alike above criticism and praise.
   For the reasons already given, the less familiar but
more important - indeed, the greatest - of Herbert's poems,
'Man,' cannot be left out, though it must close this over-
long list of poetical citations. The Miltonic character of
the poem has been often noted, as well as its apparent
anticipation of modern scientific knowledge. Echoing the
amazed admiration of King David and Hamlet - names sufficiently wide apart - for the supreme handiwork of Creation,
it implicitly recognises the fact that man and his earthly
house have been of united growth: such at least seems to
be its incidental teaching. We are part and parcel of the
natural scheme of things: man is an animal, if a rational
one, with only reason and speech to lift him above his
humbler brethren. He is affected by the months and
seasons; by reason of a common origin, the herbs of the

field cure his body, even those he tramples under foot.
The centre and summit of the world, he is its complete epi-
tome, an atom yet the sum of all:

[Quotes 'Man' in full.]

Here, even more than in 'The Pulley,' are the 'weight,
number, and expression of the thoughts' admirable, as well
as the 'simple dignity' of the language; (4) though again
the faults incident to the metaphysical and other verse of
the age are apparent - obscurity from over-compression,
archaisms, and the like. The lapse, however, into the
Ptolemaic astronomy, in the fifth stanza ('For us ... the
earth doth rest, heaven move,' etc.), may be regarded as
merely rhetorical; the Copernican system having been well
established by Herbert's time. (5)
Such explanation as is possible for the sudden and lasting popularity of 'The Temple' poems may now, perhaps, be
considered as offered. The examples here given, it is
hoped, show that they appeal not merely to the plain man,
and that the qualities which may be said to have contributed to the best and happiest hours of the best and happiest people for nearly ten generations, place them among
the first of their kind in the language. The common criticism, that their value as religious verse is in excess of
their purely literary merits, seems to be easily dealt
with. Of the eight score and one poems, short or long,
making up 'The Temple,' at least twelve are in the very
front rank of English poetical compositions, by reason of
their strength of invention, excellence of form, and felicity of expression. To 'The Church Porch,' and to the
shorter poems, 'Man,' 'Virtue,' 'Decay,' 'Sin,' 'The Quip,'
'The Pulley,' 'Love Unknown,' 'The Pilgrimage,' 'The
Collar,' 'The Elixir,' and the second (6) poem called
'Love,' no valid objection can be made on the usual grounds
- verbal conceits, false taste, and so on; while their
positive merits are beyond praise. Quite as many more -
'The Sacrifice,' 'The Agony' (a great poem disfigured at
the end), 'Affliction,' 'Constancy,' 'The British Church,'
the two 'Antiphones,' 'Hope,' and several others - are
only just below them; while the list of poems containing
striking and effective passages or lines might be extended
almost indefinitely. The question of 'purely literary'
value is always a difficult one, and turns largely on individual tastes and opinions; but perhaps the saying of
Matthew Arnold, in his defence of Wordsworth, that the
Lake Poet excelled in 'the application of ideas to life,'
applies equally to Herbert. To deal as a poet with the
vital facts of life with power and mastery is a great

thing; and Herbert so deals with the facts of the spiritual
life. If he is not 'simple and sensuous,' (7) and sometimes overloads his verses with weighty and trenchant matter, to their poetical hurt, the practice has had its able
apologists. 'Give me a manly, rough line, with a deal of
meaning in it,' says Cowper, 'rather than a whole poem full
of musical periods that have nothing but their oily
smoothness to recommend them;' and the world at large has
persistently made the same demand, and will continue to
make it. Yet Herbert's lines abound in music; and he
rarely, like Donne, comes under Ben Jonson's censure of
deserving to be hanged 'for breaking of quantity.' (8)

Notes

1 See above, No. 36.
2 The reference is, clearly, to the third poem entitled
   'Love'.
3 No. 64.
4 The phrases are borrowed from Coleridge, as above,
   p. 166.
5 In fact, of course, it was not 'established' much before
   Newton's time.
6 Actually, the third.
7 From Milton's description of poetry in 'Of Education' as
   'simple, sensuous and passionate'.
8 From the remark reported by William Drummond of Haw-
   thornden (as above, No. 65: note 6).

68. FRANCIS THOMPSON, GEORGE HERBERT, IN THE 'ATHENAEUM'

1907

Thompson's most important tribute to Herbert was written
as a review of A.G. Hyde's biography (No. 67). It is not
a commentary on Herbert's poetry, but the tribute of a
fellow-poet who recognises the 'conflict' at the core of
'The Temple' and the life of its author. See also above,
p. 32.
   Source: Thompson, George Herbert, in 'Literary Criticisms by Francis Thompson', ed. Terence L. Connolly (1948),
pp. 79-82. First published in the 'Athenaeum' for 16 March
1907.

So little new material has been recovered, as Mr. Hyde
says, that a modern biography of George Herbert can be
scarcely more than a commentary on Walton. Except a je-
june memoir prefixed to 'The Country Parson,' and the few
references of Herbert's brother, the Lord of Cherbury
(with, of course, his own too scanty letters), old Izaak's
'Life' of the poet remains the one source of knowledge.
Mr. Hyde claims, however, the merit of correlating Herbert's
life and writings with the history and life of his time -
with his environment, in fact; the inevitable attempt of
every such biographer since Taine. Here it amounts mainly
to some chapters reviewing, from the standpoint of a moderate, but more or less High Church sympathiser, the religious movement which had Laud for its militant apostle and
Herbert for its most representative singer. (Its *first* we
cannot say, with Donne's later poems in view.) For the
rest, Mr. Hyde as a biographer, without being in any way
inspired, is careful, competent, straightforward, and not
extreme. He has accumulated whatever minutæ of information might throw light on Herbert's surroundings throughout his career, and related them in an orderly, direct
fashion. He has hardly, it is true, managed to create Herbert's environment in the larger sense of the term - mainly
because he is not an artist. He cannot vitalise his material. He comes, indeed, as near to being dull as may be
with such a subject and his wisely close following of
Walton. But such virtues as the merely careful and temperate writer, whose gifts do not include art or style, may
command, his book has.
   Among these virtues cannot be reckoned grammatical precision. In one place, after referring - with a nice de-
rangement of relatives - to a certain letter of Herbert's,
he begins a new sentence by stating: 'Never yet recovered,
a Latin letter ... has been preserved,' and gives us the
contents of the other epistle. Which means that a Latin
letter never yet recovered has (by a fortunate if imperfect
compensation) been preserved. On the other hand, Mr.
Hyde's intention, though certainly not preserved, may yet
be recovered from this curious sentence. The 'never yet
recovered' of course relates to the letter discussed in a
previous sentence, not the Latin letter so happily 'preserved' in the later sentence. But 'you know what I mean'
is an excuse that can only pass in talk. Nowadays, however, we have often to be thankful for technical ambiguity
which (like this) leaves the sense but momentarily obscured.
And this, be it said, is an extreme instance. Mr. Hyde,
indeed, is moderate in all things; even his admiration of
Mr. Herbert's poetry is tempered to something below
scalding-point.

Herbert, without Walton's charm of style, and doomed to
carry his archaeology and 'environment' and 'such odd
branches of learning' on his back, presents a slight and
undiversified life. His letters scarcely lift the veil
which covers most men of his time. Men had not then learnt
the art of correspondence: from Herbert to Swift or Cowper
is a far cry, unless perhaps we except one or two delight-
fully Charles-Surface-like letters of Suckling. If you are
interested in that disputed influence of race on poetry to
which the 'Celtic Movement' has called attention, Herbert
is a case to your hand. His lyrical work is a remarkable
fusion of poetic fantasy and mystic imagination with
strong, homely practical sense, loving an aphoristic terseness - a blend to Mr. Hyde 'curious,' to some others
delightful.

The poet was of mixed blood. The Herberts, in their
border fastness of Montgomery, had a Cymric streak across
their ancestry; while Magdalen, his mother, came from the
old Princes of Powysland. No one, indeed, has observed
how much that mystic or religious revival of the seventeenth century went to the Cymry for its singers. Of the
brilliant five - Donne, Herbert, Crashaw, Vaughan,
Traherne - Herbert was semi-Cymric, Vaughan entirely Welsh,
while Traherne, if there be any faith in names, must have
been Cornish at least by descent. Even from a portrait
not much better in art than the outrages on Shakespeare,
one knows the delicate, valetudinarian poet. He has
straight hair flowing almost to the sloping shoulders from
the brow, high, narrow, and domed above well-opened eyes;
and a sharp, hooked nose, the tip being an elongated ap-
pendage to the nose proper, as though it had been nipped
and stretched between one's finger and thumb - nose, shall
we say, as of a mortified Punch? We see a long upper lip;
long, somewhat apple-shaped chin; high-boned cheek and
hollow; and a well-proportioned upper face, marred by excessive elongation of all below the junction of nose and
lip, and by that comma-like downward dip of the extreme
nose. Set this face atop of a meagre, tallish, bottle-
shouldered figure, and you have George Herbert, a man with
the austere, almost Puritanic look which comes of bodily
pain and effort of inward restraint, not of morose nature.

For the meagre scholar was not only a courtly gentleman, but also quick-tempered, of keen physical sensibili-
ties, with a relish for that world which he never found it
an easy matter to despise. He was among those (in Pat-
more's grim jibe)

Who sing 'O easy yoke of Christ!'
But find 'tis hard to get it on.

Mr. Hyde is somewhat reluctant to admit this feature in
'holy' George Herbert. But the fact is sufficiently
plain, and excuse is needless. Were despising the world
so easy a process, why should we admire the despising of
it? Herbert, plainly, as a brilliant young man found university honours much to his taste, a career of Court ambition very attractive, the favour of kings not to be
'sneezed at'; and (most humanly) having a mind to the
serving of kings, he found excellent good reason why a
little serving of kings was not irreconcilable with the
serving of God. The flattering of them was still easier -
was it not part of his official duty as Public Orator of
Cambridge? - and perhaps he once stretched it a point too
far. So he finally launched on a definite, though brief
Court career, satisfied that pitch need not always defile.
Happily he was not brought to the trial where men as good
did not keep clean hands. You could choose your circle at
Court; and to please a learned king, to chat with brilliant Donne, discourse with wise Verulam, was no such
giddy worldliness for a religious-minded man. Ambition
itself may be exalted and grave. One guesses the dreams -
serious dreams and very pleasant. But the deaths of two
noblemen and the royal pedant, James, left the young courtier patronless; and so Providence decided for Master
George Herbert. It took him some time to stomach that decision. Even when he had made his ecclesiastical election,
and Bemerton parsonage came his way, it needed Laud to
overrule his shrinking from that final step.
     But then, according to Mr. Hyde, it was all over.
After that, all was serene and whole-hearted saintliness.
We know his life at Bemerton, touching and admirable to
read - a life that reformed the neglected parish. His
zealous and cheerful performance of duty amidst failing
health; his charity and accessibility to the poor; the
periodical music-meeting in town which was his one re-
laxation; his sweetness of spirit, shown in those charming stories of Walton's which bear out the idea of a soul
at peace and quiet - these we know, and the death-scene,
meet close for such a life. Yet the poems tell another
story. They show that (however Herbert may have found
peace at the last) for long the parson's life failed to
yield him the anticipated content. Under that sweet and
devoted external life the old conflict between worldly
desires and the spiritual life was renewed and persistent.
The dual nature was still at civil strife, not to be har-
monised and subdued by a single act of decision; and the
war was painful and keen. It is just this which gives to
his poetry the human and sympathetic element - that it reflects a weakness and struggle common to all men. Both its

lesson and the lesson of his life are lost if we insist on
regarding him as a saint completed at a stroke, by one
final act of self-abnegation. The true George Herbert is
closer to us than that; and therefore secure of appeal to
all generations, both as poet, and here in his life as
man.

69. EDWARD BLISS REED, FROM 'ENGLISH LYRIC POETRY'

1912

Reed, an assistant professor at Yale College, in his ambitious survey of the development of English lyric poetry,
reiterated many of the long-standing prejudices against
Herbert but sanctioned also his 'struggle for holiness'
and recognised in particular the novelty of the poet's
efforts. See also above, p. 32.
    Source: Reed, from The Jacobean and Caroline Lyric,
in 'English Lyric Poetry from its Origin to the Present
Time' (New Haven, Conn., 1912), pp. 278-83.

George Herbert (1593-1633), distinguished at Cambridge and
at the court, entered the church in 1626; in 1630 he was
made priest at Bemerton, where he died. On his deathbed
he sent the manuscript of the 'Temple' to Nicholas Ferrar,
who published it within a few months. It became popular
at once and six editions were brought out in eight years.
    Though Herbert was not the first Englishman to compose
religious lyrics, he created a new school of verse. The
religious poetry before him had been Scriptural paraphrases (chiefly of the Psalms), penitential verses, hymns,
and meditations. Generally, as in the case of Ben Johnson,
they formed but a small part of any writer's work; often,
especially in the sonnet sequences, they served as foils
for the secular verse. No poet, except Southwell, had
written religious poetry exclusively; no one had analyzed
the religious experience, or pondered deeply on the life
of the spirit, or recorded the defeats and victories of
his own soul. Herbert, therefore, adopted deliberately a
style and a theme for which he had no models. As an undergraduate he had regretted that poetry wore the livery of
Venus; as a priest he felt the need of expressing his own
spiritual conflicts and thus from piety, from the impulse
of confession and the desire to give sorrow words, sprang

the lyrics of the 'Temple.'

Among Herbert's warmest friends was John Donne; in his
poetic method Herbert stands with him and not with the
Elizabethans, for his keen and brilliant mind expressed
itself readily in Donne's manner. We certainly can not
say that without Donne's poems the 'Temple' would not have
been written, yet without his example Herbert's book would
not have assumed its present form. To us Herbert's conceits may seem too ingenious to be anything but artificial,
but they are not a mere ornament to his verse, for he uses
them when he is most deeply moved. Because the great emotions of life do not vary from generation to generation,
we forget that the natural method of expressing these
feelings has constantly changed. When Herbert calls aloud
to England: 'Spit out they phlegm and fill thy breast with
glory' ['The Church-porch,' 1. 92], he is not endeavouring
to startle us by a strange phrase; he is deeply stirred
and wishes to arouse his country. Few of his poems con-
tain more conceits than 'Sunday' - the sabbath is man's
face while the week days are his body; Sundays are the
pillars of Heaven's palace while the other days are the
empty spaces between them; Sundays are the pearls
threaded to adorn the bride of God - yet Walton asserts
that Herbert sang this song on his deathbed. He has many
conceits that mar his work - we could do without the comparison of spring to a box of sweetmeats in 'Sweet day, so
cool, so calm, so bright' - yet they are an essential element in his writing.

Like Donne, Herbert is impatient of melody; his verse
is grave and lacks the sweetness of Crashaw's hymns.
Though full of striking felicities of phrase, his lyrics
are rarely metrically perfect throughout. He knew the
work of the sonneteers and in the style of their sonnets
on sleep he composed one on prayer:

Prayer, the Churches banquet, angel's age,
    God's breath in man returning to his birth,
    The soul in paraphrase, heart in pilgrimage,
The Christian plummet sounding heaven and earth;
                        ['Prayer' (I), 11. 1-4]

but there is little of Elizabethan music here. His most
impressive sonnet, *My comforts drop and melt like snow,*
has a splendid opening and is suffused with the deepest
feeling, but it too, drops and melts into such a line as
'But cooling by the way, grows pursy and slow.' He en-
vied, so he said, 'no man's nightingale or spring'; he
lacks the graces of his contemporaries; yet 'The Quip,'
'The Collar,' 'Virtue,' have a music rarer than the facile

strains of the earlier age. At his best he has a sober
harmony that grows in impressiveness the more it is heard,
for with few exceptions, the musical appeal of Herbert's
verse is not an immediate one.

The great value of Herbert's lyrics consists in their
revelation of his character, for the religious lyric gains
in power according to the degree in which it discloses a
man's soul. In many of the lyrics we see the struggle for
holiness, but more impressive is his struggle for peace;
this it is that makes him such a human figure. The aver-
age man does not long for spiritual perfection, but he does
desire the calm and steadfast mind. What Herbert could not
say from the pulpit he wrote in his lyrics. Of a noble
family, the friend of courtiers and the King, famed for his
scholarship and wit, he found himself ministering to the
needs of fifty peasants - his little church would not hold
more. He could not forget the things of earth, his old
dreams and hopes of worldly greatness; he is 'full of rebellion,' and longs to fight, to travel, to deny his service. Sickness and doubt overtake him; he has drunk from
a bitter bowl; he believes his nature has been thwarted:

[Quotes 'Affliction' (I), ll. 37-40.]

He feels that he accomplished nothing in the world, that
the struggle naught availeth:

[Ibid., ll. 55-60.]

He is constantly reproaching himself with his empty days;
the very plants and bees do more than he:

>   Poor bees that work all day
>   Sting my delay.
>   ['Praise'(I), ll. 17-18]

When, moreover, we remember that the world and its train-
bands still call him; that Beauty creeps into a rose and
tempts him; that he feels the scorn of 'proud Wit and
Contemplation,' we can understand why he writes so often
on affliction. The frankness of these poems points to a
new era in the lyric; Herbert conceals nothing, and his
heart, so he tells us, bleeds on his writing.

It must not be presumed that these lyrics are depress-
ing reading; with few exceptions they are not morbid, for
Herbert has reconciled these unhappy experiences with a
divine plan to bring the soul to felicity. This restlessness and discontent is thrust upon him to draw his sould
to God:

> If goodness lead him not, yet weariness
> May toss him to my breast.

['The Pulley', ll. 19-20]

The lyrics of the 'Temple' lead not to pessimism but to
hope.
    Looking at the lyrics from the artistic standpoint,
'Virtue,' to which Isaac Walton has given a perfect prose
setting, deserves its popularity, for it is the most beautiful of all his poems. 'The Elixir' is equally well
known, because of those lines quoted as frequently as
Pope's epigrams:

> Who sweeps a room but for thy cause
>   Makes that and the action fine,

[ll. 19-20]

but more characteristic than either of these two lyrics is
'Man.' It has his peculiar music, his quaintness of style,
and deep thought:

> Man is all symmetry,
> Full of proportions, one limb to another,
>   And all to all the world besides,
>   Each part may call the farthest, brother;
> For head with foot hath private amity,
>   And both, with moons and tides.

[ll. 13-18]

The lyrics of Herbert make a man look more deeply both into his own heart and into the world about him.

70. A. CLUTTON-BROCK, FROM 'MORE ESSAYS ON BOOKS'

1921

Palmer's edition of Herbert's poems in 1905 (see headnote
to No. 65) continued over the ensuing years to occasion
reviews and essays. The widely respected critic and
essayist A. Clutton-Brock provided one such essay, notable
for his acceptance of the conflict at the heart of Herbert's poetry and for his several excellent judgements inclusive of his rejection of the notion of the poet's
quaintness. See also above, p. 32.
    Source: A. Clutton-Brock, George Herbert, in 'More

Essays on Books' (1921), pp. 13-23. First published in a
more expansive form in 'The Times Literary Supplement' for
1 April 1920.

In the preface to his edition of Herbert, Mr. Palmer says
that there are few to whom it will seem worth while, 'but
its aim is lavishness'; he was named after Herbert by a
lover of Herbert, and knew a large part of his verse before he could read. 'I could not die in peace if I did
not raise a costly monument to his beneficent memory.'
    He himself, he tells us, is a Puritan and often re-
pelled by Herbert's elaborate ecclesiasticism; but the
New England Puritan of to-day keeps the cleanness and
sweetness of seventeeth-century piety, transplanted across
the Atlantic and there naturalized and still thriving.
That piety was clean and sweet because it was intellectual,
never content to hypnotize itself with old formulas, or to
imitate sexual infatuation with religious ecstasy. Reason
kept it modest; and this modesty the New England Puritan
admires and shares. It is not mere innocence and pretti-
ness, because it is always restlessly intellectual,
richer not poorer in content than mere rapture, more full
of experience, more interesting and, when it attains to
beauty, more beautiful. Mr. Palmer says that Herbert even
now, when his name is respected, is more bought than read.
'Half a dozen of his poems are famous; but the remainder,
many of them equally fitted for household words, nobody
looks at.' We do not know whether this is true, but we do
know that he is one of the most interesting of poets, one
who can be read in a prosaic mood, and the reading of whom
will lift one gently out of that mood to the height of his
own sudden yet not incongruous beauties.
    Mr. Palmer prints in his text no readings from the
Williams MS. discovered by Dr. Grossart. (1) He believes,
rightly, we think, that this MS. represents an earlier
text which Herbert afterwards altered in many details;
and he is also right, no doubt, to accept Herbert's own
changes. But we do not agree with him that they were always for the better. The text of the Williams MS. is
rougher, but often more vigorous. Herbert seems sometimes
to have been afraid of his own vigour, and to have smoothed
it away. Thus in 'The Church Porch' the second stanza in
the text is -

    Beware of lust: it doth pollute and foul
        Whom God in Batisme washt with his own blood.
    It blots thy lesson written in thy soul;

> The holy lines cannot be understood.
> How dare those eyes upon a Bible look,
> Much lesse towards God, whose lust is all their book?

But in the Williams MS. it runs –

> Beware of lust (startle not), O beware,
> It makes thy soule a blott; it is a rodd
> Whose twigs are pleasures, and they whip thee bare.
> It spoils an Angel: robs thee of thy God.

It seems to me that the later version is more 'parsonic,'
more merely edifying than the first, which says more and
with more force and precision. In fact, if there were
question which reading was genuine, I should choose the
earlier. But Mr. Palmer gives all the readings of the
Williams MS., so that we can take our choice.
    The common notion of Herbert is false, and must be based
on small knowledge of his life and poetry; it is, indeed,
calculated to rob his poetry of interest.

> Often he is pictured as an aged saint who, through
> spending a lifetime in priestly offices, has come to
> find interest only in devout emotions....In reality Her-
> bert died under forty; was a priest less than three
> years, spent his remaining thirty-six years among men
> who loved power, place, wit, pleasure, and learning;
> and held his own among them remarkably well.

Herbert himself said when dying that his poems were 'a picture of the many spiritual conflicts that have passed betwixt God and my soul, before I could submit mine to the
will of Jesus my Master'; and this was not 'the last deliberate snuffle of a blameless prig,' but a true account
of them. He is an interesting poet because this conflict
in his life was real and because he expressed it in his
verse. It was a conflict between ambition and beauty; he
saw more and more clearly that worldliness is ugly, yet he
could not rid his mind of it. There were in him the courtier and the artist, and only gradually and painfully did
the artist win. Nowadays the artist would not express himself like Herbert; but he would feel the same temptations
and need the same renunciation, not for nothingness, but
for the beauty that is his deepest and most permanent desire. Some artists never have to make the choice; beauty
is to them the only temptation; the world does not exist
except as an outside enemy. But for Herbert it was an

enemy within, and that is why he fortifies himself with
incessant self-analysis, why he must be telling himself,
sometimes dully and with too much argument, that beauty,
which he calls God, is his true desire.

Like his master Donne, he is not an easy, confident
lover of beauty; he will not throw himself into the poet's
attitude and trust to rhythms or poetic words to inspire
him; he begins with prose and labours upwards to poetry.
No poet is more conscious of the double problem of art, the
counterpoint of sense and music. There is Donne between
him and the Elizabethan lyric, with its predominance of
music so great that it makes the problem of art almost
single; and his contempt of love-poetry is as much aesthetic as moral. Love seems to him too easy an incitement
to verse:-

[Quotes ll. 6-14 from the second of the sonnets printed by
Walton (above, p. 97).]

That last line expresses his whole poetic faith and method;
for him beauty always lies, and is achieved, in discovery;
it is to be sought where you would not expect to find it,
and wrought of unwilling materials.

[Quotes 'Jordan' (II), ll. 7-18.]

Here he describes his own method and also criticizes it;
he longs for a sweetness ready penned, but will not pretend
to it when he has not achieved it. Beauty ought to take
the pen and write for him; but he must train himself to be
her servant and must not find her where she is not. So behind his piety, or pietism, there is always the artist's
problem and the artist's labours, though he does not believe in art for art's sake. He would do all things for
the glory of God; but he sees that it is not only duty but
also beauty, and beauty made more exact and profound by
duty.

Herbert is not one of those poets who lose themselves in
the richness of the external world or can satisfy themselves in expressing it. The external throws him back into himself, and then his thoughts turn outwards for confirmation. Beauty troubles him with his own inadequacy,
and to escape from that he seeks again for beauty. He is,
in the language of modern psychology, both introvert and
extrovert, yet never an egotist. For his problem is always
universal, the problem not of himself and his own salvation
but of all mankind; and in the poems that express his most
intensive experience we recognize our own, heightened and
elucidated, though the terms of his expression may not be

what we should choose.

> How should I praise thee, Lord. How should my rymes
>   Gladly engrave thy love in steel,
> If what my soul does feel sometimes,
>   My soul might ever feel!
>
> Although there were some fourtie heavens, or more,
>   Sometimes I peer above them all;
> Sometimes I hardly reach a score,
>   Sometimes to hell I fall.
>
> ['The Temper' (I), ll. 1-8]

That expresses all the insecurity, not merely of human joy,
but of human incapacity. 'We live in a world where too
much is required,' and Herbert consents to this tax upon
the spirit, and justifies it in words that are convincing
in their beauty:

> Yet take thy way, for sure thy way is best
>   Stretch or contract me thy poore debter.
> This is but tuning of my breast,
>   To make the music better.
>
> [Ibid., ll. 21-4]

Still more intimate and close to actual experience is 'The
Flower,' with that famous verse which seems written for
every man who tries to live the life of the spirit:-

> And now in age I bud again,
> After so many deaths I live and write;
>   I once more smell the dew and rain,
> And relish versing. O my onely light,
>   It cannot be
>   That I am he
> On whom thy tempests fell all night.
>
> [ll. 36-42]

   Herbert's poems are the autobiography of a mind with a
rich and difficult content. He himself says as much;
though he may call himself a sinner, he has not the 'umble-
ness of Uriah Heep, (2) but seems to take a pride in the
diversity of his unregenerate experience. He is a sinner
worth saving - one who knows the worth of what he
renounces:

I know the ways of pleasure, the sweet strains,
    The lullings and the relishes of it;
The propositions of hot blood and brains;
    What mirth and music mean; what love and wit
Have done these twentie hundred years and more;
    I know the projects of unbridled store;
My stuffe is flesh, not brasse; my senses live,
And grumble oft that they have more in me
    Than he that curbs them, being but one to five;
        Yet I love Thee.
                                        ['The Pearl', ll. 21-30]

Here he shows himself one of the cleverest of poets, as
clever as Browning; with all the arts of prose, yet with
the momentum and controlling power of poetry. It is a mis-
fortune that he should be known mainly by a few simple lyrics and outrageous quaintnesses, as if he were half a
child and half a pedant. The phrase 'Quaint old Herbert'
misdescribes him completely. He was always young, and his
thought is less old-fashioned than that of most poets of
the eighteenth or even the nineteenth century. What seems
old-fashioned to us is the disregard of poetic usage, the
homeliness which he never tries to avoid, because poetry
for him is in the subject-matter and the effort to express
it, not in select words or images. He will say what he has
to say by whatever means he can find, and he seldom fails
to say it. He may surprise us, but, unless we are conventionally fastidious, we enjoy the surprise; for often beyond it there is beauty, the more delightful for the unexpected means by which it is achieved. Few poets are so
continually interesting, for in few do we so often recognize truth. If Herbert were a painter, we should say that
he could draw; there is nothing in his verse evaded or
left vague; he gives us a good likeness of experience,
and is a master of circumstance, never mastered by it.
Details are there full and exact, but controlled by the
purpose and theme; indeed, few poets have such cumulative power or such a command of real form. The prose virtues are his but in subordination; he will not lose them
in music, but his music persists through them, often difficult to grasp, sometimes harsh and laboured, but always
serious, and at any moment likely to surge up in divine
sweetness. It is never safe to reject a poem of Herbert's
as a failure; the failure may be in you, and with another
attempt you may discover a secret beauty which seems all
the more beautiful for having lain hid so long. This Mr.
Palmer knows by long intimacy with his favourite poet,
and his edition should help others to the same intimacy.

Notes

1 Alexander Grosart (as above, p. 28).
2 In Dickens's 'David Copperfield'.

71. HERBERT J.C. GRIERSON, FROM HIS INTRODUCTION TO
'METAPHYSICAL LYRICS AND POEMS OF THE SEVENTEENTH
CENTURY'

1921

The successor to George Saintsbury in the Chair of Rhetoric
and Belles Lettres at the University of Edinburgh, Grierson
was instrumental in the revival of Donne, capitally through
his edition of Donne's poetry in 1912. Donne, indeed, became the norm; and when other poets were judged in the
light of his performance - as Herbert was judged in the ensuing extract - they were invariably found wanting. Grierson was much too discriminating a scholar to be hostile to
Herbert; but his reserve is unmistakable. See also above,
p. 33.
    Source: Grierson, from the introduction to his edition
of 'Metaphysical Lyrics and Poems of the Seventeeth Century: Donne to Butler' (Oxford, 1921), pp. xl-xliv.

The poet in whom the English Church of Hooker and Laud, the
Church of the *via media* in doctrine and ritual, found a
voice of its own, was George Herbert, the son of Donne's
friend Magdalen Herbert, and the younger brother of Lord
Herbert of Cherbury. His volume 'The Temple, Sacred Poems
and Private Ejaculations, By Mr. George Herbert,' was
printed at Cambridge in the year that a disorderly collection of the amorous, satirical, courtly and pious poems of
the famous Dean of St. Paul's, who died in 1631, was shot
from the press in London as 'Poems, by J.D., with Elegies
on the Author's Death.' As J.D. the author continued to
figure on the title-page of each successive edition till
that of 1669; nor were the additions made from time to
time of a kind to diminish the complex, ambiguous impression which the volume must have produced on the minds of
the admirers of the ascetic and eloquent Dean. There is
no such record of a complex character and troubled progress
in the poetry of Herbert. It was not, indeed, altogether
without a struggle that Herbert bowed his neck to the

collar, abandoned the ambitions and vanities of youth to
become the pious rector of Bemerton. He knew, like Donne,
in what light the ministry was regarded by the young courtiers whose days were spent

> In dressing, mistressing and compliment.
>
> ['The Church-porch', 1. 80]

His ambitions had been courtly. He loved fine clothes. As
Orator at Cambridge he showed himself an adept in learned
and elegant flattery, and he hoped 'that, as his predecessors, he might in time attain the place of a Secretary of
State'. When he resolved, after the death of 'his most
obliging and powerful friends', to take Orders, he 'did
acquaint a court-friend' with his resolution, 'who persuaded him to alter it, as too mean an employment, and too
much below his birth, and the excellent abilities and endowments of his mind'. All this is clearly enough reflected in Herbert's poems, and I have endeavoured in my selection (1) to emphasize the note of conflict, of personal experience, which troubles and gives life to poetry that
might otherwise be too entirely doctrinal and didactic.
But there is no evidence in Herbert's most agitated verses
of the deeper scars, the profounder remorse which gives
such a passionate, anguished *timbre* to the harsh but resonant harmonies of his older friend's 'Divine Poems':

> Despair behind, and death before doth cast
> Such terror, and my feeble flesh doth waste
> By sin in it, which it t'wards hell doth weigh.

Herbert knows the feeling of alienation from God; but he
knows also that of reconciliation, the joy and peace of
religion:

> You must sit down, says Love, and taste my meat;
>   So I did sit and eat.
>
> ('Love' (III), 11. 17-18]

Herbert is too in full harmony with the Church of his country, could say, with Sir Thomas Browne, 'There is no Church
whose every part so squares unto my Conscience; whose
Articles, Constitutions and Customs, seem so constant unto
reason, and as it were framed to my particular Devotion, as
this whereof I hold my Belief, the Church of England':

[Quotes 'The British Church', 11. 5-9, 25-30.]

It was from Donne that Herbert learned the 'metaphysical'

manner. He has none of Donne's daring applications of
scholastic doctrines. Herbert's interest in theology is
not metaphysical but practical and devotional, the doctrines of his Church - the Incarnation, Passion, Resurrection, Trinity, Baptism - as these are reflected in the
festivals, fabric, and order of the Church and are capable
of appeal to the heart. But Herbert's central theme is
the psychology of his religious experiences. He transferred
to religious poetry the subtler analysis and record of
moods which had been Donne's great contribution to love
poetry. The metaphysical taste in conceit, too, ingenious,
erudite, and indiscriminate, not confining itself to the
conventionally picturesque and poetic, appealed to his
acute, if not profound mind, and to the Christian temper
which rejected nothing as common and unclean. He would
speak of sacred things in the simplest language and with
the aid of the homeliest comparisons:

> Both heav'n and earth
> Paid me my wages in a world of mirth.
> > ['Affliction' (I), ll. 11-12]

Prayer is:

> Heaven in ordinary, man well drest,
> The milky way, the bird of Paradise.
> > ['Prayer' (I), ll. 11-12]

Divine grace in the Sacramental Elements:

> Knoweth the ready way,
> And hath the privy key
> Op'ning the soul's most subtle rooms;
> While those, to spirits refin'd, at door attend
> Dispatches from their friend.
> > ['The H. Communion', ll. 20-4]

Night is God's 'ebony box' in which:

> Thou dost inclose us till the day
> Put our amendment in our way,
> And give new wheels to our disorder'd clocks.
> > ['Even-song', ll. 22-4]

> Christ left his grave-clothes that we might, when grief
> Draws tears or blood, not want an handkerchief.
> > ['Dawning', ll. 15-16]

These are the 'mean' similies which in Dr. Johnson's

view were fatal to poetic effect even in Shakespeare. We
have learned not to be so fastidious, yet when they are not
purified by the passionate heat of the poet's dramatic imagination the effect is a little stuffy, for the analogies
and symbols are more fanciful or traditional than natural
and imaginative. Herbert's nature is generally 'metaphysical', - 'the busy orange-tree', the rose that purges,
the 'sweet spring' which is 'a box where sweets compacted
lie'. It is at rare moments that feeling and natural image
are imaginatively and completely merged in one another:

> And now in age I bud again,
> After so many deaths I live and write;
> I once more smell the dew and rain,
> And relish versing: O my only light,
> It cannot be
> That I am he
> On whom thy tempests fell all night.
>
> ['The Flower', ll. 36-42]

But if not a greatly imaginative, Herbert is a sincere and
sensitive poet, and an accomplished artist elaborating his
argumentative strain or little allegories and conceits with
felicitous completeness, and managing his variously patterned stanzas - even the symbolic wings and altars and
priestly bells, the three or seven-lined stanzas of his
poems on the Trinity and Sunday - with a finished and delicate harmony. 'The Temple' breathes the spirit of the
Anglican Church at its best, primitive and modest: and
also of one troubled and delicate soul seeking and finding
peace.

Note

1 Grierson reprints thirteen poems: 'Redemption', 'Easter-
   wings', 'Affliction' (I), 'Jordan' (I), 'The Church-
   floore', 'The Windows', 'Vertue', 'Life', 'Jesu', 'The
   Collar', 'Aaron', 'Discipline', and 'Love' (III).

72. T.S. ELIOT, GEORGE HERBERT, IN THE 'SPECTATOR'

1932

Eliot's celebrated essay on The Metaphysical Poets (1921),

occasioned by Grierson's edition of 'Metaphysical Lyrics
and Poems' (see No. 71), adhered to the latter's circumscribed response to Herbert. But eleven years later, within the framework of the series Studies in Sanctity published in the 'Spectator', Eliot publicly confirmed his
drastically changed outlook. The ensuing essay, it should
be noted, was to lead to his longer performance in 'George
Herbert' (Writers and their Work, 1962), the only sustained
account of any of the 'metaphysical' poets ever written by
Eliot. See further above, p. 33.
    Source: T.S. Eliot, George Herbert, 'Spectator',
CXLVIII (12 March 1932), pp. 360-1; reprinted from 'Spectator's Gallery: Essays, Sketches, Short Stories & Poems
from "The Spectator" 1932', ed. Peter Fleming and Derek
Verschoyle (1933), pp. 276-80.

In 'The Oxford Book of English Verse,' (1) George Herbert
is allotted five pages, the same number as Bishop King and
many less than Robert Herrick. This does I imagine, gauge
pretty accurately the measure of Herbert's reputation: he
is known as the author of a few fine devotional poems suitable for anthologies, which serve to illustrate his debt to
Donne; and his figure is preserved, chiefly by Walton's
Life, as one of genuine though rather conventional piety.
For poetic range he is compared unfavourably with Donne,
and for religious intensity he is compared unfavourably
with Crashaw. This latter opinion, it may be suspected, is
supported by those who choose to take a view of the Church
of England into which a very temperate and 'reasonable'
kind of personal devoutness will best fit. The author of
the Introduction to the little World's Classic edition seems
to me representative of this attitude. 'The strength and
support of that branch of the Catholic Church militant in
our own country,' he says, 'has always lain upon the middle
way; it has never been her method either to "waste in passionate dreams" or to protest overmuch with the voices of
prophecy or denunciation.' But he adds, with true British
tolerance, 'to say this is not to presume to depreciate the
excellence of those kinds of enthusiasm which are congeni-
tally foreign to the English character.' He completes his
picture of the Church of England in the spirit of Tenny-
sonian pastoral: 'There, as the cattle wind homeward in
the evening light, the benign, whitehaired parson stands at
his gate to greet the cowherd, and the village chime calls
the labourers to evensong.' (2)
    In our time such a happy picture of a social fabric of
moderate and complacent piety - a picture which at once
idealizes society and travesties the Church - may provoke

a smile; yet it does represent the false setting in which
we still place the figure of George Herbert. We know but
little of his life, it is true; but what we do know, and
the very much more that we know about his period, concur to
demonstrate the falsity. Whatever Herbert was, he was not
the prototype of the clergyman of Dickens' Christmas at
Dingley Dell. Walton's portrait is certainly formalized
and starched, but probably true so far as it goes; sug-
gesting as it does, that he was not himself imaginative or
spiritually minded enough to appreciate, though he could
respect.

Of all the 'metaphysical' poets, Herbert has suffered
the most from being read only in anthologies. Even in
Professor Grierson's admirable specialized anthology of
metaphysical verse, he is at a disadvantage compared with
several writers of less importance. The usual option, I
believe, is as I have already said in other words, that we
go to Donne for poetry and to Crashaw for religious poetry:
but that Herbert deserves to be remembered as the representative lyrist of a mild and tepid church.

Yet, when we take Herbert's collected poems and read in-
dustriously through the volume we cannot help being aston-
ished both at the considerable number of pieces which are
as fine as those in any anthology, and at what we may call
the spiritual stamina of the work. Throughout there is
brain work, and a very high level of intensity; his poetry
is definitely an *oeuvre,* to be studied entire. And our
gradual appreciation of the poetry gives us a new impression of the man.

All poetry is difficult, almost impossible, to write:
and one of the great permanent causes of error in writing
poetry is the difficulty of distinguishing between what one
really feels and what one would like to feel, and between
the moments of genuine feeling and the moments of falsity.
There is a danger in all poetry: but it is a peculiarly
grave danger in the writing of devotional verse. Above
that level of attainment of the spiritual life, below which
there is no desire to write religious verse, it becomes extremely difficult not to confuse accomplishment with intention, a condition at which one merely aims with the condition in which one actually lives, what one would be with
what one is: and verse which represents only good intentions is worthless - on that plane, indeed, a betrayal.
The greater the elevation, the finer becomes the difference
between sincerity and insincerity, between the reality and
the unattained aspiration.

And in this George Herbert seems to me to be as secure,
as habitually sure, as any poet who has written in English.
With the religious verse of Donne, as with that of Milton,

one is aware of a prodigious mastery of the language employed upon religious subjects; with that of Crashaw, of a
passionate fancy and a metrical ability which might also
have employed themselves upon other than religious themes;
and even with Gerard Hopkins, I find myself wondering
whether there is an essential relation between his contribution to poetry and his religious vocation. Of George
Herbert, as of St. John of the Cross, I feel that no lower
theme could have evoked his genius. This, no doubt, sounds
like excessive praise; but I am not for a moment comparing
the accomplishment of Herbert with that of the Spaniard.
I am only putting forward the suggestion that it is very
rare to find a poet of whom one may say, that his poetic
gift would have remained dormant or unfulfilled but for his
religious vocation. Crashaw (or so I believe) had he remained in the world, might still have been the great poet
that he is; Herbert, had he remained in the world, would
(I think) at most have produced a few elegant anthology
pieces like those of Herbert of Cherbury. But you will not
get much satisfaction from George Herbert unless you can
take seriously the things which he took seriously himself
and which made him what he was.

   That age of violent religious dissensions, a time in
which even the most retired clergyman might find himself
called upon to suffer extremely for his faith, was an age
of strong passions, including religious passions; in which
those who, like the Herbert family, had the best opportunity
of enjoying the pleasures and glories of this world were
also sometimes the most aware of the other. Of all devotional poets, certainly of all Anglican poets, George Herbert
seems nearest in feeling to Christina Rossetti – who indeed,
in a humble way, found herself obliged to make as great,
and perhaps a greater, sacrifice of this world than did
Herbert. But a certain resemblance of temperament immediately suggests also profound differences. Christina's religious verse suffers, when we read much of it together,
from a monotony due to a narrower range of emotion and an
inferior intellectual gift. Herbert is an anatomist of
feeling and a trained theologian too; his mind is working
continually both on the mysteries of faith and the motives
of the heart.

   I know the ways of Learning; both the head
   And pipes that feed the press, and make it run....

   I know the ways of Honour, what maintains
   The quick returns of courtesy and wit....

I know the ways of Pleasure, the sweet strains,
The lullings and the relishings of it;
The propositions of hot blood and brains....
                    ['The Pearl', ll. 1-2, 11-12, 21-3]

He knew all these various motions far better than Christina
Rossetti did; and his poetry expresses the slow, sometimes
almost despairing and always agonizing toil of the proud
and passionate man of the world towards spiritual life; a
toil and agony which must always be the same, for the similar temperament, to the end of the world. I never feel
that the great Dean of St. Paul's, with his mastery of the
spoken word, his success and applause to the end, quite
conquered his natural pride of mind; Herbert, the vicar of
Bemerton, in his shorter life went much farther on the road
of humility.

Notes

1 Edited by Arthur Quiller-Couch (1919).
2 Arthur Waugh, Introduction to 'The Poems of George
   Herbert' (1907), pp. v, vi.

73. BASIL DE SELINCOURT, GEORGE HERBERT, IN 'THE TIMES
LITERARY SUPPLEMENT'

1933

───

Of the several essays published in 1933 apropos the tercentenary of Herbert's death and the initial appearance of
'The Temple', only the ensuing one by Basil de Selincourt
merits one's attention now. An energetically articulated
essay, it is especially noteworthy because of its recognition of Herbert's 'precision', 'technical playfulness',
and 'magical surprises'.
   Source: George Herbert, 'The Times Literary Supplement', XXXII (2 March 1933), 133-4. Initially published
anonymously; de Selincourt's authorship is now acknowledged for the first time.

───

George Herbert suffers as a poet from having been too
easily and too simply beatified. A few of his lyrics, being in the popular anthologies, are known to every one;

they are not the most representative; his work when read
through is more often read devotionally than poetically;
and his life, like his work, is generally believed to exemplify the solemn-sweet moderation of the English Church, in
its settled atmosphere of rustic benevolence. We associate
him with the comfortable quiet tower among the trees,
beautiful in its retirement, an established home of peace
and piety. Izaak Walton, at the close of a Life which, for
all its melodious grace and charm, is almost obsequious in
its attitude of spiritual adulation, reinforces the sweet
picture when he narrates how, on the Sunday before his
death, Herbert called for his lute and, having tuned it,
played and sung:-

>   The Sundaies of man's life
>   Thredded together on time's string,
>   Make bracelets to adorn the wife
>   Of the eternall glorious King.
>
>   ['Sunday', ll. 29-34]

a verse in which simplicity and innocence appear to take
hands in Blake-like meekness and put on ingenuity as a
crown. These lines are certainly in 'The Temple'; but
perhaps 'The Temple' would have found more, and more
assiduous, readers if they had not been accidently brought
into unmerited prominence. Not but what the accident may
have been of Herbert's making. He was truly saintly, but
he also cultivated saintliness, and may have comforted himself in his last hours with this pious conventionality.
    In his substance, however, he is anything but a con-
ventionalist; there is not one of our poets whose style
is less easy-going, whose sweetness is less mild. Herbert
is unsurpassed for the fineness of his temper:-

> How should I praise thee, Lord, how should my rymes
>   Gladly engrave thy love in steel -
>   ['Temper' (I)', ll. 1-2]

That was his wish; and it is his achievement. His inspiration is a disciplined and disciplinary energy:-

> He that is weary, let him sit.
>   My soul would stirre
> And trade in courtesies and wit,
>   Quitting the furre
> To cold complexions needing it.
>   ['Employment' (II), ll. 1-5]

That is a recurring note. He finds the chief fault of the

England of his time (and in his time the Bible was translated and Shakespeare, Raleigh, Drake were not far off) to
be sloth, wool-gathering; the English have, above all, no
education. 'England,' says he,

> Thy Gentrie bleats, as if thy native cloth
> Transfus'd a sheepishnesse into thy storie -
> > ['The Church-porch', ll. 93-4]

When he writes the character of the honest man he lifts
morality, as Kant and Wordsworth were afterwards to do, to
kindred sublimity with Nature in her greatest manifes-
tations of uniformity and power - so passionate is his insistence on an inflexible constancy:-

> When the day is done,
> His goodnesse sets not, but in dark can runne:
> > The sunne to others writeth laws
> And is their vertue; Vertue is his Sunne.
> > ['Constancie', ll. 22-5]

Till, finally, in that lyric of exemplary beauty:-

> Sweet day, so cool, so calm, so bright
> The bridal of the earth and skie,

there is still an emphasis, so quietly given that there is
a risk it may escape us, on the distinction between tempered and untempered sweetness, and upon the achievement
of virtue:-

> Only the sweet and vertuous soul
> Like season'd timber *never gives.*
> > ['Vertue', ll. 1-2, 13-14]

Herbert's insistence on energy had a double motive. He
was physically frail; and yet he was a man of singular intellectual power and strong worldly ambition. While still
a schoolboy at Westminster he had plunged into the ecclesiastical controversies of the day and in a resounding Latin
poem of fifty sapphic stanzas attacked the leading exponent of Scottish Puritanism. (1) When later he became
Public Orator at Cambridge he valued the post because it
enabled him, not to bring Cambridge before the world, but
to be of the world though still at Cambridge. This Walton
himself allows. Narrating, first, how he had received
from the King a valuable *Sine Cure,* formerly given by
Elizabeth to her favourite Sir Philip Sidney, he goes on:-

> With this and his Annuity, and the advantage of his
> Colledge and of his Oratorship, he enjoyed his gentile
> humour and cloaths and Courtlike company, and seldom
> look'd towards Cambridge unless the King were there,
> but then he never fail'd -
>
> [above, p. 101]

Briefly, his life, up to the age of thirty-four, though
founded in high scholarly attainment and limited by the
professional religious celibacy required of a Fellow of a
college, was spent in strenuous and calculated endeavour
to achieve political and worldly distinction. As a member
of one of the most ancient and honourable families in the
realm he had every reason to believe that his qualifications would be recognized; and his religious convictions, however fostered by his mother, did not weigh
further with him than to provoke the desire for a compro-
mise between piety and ambition. In his own words:-

> Such starres I counted mine: both heaven and earth
> Payd me my wages in a world of mirth.
>
> ['Affliction' (I), ll. 11-12]

When, at last, after his marriage in 1628, he was offered
the incumbency of Fulston and Bemerton (and Bemerton, says
Walton, 'is but a Chappel of ease'), he was already in re-
ceipt of the income of two other ecclesiastical benefies,
yet hesitated to commit himself to the priesthood, because
it involved the final renunciation of his hopes. He had,
indeed, never been ordained; and was so far from imper-
sonating the normal kindly and accommodating village parson, that, one may fairly say, to accept the life was, in
his estimation, to put on sackcloth. And he had hardly
put it on when he realized that he must prepare himself
for the swift decay and early extinction of his powers.
He had been menaced with consumption from the beginning;
the collapse of his political prospects at the death of
James I had produced in him a physical prostration from
which it took him a year to recover; nor did his marriage
re-establish him. So when, four or five months later, he
took up duty at Bemerton, the ardours of his mind converged
and seized upon the attainment of a pure spiritual excellence; to be pursued not in the atmosphere of peaceful
mildness commonly associated with his name, but by way of
a stern, even a bitter, renunciation.
    The three years of his cure at Bemerton were, in fact,
not representative but critical years. Like that of his
more spectacular contemporary Donne, Herbert's admission
to the Church was a surrender: a surrender of the world

rather than of the flesh; and if more thoroughly, perhaps
more easily accomplished. For if Herbert has a fault, it
is that he is a little dry, a little too ready for the
ascetic rigour. His marriage was decked out by Walton in
fantastically romantic colours; but in the whole of 'The
Temple' there is hardly a line that reveals the human
lover or husband.

Even the lusts and passions are somewhat conventional
figures; and although we are told more than once that his
youth was fierce, and that he knows the 'propositions of
hot blood and brains,' we feel that those propositions were
very summarily dealt with. Vice, moreover, is sometimes
relegated with so broad a brush, that one is inclined to
wonder if anything is left for virtue or for praise.

> Farewell sweet phrases, lovely metaphors,
> But will ye leave me thus? when ye before
> Of stews and brothels onely knew the doors,
> Then did I wash you with my tears, and more
>   Brought you to Church well-drest....
> ['The Forerunners', 11. 13-17]

English poetry, if not all divine before 'The Temple,' was
certainly not all dissolute; the normal sobriety and justice of Herbert's diction makes the exaggeration specially
unpleasing. Certainly he too often treats the poetry of
the religious life as if it were essentially opposed to the
poetry of common human interests. The Son of Man, we hear
in the Gospel, came eating and drinking. Herbert's emphasis is hardly ever on his life: 'Have ye not heard,' he
repeats to us continually, 'that my Lord Jesus died?'

'The Temple' is generally regarded as the work of his
last three years alone. No doubt, as a whole, or so far
as it is a whole, it was so. But, for its individual numbers, he must have drawn largely on the work of earlier
years; for high and consistent technical achievement is
not compassed in a day. It had always been a part of Herbert's ambition to consecrate his poetical gift; he accepted and emphasized the distinction current in his day
between the sacred and the profane in poetry; but his
character was from the first too closely knit to allow in
his own work the kind of cleavage we see in the writings
of Herrick or even of Donne. Donne influenced him powerfully, as a man possessed of such a wealth of music and
imagination could not fail to do. But an equal and a
countervailing influence was his long apprenticeship in the
classics. A boyhood, youth and manhood spent in the composition of Greek and Latin verse, and in the study of
writers in whom beauty and economy of speech were always

closely allied, could not go for nothing; the boisterous
effluence of self-confident Elizabethanism must often have
shocked his scrupulous and discriminating sense. His bent
is all towards precision and the close-packing of the
thought. And as his experience develops, he realizes increasingly that the more we love Truth the less inclined
we are to obscure or decorate her features. So in the end
religious poetry, which he first envisages as a mere trans-
ference of favour, as if one placed the wreath on Christ's
head instead of on a lady's table, evokes in his mind an
ideal of essential truth of expression and reveals to him
the ultimate problem of all poetry - the purification together of the passionate feeling and the passionate word:-

> When first my lines of heav'nly joyes made mention,
> Such was their lustre, they did so excell,
> That I sought out quaint words and trim invention:
> My thoughts began to burnish, sprout, and swell,
> Curling with metaphors a plain intention,
> Decking the sense as if it were to sell....
>
> As flames do work and winde when they ascend,
> So did I weave my self into the sense;
> But when I bustled I might heare a friend
> Whisper, 'How wide is all this long pretence.
> There is in love a sweetnesse readie penn'd;
> Copie out onely that, and save expense.'
>
> ['Jordan' (II), ll. 1-6, 13-18]

Of course the bulk of 'The Temple' is not, and does not
aim at being *poésie pure*. In one of its purest moments
Herbert, describing his own artistic activity, relegates it
as happy craftsmanship:-

> And now in age I bud again,
> After so many deaths I live and write;
> I once more smell the dew and rain
> And *relish versing*:
>
> ['The Flower', ll. 36-9]

reminding us even in his ecstasy of the sober exordium:-

> Hearken unto a Verser, who may chance
> Ryme thee to good;
>
> ['The Church-porch', ll. 3-4]

His work is largely, perhaps predominantly, versified description, admonition, exhortation. Of course, too, he
suffers to some extent as a religious poet from the very

fact that the outlines of religious belief in his time were
too limited and clear. There was no doubt, or only the
first vestige of doubt, even in minds enlightened as his
was, that the earth was made for man, and that earth and
man were centres of creation. His long poem 'Providence'
is of child-like literalness in its ingenuous assurance of
a universal disposal of nature to the service of mankind.
God, we are even told, sometimes forsakes uniformity, lest
men should think him uninventive:

> To show thou are not bound, as if thy lot
> Were worse then ours, sometimes thou shiftest hands;
> Most things move th'under-jaw, the Crocodile not;
> Most things sleep lying, th'Elephant leans or stands.
> [ll. 137-40]

All this, all thinking of which such thought as this is the
extreme example, naturally predisposed the Christian not
merely to repose in, but to emphasize, the uniqueness and
finality of the Christian revelation; and whether or no
such finality is of value for religion, there can be no
doubt that it depresses poetry, because vision cannot be
vicarious, and poetry cannot have a double function simul-
taneously; in the last resort it is either vision or interpretation, it cannot be both. With Herbert it was
mainly interpretative, the sermon in verse; and his more
specifically poetical movements are incidental to that
large purpose, or arise within him either out of his soul's
conflict as he strives to adapt himself to the position he
believes assigned to him in the great dispensation, or in
those moments of peace when he achieves harmony with it.
He himself defines the quality of the inspiration he seeks
in 'The Quidditie,' a little piece which, with its quaint
and copious negatives, reveals in its course the confinement or uneasiness which it denies in its conclusion:

> My God, a verse is not a crown,
> No point of honour, or gay suit,
> No hawk, or banquet, or renown,
> Nor a good sword, nor yet a lute....
>
> It is no office, art or news,
> Nor the Exchange, or busie Hall;
> But it is that which while I use
> I am with thee, and MOST TAKE ALL.
> [ll. 1-4, 9-12]

There, indeed, is the esssence of poetry for all poets;
but few of them have found, in practice, that they 'most

take all' by excluding the crown, or the lute, or even the
office and the busie hall; and of course Herbert himself,
when he achieves his end, overflows all these exclusions.

'The Temple,' one must admit, is a difficult work to
read, and this not only because the economy of its style
has a certain angularity, turning many a sentence and even
many a poem into a riddle (what, for instance, is the
meaning of

> The grosser world stands to thy word and art,
> ['The Temper' (II), 1. 5]

or of

> Man and the present fit; if he provide
>   He breaks the square?)
> ['The Discharge', 11. 31-2]

but also because it seems to promise a unity, or at least
a progression, which is never realized. At first we think
we are to be taken round the church, with appropriate meditations; but soon we realize that the round we are following is that of the Christian Year, beginning with and returning to Good Friday. Parallel references to the religious experience of the individual are clearly indicated
at the start; and one imagines that Herbert had in his
mind to achieve construction on a triple principle - to
build the church and the soul together and to set both in
a frame of revolving seasons, a calendar of holy days. But
soon the calendar is the only recognizable thread, and even
this disappears before the middle of the collection is
reached. The rest is frankly kaleidoscopic, a litter of
stained glass, in fragments of the first lustre, but pat-
ternless, or at best occasionally paired. Toys and fancies
jostle in the box against intimate and impassioned plead-
ings and confessions; the artifice is sometimes trans-
parent, sometimes subtly concealed. Such changes and re-
liefs may serve to hold the attention, if any principle is
at work. But in this medley no sequence is obtained, and
the very perfection of the pieces isolates them.

Yet, if such inconsequence at first perplexes the
reader, in the end it sets him free. He turns the pages
forward and backward, sipping where he will; recognizing
by degrees that he is in the presence of an artist who delights in the curious limitations of his instrument, since
by their means he can throw into relief the transcendence
of his theme. Naturally the greater moments only come to
the hand that knows every degree of preparation for them

and therefore the bulk of the work exhibits these trials
and approaches, these playful solemn preludes in the porch
or precincts of the temple. And here Herbert's long literary apprenticeship and all his courtly accomplishment
stand him in good stead. He has

>   the pliant mind, whose gentle measure
>   Complies and suits with all estates.
>
> ['Content', ll. 13-14]

He has bidden the world good-bye, but his imagination still
moves as easily in any and every society as once his person
did. He is the gentleman saint of English history, never
discountenanced, never at a loss. He anticipates La Fontaine with the fable in verse, and, though he uses more
exacting and more restricted measures, can be no less agile
in his turns, no less vivid in his impersonations:

>   Meeting with Time, 'Slack thing,' said I,
>   'Thy sithe is dull, whet it, for shame!'
>
> ['Time', ll. 1-2]

Before Bunyan, he writes a Pilgrim's Progress:

>   The gloomy cave of Desperation
>   I left on th'one, and on the other side
>   The rock of Pride.
>
> ['The Pilgrimage', ll. 4-6]

putting the pith of the thing in six stanzas, 'loading
every rift with ore.' Who can fail to admire the excellent
moderation and practical good sense with which he presents
the rule of life and the recommendations of religion to
common readers? His professed object is to make religion
attractive and catch the pleasure-lover with a verse; to
realize that extraneous motive he deploys all his art, developing a kind of technical playfulness which is both a
decoy for his audience and a diversion and solace for himself. So at one time he will cajole the reader, here with
an anagram, there with a puzzle-piece; at another he will
cajole his divine Friend and Master, incidentally revealing
thereby that his dedication is unreserved. Thus it comes
about that the tenderest thought is often conveyed by
childlike artifice, as in 'Gratefulnesse':-

>   Thou that has giv'n so much to me,
>   Give one thing more, a grateful heart;
>   *See how thy beggar works on thee*
>   *By art.*
>
> [ll. 1-4]

Or in that lyric 'Deniall,' in which the broken verse conveys the image of a heart broken by grief, to be mended at
last with the mending of the rhyme. For precision of touch
and resourcefulness of lyrical invention he resembles and
surpasses Robert Bridges, whose happy coolness and crisp-
ness he often recalls:-

      Ah my dear angrie Lord,
          Since thou dost love, yet strike:
      Cast down, yet help afford;
          Sure I will do the like.

      I will complain, yet praise;
          I will bewail, approve;
      And all my sowre-sweet dayes,
          I will lament, and love.

                                      ['Bitter-sweet']

Herbert, of course, like Bridges, was an accomplished ama-
teur musician; he handles words with musicianly severity,
with harmonious balance and compactness, with musical implications and returns. The strictness and straightness
of his diction may well conceal its power from unaccustomed
readers, to whom the idiom is strange; one must, as it
were, acknowledge his convention, and share his chains,
before one can appreciate his freedom. Yet certain passages of extreme felicity will serve to suggest the range
of his resources. Chaucer, if he had wished to put
'Worldliness' in his procession of pilgrims on the road to
Canterbury could not have bettered:-

      Then came brave Glorie puffing by
          In silks that whistled, who but he!
      He scarce allowed me half an eie....
                                    ['The Quip', ll. 13-15]

It is a symptom of exceptional command, both of thought and
form, to avail oneself as freely as Herbert does of the
spoken idiom. Was he the inventor of

      Wouldst thou both eat thy cake and have it?
                                      ['The Size', l. 18]

If not, he invented a hundred other colloquial pictures
just as good: it is his vein.

>   To Thee help appertains:
>   Hast thou left all things to their course,
>   And *laid the reins*
>   *Upon the horse*?
>
>   ['Longing', ll. 43-6]

or, again:-

>   God chains the dog till night: wilt loose they chain
>   And wake thy sorrow?
>   ['The Discharge', ll. 46-7]

He can use the simplest words, too, with inventive or creative adaptation to thought and design, with a Shakespearian
sense for the fluidity and malleability of language; as in
'The Glance,' where he first describes how, when Christ
looked upon him 'in the midst of youth and night,' at once
'a sugred strange delight' 'bedewed' and 'embalmed' his
spirit, and so goes on to reflect:-

>   If thy first glance so powerful be....
>   What wonders shall we feel when we shall see
>   Thy full-ey'd love!
>   When thou shalt *look us out of pain*....
>   [ll. 17-20]

'The Temple' is full of magical surprises of this kind;
it is difficult to leave off quoting. Language more triumphant can scarcely be imagined than in these culminating
lines of 'Confession':-

>   I challenge here the brightest day,
>   The clearest diamond; let them do their best,
>   *They shall be thick and cloudie to my breast*.
>   [ll. 28-30]

The more attentively we read Herbert the more consistently
he rewards us by the quiet completeness with which every
anticipation the verse arouses is fulfilled both in the
sound and the sense:-

>   For us the windes do blow
>   The earth doth rest, heav'n move, and fountains flow,
>   Nothing we see but means our good,
>   As our *delight*, or as our *treasure*:
>   The whole is, either our cupboard of *food*,
>   Or cabinet of *pleasure*.
>   ['Man', ll. 25-30]

It could not have been said so beautifully, unless it had
been wholly believed; and could it have been wholly believed unless it had been largely true?
But we do not read 'The Temple' to-day because it explains the world to us and justifies Providence. We read
it because, in spite of Herbert's belief that he possessed
an explanation, he passed through the strenuous and ultimate internal struggle which is imposed on every man,
whether religion comes to him as a singular or as a universal mystery. We find in it, that is, not merely his
own personal struggle against worldly ambition, though that
is the theme of at least a dozen pieces, among them some of
the most human and the most endearing; but also, and more
profoundly, faith's essential struggle against fleeting appearance and clouded vision:-

If what my soul doth feel sometimes
    My soul might ever feel!
                    ['The Temper' (I), 11. 3-4]

The main difficulty of the Christian dispensation as Herbert received it was that it was past history. On Whit
Sunday (as on so many other days) his meditation is to the
sorrowful effect that the world's Sun is set:-

Thou shutt'st the doore and keep'st within;
Scarce a good joy creeps through the chink.
                    ['Whitsunday, 11. 21-2]

That difficulty inevitably besets the religious life of
those who found their belief on a historical event. But
the same difficulty reappears and in even more baffling
forms for those who seek an unmeditated vision, an abiding
light. So baffling indeed is it that they may well find
comfort in observing how deeply Herbert was baffled in
spite of his decisive, simple creed:-

Thou tarriest, while I die,
And fall to nothing; thou dost reigne
        And rule on high,
        While I remain
In bitter grief: yet am I stil'd
        Thy childe.
                    ['Longing', 11. 55-60]

His intense preoccupation with the problem often leads him
to forms of expression which transcend the limits of any
single doctrine or tradition:-

> Oh loose this frame, this knot of man untie!
> That my free soul may use her wing.
> Which now is pinion'd with mortalitie,
> As an intangled, hamper'd thing.
>
> ['Home', 11. 61-4]

and because he thus grips the final issue, his release,
when he obtains it, has not only the sweetness and radiance
of a specifically Christian security:-

> Love took my hand, and smiling did reply,
>   'Who made the eyes but I?'
>
> ['Love' (III), 11. 11-12]

it also finds words whose simplicity and timelessness suit
all our creeds and supersede them:-

> Thy power and love, my love and trust
>   Make one place ev'ry where.
>
> ['The Temper' (I), 11. 27-8]

Note

1   'Musae responsoriae ad Andreae Melvini Scoti Anti-Tami-
Cami-Categoriam', first published in Duport's 'Ecclesi-
astes Solomonis' in 1662 (see No. 27);   trans. Mark
McCloskey and Paul R. Murphy, 'The Latin Poetry of
George Herbert' (Athens, Ohio, 1965), pp. 2-61.

74. AUSTIN WARREN, FROM GEORGE HERBERT, IN 'AMERICAN
REVIEW'

1936

_____

By the mid-1930s the tide had turned. For Austin Warren,
certainly, Herbert stood very high indeed - and so, by and
large, he was to stand thereafter (see above, pp. 34-6).
The ensuing extract begins where a preliminary glance at
Herbert's life ends.
    Source: Warren, from George Herbert, in 'Rage for
Order: Essays in Criticism' (Chicago, 1948), pp. 23-4,
25-36; first published in 'American Review,' VII (1936),
249-71.

_____

For Herbert, as for William Law, Anglican saint of the next
century, there were two ways of life, discrete, not reconciled. The world esteems energy, valor, breeding, wit,
self-respect; but, says 'The Country Parson,' 'the two
highest points of life, wherein a Christian is most seen,
are Patience and Mortification.' 'The Pearl' recalls by
its title St. Matthew's merchant who, finding a jewel of
great price, sold all that he had in order to buy. In his
poem, Herbert described what he surrendered - and for
what. The ways of learning, of honor, of pleasure:

[Quotes ll. 31-5.]

   In the pattern of their lives Herbert and Donne offer a
partial parallel. Both had an early devotion to theology;
in both it was stifled by secular ambition; both took
Orders only when their secular ambition proved frustrate.
Yet, like à Becket, who, from being King Henry's merry companion, turned his ecclesiastical judge and foe, both these
courtier poets proved capable of decision; and, having
decided, they did not look back. Their subsequent years of
discipline and devotion demonstrated the sincerity of their
resolves.
   From childhood a dweller in London or Cambridge, Herbert
sought to adapt himself and his use to his rural parish.
At the end of his first sermon - learned and elaborate as
if to show his brilliance - he announced his intention
thereafter to preach plainly and practically. An admiring
friend of Bishop Andrewes, he renounced the ingenious exe-
getical methods of that great preacher together with his
wit, learning, and eloquence; and, finding that simple
people, little heedful of exortations, relish and remember
stories and sayings, he made use of such bait.
   Adages had formed a favorite study with men like
Andrewes and John Selden. 'Jacula Prudentum, or Outland-
ish Proverbs,' first published eight years after Herbert's
death, was undoubtledly used by its compiler in his parish
sermons; and some of these homely maxims may be found in
the poems, especially in 'The Church Porch.' Indeed, this
prelude to 'The Temple' is a cento of aphorisms which,
though assembled into six-line stanzas, might fittingly
have been versified in neoclassical couplets; in a couplet, indeed, each stanza ends. 'The Church Porch' compends
a moral philosophy, classical and popular - such Aristote-
lian and Stoic thoughts as have passed into the treasury of
common sense. By way of humanistic preparation for Christian devotion, Herbert reviews the standards of decency;
like Newman in his portrait of a gentleman, he delineates
the character generally accepted as the highest - at the

level of what the eighteenth century would have called
'natural religion.' Only, Christian humanist that he was,
Herbert does not antithesize 'natural' and supernatural
virtues. There is, of course, a false wisdom of this world
which is, indeed, foolishness with God; but there is also
a wisdom which is sound so far as it goes - a classical
wisdom which revelation does not abolish but completes.
This is the wisdom represented, for the people, in the proverbs of all nations and, for the educated, in the 'Ana-
lects,' the 'Nicomachean Ethics,' and the 'De officiis.'
In the spirit of this wisdom Herbert commends temperance
('drink not the third glass'); the avoidance of smut and
profanity; in the management of money, the mean between
parsimony and prodigality; the proper use of conversation;
and, most centrally and ardently, the virtues of self-
examination, self-control, constancy, integration.

[Quotes 'The Church-porch', ll. 115-20, 139-44.]

In 'The Country Parson,' Herbert urges the preacher to
use examples, especially those drawn from daily life and
the experiences habitual with his parishioners; and he remarks that such illustration is in accord with Holy Scripture, which 'condescends to the naming of a plough, a hatchet, a bushel, leaven, boys piping and dancing - showing
that things of ordinary use are not only to serve in the
way of drudgery, but to be washed and cleansed, and serve
for lights even of heavenly truths.' Again, discoursing
on the Parson's 'completeness' as a parish *person*, able to
cure the simple legal and medical maladies of his neigh-
bors, Herbert recommends the cultivation of herbs, since
these plants will not only prove substitutes for exotic
drugs but will supply the parson himself with metaphors.
This Christ did in order that 'by familiar things he might
make his doctrine slip the more easily into the hearts even
of the meanest' and especially that 'laboring people, whom
he chiefly considered, might have everywhere monuments of
his doctrine; remembering in gardens his mustard-seed and
lilies, in the fields his seed corn and tares.' The servant is not above his master.
    None of Herbert's parish homilies survives. But even
when writing for himself, not for 'laboring people,' he
uses such analogies as they would apprehend. 'The Country
Parson, as soon as he awakes on Sunday, presently falls to
work, and seems to himself so as a marketman is when the
market day comes, or a shopkeeper when customers use to
come in. His thoughts are full of making the best of the
day, and contriving it to his best gains.' In 'The 'Temple,'
too, homely analogies and illustrations prevail.

> Who sweeps a room, as for Thy laws,
> Makes that and th'action fine.

The constant man is he

> Who rides his sure and even trot
> While the world now rides by, now lags behind.

Sunday, Christ set aside for men's spiritual life

> That as each beast his manger knows
> Man might not of his fodder miss.

In God's love, 'more than in bed, I rest.' (1)
   Were Herbert's poems, then, deliberately written for the
unlearned, the 'workers'? Presumably not. 'The Temple' is
Herbert's spiritual autobiography; dying, he left it to
his friend, Nicholas Ferrar, to determine whether it should
appear: 'if he think it may turn to the advantage of any
dejected poor soul, let it be made public; if not, let him
burn it.' But surely 'The Country Parson' provides the
best commentary on 'The Temple.' And, surely, the Christian discipline of his pride may well have led Herbert to
write such poems as might speak to all. What is the meaning of his two poems with the common title, 'Jordan'?
Perhaps he recalled the Syrian Naaman who, bidden by Elisha
to wash in the Jordan and be cleansed of his leprosy, cried
out, affronted, 'Are not Abana and Pharpar, rivers of Dam-
ascus, better than all the waters of Israel?' (2) Fuller
says of Quarles that he 'drank of Jordan instead of Helicon, and slept on Mount Olivet for his Parnassus'; and the
antithesis of rival founts and mounts recurs elsewhere.
The theme of both poems is evident. Though secular verse
may need adornment - nightingales and purling streams, metaphors and invention - not so with sacred poetry: 'Shepherds are honest people; let them sing.' That drinking
of the Jordan was an ascetic practice seems the judgment
of Lord Herbert of Cherbury, who, acknowledging the sanctity of his brother's last years, thinks his English poems
'far short of expressing those perfections he had in the
Greek and Latin tongues.' (3)
   Herbert does not eschew the 'literary' merely in his
metaphors. His diction is that of the English Bible:
habitually, as Coleridge has called it, 'pure, manly, and
unaffected.' (4) His syntax rarely admits inversion or any
other mode of poetic dislocation; his sentence structure
is that of good conversation - though firm, yet supple and
easy.
   From his secular youth Herbert allowed two aesthetic

devotions to survive: his love of music and his love of
order. Music is an audible rehearsal of order. What is a
dissonance but a tone alien to the chordal triad? Harmony
weaves individual voices into the pattern of a society.
Herbert's favorite metaphor, that of tuning the lute, sym-
bolizes the adjustment of strayed strings to the pitch of
the constant, or of all the strings to some objective standard. Since the lute stood in constant need of such attention, it aptly paralleled the unstable nature of man.
Herbert's poems portray, as he said, the 'many spiritual
conflicts that have passed betwixt God and my soul'; but
he identifies the end of religion as the submission of
man's will to God's.

Certain kinds of external order attracted Herbert's temperament: he liked hierarchy in church and state, the prescription of a common liturgy. For his poetry, he devised
intricate stanza patterns; and, having initiated a pattern,
he maintained it throughout the poem. It is Order which
gives

All things their set forms and hours
Makes of wild woods sweet walks and bowers.
['The Familie', ll. 11-12]

Art is the ordering of landscapes and loves. By the obvious kinds of spontaneity Herbert was not tempted.

His conflicts lay deeper. Religion is, in essence, the
reduction to order of the human will. The mark of that
effected order is peace. Wondering how those lowest in
Paradise can lack restless desire, Dante is assured by one
of these spirits that if they desired a higher place, their
wills would be discordant from that of God: *la sua volon-
tate è nostra pace.* (5) Yet more than of poetry, the line
is a touchstone of spiritual direction. False prophets, of
religion as well as of culture, are ever promising some
labor-saving device, some formula for getting rich or
learned without toil, wise or holy without discipline.
Like Fénélon, Herbert never betrays us to such delusion.
He sees human life - its inconstancy (our 'twenty several
selves'), the insatiability of its desires; and, in 'The
Pulley,' he represents God as having endowed man with
beauty, wisdom, honor, pleasure, reserving, as the divine
gift, only peace. To effect this inner order, this submission of his will to God's, Herbert endured those conflicts which the poems re-enact.

Occasionally Herbert seeks to incarnate the theme of a
poem in its very form. 'Denial,' with its five-line pattern, leaves the last line unrhymed until the final stanza,
when the soul, before 'untuned, unstrung,' attains to

unison with God's harmony. In 'Grief,' verses are bidden
to keep their measures for some lover.

> Whose grief allows him music and a rhyme;
> For mine excludes both measure, tune, and time.
>   -Alas, my God.
>
> [11. 17-19]

The rhymeless, truncated last line exemplifies the break-
down. In 'Home,' written on the Advent, the last stanza
practices a similar adaptation. The poem on Trinity Sunday uses three-line stanzas; 'The Altar' and 'Easter
Wings' visualize the objects they signify.

These innocent ingenuities have been duly chastised in
Addison's essay on 'False Wit' (6) and elsewhere in neoclassical criticism. Relatively few in number, they proceed from a principle analogous to onomatopoeia and equally
harmless in moderation: the expressive adjustment of
structure, phonetic or typographical, to theme.

Most of Herbert's poetry is conventionally, though variously, patterned: of his hundred and sixty-nine poems,
one hundred and sixteen are composed in stanza forms which
are not repeated. Having sacrificed learned allusion and
poetic diction, having adopted a conversational syntax,
Herbert could still, with pure conscience, retain the art
of metrical invention. In Herbert's stanzaic invention,
as in the constant precision of his craftmanship, there
survives his temperamental fastidiousness. The tension
between inner struggle and outer neatness gives its central
character to his poetry.

Herbert's instrument is delicate of timbre and limited
of gamut; not the sustainedly sonorous organ nor the im-
perious

> tuba, mirum spargens sonum
> per sepulchra regionum (7)

but viol or lute, apt for accompaniment, adjusted to the
chamber and the closet. Moderate in pitch, its tone can,
without hysterical tightening, rise to joy and, avoiding
the whine and the sob, sink to pathos. This control of
scale, this restrained modulation, are the natural con-
comitants of a remarkable poetic integrity. Whether or
not he learned his architecture from Donne, Herbert com-
poses a lyric as a whole; and he should be quoted not by
lines or by stanzas but by poems. Brilliant phrases there
are, of course, like 'church bells beyond the stars heard,'
in that brilliant and tender poem, 'Prayer.'

[Quotes 'Prayer' (I) in full.]

It remains true, however, that the verse which, in its
context and as climax, moves the reader cannot be detached;
for it is by virtue of its position in the whole poem and
as pervaded by what has gone before that it acquires this
light and warmth. In some of Herbert's miniatures, the
finale - like Milton's in 'Lycidas' and 'Paradise Lost' -
is a diminuendo. The vigor of 'The Collar' expounds dramatically the motives to rebellion; the motive to submission finds utterance in but one tender word, the acknowledgment of submission in two more.

Through the influence of Coleridge in England and Emerson in America, Herbert did not want, in the nineteenth
century, for readers capable of some justice to his spirit
and to his art; in addition to this audience of the 'literary,' he continued to reach the devout, for whom 'The
Temple' took its place with the Bible, the Book of Common
Prayer, Law's 'Serious Call,' and Keble's 'The Christian
Year.' These nineteenth-century audiences have dispersed;
but Herbert has survived many changes in doctrine and
poetic mode. With our own time, the reaction against romantic and Victorian poetry has led to a revaluation of
the seventeenth-century lyric. Donne, restored to something like the position he held for his own generation,
has drawn attention and study to those other introspective
poets, commonly called 'metaphysical,' who followed him.

Donne's program excluded mythological and other 'literary' decoration. For conventional, hyperbolic laud of
love and mistress, he substituted realistic but subtle
analysis of the experienced. Resolved to transfer the
whole of himself to his verses, he saw no reason to deny
or conceal his erudition in geography, astronomy, physi-
ology, the dialectic of the Schools. He drew his analogies from his own universe of discourse and illustrated
love from science. Chiefly Donne sought to make poetry
out of reasoning - not *de rerum natura* (8) but about his
own problems. Yet versified analysis is not poetry; to
escape being metered prose, poetry must either relieve its
statements by images or think in images. A poet's simile
may not advance his thought but merely illustrate it. But
Donne made an endeavour, at which he was frequently successful, to have analysis move *pari passu* with metaphor.
His characteristic device was a protracted 'conceit,' disclosing successive but interpenetrating points of likeness
between the objects relationally identified. Thus Christ,
between Good Friday and Easter,

> For these three days became a mineral.
> He was all gold when He lay down, but rose
> All tincture, and doth not alone dispose
> Leaden and iron wills to good, but is
> Of power to make e'en sinful flesh like his.
> > ['Resurrection, imperfect', ll. 12-16]

His close reasoning, amorous casuistry, and syntax – those long sentences parenthetically interrupted – reappear only in Lord Herbert. of Cherbury. Carew, a poet still underestimated, not only wrote the best contemporary analysis of Donne's style but achieved, with a less complex nature and a less dissonant music, some distinguished love poetry of a sort impossible without Donne's predecession. In no really significant sense is Crashaw a 'metaphysical': Giles Fletcher and Marino supply the plausible paternity; his mind, though perverse, is simple; his syntax lacks involution;   characteristic images are sensual not scientific. Traherne, an overrated discovery, completely wants Donne's grasp of the poem as a tightly woven pattern;   he sprawls. Save for 'The Night,' Vaughan composed few poems; capable of extraordinary lines and arresting inaugurations, he ordinarily cannot organize or sustain. What chiefly gives these poets their legitimate connection with the name of Donne is their production not of hymns, justifications of Deity, metrical paraphrases of Scripture and Creed, but of autobiographical lyrics in analysis of religious experience.

George Herbert's relation to Donne seems to have been personal rather than literary. Sometimes attributed to Donne are his surrender of the mythological allusions frequent in his Latin poems, his structural neatness, his 'conceits.'

> Only a sweet and virtuous soul,
> > Like seasoned timber, never gives,
> But, though the whole world turn to coal,
> > Then chiefly lives.
> > > ['Vertue', ll. 13-16]

Yet the student of 'The Country Parson' will be aware of alternative explanations for these traits. 'The Temple,' written chiefly during the years at Bemerton, rarely draws its metaphors from travel, science, or philosophy. Herbert's 'seasoned timber' offers a shock not because the simile is researched but because, unexpectedly, it juxtaposes the world of ethics and the world of the carpenter.

That he should approach Herbert through Donne is a proper procedure for the literary historian but not necessary for the reader of poetry. There are eighteenth-century essays in blank verse - like Dyer's 'Fleece' and Akenside's 'Pleasures of the Imagination' - which become intelligible only when we know their Miltonic lineage; when we are possessed of that knowledge, 'Paradise Lost' shames them into the status of period pieces. But Herbert's poetry evokes no comparison with epic or dramatic grandeur and, put beside Donne's, is seen to have its own 'end' - as coherent and 'pure' as Donne's, but other.

Notes

1 Seriatim: 'The Elixer', ll. 19-20; 'Constancie', ll. 9-10; 'Sunday', ll. 38-9; and 'Even-song', l. 32.
2 2 Kings 5.12.
3 No. 10.
4 Above, p. 168.
5 'His will is our peace' ('Paradiso', III, 85).
6 No. 36.
7 From the thirteenth-century hymn by Thomas of Celano, 'Dies Irae': 'the trumpet, pouring forth its astonishing sound / over the graves of [all] regions' (translated by Austin Warren).
8 'About the nature of things' (the title of the poem by Lucretius).

Appendix I

Seventeenth-Century Musical Settings of Lyrics by Herbert

The first composer to provide settings for Herbert's
lyrics was John Jenkins (see above, p. 3). He was joined
in the middle and later seventeenth century by several
other composers who transformed Herbert into the author
of hymns intended sometimes for congregational use but
habitually for private devotions too (above, p. 13). In
the following five examples, the text of the poems is
borrowed from 'The English Poems of George Herbert' (above,
p. xvi).

1

John Jenkins's setting of the first four stanzas of 'The
Starre' (11. 1-16), from Christ Church, Oxford, Music MS
736-8, no. 18, pp. 254-5; transcribed and edited by Andrew
J. Sabol; reproduced from 'Major Poets of the Earlier
Seventeenth Century', ed. Barbara K. Lewalski and Andrew
J. Sabol (1973), pp. 1224-30. On Jenkins, see Vincent
Duckles, John Jenkins's Settings of Lyrics by George
Herbert, 'Musical Quarterly', XLVIII (1962), 461-75.

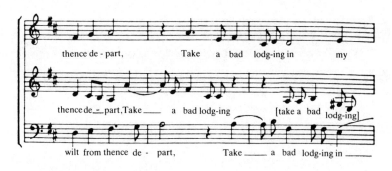

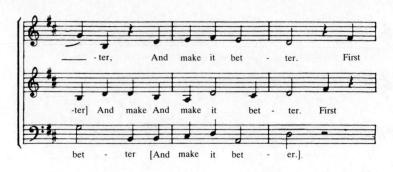

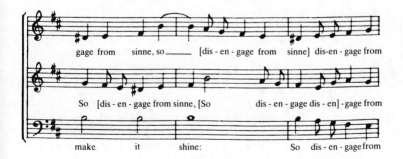

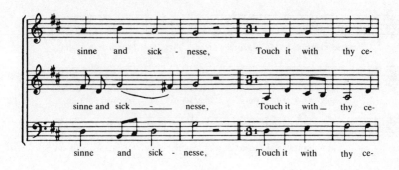

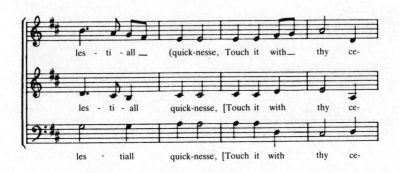

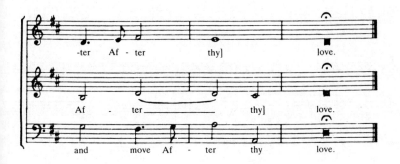

2

John Wilson's setting of four of the nine stanzas of 'Content' (11. 1-12 and 33-6, the text of the latter considerably amended), from Bodleian MS Mus. b. 1, ff. 50v-51; keyboard realisation by André Souris; reproduced from 'Poèmes de Donne, Herbert, et Crashaw mis en musique par leurs contemporains', ed. André Souris (Paris, 1961), pp. 20-2. On Wilson, see Vincent Duckles, The 'Curious' Art of John Wilson, 'Journal of the American Musicological Society', VII (1954), 93-113.

To court each place and for- tune that doth fall, _____ is wan-ton-nesse in con- tem-pla-tion.

Mark how the fire in flint doth quiet __ lie, Con-tent and warm t' it self a - lone

But when it would appeare ____ to others eye, With-out a knock it nev- er shone.

[♩ = 69]

Then peace dis- cour- sing soul, plough __ thine owne ground, Do not thy

self or friends ____ im- por- tune. He that by seek- ing

once him- self hath found, Hath ev- er found a for- tune

3

John Playford's setting of 'The Altar' (complete), from
Playford's 'Psalms & Hymns in Solemn Musick' (1671),
p. 92; transcribed by, and reproduced from, Louise
Schleiner, The Composer as Reader: A Setting of George
Herbert's 'The Altar', 'Musical Quarterly', LXI (1975),
426, which discusses the setting in detail (pp. 422-32).

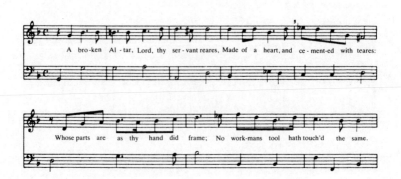

A bro-ken Al -tar, Lord, thy ser-vant reares, Made of a heart, and ce-ment-ed with teares:

Whose parts are as thy hand did frame; No work-mans tool hath touch'd the same.

A Heart a-lone Is such a stone, As noth-ing but Thy pow'r doth cut. Wherefore each part Of my hard heart Meets in this frame, To praise thy ho-ly name: That if I chance to hold my peace, These stones to praise thee may not cease. O let thy bles-sed Sac-ri-fice be mine, And sanc-ti-fie this Al-tar to be thine.

4

John Blow's setting of 'Ephes. 4.30. Grieve not the Holy Spirit, &c.' (complete), from Henry Playford's 'Harmonia sacra; or, Divine Hymns and Dialogues' (1688), I, 27-9; transcribed for the present volume by Elaine Sisman.

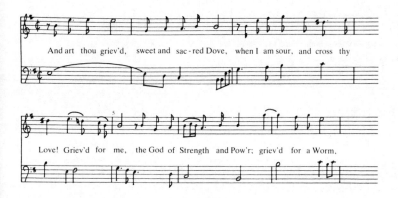

And art thou griev'd, sweet and sac-red Dove, when I am sour, and cross thy Love! Griev'd for me, the God of Strength and Pow'r; griev'd for a Worm,

there can no Dis-cord but in cea-sing be; Mar-bles can weep, and sure-ly Strings

more Bow-els have, than such hard things. Lord, I ad-judge my self to Tears and

Grief, ev'n end-less Tears with-out Re-lief;   if a clear Spring for me no

time for-bears,   but runs, al-though I be not   dry; I am no Crys-tal, what   shall I?

Yet if I wail- not still,   since still to wail, Na-tures de-nies, and Flesh would

fail,   if my De- serts were Mas-ters of mine Eyes. Lord, par-don,

for thy Son makes good my want of Tears ——, my want of Tears —

—, with   store   of   Blood.

5

Henry Purcell's setting of seven of the fourteen stanzas of
'Longing' (ll. 1-12, 19-42, 79-84), from Henry Playford's
'Harmonia sacra; or, Divine Hymns and Dialogues' (1688), I,
22-4; reproduced from 'The Works of Henry Purcell', Vol.
XXX, 'Sacred Music: Part VI', ed. Anthony Lewis and Nigel
Fortune (1965), pp. 94-7. On this setting, see Louise
Schleiner, Seventeenth-Century Settings of Herbert:
Purcell's 'Longing', in '"Too Rich to Clothe the Sunne"':
Essays on George Herbert', ed. Claude J. Summers and Ted-
Larry Pebworth (Pittsburgh, Pa, 1980), pp. 195-207.

Thy pile of dust, where-in each crumme Sayes, 'Come'. My love, my sweet - nesse, heare!

By these thy feet, at which my heart ___ Lies all the yeare. Pluck out thy dart, And heal _ my trou -

- bled breast, which cryes, Which dyes, heal _ my trou - bled breast, which cryes, Which dyes.

Appendix II

Eighteenth-Century Versions of Herbert's 'Vertue'

The adaptation of Herbert's poems during the eighteenth
century (see above, pp. 18 ff.) can be appreciated best
through a comparison of the different versions of 'Vertue'
available at the time. The original poem in 'The Temple'
(1633) reads as follows:

> Sweet day, so cool, so calm, so bright,
> The bridall of the earth and skie:
> The dew shall weep thy fall to night;
>   For thou must die.
>
> Sweet rose, whose hue angrie and brave
> Bids the rash gazer wipe his eye:
> Thy root is ever in its grave,
>   And thou must die.
>
> Sweet spring, full of sweet dayes and roses,
> A box where sweets compacted lie;
> My musick shows ye have your closes,
>   And all must die.
>
> Onely a sweet and vertuous soul,
> Like season'd timber, never gives;
> But though the whole world turn to coal,
>   Then chiefly lives.

The ensuing versions indicate the changes introduced on a
number of occasions.

1

The version in John and Charles Wesley, 'Hymns and Sacred
Poems' (1739), pp. 9-10, reads:

VIRTUE.   *Altered from* Herbert.

I.

Sweet Day, so cool, so calm, so bright,
   The Bridal of the Earth and Sky:
The Dew shall weep thy Fall to Night,
   For Thou with all thy Sweets must die!

II.

Sweet Rose, so fragrant and so brave,
   Dazling the rash Beholder's Eye:
Thy Root is ever in its Grave,
   And Thou with all thy Sweets must die!

III.

Sweet Spring, so beauteous and so gay,
   Storehouse, where Sweets unnumber'd lie:
Not long thy fading Glories stay,
   But Thou with all thy Sweets must die!

IV.

Only a Sweet and Virtuous Mind,
   When Nature all in Ruins lies,
When Earth and Heav'n a Period find,
   Begins a Life that never dies!

2

The anonymous version in 'Universal Harmony or, the
Gentleman & Ladie's Social Companion. Consisting of a
great Variety of the Best & most Favourite English & Scots
Songs, Cantatas &c. &c.' (1745), p. 23, retains Wesley's
version of the first three stanzas but provides a new
final stanza in line with the poem's remarkable new title,
'Conjugal Love'. Herbert is not mentioned.

Sweet love alone, sweet weded Love
To thee no Period is assign'd,
Thy tender joys by time improve
In death it self, the most refin'd

The same version, again without any mention of Herbert, reappeared under the title 'Song' in 'The Muses Banquet: or, a Present from Parnassus. Being a Collection of such English and Scots Songs, as are well worth preserving' (Reading, 1752), II, 201. It was in turn copied in 'A Collection of English Songs', ed. A. Dalrymple (Edinburgh, 1756; London, 1796), p. 163.

3

The anonymous version in 'The Charmer: A Choice Collection of Songs, Scots and English' (Edinburgh, 1749; 2nd edn, 1752; 3rd edn, 1765), I, 316-17, retains Wesley's version of the first two stanzas, provides a slightly different reading of the third stanza (given below), and concludes by borrowing the fourth stanza from 'Universal Harmony' (see above). There is no title, and Herbert is not mentioned.

    Sweet spring, full of sweet days and roses,
        A box, where sweet compacted lie,
    Not long ere all thy fragrant posies,
        With all their sweets, must fade and die.

4

The radically new version by W.H. Reid in the 'Universal Magazine of Knowledge and Pleasure', LXXXIII (September 1788), 159, again does not mention Herbert.

A THOUGHT.

    Sweet Day! so bland, so fair, so bright,
        The garnisher of earth and sky;
    Soft dews shall weep thy fall to night,
                For thou must die.

    Sweet Spring! full of sweet days and pleasures,
        In Expectation's youthful eye
    Thy fragrant airs and melting measures
               Alike must die.

    Sweet Rose! whose bloom such hues discover
        As quick vermillion comes not nigh;
    Thy root e'en now the grave doth cover
              Where thou may'st die.

Then since each good that time supposes,
    From changeful seasons feels decay;
From pleasure cull perennial poesies:
        Live while you may.

5

The last version of 'Vertue' attempted during the eight-
eenth century was ventured by George Horne (d. 1792).
It is here reprinted from 'The Works of the Right Reverend
George Horne, D.D. late Lord Bishop of Norwich', ed.
Williams Jones (1809), I, 236.

AN ODE.
THE SENTIMENT FROM THE DIVINE HERBERT.

I.

Sweet day, so cool, so calm, so bright,
    Bridal of earth and sky,
The dew shall weep thy fall to-night;
    For thou, alas! must die.

II.

Sweet rose, in air whose odours wave,
    And colour charms the eye,
Thy root is ever in its grave,
    And thou, alas! must die.

III.

Sweet Spring, of days and roses made,
    Whose charms for beauty vie,
Thy days depart, thy roses fade,
    Thou too, alas! must die.

IV.

Be wise then, Christian, while you may,
    For swiftly time is flying;
The thoughtless man, that laughs to-day,
    To-morrow will be dying.

Index

The index is divided into two parts: I Herbert's Works;
II Name Index.

I HERBERT'S WORKS

II   NAME INDEX

386   Index

THE CRITICAL HERITAGE SERIES

GENERAL EDITOR: B. C. SOUTHAM

Volumes published and forthcoming